A Ghetto Takes Shape

BLACKS IN THE NEW WORLD

August Meier, Series Editor

A Ghetto Takes Shape

Black Cleveland, 1870-1930

WITHDRAWN

Kenneth L. Kusmer

UNIVERSITY OF ILLINOIS PRESS

Urbana and Chicago

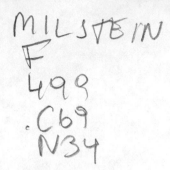
First paperback edition, 1978

© 1976 by the Board of Trustees of the University of Illinois
Manufactured in the United States of America
P 16 15 14 13 12

This book is printed on acid-free paper.

LIBRARY OF CONGRESS CATALOGING-IN-PUBLICATION DATA

Kusmer, Kenneth L.
A ghetto takes shape.
(Blacks in the new world)
Bibliography: p.
Includes index.
1. Negroes—Cleveland—History. 2. Cleveland—
History. I. Title. II. Series.
F499.C69N34   977.1'32'00496073   75-40113
ISBN 978-0-252-00690-6

FOR MY MOTHER
AND IN MEMORY OF MY FATHER

Contents

Many are the misapprehensions and misstatements as to the social environment of Negroes in a great Northern city. Sometimes it is said, here they are free; they have the same chance as the Irishman, the Italian, or the Swede; at other times it is said, the environment is such that it is really more oppressive than the situation in Southern cities. The student must ignore both of these extreme statements and seek to extract from a complicated mass of facts the tangible evidence of a social atmosphere surrounding Negroes, which differs from that surrounding most whites; of a different mental attitude, moral standard, and economic judgment shown toward Negroes than toward most other folk. That such a difference exists and can now and then plainly be seen, few deny; but just how far it goes and how large a a factor it is in the Negro problems, nothing but careful study and measurement can reveal.

W. E. B. Du Bois,
The Philadelphia Negro (1899)

Preface

Historically, the institution of slavery and the development of the black ghetto have been the two great factors that have shaped the experience of Afro-Americans in the United States. The ramifications of slavery have been the subject of almost constant scholarly debate since the beginning of this century; and during the past fifteen years the nature of the "peculiar institution" has received careful and detailed scrutiny by a number of competing schools of historical thought. In marked contrast, the development of the ghetto—a phenomenon of equal importance— has received comparatively little attention. I hope this volume will, in some small way, help to rectify this historiographical deficiency.

A Ghetto Takes Shape constitutes an attempt at what might be called comprehensive comparative history. Its chief aim is to trace a number of aspects of black life—economic, political, social, and cultural—in a single city over a period of sixty to one hundred years, and to show how changes in each of these aspects were integrally related to the developing ghetto. This study also proposes, however, to make the process of ghetto development more comprehensible by systematically surveying changing white attitudes toward blacks; by comparing, at as many points as possible, the position of blacks in the social order with the positions of immigrants and native whites; and by placing the growth of the ghetto in its urban as well as its purely racial context.

The need for comparative analysis in black urban history cannot be emphasized too strongly. In his influential article, "The Enduring Ghetto" (*Journal of American History*, 55, September 1968), the late Gilbert Osofsky concluded that "the essential structure and nature of the Negro ghetto have remained remarkably durable since the demise of slavery in the North. There has been an unending and tragic sameness about Negro life in the metropolis over the two centuries." While in many ways this statement may be true for New York (the city which Osofsky drew most of his examples) and perhaps for some other cities also, I do not think that it applies equally well to all urban areas. If we are to understand the black urban experience in its totality, we need to revise and move beyond ahistorical concepts like the "enduring ghetto" by exploring the variations that have existed in the history of black communities—in much the same manner that historians have already begun to study the diversity of slave societies in the New World. Did the ghetto as a geographical entity develop differently and at different times in various cities? Did the black communities of different cities have varying patterns of property ownership and occupational mobility? of family structure? of political participation? Thus far historians have seldom asked these questions because they have not considered the answers to be worth noting. Yet these questions are crucial to understanding why a race riot occurred in Chicago but not in Cleveland; why there was a "ghetto revolt" in the 1960s but not in the 1920s; why black leadership has been militant in one community and conservative in another; why in some cities the black ghetto has indeed been "enduring," while in others the quality of black life has fluctuated over time.

Besides studying the differences among ghettos, there is also a need to analyze more carefully differences within individual black communities. Contrary to popular assumption, the black ghetto is not an undifferentiated mass of slum dwellers. To use St. Clair Drake's expression, there are —and have been—many "folkways and classways" in the black community. The emphasis, in some quarters, on the "pathological" effects of racism (however important these effects may intrinsically be) has led to a neglect of the study of the historical development of class structure in the black community and the positive ways in which blacks have responded to the growth of the ghetto. The functions of black organizations, institutions, and leadership at the local level require much more study than they have thus far received. We cannot assume that local branches of nationwide black organizations always functioned in the same manner as their parent organizations; nor can we assume that the ideologies, divisions, and strategies of black leadership groups in specific cities necessarily duplicates, during any given time period, divisions among those black leaders who claimed to speak for larger constituencies.

Exploring differences among and within black communities, however, is not sufficient. For a more comprehensive understanding of the development of black ghettos, comparative studies of Afro-Americans and other groups in the population, especially immigrants, are needed. It is hardly possible to assess adequately the position of blacks in the social order without measuring their progress (or lack of progress) against general trends. In analyzing occupations and patterns of residential change, in particular, I have sought to draw parallels between the experience of blacks and that of native whites and the various immigrant groups.

It should be evident from the nature of the questions raised in this preface that no one study can possibly explain all of the ramifications of the development of black ghettos. That will take many studies of many cities. Therefore, although one of the purposes of this study is to show that there were important differences among black communities before 1930 (and especially before 1915), I make no claims for the typicality of the Cleveland model. In many ways the history of Cleveland's black population parallels that of other cities; in other ways that history is exceptional, perhaps, or even unique. Wherever possible, I have tried to follow the astute advice which Gunnar Myrdal gave scholars in an appendix entitled "Research in a Negro Community," in *An American Dilemma* (1944): "When only a single community can be studied it should not be assumed to be typical nor should the question of its uniqueness or typicality be ignored. Rather, the investigator must attempt to place it in the Southern scene, or in the American scene, or even in the whole Western Civilization scene, by comparing it with the average and range in many significant respects." Throughout the present study I have compared Cleveland's developing ghetto and its black population with their counterparts in many other communities in both the North and the South. I have noted similarities where they have existed, but I have also noted differences and attempted to account for them. I have tried, perhaps unsuccessfully at times, to avoid reducing a complex and variegated historical problem to a series of pat, easily digested formulas.

Of the many librarians who helped me during the long process of researching this study, a few stand out as particularly praiseworthy. A special word of thanks is due the staffs of the Ohio State Historical Society, the Sociology Division of the Cleveland Public Library, the Joseph Regenstein Library of the University of Chicago, and the Western Reserve Historical Society Library. At Western Reserve, Virginia Hawley (who has assisted countless researchers during her tenure at the Library) and Olivia Martin were especially helpful.

I would like to express my deep appreciation to James Louis, Henry Leonard, Allan Spear, Christopher Wye, Paul Finkelman, Stanley Katz, August Meier, and John Hope Franklin for taking the time and trouble to read the manuscript of this study at various stages in its development, to point out errors, and to offer valuable criticisms. Professor Franklin, in particular, rendered a great service in drawing my attention to a number of critical issues in black urban history. Paul Lammermeier, of Kent State University, generously lent me data from his forthcoming dissertation on nineteenth-century black communities of the Ohio River Valley. Thanks also must go to Richard L. Wentworth and Carole S. Appel, of the University of Illinois Press, for their patience and editorial guidance. My greatest debt is to August Meier. This study began as a master's thesis under his direction, and I can say unequivocally that without his encouragement and inspiration I would never have enlarged upon my original ideas and brought them to their present fruition. I would also like to thank Leon C. Soulé, whose lectures first introduced me to American history; his intellectual guidance and moral support over the years have been invaluable. None of the individuals mentioned in this paragraph, of course, is responsible for any errors of fact or judgment that remain in this volume.

During the period of time that book has been in the making I received financial assistance from Kent State University, the history department of the University of Chicago (the James L. Cate Fellowship), and the Ford Foundation. I am very grateful for this aid.

An earlier version of this study was typed by Martha Siegwarth and Vitalija Mekesa Butkus. I am glad to have this opportunity to thank them for the valuable help which they rendered at the time.

Finally, I want to thank Holly—for everything.

PART I

---

*The Nineteenth-Century
Heritage*

CHAPTER 1

Almost Equal:
Black Cleveland before 1870

I

December 2, 1859, was a day that the citizens of Cleveland would not soon forget. That morning, John Brown had been executed at Charlestown, Virginia. As news of his death reached Cleveland, there was an immediate reaction among the populace. A number of shopkeepers closed their doors for the day. For one half hour, from 10:30 to 11 that morning, the bell of the Second Baptist Church tolled in commemoration of the departed hero. One group of citizens stretched a banner, bordered in black, across Superior Avenue, with Brown's words, "I do not think I can better honor the cause I love than to die for it," inscribed on it. Flags hung at half staff in several places, and a general gloom settled over the usually bustling town on the shores of Lake Erie.

The weather that Tuesday seemed to match the mood of the people. It was a stormy day, and the sun failed to break through a thick layer of clouds; a fine drizzle that began in the morning turned first to sleet and then to snow. That evening Melodeon Hall, one of the city's largest auditoriums, was draped in mourning for a public meeting in memory of the man who had tried unsuccessfully to liberate the slaves at Harpers Ferry. The meeting proved to be one of the largest the young metropolis had witnessed up to that time. Fourteen hundred people—about one of every fifteen adults in the community—turned out for the occasion. During the 1850s, southern slaveholders were fond of depicting the northern abolitionists as a rabble-rousing minority of troublemakers and ne'er-do-wells, bent on dividing communities and sundering the Union. The meeting at Melodeon Hall, however, belied at least the first half of this description: it contained a broad cross section of the community and included many people of wealth and standing. Among the speakers that night were two judges, three well-known ministers, and several aspiring local politicians, as well as John M. Langston, the prominent black abolitionist from Oberlin. One after another of these individuals rose to eulogize Brown, to condemn the state of Virginia for his execution, and to denounce the institution of slavery. "John Brown has gone to his grave," said one speaker, "and we can't call him back, but I propose that we baptise ourselves in his spirit, and stand upon a foundation of adamant in unalterable hostility to slavery." Several resolutions, adopted unanimously, highlighted the emotion-filled evening. "However much we may lament the death of the devoted Brown," read one of these that summed up the feelings of the crowd, "we are satisfied that his execution will bring confusion upon his enemies, and do more to overthrow the bulwarks of Slavery than a long life of philanthropic deeds with a peaceful exit. We honor his memory! Posterity will give him a monument as indestructable as their aspirations for FREEDOM."[1]

The outpouring of sentiment for John Brown was indicative of the growing sympathy of white Clevelanders, on the eve of the Civil War, for the plight of black Americans. Yet it had not always been this way. The delegates from the northeastern section of Ohio who attended the state Constitutional Convention in 1802 had evinced no marked concern for the rights of Negroes, and the constitution that emerged from the convention's deliberations was distinctly a white man's document. Slavery was excluded (by a single vote!), but blacks were denied suffrage and the right to give testimony in court against white persons, and they were declared ineligible to hold public office or to serve in the state militia. In addition to these constitutional provisions, a series of Black Laws were soon passed that further degraded the state's Afro-American population. Blacks were prohibited from settling in the state without filing a five-hundred-dollar bond. They were required to register their certificate of freedom in a county clerk's office before they could obtain employ-

---

[1] *A Tribute of Respect, Commemorative of the Worth and Sacrifice of John Brown, of Ossawatomie: It Being a Full Report of the Speeches made and the Resolutions adopted by the citizens of Cleveland, at a meeting held in the Melodeon, on the evening of the day on which John Brown was sacrificed by the Commonwealth of Virginia; together with a Sermon, commemorative of the same sad event* (Cleveland, 1859). Earlier in 1859 Brown had been able to live openly in Cleveland without fear of arrest, even though President James Buchanan had offered a large reward for his arrest. See Stephen B. Oates, *To Purge This Land with Blood: A Biography of John Brown* (New York, 1970), 267.

ment. They were excluded from jury service. Prior to 1848, the state made no provision for the public education of black youths; and when the legislature finally did pass laws pertaining to their education, it specifically allowed local communities to establish separate, segregated schools—an option that most localities readily accepted. Some of the Black Laws (such as the filing of bonds and certificates of freedom) were only sporadically enforced; most of the statutes limiting the freedom of blacks, however, were carried out to the letter.[2]

Prior to the mid-1830s, most of the citizens of Cleveland, Cuyahoga County, and the surrounding counties—an area known collectively as the Western Reserve—found the provisions of the Black Laws acceptable. There may well have been some individuals in Cleveland at that time who opposed the restrictive codes, but they were too few in number to be noticed by the local press. A more ambivalent attitude prevailed on the subject of slavery. As early as 1819, two men were convicted by a Cleveland jury on a charge of kidnapping when they attempted to return two fugitive slaves who had settled in the city to their master in western Virginia. This action, however, was unique for its time and constituted only the first faint stirrings of the militant abolitionism that would later take hold in the Reserve. When some Ohioans suggested, in the same year, that the state constitution be changed to allow slavery, the Cleveland *Register* vigorously protested that the "practice of trafficking in the human species is too contemptible an occupation for a citizen of Ohio." On the other hand, while opposing the introduction of slavery in Ohio, the paper did not object to the existence of the peculiar institution in those parts of the Union where it had already gained a foothold; and in the same edition the editors took note that a slave insurrection in Georgia had "been happily defeated." During the first two or three decades of the nineteenth century, most of the antislavery sentiment in Ohio was confined to those southern parts of the state that had been founded by Quakers. Western Reserve newspapers carried adver-

[2] Charles T. Hickok, *The Negro in Ohio, 1802–1870* (Cleveland, 1896), 33–39, 40–46; Helen M. Thurston, "The 1802 Constitutional Convention and [the] Status of the Negro," *Ohio History*, 81 (Winter 1972), 15–37; Robert E. Chaddock, *Ohio before 1850: A Study of the Early Influence of Pennsylvania and Southern Populations in Ohio,* Columbia University Studies in History, Economics, and Public Law, vol. 31, no. 2 (New York, 1908), 82–86; Franklin Johnson, *The Development of State Legislation Concerning the Free Negro* (New York, 1918), 161–63. For a survey of the legal disabilities facing Negroes throughout the North at this time, see Leon Litwack, *North of Slavery: The Negro in the Free States, 1790–1860* (Chicago, 1961), 64–112. See also Frank U. Quillin, *The Color Line in Ohio: A History of Race Prejudice in a Typical Northern State* (Ann Arbor, 1913), 13–34, 44–59.

tisements for fugitive slaves, and—notwithstanding the 1819 kidnapping case—runaways captured in northern Ohio were often routinely returned to their masters.[3]

In confronting the questions of slavery and race during the 1820s and much of the 1830s, the chief hallmark of white opinion in Cleveland was the desire to avoid sectional conflict. The Cuyahoga County Colonization Society was founded in 1826, and its proposed "solution" to the race question—gradual abolition and the colonization of blacks in Africa or South America—rapidly gained adherents and was soon being advocated by the Cleveland *Herald*, the city's leading newspaper at that time. The *Herald* defended the Colonization Society as "a highly useful institution" and opposed any scheme of emancipation that did not include a plan to reimburse the slave owners for the loss of their "property." Commenting in 1833 on the more militant advocates of abolition that were beginning to organize in New England, the *Herald* stated with satisfaction that "The visionary schemes of enthusiasts who would, to effect their purposes, jeopardize even our happy form of government, find but few advocates in this place [the Western Reserve]." Two years later a large proslavery meeting in the city resolved to "distinctly disclaim any right to interfere with the subject of slavery in the southern states" and condemned the abolitionists for menacing "the peace and permanence of the union. . . ."[4]

During the next two decades, however, while white sentiment throughout much of the North turned against the Negro in an effort to placate southern opinion, the attitude of people in the Western Reserve shifted dramatically in the opposite direction. Inundated by settlers from New England, many of whom were steeped in evangelical religion and were hospitable to reform causes of all types, the Reserve exhibited a growing hostility to slavery during the years preceding the Civil War. Much of northern Ohio became, in fact, a hotbed of abolitionism, and Cleveland and surrounding towns became regular stopping points on the underground railroad. "It is well known," William Wells Brown, the

[3] Cleveland *Herald*, November 14, 1820, January 2, 1821; Cleveland *Register*, April 27, June 8, 15, 1819, in Works Projects Administration, *The Annals of Cleveland* (Cleveland, 1937–38), III, 77, IV, 148, I, 499, 579, 587, 589 (hereafter cited as *Annals*); Chaddock, *Ohio before 1850*, 88–93; A. G. Riddle, "Rise of the Anti-Slavery Sentiment on the Western Reserve," *Magazine of Western History*, 6 (1887), 154; Wilbur Henry Siebert, *The Mysteries of Ohio's Underground Railroads* (Columbus, 1951), 26–132.

[4] Cleveland *Herald*, November 3, 1826, January 11, 25, 1828, April 9, 23, August 17, October 26, 1833; Cleveland *Whig*, September 16, 1835, in *Annals*, IX, 40, XI, 252, 253, XV, 138, 139, 141, XVIII, 107.

black abolitionist, noted in 1848, "that a great number of fugitives make their escape to Canada, by way of Cleaveland; and while on the lakes, I always made arrangements to carry them on the boat to Buffalo or Detroit, and thus effect their escape to the 'promised land.' The friends of the slave, knowing that I would transport them without charge, never failed to have a delegation when the boat arrived at Cleaveland." As one historian has noted, the Fugitive Slave Act of 1850 became virtually a dead letter throughout the Reserve; and local abolitionists, as illustrated most dramatically by incidents like the Oberlin-Wellington rescue of 1858, made it very difficult for southern slaveholders to capture runaways once they reached the northeastern part of the state.[5]

As a number of scholars have recently shown, supporters of the anti-slavery cause did not necessarily also favor racial equality. In Cleveland, however, the two ideas were frequently conjoined, and militant abolitionists were almost always in the forefront of the struggle for equal rights. Beginning in 1838, the Cuyahoga County Anti-Slavery Society began pressuring office-seekers to take a strong stand against the Black Laws, and during the 1840s the repeal of the codes became a leading issue on the Reserve. Even the moderate Cleveland *Herald* came out against the codes in 1844, stating that in the future such laws would "be cited as evidence of the barbarous character of the state of Ohio in the early part of the 19th century." In 1848 the abolitionist congressman Joshua Giddings and other "conscience Whigs" led a mass defection to the Free Soil party. The Reserve sent an entire slate of Free Soil legislators to the state capitol, where they held the balance of power and were partially responsible for the repeal of most of the state's notorious Black Laws. The region remained a stronghold of radicalism during the crisis of the next two decades. In the Ohio Constitutional Convention of 1851, the delegates from Cuyahoga County voted unanimously against the anti-Negro provisions that were eventually included in the revised document, and in 1867 the county voted heavily in favor of granting

[5] Riddle, "Rise of the Anti-Slavery Sentiment on the Western Reserve," 145–46; Chaddock, *Ohio before 1850*, 104; Samuel P. Orth, *A History of Cleveland, Ohio* (Chicago, 1910), I, 290–99; Karl Geiser, "The Western Reserve in the Anti-Slavery Movement, 1840–1860," Mississippi Valley Historical Society *Proceedings*, 5 (1911–12), 73–98; William C. Cochran, *The Western Reserve and the Fugitive Slave Law: A Prelude to the Civil War*, Western Reserve Historical Society Collections, no. 101 (Cleveland, 1920), 78–211; *The Narrative of William W. Brown, A Fugitive Slave* (Reading, Mass., 1969; first published 1848), 46, 48; Russell H. Davis, *Memorable Negroes in Cleveland's Past* (Cleveland, 1969), 23. The description of the Fugitive Slave Act as a "dead letter" in the Reserve was made by Wilbur Siebert; see his *Mysteries of Ohio's Underground Railroads*, 264–79.

suffrage to Ohio Negroes (unfortunately, a majority of the state's voters rejected the proposal). During the 1850s and 1860s Cleveland sent two Radical Republicans, Edward Wade and Rufus Spaulding, to Congress. The entire region remained staunchly Republican during the next half-century.[6]

[6] Cleveland *Herald and Gazette*, September 23, 1838; Cleveland *Herald*, October 5, 1839, December 20, 1844, November 1, 21, 1845; Cleveland *Whig*, February 10, 1847, in *Annals*, XXI, 394–95, XXII, 132, XXVII, 560–61, XXVIII, 189; Cochran *The Western Reserve and the Fugitive Slave Law*, 81, 84–85; Quillin, *The Color Line in Ohio*, 38–40, 43, 100 (map showing 1867 vote on Negro suffrage by counties); Theodore C. Smith, *The Liberty and Free Soil Parties in the Northwest* (New York, 1897), 23, 35, 90–91; Cleveland *Daily True Democrat*, December 9, 1848, October 1, 1852; Cleveland *Leader*, April 9, 1867; A. G. Riddle, "Recollections of the Forty-Seventh General Assembly of Ohio, 1847–48," *Magazine of Western History*, 6 (1887), 341–51 (the assembly actually met 1848–49); N. S. Townshend, "The Forty-Seventh General Assembly of Ohio—Comments upon Mr. Riddle's Paper," *ibid.*, 6 (1887), 623–28; Thomas A. Flinn, "Continuity and Change in Ohio Politics," *Journal of Politics*, 24 (1962), 521–44. Giddings's career is surveyed in George W. Julian, *The Life of Joshua R. Giddings* (Chicago, 1892), and in Jane H. Pease and William H. Pease, *Bound with Them in Chains: A Biographical History of the Antislavery Movement* (Greenwood, Conn., 1972).

Several scholars have contended that it was the small size of the black population in the counties of the Western Reserve that was responsible for the lenient racial attitudes of many whites. "The blacks were not numerous enough in the Western Reserve to excite hostility," said William Cochran (*The Western Reserve and the Fugitive Slave Law*, 80). Frank Quillin carried this thesis further; after surveying racial attitudes in different parts of Ohio in the nineteenth century, he concluded that "the greater the negro population, the greater the white man's prejudice" (*The Color Line in Ohio*, 73). While this contention has some validity, it would be a mistake to push the point too far. There was only a very rough correlation between proportional vote against Negro suffrage in 1867 (one of the most readily available indicators of prejudice) and the size of a county's black population. The four counties with the largest number of blacks did vote heavily against suffrage, but counties with moderate-sized or small black populations followed no set pattern. There were some parts of the state that contained very few Negroes but still strongly opposed equal rights, both in the Constitutional Convention of 1851 and in the suffrage vote. (See maps in *ibid.*, 74–75, 100–101.) In explaining the egalitarianism of some whites, one is inclined to give considerable weight to the statement of one delegate from the Reserve who attended the 1851 convention: "Our sympathy for them [blacks] does not spring from our ignorance of them, but from the conviction that they are human beings and therefore entitled to all the rights and privileges and sympathies due to humanity, and from the conviction that they, equally with other men, are susceptible of intellectual and moral elevation" (*ibid.*, 70). The ideology of Radical Republicanism in the Western Reserve (as in other abolitionist centers of the North) was based fundamentally upon a moral opposition to slavery, but it also frequently entailed a rejection of nativism and an acceptance of the idea of equality between the races. For a general discussion, see the brilliant study by Eric Foner, *Free Soil, Free Labor, Free Men: The Ideology of the Republican Party before the Civil War* (New York, 1970), especially chs. 4, 7, 8, and 9. Also useful is James McPherson, *The Struggle for Equality* (Princeton, N.J., 1964), ch. 6.

Whites in southern and central Ohio, where hostility to blacks was widespread and growing during the 1850s, often expressed incredulity over the egalitarian or antislavery sentiments of many Clevelanders. When the Cleveland *Leader*, the city's leading Republican paper, quoted Frederick Douglass at length on the Kansas-Nebraska controversy in 1855, it drew fire from a Columbus newspaper. "What is the matter with the *Leader?*" asked the Columbus editor. "Does it go for Fred[erick] Douglass[?] Will no white man do?" The response of the *Leader* was unequivocal. "We infinitely prefer Fred[erick] Douglas[s] to the Chicago [i. e., Stephen A.] Douglas, or any of the Nebraska conspirators. We judge men by their principle."[7]

Such statements did not represent the opinion of all segments of the white population of Cleveland. If the *Leader* reflected what was undoubtedly the dominant view in the community, the Cleveland *Plain Dealer*, its Democratic competitor, accurately mirrored the views of those whites who believed in Negro inferiority and distrusted the abolitionist fervor of the majority. Although it changed course a number of times on specific issues, the *Plain Dealer* generally supported the "popular sovereignty" position on the extension of slavery into the territories. The paper also backed the Fugitive Slave Act. "The right to reclaim fugitives from labor," it editorialized vehemently in January, 1859, "*is in the Constitution.*" For many years, the paper was not above making racist jibes at the black citizens of Cleveland, Oberlin, and elsewhere, and it looked to the voluntary colonization of Negroes in Africa, rather than the attainment of equal rights in the United States, as the key to the nation's racial problems. "We have ever contended that Africa was the spot, the quarter of the Globe," the paper's editor stated in 1859, "originally designed for them and to which our free colored population should be *encouraged*, not *driven*, to go. . . . This is a government of white men; let them establish a government of colored men."[8]

The persistence of such views in nineteenth-century Cleveland insured a residue of prejudice and discrimination and made the achievement of absolute equality on the part of the city's black residents an impossibility. But until the end of the nineteenth century, if not later, the views expressed by the *Plain Dealer* were very far from being dominant among whites in the community. The racial egalitarianism of most whites, combined with the fluid social and economic conditions preva-

[7] Cleveland *Leader*, November 10, 1855.
[8] Archer H. Shaw, *The Plain Dealer: One Hundred Years in Cleveland* (New York, 1942), 82; Cleveland *Plain Dealer*, January 13, 1859.

lent in a rapidly growing frontier city, made nineteenth-century Cleveland much less oppressive for blacks than most other municipalities in the United States.

II

The growth of Cleveland during the nineteenth century was remarkable. Prior to 1832 the village remained a small, struggling frontier settlement. But in that year the Ohio and Erie Canal, connecting the Ohio River and Lake Erie, was completed, and Cleveland became the northern terminus of that important waterway. This gave the town the economic boost that it needed, and the completion of the first railroad linkages to New York and Cincinnati in the 1850s insured Cleveland's commercial dominance of northern Ohio over all rivals. The total population of Cleveland increased from a few thousand in 1830 to over ninety thousand, four decades later. Yet even this was insignificant compared with the expansion that lay ahead.[9] (See Table 1.)

TABLE 1. *Negro population of Cleveland, 1850–1930*

| | | | | Percentage of increase | |
Year	Total population	Negro population[a]	Percentage Negro	Total population	Negro population
1850	17,034	224	1.3		
1860	43,417	799	1.9	142.0	180.0
1870	92,829	1,293	1.4	107.0	62.1
1880	160,416	2,062	1.3	72.5	59.3
1890	261,353	3,035	1.2	63.0	46.9
1900	381,768	5,988	1.6	46.0	98.7
1910	560,663	8,448	1.5	46.9	40.9
1920	796,841	34,451	4.3	42.1	307.8
1930	900,429	71,899	8.0	13.0	108.3

SOURCE: U.S. Census Bureau Reports, 1850–1930.
   [a] Figures for years before 1900 include Chinese, Japanese, and "civilized Indians." These groups, however, were very small compared with the Negro population.

Cleveland's black community was almost as old as the city itself, but it grew at a slower rate. The first permanent black resident was a free Negro who migrated from Maryland in 1809, only a dozen years after Moses Cleaveland had staked out his original claim on the shores of Lake Erie. By 1850 the black population had increased to more than three hundred and comprised 1.8 percent of the inhabitants of the

   [9] Orth, *A History of Cleveland*, I, 98–116; Department of the Interior, Census Office, *Report on the Social Statistics of Cities*, pt. II (Washington, 1887), 377–78.

Forest City. During the following decade, this community of "free persons of color" (as they called themselves) almost tripled in size, and between 1860 and 1880 their numbers continued to grow at a steady, if somewhat slower, rate. At the close of the Reconstruction era there were slightly more than two thousand Afro-Americans residing in the city.[10]

The demographic characteristics of this small but growing black community ran counter to almost all of the stereotypes—then and now— about black urban life. There was not, as in most eastern and southern cities, a higher proportion of females to males; in 1850 males constituted 51.8 percent of the Cleveland Negro population. Nor was there an unusually large number of children or young people in the city's black community. In 1850, 52.4 percent of the blacks residing in Cuyahoga County were under the age of twenty-one; but by 1880, as a result of the migration of childless adults from other states, this percentage declined to 39.9. Almost all of the black families (93.1 percent in 1850; 85.2 percent twenty years later) were headed by males, and large families were clearly the exception rather than the rule: in 1880 68.4 percent of all black households in the county contained four persons or less.[11]

[10] Harry E. Davis, "Early Colored Residents of Cleveland," *Phylon*, 4 (July 1943), 235–36.

[11] This information is taken from Thomas J. Goliber's study of manuscript census data, "Cuyahoga Blacks: A Social and Demographic Study" (M.A. thesis, Kent State University, 1972), 22–34. It is now becoming clear that the sociological description of urban black lower-class families as "disorganized" and "matriarchal" as a result of "the impact of urban life on the simple family organization and folk culture which the Negro has evolved in the rural South" (E. Franklin Frazier, *The Negro Family in the United States*, New York, 1939, 341) is far from accurate when applied to families of the nineteenth century. In 1880, 82 percent of black households in Boston had two parents, and southern black migrants who came to that city at that time did not seem to experience any trend toward family "disorganization." In Philadelphia, where conditions were worse than in Boston, there was a somewhat higher proportion of female-headed households, especially among the poorer black families. But there is reason to believe that Philadelphia was not typical in this regard. An extensive study of black families in Pittsburgh, Cincinnati, Louisville, and several smaller Ohio River Valley cities between 1850 and 1880 shows that nuclear, male-headed households were predominant at that time; the percentage of black families in 1880 headed by males in Ohio Valley communities averaged over 80 percent. See Elizabeth Pleck, "The Two-Parent Household: Black Family Structure in Late Nineteenth-Century Boston," *Journal of Social History*, 6 (Fall 1972), 3–31; Theodore Hershberg, "Free Blacks in Antebellum Philadelphia: A Study of Ex-Slaves, Freeborn and Socioeconomic Decline," *ibid.*, 5 (Winter, 1971), 186; John W. Blassingame, *Black New Orleans, 1860–1880* (Chicago, 1972), 79–104; Paul Lammermeier, "The Urban Black Family in the Nineteenth Century: A Study of Black Family Structure in the Ohio Valley, 1850–1880," *Journal of Marriage and the Family*, 35 (August 1973), 454. Herbert Gutman's forthcoming history of the black family in the United States will analyze this problem in great detail.

As early as 1860, most of Cleveland's black population resided on the East Side, and the center of the Negro community was the old haymarket district on Central Avenue. Prior to the 1880s, however, there was no noticeable trend toward the ghettoization of the black population. Before then, in fact, no ward in the city was more than five percent black; and although blacks were concentrated essentially in three wards (the First, Fourth, and Sixth), they were thoroughly integrated in each. No segregated neighborhoods as such existed. Nor were blacks housed primarily in multiple-unit dwellings; in 1880 almost 70 percent of the city's Negroes lived in single-household units.[12]

The residential distribution of blacks in Cleveland before 1880—a clustering in certain areas of the city coupled with a high degree of integration *within* those areas—was probably quite similar to that of most other cities. On the basis of recently completed research, it now appears that the pattern of life in nineteenth-century urban America was usually not amenable to the formation of ghettos, either black or immigrant. Although in a few isolated instances (the best example is the Irish in Boston) a significant level of residential segregation was in evidence, this was the result of unique local conditions. Generally speaking, the high geographic mobility of urban workers, the rapid growth of many cities, unpredictable patterns of land use, and the need for people of all classes to live fairly close to their place of employment made the strict residential separation of any one group or class difficult. To be sure, blacks—more so than immigrants or native whites—tended to be restricted quite often to the poorer sections of many cities, but this was primarily the result of economic factors (the lower income of many Negroes) and only indirectly the result of racial prejudice. And in spite of this, it seems doubtful that anything even remotely resembling a real black ghetto existed in American cities, north or south, prior to the 1890s.[13]

---

[12] William Ganson Rose, *Cleveland: The Making of a City* (Cleveland, 1950), 218, 235; Works Projects Administration, "The Peoples of Cleveland" (typewritten manuscript [1942], Cleveland Public Library), 185, 195; Goliber, "Cuyahoga Blacks," 53, 60.

[13] For perceptive comments on this point, see Zane L. Miller, *Boss Cox's Cincinnati* (New York, 1968), 11; Sam Bass Warner, Jr., *The Private City: Philadelphia in Three Periods of Its Growth* (Philadelphia, 1968), 56–57, and Sam Bass Warner, Jr. and Colin Burke, "Cultural Change and the Ghetto," *Journal of Contemporary History*, 4 (October 1969), 173–87. On geographic mobility, see Stephan Thernstrom and Peter R. Knights, "Men in Motion: Some Data and Speculations about Urban Population Mobility in Nineteenth-Century America," *Journal of Interdisciplinary History*, 1 (Fall 1970), 1–19. On the segregation of the Irish in Boston, see Oscar Handlin, *Boston's Immigrants: A Study in Acculturation*, rev. ed. (New

Chicago and New York may be partial exceptions to this observation. In the late nineteenth century, *some* blacks in these cities undoubtedly lived in all-black sections of perhaps a few square blocks in size. Although Chicago had no clear-cut ghetto at the time, most of its black population was residentially restricted at an early date. A good deal of this may have been one of the indirect results of the fire of 1871 that almost destroyed the city; it allowed various groups to resettle in new areas and provided an opportunity to exclude blacks from neighborhoods where they had previously resided. Even before the fire, however, Afro-Americans were more segregated in Chicago than elsewhere, and the exact reason for this is unclear. The key may lie in the peculiar distribution of the city's ethnic elements, especially in the perhaps accidental tendency of blacks to settle in an area so close to hostile immigrant groups.[14]

Conditions in New York and Chicago were not typical, however. Even in such relatively "racist" cities as Detroit and Cincinnati there is no evidence of the existence of well-defined ghettos before 1890. A historian of Detroit's nineteenth-century black community found that in 1880 "even in the area of highest Negro concentration, blacks and whites lived next to one another." Summarizing conditions in Cincinnati in 1880, another scholar notes that "while the black population was concentrated in the poorer areas of the city, two-thirds of them lived in mixed blocks, inhabited chiefly by low-income Irish immigrants." In a number of smaller, more recently founded cities, blacks were also fairly well integrated residentially, and may in addition have been dispersed over a much wider area of the city than in older urban centers.[15]

York, 1959), 88–100. Even in Boston the Irish were not confined to a single unified ghetto; clusters of Irish immigrants were located in many parts of the city.

[14] Gilbert Osofsky, *Harlem: The Making of a Ghetto, Negro New York, 1890–1930* (New York, 1966), 12; St. Clair Drake and Horace R. Cayton, *Black Metropolis: A Study of Negro Life in a Northern City* (New York, 1945), 46–47, 62. Osofsky's description, "Handfuls of small and densely populated ghettos, usually a block or two in length, were found throughout Manhattan," stretches the definition of ghetto too far, however. Such small units of population are more accurately portrayed as "clusters" or "enclaves" than as ghettos.

[15] David M. Katzman, *Before the Ghetto: Black Detroit in the Nineteenth Century* (Urbana, Ill., 1973), 69; Paul J. Lammermeier, "Cincinnati's Black Community: The Origins of a Ghetto, 1870–1880," in John H. Bracey, August Meier, and Elliott Rudwick, eds., *The Rise of the Ghetto* (Belmont, Calif., 1971), 26; W. E. B. Du Bois, *The Philadelphia Negro: A Social Study* (Philadelphia, 1899), 58–62 and the map preceding the title page. Prior to about 1880, the amount of residential segregation in southern cities was quite minimal. Although as early as 1850 some very small predominantly Negro sections existed on the outskirts of Richmond, New Orleans, and Charleston, South Carolina, as well as elsewhere in

Although fairly typical in their patterns of residency, in other respects
the social and economic status of blacks in Cleveland throughout most
of the nineteenth century was much superior to that of blacks in most
other parts of the state or country. Prior to the passage of the Fifteenth
Amendment, of course, all Negroes in Ohio were excluded from holding
public office, and most were denied the right to vote.[16] But with these
significant exceptions, most of the disabilities that free blacks suffered
in other localities usually did not occur in Cleveland. Segregation in
public accommodations, for example, was infrequent and usually short-
lived. As late as 1883, the editor of Cleveland's weekly black newspaper,
the *Gazette*, claimed that no hotel in the city excluded Negroes—a statement that could be made of few municipalities outside of New England
at that time. Integrated facilities were also the rule rather than the

---

the South, these districts housed only a small minority of the aggregate black
populations of these metropolises. At that time most southern black urban dwellers
were servants who lived in or near the residences of the whites for whom they
worked; but even self-employed black artisans and entrepreneurs tended to be
residentially integrated. See Richard C. Wade, *Slavery in the Cities: The South,
1820–1860* (New York, 1964), 273–80; Karl E. Taeuber and Alma F. Taeuber,
Negroes in Cities: Residential Segregation and Neighborhood Change (Chicago,
1965), 45–46; John W. Blassingame, "Before the Ghetto: The Making of the Black
Community in Savannah, Georgia, 1865–1880," *Journal of Social History*, 6 (Summer 1973), 481.

[16] Many scholars incorrectly list Ohio among those states which categorically
prohibited Negro voting before the Civil War. Although the constitution of Ohio
stated that only white males were entitled to vote, the state Supreme Court in 1842
upheld the right of suffrage of mulattoes with less than one-half Negro blood, on
the grounds that such persons were more white than Negro. (*Parker Jeffries* v. *John
Ankeny et al.*, 11 Ohio 372; *Edwin Thacker* v. *John Hawk et al.*, 11 Ohio 377.)
These decisions, as well as other liberal interpretations of the Black Laws, led to
much bitterness among whites in central and southern Ohio, and in 1859 the state
legislature passed a bill excluding from the franchise anyone with "a distinct and
visible admixture of African blood." (*Ohio Laws, 1859,* 120.) Yet this legislation
did not prevent mulattoes from voting in the Western Reserve. Shortly after the
passage of the 1859 law Freeman Morris, a Cleveland tailor of one-quarter Negro
ancestry, brought suit in common pleas court when an election judge denied him
the right to vote. Judge John A. Foote, a Radical Republican, ruled in favor of
Morris and declared the law unconstitutional. The decision was not appealed, and
apparently mulattoes continued to vote without interference in Cleveland and perhaps in other parts of the state as well. (*Weekly Anglo-African*, July 30, 1859;
Cleveland *Leader*, April 18, 1867, January 20, April 6, 1868; Russell H. Davis, "The
Negro in Cleveland Politics: Negro Political Life Begins," Cleveland *Call and Post*,
September 10, 1966.) In 1868 the state legislature passed a much more elaborate
"visible admixture" law, this time allowing any bona fide white voter to challenge
the vote of any person whom he suspected to be Negro. (*Ohio Laws, 1868–69,*
97.) The Ohio Supreme Court immediately declared this law unconstitutional also
(*James Monroe et al.* v. *George Collins*, 17 Ohio State Reports 666), reasserting
the doctrine it had laid down in 1842. With the passage of the Fifteenth Amendment in 1870, of course, all blacks in Ohio gained the right of suffrage.

exception in most of the city's restaurants, lecture halls, and other public facilities. "An indication of the civilized spirit of the city of Cleveland," boasted the *Leader* in 1865, "is found in the fact that colored children attend our schools, colored people are permitted to attend all public lectures and public affairs where the fashion and culture of the city congregate, and nobody is offended."[17]

The *Leader's* statement was not, unfortunately, accurate in every respect. Racial prejudice was not completely absent from mid-nineteenth-century Cleveland. When, for example, Frederick Douglass visited the city in 1852, he was allowed to lodge at the Forest City House but was denied the right to take his meals at the common table with the rest of the hotel's guests. In 1851 the first attempt was made to establish a "colored gallery" in a Cleveland theater (whether the move was successful, or how long the policy of segregation lasted, is unclear), and throughout the Reconstruction era the Cleveland Academy of Music successfully barred black patrons from its dress circle. The fact that the *Leader* castigated the proprietor of the Academy as a "negro hater" did not make it easier for blacks to accept the policy of segregation.[18]

While such examples of discrimination existed, however, they were not (at least prior to 1890), typical of conditions in the city. Most theaters and other public facilities did not segregate blacks, a fact that surprised and sometimes infuriated visitors from other parts of the country where rigid segregation was the rule. When two Texans traveling through the North in 1865 stopped at Cleveland for supper, they related that "[we] had not more than taken our seats at the principal hotel when two buck negroes deliberately seated themselves opposite." This proved too much for their "Southern raising" and they promptly "left the table in great disgust." In large measure (though not invariably) the policy of integrated facilities received the backing of the judges and juries who interpreted the laws. An attempt to segregate Negroes by one of the city's streetcar companies in 1864 lead to a court decision making integration mandatory. In another case brought before a local court in 1868, a young Afro-American who had been excluded from a city skating rink sued the owner of the establishment and won a settlement of three hundred dollars—a considerable sum at that time. Undoubtedly the possibility of such action on the part of the legal authorities made owners

[17] David A. Gerber, "Ohio and the Color Line: Racial Discrimination and Negro Responses in a Northern State, 1860–1915" (Ph.D. dissertation, Princeton University, 1971; to be published as *Black Ohio and the Color Line, 1860–1915*, Urbana, Ill., 1976), 102; Cleveland *Leader*, March 7, 1865.

[18] Cleveland *Daily True Democrat*, September 4, 1851, May 20, 1852; Cleveland *Leader*, March 7, 1865. See also *ibid.*, May 3, 1856.

and managers think twice before they tried to draw the color line.[19]

Nowhere, perhaps, was the spirit of racial fairness more pervasive than in the city's school system. Despite the fact that prior to 1887 Ohio law either made no provision at all for black education or made it easy for communities to establish separate schools, Cleveland's public schools were integrated at an early date. From 1832 to 1837, before the city's school system had been formally established, the black community (with some help from white philanthropists) irregularly supported its own school, and during the early 1840s the City Council helped subsidize a private school for black children. By the end of that decade, however, the public educational system had been completely integrated, and it would remain that way until well into the twentieth century. The early policy of exclusion was probably due to the fact that state law, prior to 1848, limited access to the public schools to white children. This prohibited municipalities from establishing even segregated public schools for blacks. In addition, the legislature had inserted a statement in the original Cleveland city charter of 1835 that the schools were to be "accessible to all *white* children," and this may have had an intimidating effect.[20]

Once Cleveland's schools were integrated, few whites in the city disputed the new policy, and those that did were not numerous enough to turn back the clock. In 1859, when a group of whites living in the Sixth Ward "offered to pay for the erection of a separate school house for the exclusive use of colored children, in order to eliminate the necessity of colored children mingling with white children," the city Board of Education firmly rejected the proposal. This is not surprising, since the president of the Board at the time was the Rev. James A. Thome, a leading abolitionist and insistent advocate of racial equality who also served as pastor of the West Side Congregational Church. Other board members were equally adamant in opposing a separate school for blacks. "In the Hudson Street [Sixth Ward] school," said William Fogg, "there are 16 colored children scattered in five different rooms. I am opposed to any action like seating three or four in rooms by themselves,

[19] Cleveland *Leader*, July 1, 1864, May 6, 1865; Gerber, "Ohio and the Color Line," 76.

[20] Cleveland *Herald and Gazette*, July 11, 1837, March 29, 1839; Cleveland *Herald*, November 30, December 28, 1839, July 16, 1842, May 17, November 30, 1843, in *Annals*, XX, 379, XXII, 228, 233, 234, XXV, 223, XXVI, 296, 298; Hickok, *The Negro in Ohio, 1802–1870*, 88; James H. Kennedy, *History of the City of Cleveland* (Cleveland, 1896), 276; William J. Akers, *Cleveland Schools in the Nineteenth Century* (Cleveland, 1901), 29; Quillin, *The Color Line in Ohio*, 33, 45, 67.

thereby creating distinction and degrading these unfortunate children in their schoolmates' eyes. . . . I don't think my child is disgraced or contaminated by sitting next to these colored children. . . . Rather than consent to what I consider an act of injustice and oppression to any class or race of children I would resign my seat as a member of the board." After the Civil War, all resistance to integrated education in Cleveland faded away. In 1871, in an editorial criticizing segregation, the *Leader* stated that there "is no sound or reasonable objection" to integration of the schools, and that "the opposition to it springs wholly from that small and narrow prejudice which is no longer tolerable in this country." Most Clevelanders shared this opinion and accepted integrated schools as a fact of life, even if whites in Detroit and elsewhere did not.[21]

III

If blacks in nineteenth-century Cleveland achieved near-equality in access to public facilities, they also found the door of economic opportunity open wider in the Forest City than most other communities. At the Ohio Constitutional Convention of 1851, one white delegate from Cleveland used the general social and economic status of the city's blacks as proof enough that all Negroes deserved the right to vote. "The truth is," argued the Cleveland representative, "that if we apply to them the same measure of qualification that we do to the whites, they are as well qualified to exercise the right of suffrage as thousands of white voters in this or any other State." In 1858 the *Leader* chimed in its agreement. The city's black community, it claimed, contained many "old, intelligent, industrious and respectable citizens, who own property, pay taxes, vote at elections, educate their children in public schools, and contribute to build up the institutions and to the advancement of the prosperity of the city." Visitors to the city often agreed with these assessments. When William Wells Brown returned to Cleveland while on a lecture tour in 1857, he remarked upon "the intelligence, industry, and respectability of the colored citizens. . . . Indeed they will compare favorably with an equal number of whites in any portion of Ohio. Some of them are in good circumstances and are engaged in businesses employing their own capital." Wrote abolitionist James Freeman Clarke in 1859, "The feeling toward them [blacks] in Cleveland and throughout the Western Reserve is very kind, and there

[21] Cleveland *Leader*, May 11, December 20, 1859, January 13, 1871; Eugene H. Roseboom, *The Civil War Era, 1850–1873* (Columbus, Ohio, 1944), 194; Cochran, *The Western Reserve and the Fugitive Slave Law*, 159n.

they do better than in most places. There you find them master carpenters, master painters, shopkeepers, and growing rich every year."[22]

To be sure, not all of the city's Afro-Americans were "growing rich every year." But Cleveland's black community could boast a sizable number of success stories. George Peake, the city's first permanent black resident, owned a one-hundred-acre tract of land and invented and patented a new type of hand mill that made the production of meal from grain much easier. Alfred Greenbrier, another early resident, bred horses and cattle and became widely known for the excellence of the stock he raised. Madison Tilly, one of Cleveland's most prominent black citizens and an early political leader until his death in 1887, employed an integrated labor force of one hundred men in his lucrative business as an excavating contractor. He enjoyed social contacts with many prominent whites and left his sons an estate estimated at between $25,000 and $30,000. Dr. Robert Boyd Leach, Cleveland's first Negro physician, earned a degree from the city's Western Homeopathic College, one of the few medical colleges in the country that admitted Negroes. Leach's successful practice brought middle-class respectability; his home, the *Leader* noted in 1858, contained "all the pleasant surroundings which well-directed industry and economy usually bring with competence when directed by good taste." Freeman H. Morris owned a tailoring establishment in the Dunham House; he was described by the *Daily True Democrat* in 1850 as "a first rate workman and those who patronize him will be more than satisfied."[23]

Clearly the most prosperous black man in Cleveland before 1870, however, was the barber John Brown. Born in Virginia of free parents, Brown came to Cleveland in 1828. He soon established himself as one of the city's leading barbers, and by the early 1840s his income was large enough for him to almost single-handedly support a free school for blacks for several years. Through a judicious investment in real estate, Brown was able to accumulate about $40,000 in property by the time of his death in 1869.[24]

These successful individuals were not, of course, representative of the

[22] Quillin, *The Color Line in Ohio*, 67; Davis, *Memorable Negroes in Cleveland's Past*, foreword, n.p.; Cleveland *Leader*, February 8, 1858, quoted in introduction to Allan Peskin, ed., *North into Freedom: The Autobiography of John Malvin, Free Negro, 1795–1880* (Cleveland, 1966; first published 1879), 14; James Freeman Clarke, "Condition of the Free Colored People of the United States," *Christian Examiner*, 5th ser., 4 (1859), 255.

[23] Davis, "Early Colored Residents of Cleveland," 235–37; Davis, *Memorable Negroes in Cleveland's Past*, 7, 13, 17; Cleveland *Leader*, March 11, 1858; Cleveland *Daily True Democrat*, September 24, 1850.

[24] Cleveland *Leader*, March 31, 1869; Peskin, ed., *North into Freedom*, 72n.

entire black community, and there were, in fact, far more blacks near the lower than the upper end of the economic spectrum. Many blacks were dockworkers or unskilled laborers of various sorts. It is important, however, to place the economic and occupational structure of nineteenth-century black Cleveland in the proper context before evaluating it. Before 1870 (if not later), unskilled labor made up a relatively larger share of *all* groups in the economy, so the mere fact that many blacks were in this category does not, in itself, prove that their economic status was grossly depressed. For a more thorough understanding of the socio-economic standing of blacks it is necessary to look at both the male *and* female occupational structure of Negroes and to measure these against their native-white and ethnic counterparts.

Table 2 gives a breakdown of occupations by racial and ethnic group for Cleveland (in the case of blacks, for Cuyahoga County) in 1870. It reveals that a larger proportion of blacks were in the two lowest categories, unskilled labor and domestic service, than any other group in the economy of the city at that time. But there were also sizable numbers of the foreign-born in these two categories, and there was not a great deal of difference between the proportion of Negroes and Irish in the service jobs. Much more important was the ability of Afro-American males to gain access to the skilled trades; this job category, in fact, comprised about one-third of the black male work force. The proportion of blacks doing skilled work was little different from the rest of the city's work force, and blacks were much more likely to be artisans than were Irish immigrants. In the higher job categories blacks did not fare as well (although the number of black males in the professions was not noticeably lower than average), but in the professional and clerical occupations the foreign-born did little better.[25]

An analysis of female occupations shows that black women did not suffer any noticeable occupational discrimination because of their *race*. Sixty-two percent of all employed black women in the city were personal or domestic servants of one kind or another in 1870. In this respect, however, blacks differed little from the rest of the labor force, since 65.7 percent of *all* employed women in Cleveland worked as domestics. Gender, rather than race, was clearly the determining factor: it was females per se, not black females, whose occupational status was depressed at the time. Furthermore—perhaps because of the "stability"

[25] For a discussion of the limitations of these data, see the footnotes to Table 2. The occupational classification system used in this study is based upon that developed by Alba M. Edwards in *An Alphabetical Index of Occupations by Industries and Social-Economic Groups* (Washington, 1937) and is discussed in Appendix I.

TABLE 2. *Occupational structure of Cleveland, by ethnic and racial group, 1870*

| | Occupational category | | | | | | |
	Professional	Proprietary	Clerical	Skilled	Semiskilled	Unskilled	Domestic service
Males							
Negroes[a]	1.4%	3.2%	0.8%	31.7%	14.8%	29.6%	14.8%
All workers[b]	1.9	7.4	7.4	30.2	12.0	14.7	0.9
Females							
Negroes[a]	1.0	2.9	—	—	26.5	7.8	61.7
All workers	4.2	0.5	1.7	—	22.8	0.1	65.7
Total work force							
Negroes	1.3	3.2	0.7	26.2	16.8	25.9	22.9
Foreign-born (total)	1.1	5.3	2.2	29.7	12.8	15.9	10.0
Native whites	3.9	8.5	10.7	21.0	15.6	4.5	8.5
German immigrants	1.2	6.8	1.9	33.6	11.0	16.3	7.1
Irish immigrants	0.7	3.1	1.7	16.9	11.6	19.8	15.8
English and Welsh immigrants	1.0	5.1	3.0	34.8	17.8	7.4	6.4
All workers	2.2	6.5	5.6	26.4	13.5	12.7	9.5

SOURCE: Thomas Goliber, "Cuyahoga Blacks: A Social and Demographic Study, 1850–1880" (M.A. thesis, Kent State University, 1972), 64–96; Department of the Interior, Census Office, *Ninth Census, 1870* (Washington, 1873), I, 784.
[a] Data for Cuyahoga County. The raw data on Negro occupations were taken from Goliber's study; the data were reorganized, however, according to the classification system explained in Appendix I of this volume. All other data were computed from the 1870 published census.
[b] Because more occupations in the 1870 printed census than in the 1870 manuscript census were unclassifiable (see Appendix I), it is likely that the percentages of white workers in skilled, semiskilled, and unskilled work, as listed above, are somewhat underestimated.

of the Negro family and the superior economic opportunities afforded
black males in nineteenth-century Cleveland—there was only a slight
tendency for black women to be employed more frequently than whites.
In 1870, women made up 13.3 percent of the total work force, while
females comprised 17.5 percent of the Negro work force.[26]

By means of a proportionate weighting of the different occupational
categories, it is possible to calculate an occupational index which
measures the average occupational standing of any group in the economy. (Throughout this study, this index will be one of the main tools
used to compare the position of blacks relative to other groups.)[27] Table
3 shows that there was much less differentiation between the occupa-

TABLE 3. *Occupational indexes, by racial and ethnic group, Cleveland, 1870*

	Occupational index
Males	
Negroes	510
All workers	422
Females	
Negroes	618
All workers	617
Total work force	
Negroes	531
Foreign-born (total)	477
Native whites	414
Germans	459
Irish	528
English and Welsh	447
All workers	455

SOURCE: Table 2.

tional standing of Afro-Americans and other racial and ethnic groups in
1870 than would later become evident. The mythical "average" black
male worker stood almost one full occupational unit below his white
counterpart. But the typical employed male, regardless of the color of
his skin or place of birth, was more likely to be a manual laborer than

[26] Although the 1870 printed census does not provide enough information to
analyze female occupations by specific ethnic group, it is almost certain that Irish
women tended to be employed more often, and at lower paying jobs, than German
or English women. In 1890 German and English immigrant women made up, respectively, 12.6 percent of the total work forces of their ethnic groups; however,
20.6 percent of all employed Irish immigrants were female. U.S. *Thirteenth Census,
Occupations* (Washington, 1893), II, 654–55.

[27] The occupational index is explained in Appendix I.

anything else; only among native whites did white-collar workers make up even 10 percent of the total work force. Negroes and Irish immigrants were clearly at the bottom of the occupational ladder. Cleveland in 1870, however, was still to a large extent a commercial rather than an industrial city, and there was much less diversity in its job structure than there would be later. As a result, there were not very many "rungs" between the top and bottom of the occupational ladder, and the status discrepancy between the highest and lowest groups on the scale was considerably foreshortened.

At the close of the Civil War, a large minority of Cleveland's black population had an aura of middle-class respectability. As a result of their unusual educational and economic opportunities, a significant number of blacks in the Forest City were able to accumulate property. Mention has already been made of several early black residents who acquired modest fortunes by buying land that later grew tremendously in value. The acquisition of property, however, was not limited to these lucky few. In 1850 eighteen blacks (23.6 percent of all heads of households) owned $15,660 in real estate. According to Thomas J. Goliber's meticulous compilation of manuscript census data, the total value of real property owned by Cuyahoga County Negroes increased dramatically to $237,400 in 1870, while the total number of property owners rose to 101, or 27.8 percent of the heads of households. Furthermore, those owning property in 1870 included many unskilled laborers and domestic servants who, despite their low occupational standing, had over the years been able to acquire modest holdings. The average value of the real estate owned by black property holders in Cuyahoga County in 1870 was $2,350; the average wealth per person (real estate and personal property) for the entire black population was $198. At a time when the average annual income of many workers was less than $500, these sums were not insignificant.[28]

Although a thorough history of black economic status remains to be written, it is clear from the scattered studies that exist that the overall economic standing of Cleveland's black population was higher than

[28] Goliber, "Cuyahoga Blacks," 98–101. Comparison of the economic status of black Clevelanders with the rural free Negroes of North Carolina is instructive. In 1860 the average wealth per person of the latter was only $34. John Hope Franklin, *The Free Negro in North Carolina, 1790–1860* (Chapel Hill, N.C., 1943), 159. Even more striking are the data on blacks in rural Adams County, Mississippi, recently compiled by Herbert Gutman. In 1880 only 6 percent of the adult black males in Adams County were farmers who owned property, and only 1 percent were skilled artisans. See Gutman, "The World Two Cliometricians Made," *Journal of Negro History*, 60 (January 1975), 123 (revised and reprinted, Urbana, Ill., 1975, as *Slavery and the Numbers Game: A Critique of Time on the Cross*).

that of most black communities in the nineteenth century. Perhaps the only city where black economic status surpassed that of Cleveland was New Orleans. During the 1860–80 period the free Negroes of that polyglot metropolis were employed in an amazing variety of skilled, semi-skilled, and proprietary occupations, and were able to accumulate substantial property, despite the racial antipathy of many whites. Whether this pattern prevailed elsewhere in the South is open to question, however. The situation in Atlanta was much different. There, in 1870, seven out of ten blacks were listed as laborers or servants. At the same time the number of blacks in Baltimore "with jobs requiring no skill at all far outweighed those with skilled or business or professional positions," and few Negroes in that city were able to acquire property.[29]

In most northern cities (at least those that have been studied so far), blacks were largely restricted to low-paying unskilled jobs.[30] As early as 1860, many black communities contained a property-holding middle class and even, in some cases, an elite group of well-to-do entrepreneurs; but these groups usually remained quite small. In New York City in 1855, for example, 76.9 percent of employed Negro males were either unskilled laborers or (as was more often the case) domestic servants, and only 5.6 percent held skilled jobs; less than one Negro in ten owned taxable property. In 1847 only 6 percent of the blacks living in Philadelphia owned real estate. The pattern of occupations there was similar to that of New York, although a considerably higher proportion of blacks (16 percent) were able to gain access to the skilled trades. The free Negroes of Washington, D.C., did somewhat better; by 1860 approximately 14 percent owned real estate. Conditions in antebellum Boston were much more favorable. There, in 1850, the occupational status of

[29] Blassingame, *Black New Orleans*, 60–61, 68–69, 223–28; Richard J. Hopkins, "Occupational and Geographical Mobility in Atlanta, 1870–1896," *Journal of Southern History*, 34 (May 1968), 204; Richard P. Fuke, "Black Marylanders, 1864–68" (Ph.D. dissertation, University of Chicago, 1973), 102, 105.

[30] It is important to note that this may also have been true of many immigrant groups and even some native whites, especially in the eastern seaboard cities during the antebellum period. Quantitative studies have shown that the social order of the large urban centers was becoming increasingly stratified on the eve of the Civil War. Stuart Blumin, "Mobility and Change in Ante-Bellum Philadelphia," in Stephan Thernstrom and Richard Sennett, eds., *Nineteenth-Century Cities* (New Haven, Conn., 1969), 204–6; Edward Pessen, 'The Egalitarian Myth and the American Social Reality: Wealth, Mobility, and Equality in the 'Era of the Common Man,' " *American Historical Review*, 76 (October 1971), 989–1034. A thorough analysis of the place of blacks in the socioeconomic order of nineteenth-century America would examine regional variations in black occupations and wealth-holding, would survey differences among blacks, imigrants, and native whites in each region or city, and would trace changes in these variations over time. This type of analysis is beyond the scope of the present study.

blacks easily surpassed that of the newly arrived Irish immigrants, most
of whom were unskilled laborers or servants. A surprisingly large number of Boston Negroes (8.5 percent) operated small businesses, and an
equally high 47.8 percent were employed as skilled or semiskilled workers. Among eastern cities, Boston was clearly exceptional in the opportunities it afforded blacks. In the fast-growing metropolises of the West
and Midwest, the economic status of blacks was probably a good deal
higher than that of most eastern cities. But even in Pittsburgh and Cincinnati, the average wealth per person for blacks in 1870 was only about
two-thirds that of Cleveland.[31]

[31] Robert Ernst, "The Economic Status of New York City Negroes, 1850–
1863," Negro History Bulletin, 12 (March 1949), 139–43 (footnote 38 and the
"Special Statistical Note" at the end of the article); Gilbert Osofsky, "The Endur-
ing Ghetto," Journal of American History, 55 (September 1968), 248; A Statistical
Inquiry into the Condition of the People of Color, of the City and Districts of
Philadelphia (Philadelphia, 1849), 14, 17; Du Bois, The Philadelphia Negro, 179–
81; Hershberg, "Free Blacks in Antebellum Philadelphia," 187, 198–99; Dorothy
Provine, "The Economic Position of the Free Blacks in the District of Columbia,
1800–1860," Journal of Negro History, 58 (January 1973), 68–69; John Daniels,
In Freedom's Birthplace: A Study of the Boston Negroes (Boston, 1914), 18–19;
Handlin, Boston's Immigrants, 69–70, 250–51 (Table 13). The percentages for
black occupations in New York and Boston were computed from the manuscript
census data provided by Handlin and Ernst; the occupational classification system
used is explained in Appendix I. The data on wealth-holding in Pittsburgh and
Cincinnati were supplied by Paul Lammermeier of Kent State University, whose
forthcoming dissertation on the black communities of cities along the Ohio River
Valley will deal extensively with the question of black occupations and property
ownership, as well as with family structure and other aspects of black life.

The most thorough study of an antebellum black community, Theodore Hershberg's "Free Blacks in Antebellum Philadelphia," concludes that there was "a
remarkable deterioration in the socioeconomic condition of blacks from 1830 to
the Civil War." While this was undoubtedly true of Philadelphia and a number of
other cities, it is important to note that these circumstances did not prevail uniformly throughout the country. Although blacks everywhere suffered from prejudice
and discrimination, they were often able, in spite of handicaps, to make considerable economic progress at the time. (On this point, see E. Franklin Frazier,
The Free Negro Family, Nashville, 1932, 12–23; Provine, "Economic Position of
Free Blacks," 61–72; Letitia Woods Brown, Free Negroes in the District of Columbia, 1790–1846, New York, 1972, 140; and Blassingame, Black New Orleans,
10–11. See also the 1850 occupational data assembled by Katzman, Before the
Ghetto, 29, although Katzman draws oddly negative conclusions from his findings.)
Furthermore, our understanding of the economic status of black Americans in the
nineteenth century is still incomplete because of the almost total scholarly neglect
of northern blacks who lived outside the larger cities. It is seldom realized that
throughout most of the nineteenth century most blacks—like most whites—resided
in rural areas or small towns. While in some of these communities blacks lived in
wretched poverty, in others quite the opposite conditions were in evidence. In
rural New England, southwestern Michigan, and the Quaker settlements of Ohio,
Indiana, and Illinois, blacks encountered little animosity from their white neighbors and little competition from immigrants and may as a result have had a much

IV

The low level of prejudice and unusual economic opportunities that prevailed in Cleveland before 1870 did not lead to a sense of complacency among the city's Afro-Americans. Rather it engendered a feeling of pride and a strong belief that the barriers of inequality that existed throughout most of the United States (as well as the remnants still evident in Cleveland) could only be surmounted through concerted, militant action. Blacks expressed this attitude most vigorously in their denunciation of the Fugitive Slave Law. "We will exert our influence to induce slaves to escape from their masters," a meeting of Cleveland Negroes declared in 1850, "and will protect them from recapture against all attempts, whether lawful or not, to return them to slavery."[32]

Afro-Americans in Cleveland and throughout the Western Reserve participated actively in the abolitionist movement and aided fugitive slaves in gaining safe passage to Canada. Alfred Greenbrier's farm, for many years equipped with a number of secret hideouts, served as an important link in the underground railroad; and Greenbrier's fine horses, according to legend, helped provide the necessary transportation to the next station along the line. Several other black leaders, especially John Brown and John Malvin, regularly assisted escaped slaves. By the 1850s, the city's black community had organized a vigilance committee of five men and four women whose purpose was to find temporary residence, material aid, and sometimes jobs for fugitives until they could be safely transported to Canada. During one nine-month period in 1854–55, the committee assisted a total of 275 runaways.[33]

When civil war erupted in 1861, Cleveland's black citizens were among the first to express their desire to serve in the Union army. "Resolved," they stated in an April 19 meeting, "that today, as in the times of '76, and in the days of 1812, we are ready to go forth and do battle in

---

better chance to acquire property than did their counterparts in Philadelphia and New York. In 1870—to give one readily available example—fully 57 percent of the black families living in the southern Ohio community of Portsmouth owned real estate. (Lammermeier, "The Urban Black Family in the Nineteenth Century," 445.)

[32] Cleveland *Daily True Democrat*, September 30, 1850.

[33] Davis, *Memorable Negroes in Cleveland's Past*, 11; Peskin ed., *North Into Freedom*, 44–46, 73–74; Benjamin Quarles, *Black Abolitionists* (New York, 1969), 153. Whether Greenbrier's farm was really as important a station in the underground railroad as legend would have us believe is difficult to determine. As Larry Gara has pointed out in *The Liberty Line: The Legend of the Underground Railroad* (Lexington, Ky., 1961), the exploits of many abolitionists tended to grow larger in the minds of some as the Civil War era receded into the haze of memory.

the common cause of our country." Negroes in Cleveland, as elsewhere, however, were not immediately allowed the opportunity to join in the struggle against the Confederacy. No sooner had the city's blacks offered their services than H. B. Carrington, the state's adjutant general, informed them that the Ohio constitution (which excluded blacks from the militia) did not allow their enlistment. During the first two years of the war, Ohio governor David Tod continued to resist all offers of blacks to volunteer; as a result, a number of blacks from Cleveland (including the barber John Brown's two sons) and other Ohio cities traveled to Massachusetts to join the black regiment that had been established there. It was not until the summer of 1863 that the recruitment of Negro troops in Ohio was finally authorized; black Clevelanders who joined after that date served in the Fifth United States Colored Troops, a regiment recruited almost exclusively from Ohio. The black community aided the war effort on the home front as well by contributing liberally to the Soldiers' Aid Society and holding several fairs to benefit the Cleveland branch of the Freedmen's Aid Society.[34]

Three leaders who exemplified the activism and militancy of the Cleveland black community during its early years were John L. Watson, William Howard Day, and John Malvin. In the 1840s, Watson was active in the Young Men's Union Society, a black organization founded "for mutual assistance and improvement" of the black community. Watson, a barber, was a frequent speaker at the Lyceum organized by the YMUS for the purpose of debating the important issues of the day; in 1842 he served as secretary of the School Committee organized at that time to support black education in the city. Watson was a delegate to a number of the state conventions held by Ohio Negroes prior to the Civil War. His prestige among Ohio Negroes was such that in 1850 he was appointed president of the 1850 State Convention of Colored Citizens and was one of two individuals named by the convention to lecture throughout the state on behalf of Negro suffrage. Apparently Watson left the city after 1858, but for two decades he had served the black community well as one of its most dynamic leaders.[35]

[34] Peskin, ed., North into Freedom, 84–85; Benjamin Quarles, The Negro in the Civil War (Boston, 1953), 29, 191–93; Charles H. Wesley and Patricia Romero, Negro Americans in the Civil War (New York, 1967), 61–62; Cleveland Leader, February 2, 13, 1865.

[35] Cleveland Herald and Gazette, February 5, March 29, 1839; Cleveland Herald, March 6, 1841, January 8, July 16, 1842, April 13, 1843, in Annals XXII, 129, 131, XXIV, 141, XXV, 179, 223, XXVI, 187; Cleveland Daily True Democrat, January 21, 30, February 2, 1850; Report of Proceedings of the Colored National Convention held at Cleveland, Ohio, on Wednesday, September 6, 1848 (Rochester, N.Y.,

Though a resident of Cleveland for only a few years, William Howard Day gained more national recognition than Watson as a result of his many activities on behalf of the race. After graduating from Oberlin College in 1847, Day served briefly as a local editor for the white *Daily True Democrat*; for several years he also worked as a librarian for the Cleveland Library Association, the antecedent of the present library system. He edited the first black newspaper in Cleveland, *The Aliened American*, a militant journal which lasted from 1853 to 1855, and also published briefly in 1855 a monthly, *The People's Exposition*. A leading participant in the antebellum Negro Convention Movement, Day worked tirelessly on behalf of racial justice in the United States and also lectured abroad to raise funds for the assistance of fugitive slaves who had fled to Canada.[36]

It was not Day, however, but John Malvin, known as "Father John" by the time of his death in 1880 at eighty-five, who best exemplified both the militancy of the city's early black leaders and the high degree to which successful blacks were integrated into the general life of the community. Malvin worked at a variety of occupations, most of which entailed close contact with whites. At various times he served as cook, a sawmill operator, a carpenter and joiner, and a canalboat captain—in the latter instance, presiding over a thoroughly integrated crew. Eventually Malvin bought a lake vessel and built up a considerable business transporting limestone across Lake Erie to supply the city's first iron foundries.[37]

In the early 1830s, when Cleveland was still a village and had no public educational system, Malvin helped organize a school for blacks. Throughout most of his life, however, he fought for racial equality and the admission of blacks to white institutions, rather than for separate

---

1848); Howard H. Bell, "A Survey of the Negro Convention Movement, 1830–1861" (Ph.D. dissertation, Northwestern University, 1953), 139.

[36] Cleveland *Daily True Democrat*, September 10, 1852, June 15, 1853; Cleveland *Leader*, January 10, June 5, 1855; Davis, "Early Colored Residents of Cleveland," 24–43; J. Reuben Sheeler, "The Struggle of the Negro in Ohio for Freedom," *Journal of Negro History*, 31 (April 1946), 224; Bell, "A Survey of the Negro Convention Movement," 17, 107, 118, 141, 156, 172–73; Cleveland *Aliened American*, April 9, 1853. Day was one of the most militant black leaders of his era, and he urged Afro-Americans to use violent means if necessary to help slaves escape from bondage. (See *Proceedings of the Convention of Colored Men of Ohio, held in the city of Cincinnati, on the 23rd, 24th, 25th and 26th Days of November, 1858,* Cincinnati, 1858, 17–18.) The black editor left Cleveland in 1858 and eventually settled in Harrisburg, Pennsylvania, where he served for many years on the Board of Education. Day died in 1900.

[37] Peskin, ed., *North into Freedom*, 49–87; Davis, "Early Colored Residents of Cleveland," 237–40.

black institutions. Malvin and his wife, Harriet, were charter members of the First Baptist Church; and when the church's first permanent home was constructed in 1835, they were successful in preventing the segregation of black members in a separate "colored gallery." Malvin was a prominent member of the Cleveland Anti-Slavery Society, served as a lecturer for that organization, and personally assisted runaway slaves who were seeking safe passage to the border to the north. Though to a lesser extent than Day, Malvin was active in the Negro Convention Movement, and in 1843 he and one R. Robinson were the first blacks from Cleveland to attend a national convention. The ship captain fought vigorously against the Black Laws and was a frequent speaker at mass meetings protesting the unequal treatment that Afro-Americans received at the hands of the state legislature.[38]

Almost all of Cleveland's early black leaders were integrationists, and their success in breaking down many of the racial barriers that afflicted the race elsewhere caused them to look more hopefully to the future than did their brethren in other parts of the union. As a result, the sentiment for black emigration to Africa or Latin America that arose among an increasing number of northern black leaders during the pessimistic 1840s and '50s did not find much response among Afro-Americans in the Forest City. In a series of meetings held in the winter of 1845–46, Cleveland blacks joined with delegates from other cities to denounce the American Colonization Society as a racist organization that could only hinder the quest for equal rights in the United States. And seven years later a Cleveland delegate to the Ohio State Convention of Colored Freemen attacked the ACS as a "nefarious and diabolical" organization and supported a resolution naming the Society as "one of our worst enemies."[39]

---

[38] Peskin, ed., *North into Freedom*, 63–67, 56–57; *Minutes of the National Convention of the Colored Citizens Held at Buffalo, On the 15th, 16th, 17th, 18th and 19th of August, 1843* (New York, 1843), 11, 17–19; *Report of Proceedings of the Colored National Convention . . . 1848, passim*; Cleveland *Daily True Democrat*, June 15, 1853; *Proceedings of the National Convention of Colored Men, held in the City of Syracuse, N.Y., October 4, 5, 6, 7, 1864* (Boston, 1864), 6, 11. It is interesting to note that Malvin, unlike Day, was not willing to urge blacks to take up arms against the slaveholders. In the Negro Convention of 1843, he was one of the principal speakers against Henry Highland Garnet's resolution advocating violent rebellion by slaves.

[39] *African Repository and Colonial Journal*, 22 (1846), 265; *Cleveland Aliened American*, April 9, 1853. For the general black response to the Colonization Society and emigrationism, see Louis Mehlinger, "The Attitude of the Free Negro toward African Colonization," *Journal of Negro History*, 1 (July 1916), 271–301, and Hollis R. Lynch, "Pan-Negro Nationalism in the New World, Before 1862," in Jeffrey Butler, ed., *Boston University Papers on Africa*, II, *African History* (Boston, 1966), 149–79.

The ACS was a white organization; black Clevelanders also, however, opposed the plans of black emigrationists. In a meeting of the black citizens of the city in 1846 the question of emigrating was brought up, but "resolutions were adopted opposing the plan." And when a black emigrationist convention met in Cleveland in 1854 to promote colonization outside of North America, the *Leader* remarked "that the objects of the convention met with but little favor from our colored citizens." On the very eve of the Civil War there apparently was some upsurge of interest in emigration. "It has been announced," the press reported in March of that year, "that a party of intelligent colored citizens, mostly of Cleveland, propose to visit Africa, some to establish immediate homes, others to learn what advantages are to be found for those who wish to go." Whether the proposed trip was actually carried out is unknown, but with the coming of the Civil War no further mention of migrating to Africa was made by black Clevelanders.[40]

Equal access to most public accommodations and the integrationist ideology of Cleveland's black leadership retarded the development of separate black institutions in the city. Blacks did organize a number of informal literary and cultural groups and formed several debating societies, and in 1841 a black temperance society was formed. But unlike most cities in Ohio and throughout the North, Cleveland during these decades had few *formal* black institutions. The city had no separate schools for Negroes. The *Aliened American* was one of the earliest black newspapers in the country, but its existence was short-lived; it was less a community newspaper, in fact, than an organ for Negro leaders throughout the Midwest who were engaged in various protest activities. The small size of Cleveland's black population and the generally favorable editorial stance and news coverage of the *Leader* delayed the establishment of a regularly published black weekly until 1883.[41]

[40] Cleveland *Herald*, April 9, 1846, in *Annals*, IXXX, 177; Cleveland *Leader*, August 25, 1854, March 19, 1859. One black leader who did play an active role in the emigrationist movement was William Howard Day. Throughout the early 1850s, Day attempted to remain neutral on the emigration issue, but in 1856 he came out strongly for the plan and during the next six years actively promoted black migration to Africa (Cleveland *Leader*, September 18, 1858; Bell, "A Survey of the Negro Convention Movement," 141, 156, 173, 202–03, 208). By 1856, however, Day was more a national than a local leader, and he did not speak for the majority of black Clevelanders in supporting emigration.

[41] Cleveland *Herald*, April 21, 1841, 1841, in *Annals*, XXIV, 287; Davis, "Early Colored Residents of Cleveland," 240; Cleveland *Daily True Democrat*, January 1, 1850. On black support of the Cleveland *Leader*, see a letter to the editor of the *Leader*, October 12, 1874. On the *Leader's* radicalism compared with most other Midwestern white newspapers, see V. Jacque Voegeli, *Free But Not Equal: The*

Thanks to men like John Malvin, a number of Cleveland churches remained integrated until late in the nineteenth century. Cleveland's first black church, St. John's AME (African Methodist Episcopal), was founded in 1830, but it grew very slowly during its first two or three decades and was serviced primarily by a lower-class element who felt out of place attending the staid services of the integrated congregations. In 1855 it was reported that the church was having difficulty meeting the salary of its pastor, R. M. Thompson, and had to hold a "donation party" to cover these expenses temporarily. During the next ten years St. John's apparently grew in size, and the congregation was able to move from their old home on Bolivar Street to a newly constructed edifice on Ohio Street and to furnish their new pastor, John A. Warren, with a parsonage. By 1863 the church had seventy-six members and "85 scholars in its Sunday school." Though a notable improvement over earlier years, this figure still represented only about 15 percent of the black population of the city at that time.[42]

The existence of integrated schools, churches, and other institutions meant that the group life of Cleveland's black citizens would, for some time, be different in several respects from that of most other black communities. The use of black churches as all-purpose institutions proved largely unnecessary. "In addition to being a center of religious devotion and ceremony," Leon Litwack has said in describing the typical antebellum black church, "it was a school, a political meeting hall, a community recreation and social center, and not too infrequently, a haven for fugitive slaves." Black Clevelanders, however, had less pressing need for these functions that the church provided elsewhere, because they shared the schools, the meeting halls, and to some extent the recreation and social centers of the city with white citizens.[43]

In time all this would change. The growth of the commercial town of Cleveland into a major industrial metropolis, bringing with it new patterns of residency and employment; the changing racial attitudes of whites in the city as well as in the country as a whole; the influx of immigrants from southern and eastern Europe; the declining influence and changing values of the white elite of New England stock that ruled the city during the nineteenth century; the increasing migration of impoverished blacks from the South—all these changes (and more) would

Midwest and the Negro during the Civil War (Chicago, 1967), 5, 62, 79, 86–87, 164.
    [42] Rose, Cleveland, 124, 325; introduction to Peskin, ed., North into Freedom, 18; Cleveland Leader, November 21, 1855, September 22, 1863.
    [43] Litwack, North of Slavery, 188.

gradually alter the status of the black population of Cleveland and call forth diverse responses from the city's black leaders.

For the time being, however, black Clevelanders enjoyed a significant degree of racial equality. Their condition was not, it is true, unsullied by prejudice and discrimination, and even during the Civil War and Reconstruction years, when sympathy for black rights was at its peak, there were hints of trouble to come. When fraternal lodges began to become popular after the war, Cleveland Negroes found (with a few exceptions) that they had to set up separate fraternal orders if they wished to participate in this activity. The formation in 1864 of a black middle-class church, Mt. Zion Congregational, was further evidence that there were limitations to the white acceptance of blacks as equals. In 1874, in a striking reversal of some previous judicial decisions, a Cleveland judge upheld the right of the proprietor of the Academy of Music to exclude black patrons from the theater's dress circle. These were clouds on the horizon, but they were not, as yet, significant enough to be viewed as part of a dangerous trend.[44] The development of the ghetto, and all that it entailed, still lay in the future.

[44] Cleveland *Leader*, November 30, 1874. Separate black Masonic and Odd Fellows lodges in Cleveland dated to 1856, but during the early years of these institutions a few blacks were accepted in white lodges. The development of black lodges and churches is surveyed in Chapter 5.

PART II

The Black Community in
Transition, 1870-1915

CHAPTER 2

Urban Change and the Roots of the Ghetto

The period between 1870 and 1915 may be called the formative years of the black ghetto in the United States. Clear-cut black ghettos emerged in only a few cities during this period, but in most metropolises there was a noticeable increase in the residential segregation of blacks in a few fairly well defined sections. The intensification of racism during the post-Reconstruction decades (as discussed in Chapter 3) was one cause of the development of ghettos; it was not, however, the sole factor involved. Racial prejudice has always existed in the United States, but black ghettos have not. In order to understand the phenomenon of ghettoization, it is necessary to study the urban context as well as the racial context in which it occurred.

The ghettos began to take shape when they did because a period of growing racial hostility coincided with an era of dramatic change in the patterns of urban life. Between the Civil War and World War I, urban society in America underwent an enormous transformation. The increase in population alone—the total number of urban dwellers expanded from 6,200,000 in 1860 to almost 42,000,000 a half-century later—astounded European visitors as much as it delighted American boosters. During these years, New York's population approached five million; Chicago's exceeded two million; and several other cities reached or neared the one-million mark. Size was but one part of the story, however. Equally important was the reorganization that accompanied this growth in numbers. In the large urban areas, the "walking city" of the middle decades of the nineteenth century, with its haphazard arrangement of stores, businesses, and residential areas, was rapidly being replaced by a much more tightly organized urban structure. New modes of transportation—the omnibus, the electric streetcar, and by the end of the 1890s, the elevated train and subway—made possible the beginning of the exodus to the suburbs or to outlying areas of the city and allowed urban populations to sort themselves out by racial, ethnic, or socioeconomic group. At the same time, the expansion and diversification of large industries led to a more rigid system of zoning regulations than previously had existed. The result was the emergence of huge urban centers tied together by a nexus of economic relationships, but divided geographically into numerous commercial, industrial, and residential districts.[1]

Although the growth of Chicago during this period represented the archetypical model for urban change, Cleveland was no less dramatically affected. A huge influx of immigrant labor and the annexation of a number of adjacent towns helped Cleveland mushroom from a medium-sized urban center of 93,000 in 1870 to the "sixth city" in the nation, and an important industrial center, by the eve of World War I (see Table 1). The city never developed a subway or elevated system (a decision which probably retarded the development of suburbs until the 1920s, when the automobile came into widespread use), but the introduction of the electric streetcar in the 1890s made the common pattern of residential dispersion within the city possible. Geographically, Cleveland became more tightly organized during these years. For several miles along its length, the Cuyahoga River Valley became a solid industrial belt. (After World War I, the expansion of this industrial belt to the east would have an impact on the city's black population.) Lower Euclid and Superior avenues and East 9th Street became the main commercial and financial district for the city. As increasing numbers of newly arrived immigrants settled on the near East Side of the city, the exodus of Cleveland's elite, native-white constituency from that section began. Although

---

1 Charles N. Glaab, ed., *The American City: A Documentary History* (Homewood, Ill., 1963), 174; Blake McKelvey, *The Urbanization of America, 1865–1915* (New Brunswick, N.J., 1963), 35–46, 76–85; Sam Bass Warner, Jr., *Streetcar Suburbs: The Process of Growth in Boston, 1870–1900* (Cambridge, Mass., 1962); Sam Bass Warner, Jr., *The Private City: Philadelphia in Three Periods of Its Growth* (Philadelphia, 1968), 161–76; Joel Arthur Tarr, "From City to Suburb: The 'Moral' Influence of Transportation Technology," in Alexander B. Callow, Jr., ed., *American Urban History: An Interpretive Reader with Commentaries*, 2d ed. (New York, 1973), 204–5. The best overall view of these changes (using Chicago as a case study) is Sam Bass Warner, Jr., *The Urban Wilderness: A History of the American City* (New York, 1972), ch. 4.

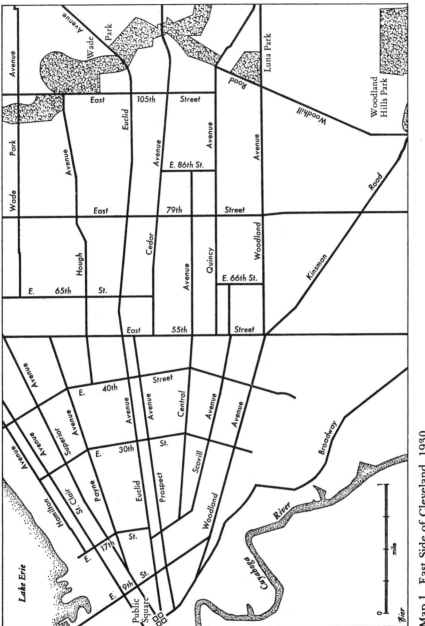

Map 1. East Side of Cleveland, 1930

much of Euclid Avenue (if not always the streets intersecting it) remained almost completely white as late as the 1950s, the noise of the streetcars, coupled with the encroachment of business firms and the foreign-born, persuaded most of the wealthy white families on that thoroughfare to leave before World War I. Many of them resettled on the quiet, tree-lined streets of the posh development beyond East 55th Street between Hough and Euclid avenues. (This area would later become the center of the city's post–World War II black ghetto.) Simultaneously, many middle-class Clevelanders also moved east and north of their previous, more centrally located residential areas, settling on the equally respectable—if less exclusive—streets between Hough and Superior avenues.[2]

It was within this context of dramatic urban change that Cleveland's black population expanded in size while simultaneously becoming more restricted to certain parts of the city. In 1870, only thirteen hundred Negroes resided in the Forest City; by 1890, this number had increased to three thousand. During the 1890s, the black population almost doubled in size, but its growth rate fell off sharply during the next ten years. In 1910, the city contained eighty-five hundred black residents.

Migration from other states accounted for most of the growth of the city's black community during these years. The black migration to Cleveland was part of a general drift of rural inhabitants to cities before World War I. Declining or unstable economic conditions in many farming regions, especially the South, caused many to move. Faced with a choice between the stagnating economy of the rural South and the booming factories of the North, the potential migrant had little trouble making a decision. But as the black sociologist George Edmund Haynes astutely noted, the beginnings of the black migration to the cities—a movement which has not yet ended—was more the product of "unconscious social forces" than reasoned alternatives. Blacks who migrated sought "better opportunities," but they did not necessarily define opportunity solely in economic terms. The desire for better schools, recreational facilities, and the need (especially evident among the younger black generation that had grown up since the Civil War) to escape the "hard, humdrum con-

[2] There is no thorough history of Cleveland for this period (or for that matter, any other). I have relied chiefly on James B. Whipple, "Cleveland in Conflict: A Study in Urban Adolescence, 1876–1900" (Ph.D. dissertation, Western Reserve University, 1951); Archer H. Shaw, *The Plain Dealer: One Hundred Years in Cleveland* (New York, 1942), 246–55; and the compilation of William Ganson Rose, *Cleveland: The Making of a City* (Cleveland, 1950). On the slower growth of Cleveland's suburbs, see W. Reynolds Farley, "Suburban Persistence" (M.A. thesis, University of Chicago, 1963), 43–45.

ditions and poor accommodations on plantation and farm" undoubtedly played an important part in motivating these early migrants.[3]

It is likely that most of the black migrants who came to Cleveland before World War I were young—in their teens or twenties—and that males predominated. Unlike in most eastern and southern cities, the black populations of Cleveland and many other midwestern cities did not have a majority of females either before or, for that matter, after the World War I migration. In Cleveland in 1900 only 46.9 percent of the black population was female, and this percentage was even lower in many other cities beyond the Alleghenies. It is also likely that few of these migrants brought children with them. The impact of relatively youthful, childless migrants on Cleveland's black population is illustrated by the distribution by ages for different groups in 1910. The black community was not overburdened by an excessively large percentage of small children; it closely resembled the city's immigrant element, in fact, in that two-thirds of its population was between the ages of fifteen and forty-four. Only 2.4 percent of Cleveland's blacks were over sixty-five, and children under five years of age comprised only 6.1 percent of the total. (See Table 4.) This contrasted sharply with the native whites and second-generation immigrants, both of whom had a much larger percentage of children.

TABLE 4. *Population by age group, Cleveland, 1910*

		Percentages			
	Total population	Native whites of native parentage	Native whites of foreign or mixed parentage	Foreign-born whites	Negroes
Under 5 years	11.1	14.1	18.6	.8	6.1
5–14 years	17.4	20.5	25.8	5.9	11.1
15–24 years	20.5	20.2	23.1	17.8	19.1
25–44 years	34.4	30.9	24.7	47.3	47.0
44–64 years	13.4	11.1	7.1	22.5	14.0
Over 64 years	3.0	2.8	0.6	5.9	2.4

SOURCE: U.S. *Thirteenth Census, 1910, Population* (Washington, 1913), I, 465.

[3] George Edmund Haynes, "Conditions among Negroes in the Cities," *Annals of the American Academy of Political and Social Science*, 49 (September 1913), 105–8; George Edmund Haynes, *The Negro at Work in New York City*, Columbia University Studies in History, Economics, and Public Law, vol. 49, no. 3 (New York, 1913), 27–32. See also the valuable discussion in Gilbert Osofsky, *Harlem: The Making of a Ghetto* (New York, 1966), 18–28.

About six out of every ten Negroes living in Cleveland in 1900 originated in states other than Ohio. (See Table 5.) Existing transportation
lines predetermined which states would contribute most to this flow of
migrants. The Baltimore and Ohio Railroad connected the city to the
southeastern seaboard, and the tier of states south of Pennsylvania
proved to be the point of departure for most black migrants who came
to Cleveland before World War I. More black residents of Cleveland

TABLE 5. *Area of birth of nonwhite residents of Cleveland, 1900*

Area of birth	Number per state	Percentage
Ohio	2,296	38.4
Middle West outside Ohio	370	6.2
Northeast	590	9.8
Upper South and Border	2,137	35.6
Lower South	300	6.0
West	17	0.3
Not specified or born abroad	153	2.6
Total	5,863	100.0

SOURCE: U.S. *Twelfth Census, 1900, Population* (Washington, 1902), 706–27.
The figures were obtained by adding the statistics from Tables 31 and 32 of the
census materials and subtracting the totals from Table 30.
    NOTE: *Middle West:* Michigan, Ohio, Indiana, Illinois, Iowa, Kansas, Wisconsin,
Minnesota, Nebraska, North and South Dakota; *Northeast:* New England states,
Pennsylvania, New York, New Jersey; *Upper South and Border:* Virginia, Kentucky,
Tennessee, North Carolina, Maryland, West Virginia, District of Columbia, Missouri,
Oklahoma, Delaware; *Lower South:* Georgia, South Carolina, Alabama, Mississippi,
Louisiana, Texas, Florida, Arkansas; *West:* all other states.

were born in Virginia than any other state except Ohio, and Maryland
and North Carolina also contributed their share. A number of rail lines
linked Cleveland, via Cincinnati, to Kentucky and Tennessee, and both
of those states sent sizable groups of Negroes to Cleveland. A smaller
but still significant number (about 10 percent) came from the Northeast,
especially the adjacent state of Pennsylvania and nearby New York. The
Lower South was not yet an important source of migration; only 6 percent of the Negroes living in Cleveland in 1900 had been born in that
region.[4]
    Although a majority of the city's black population in 1900 had mi-
grated from other states, a large minority (38.4 percent) had been born

[4] On the influence of transportation lines on migration, see Lilian Brandt, "The
Make-Up of Negro City Groups," *Charities*, 15 (October 7, 1905), 8. Chicago experienced a much larger influx of migrants from the Deep South than did Cleveland
before World War I. In 1900, 17 percent of Chicago's black population had originated in the Deep South. Allan H. Spear, *Black Chicago: The Making of a Negro
Ghetto, 1890–1920* (Chicago, 1967), 13.

in Ohio; and most of these had probably been born in Cleveland. By 1910 this figure had declined only slightly to 35.7 percent. Compared with the black communities of New York, Chicago, Cincinnati, and elsewhere, Cleveland's Afro-American population was more stable prior to World War I and contained a considerably higher proportion of individuals who had been born and reared in the North.[5]

In the late nineteenth century, most of the black newcomers to the city settled in the Central Avenue district, one of the oldest areas of the city and a district in which some blacks had lived since before the Civil War. By 1910, however, the area of settlement had expanded. Migrants now began to move into the area to the north between Central and Euclid avenues and to the south and east along Scovill and Woodland avenues. At that time the major portion of the black community lived within an area circumscribed on the north by Euclid and the wealthy residential section beyond it (from which Negroes were excluded for economic as well as racial reasons); on the south and west by the Cuyahoga River with its industrial zone, a natural boundary which would serve in the years ahead to limit the Negro population to the eastern section of the city; and on the east by East 55th Street, a major north-south thoroughfare. This area, then, constituted the nucleus of what would become Cleveland's first black ghetto.[6]

Blacks were not totally restricted to this area, but when they lived in other sections of the city they were more likely to settle near each other than to spread evenly throughout a neighborhood. Three such black "enclaves" existed before World War I.[7] One, a lower-class neighborhood of dilapidated structures, stretched along Hamilton Avenue between East 9th and East 14th streets. Close to the industrial section and the docks,

---

[5] In 1910, 19.3 percent of Chicago's Negroes were born in the state of residence. Comparative figures for other large cities are: Boston, 29.2; New York, 29.4; Philadelphia, 35.1; Pittsburgh, 34.4; Cincinnati, 28.4; Detroit, 32.2. U.S. Bureau of the Census, *Negroes in the United States, 1920–1932* (Washington, 1935), 32. The 1910 census does not give a breakdown of the Cleveland population by state of birth. The only data available for that year is for the Ohio Negro population as a whole, as listed in Appendix II.

[6] Howard W. Green, comp., *Population Characteristics by Census Tracts, Cleveland, 1930* (Cleveland, 1931), 231–32.

[7] In using the term "enclave" to describe areas of settlement outside the formative ghetto, I have followed the lead of other scholars. In particular, see Spear, *Black Chicago*, 11–17, and August Meier and Elliott Rudwick, *From Plantation to Ghetto*, rev. ed. (New York, 1970), 215. However, "enclave" connotes a compactness or density which these black sections often did not have. Like the main region of black settlement, these smaller areas of black population often exhibited an amorphous quality, with blacks tending to cluster on certain streets but still remaining, to a large extent, residentially integrated.

it was the least desirable neighborhood for blacks to live in. In three other areas outside the Central Avenue district middle-class Negroes had established themselves in small numbers. One such area lay slightly east of the intersection of Carnegie Avenue and East 105th Street, between Cedar and Euclid. Another small group of elite Negroes lived in the new middle-class Hough Avenue development north of Euclid; but they resided almost entirely in the less-exclusive area north of Hough between East 84th and East 95th streets. The third and smallest enclave lay along Kinsman Road in the southeast section of the city.[8]

The fact that most blacks lived within fairly well defined areas of the city at this time, however, does not mean that a black ghetto existed in Cleveland. Beyond the Central Avenue district and the three enclaves already mentioned, Negroes were spread throughout the eastern part of the city (very few blacks resided on the West Side) in small groups or single families. An analysis of 1910 census tract data reveals that of 155 tracts, all but 17 contained some Negro residents. Twenty-four tracts were at least 1 percent black, and no tract was more than 25 percent black. Even in the growing Negro section on Central and Scovill avenues, Negroes were still in the minority and lived in close proximity to an ever-increasing immigrant population, composed primarily of Italians and Russian Jews, who also sought refuge in that crowded and aging section of the city. "We have no 'LITTLE AFRICA' in Cleveland," Robert Drake, a Negro clerk, boasted in 1915. "There is not a single street in this city that is inhabited by nothing but Negroes."[9]

Nevertheless, despite the fact that few of the sections of the city were totally white and none were all-Negro prior to the World War I migration, the trend toward increasing segregation of the black population had already begun. As Cleveland's black community expanded in the early twentieth century, it did so primarily by filling in areas already distinguishable as "Negro sections." An analysis of population statistics by wards for 1900 and 1910 indicates that 17.8 percent of the black population in 1900 lived in wards which were less than 0.5 percent black; in 1910 only 6.4 percent lived in such wards. Furthermore, in 1900 41.8 percent of Cleveland's Negroes lived in wards which were greater than 5 percent black, while by 1910 this figure had risen to 62.3 percent. By then one-third of the city's Negroes lived in the Twelfth Ward, while in

---

[8] Green, comp., *Population Characteristics by Census Tracts*, 231–32; interview with Dr. William P. Saunders, August 6, 1972.

[9] Robert I. Drake, "The Negro in Cleveland," Cleveland *Advocate*, September 18, 1915. See Table 14 in Chapter 7.

1900 no two wards combined could claim more than 27 percent of the total Negro population.[10]

In order to properly assess the significance of this trend, it is necessary to take a longer view and to compare the residential distribution of blacks with that of other groups. To do this, indexes of dissimilarity (a basic measurement of segregation between any two groups in the population, ranging from 0 to 100) for a number of ethnic and racial groups in Cleveland were calculated from ward data available for 1870 and 1910. These calculations demonstrate that the late-nineteenth- and early-twentieth-century trend toward residential segregation was not limited to blacks. Between 1870 and 1910 the index for Negroes v. all native whites (a category that includes native-born of foreign or mixed parentage as well as those of native parentage) rose from 49 to 61, while that of Negroes v. the foreign-born increased from 52 to 66. During the same period, however, the index for native whites v. the foreign-born also rose, from 13 to 36. Furthermore, this last statistic obscures a much higher degree of segregation among specific immigrant groups. No data on individual ethnic groups are available for 1870, but in 1910 Cleveland's Italians were considerably more segregated from the dominant native-white element than were blacks, and the city's Hungarian, Russian, and Romanian immigrant communities also displayed a fairly high degree of spatial isolation.[11]

Other "new immigrant" groups, such as the Poles, Slavs, and Croatians, also tended to cluster in a few areas; but unlike the Italians and Romanians, they were slightly more segregated from blacks than from the dominant native-white element or the older immigrant groups. The Polish neighborhoods along Broadway Avenue lay well to the south of the major area of black settlement; the Slavs and Hungarians along Kinsman Road and Woodland Avenue were well to the east; and the Polish and Croatian areas along Superior and St. Clair avenues were far to the north of Central Avenue. The older Italian neighborhoods along Mayfield and Woodhill roads, on the border between Cleveland and its east-

[10] U.S. *Twelfth Census, 1900, Population* (Washington, 1902), 672–73; U.S. Bureau of the Census, *Negro Population in the United States, 1790–1915* (Washington, 1918), 107.

[11] For a discussion of the index of dissimilarity, see Karl Taeuber and Alma Taeuber, *Negroes in Cities: Residential Segregation and Neighborhood Change* (Chicago, 1965), 235–38. After the completion of this study I learned that a number of the indexes that I had computed for Cleveland for 1910 and 1920 had already been tabulated by Stanley Lieberson; see the statistical appendix to his study *Ethnic Patterns in American Cities* (Glencoe, Ill., 1963), 213. Since there are occasional discrepancies in our respective data, I have retained my own figures.

TABLE 6. *Index of dissimilarity, selected immigrant groups with native whites and Negroes, Cleveland, 1910*

	Native whites[a]	Negroes
Italians	76	66
Germans	21	74
English	17	57
Hungarians	45	72
Irish	28	67
Russians	52	62
Romanians	65	54
Swedes	40	65
All foreign-born	36	66

SOURCE: U.S. Census Bureau, *Thirteenth Census, 1910* (Washington, 1912), I, 427.

[a] Computed by adding together the categories "native white—native parentage" and "native white—foreign or mixed parentage" for each ward before calculating the index.

ern surburbs, were also well removed from the black community. These ethnic communities were not homogenous, but they did occupy fairly distinct sections of the city; relatively few of the new immigrants lived outside these areas. Thus, in one sense, the trend of increasing segregation of blacks was part of a general urban phenomenon of the prewar decades. The half-century before 1920 was, in the phrase of one historian, the age of "the segregated city," and it would indeed have been surprising if blacks had not shared the same experience that other urban groups were undergoing.[12]

[12] Eleanor E. Ledbetter, *The Slovaks of Cleveland, With Some General Information on the Race* (Cleveland, 1918), 11; Eleanor E. Ledbetter, *The Jugoslavs of Cleveland, With a Brief Sketch of their Historical and Political Backgrounds* (Cleveland [1918]), 13, 21; Green, comp., *Population Characteristics by Census Tracts*, 23, 219–29; Josef J. Barton, "Immigration and Social Mobility in an American City: Studies of Three Ethnic Groups in Cleveland, 1890–1950 (Ph.D. dissertation, University of Michigan, 1971); Warner, *The Urban Wilderness*, 85–112. See Table 14 in Chapter 7 for segregation indexes for Poles, Czechoslovakians, and Yugoslavians for 1920. No data are available on these groups for 1910.

Recently, historians who have studied ethnic segregation patterns in detail have emphasized the rapid geographic mobility of immigrants, the instability of ghettos and the lack of complete ethnic homogeneity in sections of cities supposedly dominated by one ethnic group. See Humbert Nelli, *The Italians in Chicago, 1880–1930: A Study in Ethnic Mobility* (New York, 1970), 22–54, and especially Howard P. Chudacoff, *Mobile Americans: Residential and Social Mobility in Omaha, 1880–1920* (New York, 1972), 35–83. While I am in general agreement with these authors that the monolithic quality of immigrant districts has been overstressed in the past, I think it would be a mistake to go too far in the opposite direction in emphasizing the instability of ethnic neighborhoods. Though never uniform or homogeneous, immigrant neighborhoods in *major* cities during the 1880–1920 period were an

Yet the context of urban change does not entirely explain the situation that blacks found themselves in. There were some forbidding signs indicating that the black urban experience was destined to be different from all other groups. There was a striking divergence, for example, between the residency patterns of blacks and those of Irish and German immigrants, even though the black community was older than either of these two groups. By 1910 only a few predominantly Irish neighborhoods survived in the city, primarily along Detroit Road on the West Side and in the area between Union Street and Miles Avenue to the southeast. With those exceptions, the Irish were well distributed throughout the city, as indicated by their relatively low index of dissimilarity, 28. The Germans were even more dispersed, and, although they tended more often to reside on the West Side than the East Side, no good-sized "German sections" existed on the eve of World War I. What is surprising about the residential assimilation of these two groups is that it occurred despite the fact that both continued to supplement their populations with immigrants from abroad during the prewar years. The "new immigration" from eastern and southern Europe was proportionately smaller in Cleveland than elsewhere in the North, and in 1910 the German-born continued to be the city's largest immigrant group, with a population of 41,406; the Irish remained fourth (exceeded by the Russians and the Hungarians) with 11,316. Thus the divergent patterns of residential distribution between blacks on the one hand and the Irish and, especially, the Germans on the other cannot be ascribed to the fact that the black community was burdened with a constantly increasing horde of newcomers, making assimilation difficult and resulting in segregation, whereas the Germans and Irish were relieved of this burden and could as a result assimilate their numbers more easily into the general life of the community. Although Cleveland's black community was growing during the late nineteenth and early twentieth centuries, its rate of increase was hardly exceptional compared with other groups. With the exception of the 1890s, in fact, the city's total population outstripped the growth rate of its black community for every ten-year period between 1860 and 1910. Cleveland's black population, while exanding absolutely, declined relatively from 1.9 to 1.2 percent of the city's total population between 1860

---

important factor in shaping the urban milieu. Badly needed are broad, comparative studies that will trace the residential development of a *variety* of ethnic groups in several different types of cities over a prolonged period of time; the present approach too often overgeneralizes from the experience of ·a single ethnic group in a single city.

and 1890; by 1910 this figure had increased only slightly to 1.5 percent.[13]

One cause of the widening gap between the residency patterns of Negroes and certain ethnic groups was the economic discrimination that
blacks suffered at the time. This limited the size of the black middle
class and made it impossible for many blacks to take part in the general
exodus to newer parts of the city. The occupational difference between
German and Irish immigrants and blacks (as will be explained in a later
chapter) was not great enough to account for the huge discrepancy in
residency patterns, however. A more significant cause was the growing
reluctance of white property-holders outside the Central Avenue district
to sell to blacks. Growing white opposition to black families moving into
their neighborhoods is difficult to document in Cleveland for the prewar
period because, unlike Chicago, there was no evidence of violent action
aimed at driving black families out of predominantly white sections of
the city. Rather the strategy appeared to be one of selling to "whites
only," thereby preventing any further integration of the black population in outlying residential districts. Census statistics for 1900 and 1910
indicate that the number of black families living in such areas remained
virtually unchanged during the first decade of the twentieth century;
thus the slowly increasing black middle class was forced more and more
to settle near Central Avenue. Whether the reluctance to sell to blacks
was due to a fear of deteriorating property values or was just another
aspect of the racism of the times (if, indeed, the two can be separated)
is impossible to document; the ultimate motivation of these whites
eludes the historian in this instance. What is clear is that, on the eve of
the "Great Migration" of 1916–19, racial discrimination in property
sales had become widespread in Cleveland. There was a "noticeable
tendency" toward the use of restrictive covenants, and in 1916 one
prominent black Clevelander complained that such discrimination had
become unofficial policy among members of the Cleveland Real Estate
Board. There were some desirable neighborhoods, he claimed, where
realtors would not sell or rent to Negroes, "no matter how much money
we have to pay for the desired property."[14]

[13] U.S. *Thirteenth Census, 1910, Population* (Washington, 1912), I, 427. See
Table 1 in Chapter 1 for full information on population growth during the 1860–
1910 period.

[14] Untitled description (dated April 25, 1914) of the formation of the Cleveland
branch of the National Association for the Advancement of Colored People, by
Harry E. Davis, NAACP branch files (Container G157), Papers of the National
Association for the Advancement of Colored People (referred to hereafter as
NAACP Papers), Manuscript Division, Library of Congress; George A. Myers to
F. H. Goff, January 17, 1916, George A. Myers Papers, Ohio Historical Society. On

In a very unspectacular way, such a policy helped push Cleveland's black community one step further down the road to the ghetto. It forced the city's black newcomers to settle increasingly within a rather circumscribed area; and although this area was very far from being all-Negro in composition, it was nevertheless one of the oldest in the city and suffered from over a half-century of constant use. "The quality of shelter occupied by the vast majority of Negroes in the North," Robert C. Weaver has said in describing the prewar era, "was generally similar to that occupied by other low-income families." As in the case of residential segregation, however, the comparison with poorer immigrant groups could be carried only so far, because black housing "was usually in the least desirable segments of the low-income areas, and often commanded higher rents than comparable shelter for whites." Cleveland's Central Avenue district and the black section on Hamilton Avenue fitted this description well. Four census tracts in the Central-Scovill area, housing altogether about one-half of Cleveland's Negro population in 1910, were among the most crowded in the city. Their densities ranged from forty-eight to eighty-two inhabitants per acre, while that of Cleveland as a whole was only thirteen per acre. Upon arriving in the city in 1905, Jane Edna Hunter, a nurse who later founded the local Phillis Wheatley Society, soon encountered the experience undoubtedly shared by most Negro migrants who came to Cleveland: "the despairing search for decent lodgings—up one dingy street and down another, ending with the acceptance of the least disreputable room we encountered." The small minority of Negro families who owned homes outside the Central Avenue district frequently refused, because of middle-class pretensions, to take in roomers; and newcomers invariably found themselves "restricted to the unsightly, run-down sections of the city where houses rented for

---

the earlier and more violent opposition to residential integration in Chicago, see Spear, *Black Chicago*, 20–23, and William M. Tuttle, Jr., *Race Riot: Chicago in the Red Summer of 1919* (New York, 1970), 160–61. At this time housing discrimination against middle-class Negroes in Philadelphia was also on the rise, but in Boston opposition to blacks moving into "better" white neighborhoods apparently remained fairly light. See W. E. B. Du Bois, *The Philadelphia Negro* (Philadelphia, 1899), 348–49; John T. Emlen, "The Movement for the Betterment of the Negro in Philadelphia," *Annals of the American Academy of Political and Social Science*, 49 (September 1913), 88; W. E. B. Du Bois, "The Black North," *New York Times Magazine*, December 8, 1901; John Daniels, *In Freedom's Birthplace: A Study of the Boston Negroes* (Boston, 1914), 151–52. It should be noted that pre–World War I housing discrimination did not affect Cleveland's small Negro elite nearly as much as it did the black middle and lower class. Most members of this elite were of fair complexion and many had close social or business relationships with whites; this may help to account for white acceptance of them in some neighborhoods. See Chapter 5 for a fuller discussion of this group.

as little as fifteen dollars a month and the landlady, who secured two roomers at one dollar and a quarter [per week], could realize two-thirds of her rent." Under these circumstances, a "small, low-roofed, poorly furnished room" was rapidly becoming standard fare for many Cleveland Negroes.[15]

The existence of vice districts in close proximity to black residential sections further hampered Negroes in their efforts to find decent housing in Cleveland. As early as 1905 Hamilton Avenue was well known as an area of gambling houses, "dives," and brothels, many of which were, according to Jane Hunter, engaged in "wholesale organized traffic in black flesh." During the next ten years, a second, larger red-light district developed, this time in the vicinity of East 30th and Central, in the very heart of the developing black community. By the eve of the war time migration, the editor of the Cleveland Gazette, a Negro weekly, noted with dismay the proliferation of "speakeasies, gambling, and questionable houses" in that decaying section of the city, catering in a most democratic manner to whites and blacks, immigrants and the native-born alike.[16]

The development of vice districts in or near predominantly Negro neighborhoods was a phenomenon that Cleveland shared with many northern cities. New York had its Tenderloin district, Columbus its "Badlands," Detroit its "Heights" area, and each catered to the same kind of disreputable clientele. Although this phenomenon has not received systematic study from historians, it appears that the association of blacks with vice amounted to a kind of self-fulfilling prophecy on the part of the white population. In the late nineteenth century many whites, in accordance with the stereotypes then in vogue, conceived of blacks as prone to loose morals and illicit (if often humorous) behavior. Yet the predominantly white police forces of cities, responding to the pressures of white public opinion, often refused to allow red-light districts to develop anywhere *except* in or near a black neighborhood. "In more than one city," said R. R. Wright, Jr., surveying Negro housing in the North in 1908, "the distinctively Negro neighborhood is the same as, or next to, that district which seems, *by consent of civil authorities*, to be given up to vice." In New York, Chicago, and Philadelphia, where more than one red-light district existed, vice areas could also be found in immigrant neighbor-

15 Robert C. Weaver, *The Negro Ghetto* (New York, 1948), 21; Howard W. Green, comp., *Population by Census Tracts, Cleveland and Vicinity, with Street Index* (Cleveland, 1931), 7–8; Jane Edna Hunter, *A Nickel and a Prayer* (Cleveland, 1940), 70–85. The tracts described are I–2, I–3, H–7, and H–9.

16 Hunter, *A Nickel and a Prayer*, 68–69, 124; Cleveland *Gazette*, April 1, 1916.

hoods. But taking the North as a whole, and considering the small size of the black population of most northern cities at this time, it is clear that the police were far more prone to allow vice in or near black neighborhoods than in white sections.[17]

Occasionally a few civic-minded individuals, white as well as black, attempted to eliminate some of these unsavory aspects of urban life, but the resultant reforms were usually ineffectual or short-lived. In 1908 a number of prominent black leaders mounted a campaign against vice and crime on Central Avenue; but their original enthusiasm soon withered in the face of an uninterested community, and the movement for reform died. A few years later a more serious reform effort arose, only to meet the same fate. In 1911 and 1912 a number of prohibitionists and members of the clergy had launched a drive to curtail the activities of the numerous dance halls and saloons in Cleveland's lower-class neighborhoods. These establishments served as social centers in the immigrant and black communities, but many of them were also undoubtedly fronts for various kinds of illegal activity, especially gambling and prostitution; they were often the scene of raucous arguments, drunken brawls, and general disorder. It was while this reform movement was gaining ground that a particularly brutal murder occurred on Central Avenue. Incensed by this outrage, black leaders called a mass meeting to protest the lack of police protection in the black sections of the city. The meeting was well attended and a committee was formed to meet with Mayor Newton D. Baker, who agreed to crack down on the saloons. The city's dance halls also came under scrutiny. After an investigation by a committee headed by the progressive Twelfth Ward councilman Daniel E. Morgan, the city council passed an ordinance which allowed the mayor to license dance halls, impose a curfew on dances, and appoint a dance-hall inspector to enforce the regulations.

The entire effort for reform, however, soon came to nought. Baker did order the police to close several saloons, but this had little effect. The dance-hall ordinance also had no noticeable impact on the situation and soon became a dead letter; within a few years it had been largely nullified by pressure exerted by local musicians who were fearful of a cutback in their employment if the regulations were strictly enforced. At

[17] Du Bois, *The Philadelphia Negro*, 314; R. R. Wright, Jr., "Recent Improvement in Housing among Negroes in the North," *Southern Workman*, 37 (November 1908), 602 (emphasis added). See also J. S. Himes, "Forty Years of Negro Life in Columbus, Ohio," *Journal of Negro History*, 27 (April 1942), 140; David M. Katzman, *Before the Ghetto: Black Detroit in the Nineteenth Century* (Urbana, Ill., 1973), 172; Osofsky, *Harlem*, 14–15; Spear, *Black Chicago*, 25; Zane L. Miller, *Boss Cox's Cincinnati* (New York, 1968), 11.

the same time Morgan, who had received the Republican party's nomination for city solicitor and planned a further move against gambling and prostitution in the city, was defeated in the next election. His successor in city council, Thomas W. Fleming, was too closely allied with the notorious black racketeer Albert D. ("Starlight") Boyd to consider mounting a campaign against organized vice. In retrospect, however, it would appear that the whole campaign against the saloons and dance halls had a basic flaw that would have made its success difficult under any circumstances. In attempting to curtail these institutions, the city's white leaders offered no alternatives to a black community that suffered from a lack of public recreational facilities and was increasingly being excluded from such private facilities as the YMCA and amusement parks. Nor were the police or civic leaders particularly eager to drive vice from Negro neighborhoods, when they realized that red-light districts might spring up again in white areas. If, on the eve of the Great Migration, Central Avenue's reputation as an "open," "loose" section of the city seemed secure, most of the blame must be laid at the doorstep of the city's white population.[18]

With eighty-five hundred Negro inhabitants in 1910, Cleveland looked rather insignificant besides the "black metropolises" of Chicago (forty-four thousand Negroes), Philadelphia (eighty-four thousand) and New York (ninety-two thousand). In Cleveland, blacks were much less segregated than in Chicago, which in 1910 had four census tracts that were over 50 percent Negro, or New York, which had many predominantly Negro neighborhoods and which was in the process of transforming Harlem from an upper-middle-class white community to a black ghetto. Nevertheless, the same dramatic forces of urban change, black migration, and discrimination in housing that were creating Chicago's South Side black belt and New York's Harlem were at work in the Forest City. Although no ghetto existed, the groundwork for future concentration had been laid. A definite trend toward the segregation of the city's black population was evident, and about 80 percent of black Cleveland resided within four well-defined areas of settlement. Most significant was the emergence of the Central Avenue district as a potential black belt. By 1915, this area, with its cheap lodging houses, deteriorating

[18] Cleveland *Leader*, February 19, 1912; Cleveland *Gazette*, February 24, March 9, 16, May 11, 1912, September 15, 22, 1917; Frederick Rex, "Municipal Dance Halls," *National Civic Review*, 4 (1915), 413–19; Hunter, *A Nickel and a Prayer*, 68–69, 131–32; Thomas F. Campbell, *Daniel E. Morgan, 1877–1949: The Good Citizen in Politics* (Cleveland, 1966), 19, 35, 37, 41. The careers of Fleming and Boyd are examined in detail in Chapter 6.

homes, and vice conditions, housed a majority of the Negro population under conditions that were decidedly inferior to that of most of the city's residential sections.[19]

Although almost all cities exhibited some increase in the residential segregation of blacks in the late nineteenth and early twentieth centuries, it is important to note that there was still, in 1910, great variation in the spatial distribution of blacks in American cities. If the development of ghettos proceeded at a faster pace in New York, Philadelphia, and Chicago than in Cleveland, it occurred at a slower rate in western cities like Omaha, Minneapolis, and Los Angeles and in most southern cities. This slower development in some cities was due not to a more liberal racial atmosphere (this was hardly true of southern cities) but to their divergence from the pattern of urban change that was affecting the industrial centers of the East and Midwest. The western cities were small, rapidly growing metropolises that in many ways resembled the Cleveland and Chicago of a half-century before. High levels of geographic mobility, combined with excessive population turnover and unstable housing markets, kept the black populations of these cities fairly well dispersed at the turn of the century. Southern cities were also small but, with few exceptions, they were not rapidly growing; urban growth in the South lagged far behind that of the rest of the country during the 1860–1910 period. It is true that even in the antebellum period, small sections inhabited almost exclusively by free Negroes had existed in Charleston and other southern cities; but at that time most blacks in the urban South—whether slave or free—lived in alleys behind the residences of the whites whose servants they were, or in shacks nearby. The languishing economy and slow growth of these cities between the Civil War and World War I had the effect of freezing this earlier pattern of racial intermingling in residency patterns and retarding the growth of the ghetto. Thus, in 1910, even though blacks in southern cities comprised a much larger proportion of the total urban population, they remained much more dispersed than in the North.[20]

[19] Spear, *Black Chicago*, 145; Osofsky, *Harlem*, 12, 105–23. Chicago also had a much higher percentage of census tracts from which blacks were excluded entirely. Ninety-four of 431 tracts (or 21.8 percent) in Chicago, as opposed to only 17 of 155 tracts (10.9 percent) in Cleveland, were completely white in 1910. Spear, *Black Chicago*, 17; Green, comp., *Population Characteristics by Census Tracts*, 160–62.

[20] Richard C. Wade, *Slavery in the Cities: The South, 1820–1860* (New York, 1964), 273–80; C. Vann Woodward, *Origins of the New South, 1877–1913* (Baton Rouge, La., 1951), 139; Blaine Brownell, "Urbanization in the South: A Unique Experience?" *Mississippi Quarterly*, 26 (September 1973), 116. The effects of rapid population turnover in Omaha in the late nineteenth and early twentieth centuries are illustrated in Chudacoff, *Mobile Americans*; on Los Angeles, see Lawrence B. De

While it would be incorrect to state that the pattern of residency of Cleveland blacks in the prewar years was typical, it would be fair to say that it lay at or near the middle of the spectrum when conditions in various cities are compared. The ghetto was in its formative stage, but it had not yet taken shape. This was but one aspect of black life that was in transition.

Graaf, "The City of Black Angels: Emergence of the Los Angeles Ghetto, 1890–1930," *Pacific Historical Review*, 39 (August 1970), 328–29. In 1910, Los Angeles had an extraordinarily low segregation index (for Negroes v. native whites) of 29, and in Minneapolis, Portland, and San Francisco the index was under 40. These statistics, as well as the general conclusions of this paragraph, are drawn from an in-progress study by the author of the residential segregation patterns of immigrants and blacks in thirty cities between 1870 and 1930.

CHAPTER 3

The Eclipse of Equality:
Racial Discrimination

The period of the late nineteenth and early twentieth centuries was marked by what one historian has called "the betrayal of the Negro." In the South, the end of Reconstruction brought the return of white supremacy and the slow but steady disfranchisement and segregation of the black population, and a string of Republican administrations in Washington left the freedmen to fend for themselves in an increasingly hostile environment. The Supreme Court abetted this process in a series of decisions, beginning with the civil rights cases of 1883, which declared unconstitutional the Civil Rights Act of 1875, and culminating in *Plessy* v. *Ferguson* (1896), which established the "separate but equal" doctrine for public facilities. In a number of states blacks struggled vigorously against these trends, and as late as 1906 they boycotted streetcars in Savannah, Georgia, in an attempt to prevent the segregation of passengers by race. But in the end all such tactics were doomed to failure, and the victory of Jim Crow was assured for decades to come.[1]

[1] Of the many studies of the growth of racism between 1865 and 1915, I have found most useful Rayford W. Logan, *The Betrayal of the Negro: From Rutherford B. Hayes to Woodrow Wilson* (New York, 1965), chs. 6, 9, 10, 11, 13; C. Vann Woodward, *The Strange Career of Jim Crow*, 2d rev. ed. (New York, 1966), ch. 3; John Higham, *Strangers in the Land: Patterns of American Nativism, 1860–1925* (New Brunswick, N.J., 1955), chs. 4–7; Barton J. Bernstein, "*Plessy v. Ferguson*: Conservative Sociological Jurisprudence," *Journal of Negro History*, 48 (July 1963), 196–205; I. A. Newby, *Jim Crow's Defense: Anti-Negro Thought in America, 1900–1930* (Baton Rouge, 1965), part I; George M. Frederickson, *The Black Image in the White Mind: The Debate on Afro-American Character and Destiny* (New York, 1971), 256–319; and John S. Haller, *Outcasts from Evolution: Scientific Attitudes of Racial Inferiority, 1859–1900* (Urbana, Ill., 1971).

Historians who have studied race relations between the Civil War and World War I have for the most part focused on events in the South. Yet shifts in public opinion on the race question during this period were actually national rather than sectional in nature. During the quarter-century following the war, race relations were extraordinarily fluid in *both* sections. Interracial violence and discrimination in schools and public accommodations declined substantially in many parts of the North, and a number of northern states (beginning with New York in 1874) passed civil rights acts.

This favorable climate of opinion gradually faded, however. As memories of the war dimmed, so too did sympathy for the former slaves, and instead the late nineteenth century witnessed the growth of racial stereotypes and the emergence of a new "scientific" racism whose appeal transcended sectional boundaries. The new racism pictured the Negro as inferior to the white man in most respects (physical endurance and musical ability usually excepted) and morally deficient; in 1910 a leading sociologist categorized the black race as "improvident, extravagant, lazy . . . , easily adaptable, imitative, lacking initiative, dishonest and untruthful, with little principle of honor or conception of right and virtue, superstitious, over-religious, suspicious and incapable of a comprehension of faith in mankind." With such ideas in the ascendancy, it is not surprising that the mass of white opinion in the North began to look less favorably on the struggle for equal rights. In the early years of the twentieth century, "institutional racism" was on the rise throughout the North, and discrimination in restaurants, theaters, and other places of public accommodation was increasing in most northern cities. In 1908 Ray Stannard Baker reported that in every large northern city he visited, "both white and colored people told me that race feeling and discrimination were rapidly increasing: that more and more difficult problems were constantly arising." As lynchings continued apace in the South, friction between Afro-Americans and whites outside the states of the old Confederacy erupted in race riots in New York in 1900 and Springfield, Illinois, in 1908, presaging the more terrible violence of the World War I era. "The Negro Problem," W. E. B. Du Bois noted laconically in 1901, "is not the sole property of the South."[2]

2 Howard W. Odum, *Social and Mental Traits of the Negro*, Columbia Studies in History, Economics, and Public Law, vol. 37, no. 3 (New York, 1910), 274; Ray Stannard Baker, *Following the Color Line: American Negro Citizenship in the Progressive Era* (New York, 1908), 111; W. E. B. Du Bois, "The Black North," *New York Times Magazine*, November 17, 1901. On racial violence in the North before World War I, see James Crouthemal, "The Springfield Race Riot of 1908," *Journal of Negro History*, 45 (July 1960), 164–81; Gilbert Osofsky, *Harlem: The*

As in the case of residential segregation, however, the growth of discrimination in public facilities was by no means uniform throughout the North. Conditions varied considerably from one area to another and ranged along a continuum from Cass County, Michigan, where a sizable group of black settlers shared governmental power and lived in integrated harmony with their white neighbors, to cities like Evansville, East St. Louis, and other "northern border" towns, where the forces of segregation and discrimination were so strong that the pattern of race relations closely resembled that of the South. Among large cities there were fewer extremes and less variation, but there were still important differences prior to World War I. Racial lines hardened most rapidly in such cities as Indianapolis and Chicago, where white hostility frequently led to violent clashes between the races. Cleveland and Boston, on the other hand, lay at the opposite end of the spectrum. In both cities the growth of racism, though quite evident, was more muted in its effects, and integrationist traditions remained influential much longer than elsewhere.[3]

Making of a Ghetto (New York, 1966), 46–52; William English Walling, "The Race War in the North," *Independent*, 45 (September 3, 1908), 529–34; Emma Lou Thornbrough, *The Negro in Indiana: A Study of a Minority* ([Indianapolis, Ind.] 1957), 277–87. Race riots, of course, were not restricted to the North. Two of the most violent racial conflicts of this period occurred in Wilmington, North Carolina in 1898 and in Atlanta in 1906. Charles Crowe, "Racial Massacre in Atlanta, September 22, 1906," *Journal of Negro History*, 54 (April 1969), 150–68; John Hope Franklin, *From Slavery to Freedom*, 3d ed. (New York, 1967), 341, 439–41.

[3] For information on race relations in cities outside the South prior to World War I, see St. Clair Drake and Horace R. Cayton, *Black Metropolis: A Study of Negro Life in a Northern City* (New York, 1945), I, 174–77; Allan H. Spear, *Black Chicago: The Making of a Negro Ghetto, 1890–1920* (Chicago, 1967), 11–50; Osofsky, *Harlem*, 35–52; W. E. B. Du Bois, *The Philadelphia Negro: A Social Study* (Philadelphia, 1899), 322–55; Mary White Ovington, *Half a Man: The Status of the Negro in New York* (New York, 1911), 209–16 and *passim*; John Daniels, *In Freedom's Birthplace: A Study of the Boston Negroes* (Boston, 1914), 111–15, 188–90, 406–411; Robert Austin Warner, *New Haven Negroes: A Social History* (New Haven, Conn., 1940), 160–81; Thornbrough, *The Negro in Indiana*, 255–76 and *passim*; J. S. Himes, "Forty Years of Negro Life in Columbus, Ohio," *Journal of Negro History*, 27 (April 1942), 134–35; Elliott Rudwick, *Race Riot at East St. Louis, July 2, 1917* (Carbondale, Ill., 1964), 6; Earl Spangler, *The Negro in Minnesota* (Minneapolis, Minn., 1961), 57–62, 91–92; Lawrence B. De Graaf, "The City of Black Angels: Emergence of the Los Angeles Ghetto, 1890–1930," *Pacific Historical Review*, 39 (August 1970), 329; Frank Quillin, *The Color Line in Ohio* (Ann Arbor, 1913), 88–165; David Gerber, "Ohio and the Color Line: Racial Discrimination and Negro Responses in a Northern State, 1860–1915" (Ph.D. dissertation, Princeton University, 1971), *passim*; Frank F. Lee, *Negro and White in Connecticut Town* (New York, 1961), 26–28. Racial conditions in Cass County, Michigan, are described in R. R. Wright, Jr., "Negro Governments in the North," *Southern Workman*, 37 (September 1908), 486–89, and George Hesslink, *Black Neighbors: Negroes in a Northern Rural Community* (Indianapolis, Ind., 1968), 59–61, 215. The information on northern black communities in Ray Stannard Baker's *Following*

There might be a major city with more harmonious race relations than
Cleveland, Robert I. Drake conceded half seriously in 1915, but he
hastened to add that "doubtless no such place exists." Noted Drake with
undisguised pride, "We have no such marked and blighting discrimination in Ohio's [largest] metropolis, as our people have to contend with
in other cities. . . ." He acknowledged that blacks in Cleveland had "some
troubles" with racism, but on the whole he concluded that "we have more
privileges and a greater freedom of opportunity than is accorded our
people in any other city on American soil." Such views more accurately
reflected the middle-class Negro's perception of race relations than that
of the average black resident of the city; and even for the black middle
class, conditions were becoming less tolerable with each passing year.
Yet, comparatively speaking, Drake was correct in his assessment of
Cleveland's racial scene. The smaller size of the city's black population
made it less conspicuous than elsewhere; the higher proportion of
Cleveland blacks born or raised in the North made it easier for them to
be assimilated into the general life of the community. Equally if not
more important was the city's nineteenth-century integrationist heritage.
Traditional sympathy for the cause of Negro rights, though often
amounting to little more than paternalism by the beginning of the twentieth century, continued to influence the attitudes and actions of a segment of Cleveland's old-line white Protestant element. This group was,
of course, rapidly declining as a percentage of the total population, but it
continued to dominate the political, financial, and social life of the community to a large extent, and this helped to retard the growth of discrimination to some degree.[4]

The posture of the white press on the race issue, though far from
ideal, also helped keep down racial tensions in Cleveland. The Progressive era was a period of widespread and sometimes violent Negro-
phobia among white journalists. But while other white newspapers in
the northern and border states (such as the Cincinnati *Enquirer*, the
Washington *Star*, and the St. Louis *Globe-Democrat*) inflamed racial
hatreds with lurid stories of lynchings and black criminal activity,
Cleveland's two major dailies for the most part adopted a policy of ig-
noring the Negro. Since the Cleveland *Leader* remained a Republican
newspaper and the Cleveland *Plain Dealer* an avowedly Democratic

---

the Color Line, though sometimes useful, must be used with caution. Baker by no
means systematically surveyed black life in the North, and his analysis was often
based on a superficial impression of local conditions.

[4] Robert I. Drake, "The Negro in Cleveland," Cleveland *Advocate*, September
18, 1915.

organ, the two rivals continued to dispute national issues that touched upon the Negro question. As late as 1915, for example, the *Leader* editorially attacked the disfranchisement of blacks in the South and urged the enforcement of the Fourteenth Amendment to limit southern congressional power. When it came to *local* race relations, however, both papers gradually put aside the contentiousness of an earlier day in favor of a mutual desire to avoid the problem. On most occasions the white press paid little attention to the city's black community.[5]

These factors enabled Cleveland to avoid the more virulent forms of racism that infected many other cities during the period between about 1890 and 1915. No lynchings or even near-lynchings marred the city's history during these years, and although Central Avenue was sometimes the scene of drunken brawls, no clash remotely resembling a race riot transpired at this time.

In more subtle ways, however, the racial egalitarianism that had been so prominent an aspect of nineteenth-century Cleveland was beginning to weaken. With increasing momentum during the prewar years, a pattern of discrimination was becoming established in many areas of public service. This pattern was not yet a rigid one, and the practices of businesses outside the Central Avenue district varied widely. A number of exclusive downtown restaurants and hotels (including the prestigious Hollenden and Statler establishments) which had opened their doors, several decades before the Great Migration, to the city's light-skinned Negro elite continued their policy of serving anyone who could afford their exorbitant prices—regardless of race. Cleveland's City Club, a popular gathering place for businessmen and politicians, welcomed successful Negroes like the barber George Myers from its inception in 1912; by 1919 nine black men were members.[6] The exclusive Hippodrome Theater and the Opera House were open to members of both races. Such liberal policies, however, did not always extend to other parts of the city, and Negroes with less than middle incomes found it increasingly difficult to obtain adequate accommodations. Many restaurants refused to serve Negroes altogether, and a number of theaters attempted to segregate black patrons in the balcony; the increasing number of small black hotels and lodging houses on Central Avenue testified to the discrimination that blacks were beginning to encounter in similar white institutions.

[5] Cleveland *Leader*, June 23, 1915; Logan, *Betrayal of the Negro*, 195–241; Gerber, "Ohio and the Color Line," 469–71, 490.

[6] Helen M. Chesnutt, *Charles Waddell Chesnutt: Pioneer of the Color Line* (Chapel Hill, N.C., 1952), 294; Cleveland *Advocate*, April 1, 1916; R. H. Terrell to George A. Myers, April 14, 1916, George A. Myers Papers, Ohio Historical Society; *Crisis*, 19 (December 1919), 86.

Only through the painful process of trial and error could blacks discover which establishments were open to both races on a nondiscriminatory basis.[7]

Far more blatant than the exclusion of blacks from some hotels and restaurants was the discrimination they faced in the use of recreation areas. As was true of most cities, Cleveland had no parks anywhere near the main district of black settlement. "Playgrounds in Negro neighborhoods," George Edmund Haynes reported in a survey of Negro urban life in 1913, "are so rare as to excite curiosity. . . ." Private recreational facilities were also off-bounds to the black community most of the time. In 1896 the editor of the Gazette was surprised to learn that blacks were being excluded from the dance hall at Euclid Beach Park, but within fifteen years this policy had become the rule rather than the exception in all of the city's well-known amusement parks. Luna Park, a favorite entertainment center for Clevelanders, adopted the procedure around 1910 of allowing Negroes into the park only on designated Jim Crow days—almost all of the time the park was for whites only. Even on Jim Crow days, the management refused to allow Negroes to use the bathing facilities. The ruse they used to achieve this end became almost comical in its transparency after awhile. "Everything worked at the park on those days except the swimming pool," an old black resident explained several decades later. "The pool always 'happened' to be out of order on that day."[8]

Before 1900 blacks had participated in the programs and facilities of the Cleveland Young Men's Christian Association, but by 1910 there were signs of growing white hostility to Negro membership in the Y. In 1914 Charles W. Chesnutt, one of the city's most prominent colored residents, noted in a letter to a leading white citizen that those branches of the YMCA and YWCA which did not openly exclude blacks did "not welcome them with open arms." Chesnutt was apparently unaware that blacks had recently been barred entirely by the local YWCA; and by 1915 the YMCA had adopted a similar whites-only policy. This trend

[7] Drake, "The Negro in Cleveland." For examples of discrimination in theaters, see Cleveland Gazette, March 21, 1903, September 10, October 15, 1904, October 6, 1906, February 1, April 18, 1908, April 12, 1911, November 14, 1914, January 30, August 14, 1915. For discrimination in restaurants, see Cleveland Journal, May 9, 1908; Cleveland Gazette, April 12, 1911, January 30, 1915, August 14, 1915; George A. Myers to F. H. Goff, January 17, 1916, Myers Papers.

[8] George Edmund Haynes, "Conditions among Negroes in the Cities," Annals of the American Academy of Political and Social Science, 49 (September 1913), 117; Cleveland Gazette, July 4, 1896, October 20, 1913, February 14, 1914, July 31, 1915, August 11, 1917; Perry B. Jackson quoted in Julian Krawcheck, "Society Barred Negroes—They Formed Own Groups," Cleveland Press, May 30, 1963.

of discrimination was partially responsible for the formation of the all-Negro Phillis Wheatley home for girls in 1912 and later resulted in the opening of a YMCA on Cedar Avenue designed primarily for Negroes. Recreational facilities in the black community remained inadequate for many years, however.[9]

None of the exclusionary policies of theaters, hotels, or amusement parks was legal. Ohio had passed a Civil Rights Act in 1884 which, when amended in 1894, clearly prohibited discrimination in public facilities on the basis of race. The law provided that all persons "shall be entitled to the full and equal enjoyment of the accommodations, advantages, facilities, and privileges of inns, restaurants, eating houses, barber shops, public conveyances on land and water, theaters and all other places of public accommodation or amusement. . . ." Violations could result in fines up to five hundred dollars and jail terms of thirty to ninety days, in addition to damages awarded the party discriminated against.[10]

From time to time blacks used this law to initiate suits against discriminatory managers and proprietors, but the time was past when Cleveland's black community could expect almost automatic vindication in the courts. Blacks were probably somewhat more successful in Cleveland than elsewhere in bringing civil-rights suits. But no clear-cut victory for equality emerged as a result of such activity, and discrimination, in fact, seemed to be gaining ground in the years just before the Great Migration. There were several reasons for this lack of success. First, many Negroes had neither the time nor the inclination to take a case to court. When two black attorneys were denied service in a Cleveland restaurant in 1915, they quickly brought suit against the manager and won the case. The average Negro, confronted with a similar situation, would be more likely to leave with a shrug and seek out a more hospitable place to eat. Nor was it always easy to obtain convictions in civil-rights cases. In 1901, for example, a Negro brought suit against a Cleveland bowling alley proprietor who kept Negroes out of his establishment, only to have the case dismissed when the court decided "there was no cause for action." Judges sometimes interpreted the law so narrowly that they allowed blatant examples of discrimination to go unpunished, and appeals to higher courts—even to the State Supreme Court—did not guarantee the plaintiff success. Finally, there was the hard fact that most

[9] Cleveland *Journal*, October 6, 20, 1906; Cleveland *Gazette*, February 4, 1911, February 14, 1914; Chesnutt, *Charles Waddell Chesnutt*, 261. The formation of the Phillis Wheatley home is discussed in Chapter 6.

[10] Franklin Johnson, *The Development of State Legislation Concerning the Free Negro* (New York, 1918), 164, 166.

blacks simply did not have the necessary funds to carry out legal action. For those who did, a civil-rights suit was still a risky venture. "When we look back over the court decisions," one observer wrote in 1913, "and see the failures of the colored people to get damages, as provided in the equal rights law of the State, see the amount of litigation necessary, and consider how unable the negroes generally are to bear the expense of going to law, there can be but one conclusion arrived at; and that is that equal rights in Ohio for blacks and the whites is a myth."[11]

If black Clevelanders encountered discrimination in some public accommodations during the prewar years, however, there were other areas of public service where racism was noticeably less evident. There is no indication, for example, that any of the city's hospitals either excluded or attempted to segregate black patients prior to 1915. Complete documentation is not available, but it is clear that two major institutions, Huron Road Hospital and the Catholic St. Alexis Hospital, were open to both races on a nondiscriminatory basis during the years just preceding the Great Migration, and other hospitals were probably also integrated. The first change in this policy to be noted in the black press occurred in 1915, when Women's Hospital on East 107th Street instituted a new procedure of admitting black patients only on Saturday. The institution's directors not very successfully tried to hide its real motives by claiming that they were establishing a special "clinic" for black patents, rather than trying to restrict black use of the facilities. This change in policy came as a rude shock to those members of the black middle class who had come to take much of Cleveland's integrationist heritage for granted. "What does this mean?" one black woman asked. "Are we to arrange to get sick on Saturday only or is it possible that we are to be exempted from privileges enjoyed by every other nation or nationality?" Such incredulity would, within but a few short years, turn to cynicism as one medical institution after another adopted some kind of racist policy toward black patients.[12]

If institutions generally accepted black patients on an equal basis before 1915, however, white physicians and hospital administrators were united in their opposition to the admission of black doctors and nurses to hospital staffs. Prior to 1919, when Dr. Charles Garvin joined Lakeside Hospital, no black physician served on the staff of any Cleveland hospi-

[11] Cleveland Gazette, August 14, 1915; Cleveland Advocate, August 14, September 4, 1915; Quillin, The Color Line in Ohio, 118–19, 120.

[12] Chesnutt, Charles Waddell Chesnutt, 238; Jane Edna Hunter, A Nickel and a Prayer (Cleveland, 1940), 73; Cleveland Advocate, July 24, 1915, November 11, 1916.

tal. Black nurses also experienced the sting of racial prejudice. When Jane Edna Hunter arrived in Cleveland in 1905, she repeatedly met rebuffs in her effort to find suitable employment. One physician bluntly told her "to go back South—that white doctors did not employ 'nigger' nurses." Prospective Negro physicians and nurses also found it difficult to finish their training in the Cleveland area, since as late as 1930 no hospital would admit Negroes to internships or nurses' training programs. Nor were these discriminatory policies restricted to private institutions. City Hospital, a tax-supported facility, did not integrate its staff and training programs until 1931—and only then because the city manager ordered it to do so over the protests of white physicians.[13]

To a much greater extent than hospitals, Cleveland's educational facilities were able to avoid the racist trend that was affecting other areas of urban life. In the city's public school system the nineteenth-century tradition of racial equality remained intact to a remarkable degree. The public schools had been thoroughly integrated since the 1840s, and this policy seemed to retain the support of most citizens, black and white, during the Progressive era. In 1887 the *Gazette* proudly announced that in "Cleveland, Ohio, the white citizens do not feel themselves at all disgraced by their children associating with colored children in the same school room. . . ." There is no evidence that these values changed much during the next twenty-five years. Before World War I, there was no attempt to segregate black students in separate schools or classrooms (a procedure that was prohibited by law in Ohio but nonetheless occurred to some extent in Cincinnati, Columbus, and other cities). No racial violence significant enough to be noted in either the black or the white press occurred in Cleveland schools during these years; and compared to Chicago, where "there were frequent instances of discrimination and interracial friction after 1890," public education generally exuded an air of racial harmony.[14]

This philosophy of integration extended to the teaching staffs as well as the students. Negro teachers (there were four on the payroll as early as 1888) were fully integrated within the school system. In 1896 the

[13] Quillin, *The Color Line in Ohio*, 155; Russell H. Davis, *Memorable Negroes in Cleveland's Past* (Cleveland, 1969), 56; Hunter, *A Nickel and a Prayer*, 70–71; Mercy Hospital Association of Cleveland, *Does Cleveland Need a Negro-Manned Hospital?* (n.p. [1927], pamphlet); Thomas F. Campbell, *Daniel E. Morgan: The Good Citizen in Politics* (Cleveland, 1966), 115–17; Charles H. Garvin, "Pioneering in Cleveland," *The Women's Voice*, I (September 1939), 14–15 (copy in Charles Herbert Garvin Papers, Western Reserve Historical Society).

[14] Cleveland *Gazette*, October 29, 1887; Drake, "The Negro in Cleveland," Cleveland *Advocate*, September 18, 1915; Spear, *Black Chicago*, 44.

Gazette noted that black instructors were frequently placed in charge of all-white classes. Despite the steadily increasing size of the black population, this policy remained in effect during the years before the Great Migration (and even for a while after it). In 1911 the city's black teachers were located in nine different schools in widely scattered sections of the city, and four years later the *Advocate*, a black weekly, reported that in most cases "not more than one or two Colored teachers are assigned to any one school. There is absolutely no tendency or inclination on the part of the school authorities to segregate them." The result was that only a few of the city's Negro instructors had "even a few Afro-American pupils in the rooms over which they preside[d]." Nor were black teachers in Cleveland restricted to employment in elementary schools—a practice that was common in many cities. Two black teachers were on the staff of Central High School during the prewar years. Helen Chesnutt, an instructor of Latin, was hired in 1910, and Cora Fields, a music teacher, joined the staff in 1915.[15]

In spite of these liberal policies, black students did not always receive equal treatment in the schools. When the daughters of Charles Chesnutt began their final year at Central High School they soon discovered that even light-skinned Negroes with middle-class upbringings were not immune to the more subtle aspects of racial prejudice. "When the Senior Class was organized, and its activities under way, they realized with shock and confusion that they were considered different from their classmates; they were being gently but firmly set apart, and had become self-conscious about it." And although the Board of Education adopted no policies of segregation, it sometimes assisted the formation of racist attitudes by authorizing textbooks portraying the Negro in a stereotyped or prejudiced manner. It was discovered in 1913 and again in 1916 that a number of elementary schools were using a reader which employed the obnoxious term "darkies" in describing Negroes. Such problems were indeed minor compared with those that blacks encountered in schools in many other cities, but they were prophetic of the much greater difficulties that the future would hold.[16]

[15] Cleveland *Gazette*, March 3, 1888, May 16, 1896, September 16, 1911, February 28, 1914; Frank U. Quillin, "The Negro in Cleveland, Ohio," *Independent*, 72 (March 7, 1912), 519; Chesnutt, *Charles Waddell Chesnutt*, 276; Cleveland *Advocate*, May 15, 1915.

[16] Chesnutt, *Charles Waddell Chesnutt*, 75; Cleveland *Gazette*, December 20, 1913; Cleveland *Advocate*, February 5, 1916. (It is likely that texts containing racial slurs continued to be used in many schools until fairly recently. The author, who attended a Cleveland elementary school in the 1950s, vividly recalls a reader in which the word "nigger" was used.)

Prior to World War I, the schools were also integrated in Boston, New Haven,

With the possible exception of Boston, Cleveland was unsurpassed in the opportunity it afforded blacks to attend college. Nearby Oberlin College, of course, had a long tradition of integrated education, and a number of Cleveland Negroes took advantage of its proximity to attend classes there. Western Reserve University, which produced most of the city's black teachers, graduated its first black student in 1892; by 1910 a dozen more blacks had received degrees. The University's professional schools of law and medicine were also open to Negroes, and one of the city's first Negro dentists graduated from Western Reserve's School of Dentistry in 1903. (There may have been some effort to exclude blacks from certain training programs through various subterfuges, but these do not seem to have been successful. One of Western Reserve's first

---

and probably throughout most of New England (Daniels, *In Freedom's Birthplace*, 185; Warner, *New Haven Negroes*, 174–75). In other states, conditions varied widely from one locality to another. In northern Ohio blacks and whites generally attended the same schools and received fairly equal treatment. In the central and southern parts of the state, however, there was a good deal of hostility to interracial education, and local boards of education often set up segregated or quasi-segregated facilities. Similar differences between northern and southern Illinois developed during this period, but blacks in Chicago never attained the equality of treatment common in Cleveland's schools. In Indiana, where discrimination of all kinds was more widespread than elsewhere in the North, separate schools were everywhere more the rule than the exception. In Indianapolis and Gary, however, some blacks attended integrated elementary schools, and these cities did not establish separate black high schools until after the Great Migration. In Michigan there was no geographic pattern, but segregated facilities did exist in some localities outside of Detroit in the late nineteenth century. In Philadelphia the 1881 state law abolishing separate schools was to some extent evaded through subterfuges. In 1911 less than one-quarter of that city's black elementary-school pupils were attending separate schools; but most of the other black students were concentrated in a fairly small number of schools, and a pattern of de facto segregation was beginning to emerge as a result of the growth of the ghetto. See Mame Charlotte Mason, "The Policy of Segregation of the Negro in the Public Schools of Ohio, Indiana, and Illinois" (M.A. thesis, University of Chicago, 1917), 14–60; Himes, "Forty Years of Negro Life in Columbus, Ohio," 138–39; David Gerber, "Education, Expediency, and Ideology: Race and Politics in the Desegregation of Ohio Public Schools in the Late Nineteenth Century," *Journal of Ethnic Studies*, 1 (Fall 1973), 1–31; Michael W. Homel, "The Negro in the Chicago Public Schools, 1910–1941" (Ph.D. dissertation, University of Chicago, 1971), 1–21; Thornbrough, *The Negro in Indiana*, 332–37, 341–43; Emma Lou Thornbrough, "Segregation in Indiana during the Klan Era of the 1920's," *Mississippi Valley Historical Review*, 47 (March 1961), 600, 604; David M. Katzman, *Before the Ghetto: Black Detroit in the Nineteenth Century* (Urbana, Ill., 1973), 90; Du Bois, *The Philadelphia Negro*, 88–89, 349–50; Howard W. Odum, "Negro Children in the Public Schools of Philadelphia," *Annals of the American Academy of Political and Social Science*, 49 (September 1913), 45. August Meier and Elliott Rudwick, "Negro Boycotts of Jim Crow Schools in the North, 1897–1925," *Integrated Education*, 5 (August–September 1967), 57–68, has useful information on conditions in Alton, Illinois; East Orange, New Jersey; and Dayton and Springfield, Ohio.

medical students, for example, complained that the University refused to allow him to register for a course in clinical medicine because they feared the hostile reactions of white patients to a Negro doctor. The Cleveland branch of the National Association for the Advancement of Colored People investigated the case, however, and "failed to find convincing proof of actual discrimination." In any case, within a few years the student had received his degree and was practicing medicine in the city.) Most other specialized schools in the Cleveland area had no qualms about accepting Negroes. The Cleveland University of Medicine and Surgery and the Spencerian Business College admitted blacks on a nondiscriminatory basis by the end of the 1890s; and Union College of Law, which had accepted blacks as early as 1870, remained integrated in the early twentieth century. Blacks who wanted preparation for teaching without going through a four-year college course had no difficulty in obtaining the necessary training. The Cleveland Normal Training School graduated several Negroes during the prewar years, and in 1915 the *Advocate* reported that a "score or so of the school girls" at nearby, recently established Kent State Normal School (now Kent State University) were Negroes.[17]

Cleveland's continuing tradition of integrated schools and colleges and its relative lack of interracial violence during the years before the wartime migration marked it as exceptional among northern cities. But in other ways it was becoming painfully evident, even to middle-class Negroes who were able to maintain good relations with whites, that blacks were being gradually set apart as a group distinct from, and inferior to, the rest of the population. Indicative of the changing racial attitudes of whites was the decline in black office-holding during the so-called Progressive era. During this period, the black population was still too small to elect black candidates without the help of white votes. Yet at one point in the 1890s, two blacks from Cleveland served simultaneously in the Ohio House of Representatives, and another black politician, John P. Green, was elected to the Ohio Senate from a district that was overwhelmingly white. After 1900, however, whites backed black candidates less often, and between 1910 and 1920 no Negro politician

[17] John P. Green, *Fact Stranger than Fiction: Seventy-Five Years of a Busy Life with Reminiscences of Many Great and Good Men* (Cleveland, 1920), 119; Thomas W. Fleming, "My Rise and Persecution" (manuscript autobiography, Western Reserve Historical Society [1932]), 20; Quillin, *The Color Line in Ohio*, 155; W. E. B. Du Bois, *The College-Bred Negro American*, Atlanta University Publications, no. 15 (Atlanta, 1910), 48; Davis, *Memorable Negroes*, 40; Chesnutt, *Charles Waddell Chesnutt*, 75, 165; Cleveland *Journal*, May 20, 27, 1905; Cleveland *Gazette*, March 7, 1914; Cleveland *Advocate*, May 15, July 3, 1915.

in Cleveland could garner enough white support to win election to the state legislature—although several tried and failed. The growing distaste of whites for black candidates was but one sign of the times. Segregated facilities, once a rare phenomenon, were in some areas of public service becoming more the rule than the exception.[18]

Nothing revealed the unfortunate consequences of this change in racial attitudes better than the 1908 Cleveland Convention of the National Education Association, which drew hundreds of black teachers to the city. Many of the blacks found it all but impossible to get hotel accommodations, and a number of white-run restaurants either turned them away altogether, overcharged them, or gave them bad service.[19] These visitors to the Forest City were discovering what native blacks already knew: racism was on the rise in Cleveland. Denied admittance to many hotels, restaurants, amusement parks, and theaters at the same time they were accepted as equals in the city's schools and colleges, members of Cleveland's black community looked to the future with a good deal of uncertainty.

[18] The careers of black politicians during this period are discussed in detail in Chapter 6.

[19] Cleveland *Plain Dealer*, May 3, 1908; Cleveland *Journal*, May 9, 16, 30, 1908; Cleveland *Gazette*, July 11, 1908.

CHAPTER 4

Occupational Decline

If integrated facilities were in decline by the early 1900s, so too were the economic opportunities that Afro-Americans had enjoyed in Cleveland during the mid-nineteenth century. As in the case of access to public accommodations, however, the changing status of black occupations during the decades before the World War I migration was complex and not uniform in all areas. To understand the significance of these trends it is necessary to place the changing black occupational structure in comparative context.

The transformation of urban America in the late nineteenth and early twentieth centuries was closely related to the economic changes that were occurring during these years. The half-century after 1865 was marked by massive industrialization, and the new firms producing steel, oil, rubber, machinery, and refrigerated meat seemed to demand an ever-increasing supply of laborers. Almost every indicator of economic change recorded dramatic growth. During these years, steel ingot production rose from twenty thousand to thirty million tons per year, while the total index of manufacturing output increased from 17 to 200. Everywhere in America, with the exception of most of the South, the "triumph of the industrial spirit" was much in evidence.[1]

For the most part, unfortunately, black workers did not participate very much in this new upsurge of industrial activity. In Cleveland in 1890, only three blacks were employed in the city's rapidly expanding steel industry, and virtually no black males worked as semiskilled oper-

[1] Edward Chase Kirkland, *Industry Comes of Age: Business, Labor, and Public Policy, 1860–1897* (New York, 1961), and Douglass C. North, *Growth and Welfare in the American Past: A New Economic History* (Englewood Cliffs, N.J., 1966), 149–64, survey the changing economy.

atives in factories. By 1910 this situation had improved to some extent; several hundred Afro-Americans had managed to find work in mills or foundries, and a handful had broken the racial barrier in the city's cigar, tobacco, and furniture industries. Despite these gains, however, black workers continued to have far fewer jobs in manufacturing than their percentage of the total work force warranted. What jobs they were able to obtain in industry were almost all in the unskilled labor category; only a handful attained skilled or even semiskilled positions in factories prior to the Great Migration. With some variations, this was probably true of all northern cities. Black employment in factories was higher in Cleveland than in Chicago or, especially, New York, and considerably lower in Cleveland than in Philadelphia; but the variation among these cities was not dramatic.[2]

Why, given the booming industrial economy of Cleveland, Chicago, and other cities, did blacks find jobs in manufacturing difficult to obtain? Several factors were responsible. Employers were often reluctant to hire black workers because they shared the belief, common to many whites, that Negroes were particularly suited to agricultural employment and were therefore "inherently unfitted for industrial work." Whites felt this lack of adaptability was particularly true of those blacks who had recently migrated from the South, and as a result some manufacturers "refused even to give the Negro a trial because they considered his unfitness to be an established fact." It was true, of course, that many southern migrants lacked the skills necessary for employment in industry and the trades. Few, however, were able to acquire this knowledge in the North, since apprenticeship training was usually restricted to whites. In Cleveland, of seventeen hundred men enrolled in apprenticeship programs in 1910, only seven were Negroes. Second, no economic necessity compelled employers to hire blacks until the outbreak of hostilities in 1914 sharply reduced the stream of European immigrants that had previously provided American manufacturers with an abundant supply of cheap labor. Only during World War I would northern industrialists begin to realize the value of the Negro as an "industrial reserve." Finally, many trade unions affiliated with the American Federation of Labor refused to accept black members. Only nine AFL unions openly prohibited Negro membership through clauses in their constitutions, but others ac-

[2] U.S. *Eleventh Census, 1890* (Washington, 1893), II, 654–55; U.S. *Thirteenth Census, 1910* (Washington, 1912), IV, 548–50. Cleveland, with 22 percent of its employed black males engaged in manufacturing in 1910, stood midway between the black communities of New York (14 percent in manufacturing) and Pittsburgh (29 percent in manufacturing). Louise Venable Kennedy, *The Negro Peasant Turns Cityward* (New York, 1930), 75.

complished the same purpose by excluding Negroes from the initiation ritual; still others, although they had no national policy of exclusion, allowed locals to bar Negroes if they saw fit, or to segregate black members in subordinate Jim Crow locals. Since before the 1930s few unskilled workers were unionized, these policies of the AFL did not prevent many blacks from entering industry at the lower occupational levels. They did, however, prevent most black workers from moving into the better paying skilled jobs in factories.[3]

In Cleveland, union policies, both national and local, effectively kept most eligible Negroes out of the trade union movement. The Boilermakers' Union, the International Association of Machinists, and the Plumbers' and Steamfitters' Union had a national policy of excluding blacks. Other union locals in the city, such as the Metal Polishers and the Paperhangers, barred Negroes on their own initiative. In 1896 a group of whites refused to join a Cooks' union being organized by the Knights of Labor when they learned it was to be an integrated organization. The Paperhangers' local, established at the turn of the century, had no black members whatsoever during its first twenty-seven years; the union's leaders explained that "a storm of protest" occurred whenever the question of admitting a Negro came up. Some unions, anxious to keep their Negro membership within the labor movement, but also intent upon segregating them, set up special Jim Crow locals to achieve their purpose. This occurred in two Cleveland locals with significant Negro memberships: the Freight Handlers' Union and the Porters' Union (not to be confused with A. Philip Randolph's Brotherhood of Sleeping Car Porters). Black musicians, although they had been members of an integrated union as late as 1888, also had become part of a separate, segregated organization by the 1920s.[4]

[3] Kennedy, The Negro Peasant Turns Cityward, 114; Charles H. Wesley, Negro Labor in the United States, 1850–1925: A Study in American Economic History (New York, 1927), 238–39; U.S. Thirteenth Census, IV, 548; F. E. Wolfe, Admission to American Trade Unions, Johns Hopkins University Studies in Historical and Political Science, series 30, no. 1 (Baltimore, Md., 1912), 118–21, 125–30; Sterling D. Spero and Abram L. Harris, The Black Worker: The Negro and the Labor Movement (New York, 1931), 149, 53–86; Bernard Mandel, "Samuel Gompers and the Negro Workers, 1886–1914," Journal of Negro History, 40 (January 1955), 34–60.
[4] Spero and Harris, The Black Worker, 57, 59, 103; National Urban League, Department of Research and Investigation, Negro Membership in American Labor Unions (New York [1929]), 40, 45, 67; Cleveland Gazette, May 23, 1896, December 3, 1887; Wesley, Negro Labor in the United States, 269. Unfortunately, there is a scarcity of information on Negro-white labor relations in Cleveland prior to 1930, and it is often difficult to determine the exact date of the inception of a union's discriminatory policy.

On one level, the exclusionary policies of these new unions can be viewed as simply another example of the general elitism of the AFL under the leadership of Samuel Gompers. The AFL had no interest in organizing unskilled workers, whether black or white, and their general approach to industrial questions and social issues was conservative. A more important cause of black exclusion, however, was related to the fact that many of the trade unionists, as well as the people that they served, were members of what Robert Wiebe has called "the new middle class" of the Progressive era. As a result of their newly arrived status, these groups were particularly anxious to gain respectability, and they were eager to dissociate themselves from a racial group that was becoming stereotyped by popular writers and scientists alike as ignorant, lazy, and immoral. Thus members of the Paperhangers' Union in Cleveland objected to Negroes out of a "fear of personal contact" and because they did not "desire the close association which would naturally be expected" of union men. The city's Parquet Floor Layers, on the other hand, resisted Negro membership because they feared a loss in trade from their upper-middle-class white clientele, who disapproved of having black workmen in their homes. In both cases the underlying rationale for black exclusion was a quest for respectability and status.[5]

At a more basic economic level, a major obstacle to a rapprochement between black and white workers was the use of blacks as strikebreakers. Employers who balked at hiring Negroes on a permanent basis were quite willing to use them to break strikes. This often placed Negro workers in a peculiar situation. Excluded from many unions because of white prejudice, they were sorely tempted to accept temporary employment at good wages when the opportunity presented itself. But by acting as strikebreakers they only confirmed the worst fears of the white unionists: that all blacks were potential scabs who, because of their servile inclinations, would never be able to sympathize with the cause of labor. Friction in the North between union members and black strikebreakers frequently resulted in violence and sometimes in lynchings and race riots.[6]

[5] National Urban League, *Negro Membership in American Labor Unions*, 45, 40; Robert Wiebe, *The Search for Order, 1877–1920* (New York, 1967), 111–32. The general conservatism of the AFL has been noted by many labor historians during the last decade. A useful overview is Michael Rogin, "Voluntarism: The Political Functions of an Anti-Political Doctrine," *Industrial and Labor Relations Review*, 15 (July 1962), 521–35.

[6] Spero and Harris, *The Black Worker*, 128–29; Logan, *The Betrayal of the Negro* (New York, 1965), 156–57. Two excellent case studies of the interrelationship between black workers, white unions, and management are Elliott M. Rudwick's *Race Riot at East St. Louis, July 2, 1917* (Carbondale, Ill., 1964), ch. 11, and Wil-

In Cleveland, labor disputes involving racial conflicts occurred at least as early as 1863, when the use of Negroes to replace striking longshoremen provoked a minor riot. During the next fifty years, intermittent racial violence—although less common than elsewhere—continued to plague the city's labor relations. The most serious example was the strike at the Brown Hoisting and Conveying Machine Company, which lasted several months during the summer of 1896. Although no general racial conflict occurred, the strikebreakers, many of whom were black, found it necessary to carry arms to protect themselves from hostile white strikers who milled about the plant and attempted to discourage the strikebreakers from entering. The use of black workers to break strikes sometimes resulted in the adoption of a union policy of exclusion where none had existed previously. The Cleveland Waiters' and Beverage Dispensers' Union barred Negroes after a number had "served as strikebreakers, defeating the union and retaining their jobs, working for less wages and longer hours." During and after the Great Migration this union continued to be a thorn in the side of the black community as its members harassed or attacked Negro waiters and attempted to drive them out of many downtown establishments altogether.[7]

"The greatest enemy of the Negro," said one black leader from Indiana in 1899, "is the trade unionism of the North." Whether unions were the "greatest enemy" of blacks as a whole may be doubted, but it is clear that they were a major cause behind the decline of the number of blacks in the skilled trades, thereby undercutting one of the most important elements of the black middle class of the nineteenth century. In 1870 fully 31.7 percent of all black males in Cleveland had been employed in skilled trades; by 1910 this figure had dropped sharply to 11.1 percent (Table 9).[8] As early as 1886 Jere A. Brown, a prominent

liam M. Tuttle, Jr.'s Race Riot: Chicago in the Red Summer of 1919 (New York, 1970), 108–55.

[7] Spero and Harris, The Black Worker, 198; Cleveland Plain Dealer, July 1, 2, 3, August 4, 1896; Cleveland Gazette, July 25, 1896; Joseph A. Burns to John P. Green, October 18, 1896, John Patterson Green Papers, Western Reserve Historical Society. (Burns was one of the strikebreakers and had been arrested for carrying a concealed weapon.) On the racial conflict in the Waiters' Union, see the Cleveland Gazette, September 27, 1902; National Urban League, Negro Membership in American Labor Unions, 91; and Chapter 9.

[8] It should be noted that the printed censuses for 1870, 1890, and 1910 (the source for much of the occupational data in this chapter) did not list all occupations and that, in addition, some jobs listed were unclassifiable (see Appendix I). For these reasons, it seems likely that the numbers—of both blacks and whites—in the skilled trades were slightly larger than the figures listed in Tables 7 and 9. But it is improbable that more complete occupational data for these years would alter the general conclusions that are made in this paragraph.

TABLE 7. *Male occupational structure of Cleveland, by racial and ethnic group, 1890*

	Occupational category												
	Professional		Proprietary		Clerical		Skilled		Semiskilled		Unskilled		Domestic	
	Number	Percentage	Number	Percentage	Number	Percentage	Number	Percentage	Number	Percentage	Number	Percentage	Number	Percentage
Colored[a]	10	0.8	20	1.6	34	2.8	189	15.3	15	1.2	318	25.7	392	31.7
Native whites of native parentage	879	5.0	2,140	12.2	4,061	23.1	3,926	22.3	1,076	6.1	2,023	11.5	224	1.3
Native whites of foreign or mixed parentage	313	1.5	1,631	8.0	3,278	16.1	5,686	27.9	2,317	11.4	3,800	18.6	145	0.7
Foreign-born whites	393	0.9	3,798	8.7	2,013	4.6	11,522	26.3	5,223	11.9	15,018	34.2	470	1.1
All workers	1,495	1.8	7,599	9.1	9,407	11.3	21,263	25.6	8,631	10.4	21,159	25.5	1,231	1.5
Germans	86	0.5	1,534	8.7	594	3.3	5,270	29.5	1,941	11.9	5,747	32.1	151	0.8
Irish	29	0.5	326	5.6	174	3.0	846	14.3	860	14.8	2,628	45.3	114	2.0
English	100	1.5	562	8.3	555	8.2	2,175	32.1	1,162	17.1	1,105	16.3	111	1.6
Swedes and Norwegians	3	0.9	16	4.8	5	1.5	55	16.3	53	15.7	162	48.1	12	3.6

SOURCE: U.S. *Eleventh Census, 1890* (Washington, 1893), II, 654–55.
[a] "Colored" includes a very few Chinese, Japanese, and Indians. In 1890, 14.8 percent of the male occupations in Cleveland were either unspecified by the Census Bureau or were unclassifiable. The unclassifiable occupations are listed in Appendix I.

TABLE 8. *Female occupational structure of Cleveland, by racial and ethnic group, 1890*

	Occupational category												
	Professional		Proprietary		Clerical		Skilled		Semiskilled		Unskilled		Domestic	
	Number	Percentage	Number	Percentage	Number	Percentage	Number	Percentage	Number	Percentage	Number	Percentage	Number	Percentage
Colored[a]	9	2.6	12	3.5	2	0.6	3	0.9	62	18.0	4	1.2	243	70.6
Native whites of native parentage	448	11.6	130	3.4	600	15.8	99	2.4	1,078	27.9	53	1.4	1,185	30.6
Native whites of foreign or mixed parentage	478	6.1	76	1.0	1,114	14.3	513	6.6	2,934	37.7	153	2.0	2,005	25.7
Foreign-born whites	153	2.1	239	2.3	260	3.5	349	4.8	1,984	27.1	110	1.5	3,944	53.8
All workers	1,108	5.7	457	2.4	1,976	10.2	964	5.0	6,058	31.3	320	1.7	7,377	38.2
Germans	42	1.6	70	2.7	77	2.9	115	4.4	653	24.9	59	2.2	1,498	57.1
Irish	30	2.0	53	3.5	28	1.9	10	0.7	229	15.2	11	0.7	1,125	74.6
English	33	3.4	48	4.9	62	6.4	12	1.2	319	32.9	6	0.6	436	45.0
Swedes and Norwegians	—	—	—	—	—	—	—	—	5	6.8	—	—	69	93.2

SOURCE: U.S. *Eleventh Census, 1890,* II, 654–55.
[a] "Colored" includes a very few Chinese, Japanese, and Indians. In 1890, 5.5 percent of the female occupations in Cleveland were either unspecified by the Census Bureau or were unclassifiable. The unclassifiable occupations are listed in Appendix I.

black Clevelander, noted that many younger blacks were already losing interest in the skilled trades (Brown found only three black apprentices in the entire city) and preferred to enter occupations which entailed less friction with whites. The decline of blacks in the skilled trades, however, must be qualified in a number of ways. First, part of this decline can be traced to a general contraction in the proportion of *all* workers engaged in these trades during the decades preceding World War I. The employment of all males in skilled work in Cleveland declined from over 30 percent in 1870 to 26.2 percent in 1910. Second, the drop in black skilled employment was by no means uniform in all trades. Among the older trades that had been the mainstay of the nineteenth-century black middle class, the blacksmiths, shoemakers, and painters experienced a sharp decline in the proportion of blacks. But the proportion of blacks in the carpentry trade declined much more slowly, and the percentage of brickmasons who were black actually increased substantially between 1870 and 1910. In the newer or more specialized trades, the exclusion of Afro-Americans was almost complete. Prior to 1915, almost no blacks were employed as cabinetmakers, typesetters, bakers, tinsmiths, or electricians; the 1910 Census listed only five black plumbers in the entire city.[9]

Although detailed documentary evidence is often lacking, it appears that a similar distinction between "new" and "old" trades must be made in regard to union policies of excluding Negroes. There was a strong tendency among the newer trades (such as the paperhangers') to exclude blacks altogether. Among the more traditional skilled crafts the situation was more complex. By the 1870s, many white carpenters, masons, and others had developed a tradition of working with Negroes on a basis of relative equality; and when these workers formed unions at the end of the nineteenth century, they admitted a number of Negroes to their ranks. Since few younger blacks joined apprenticeship programs (either because they were excluded or because they sensed the hostility of the younger whites who were entering the labor movement at the time), the number of blacks who were members of these unions probably declined at a steady pace, through attrition, during the prewar years. On the eve of the Great Migration, however, one black Clevelander reported that the Carpenters', Brickmasons', Plasterers', and Lathers' Unions, among others, still had black members, and a visitor to the

---

[9] Emma Lou Thornbrough, *The Negro in Indiana: A Study of a Minority* ([Indianapolis,] 1957), 356; U.S. *Thirteenth Census, 1910*, IV, 549. The index of the relative concentration of blacks in various occupations is computed in Table 26 in Appendix II.

TABLE 9. *Occupational structure of Cleveland, by racial and ethnic group, 1910*

| | Occupational category | | | | | | | | | | | | |
| | Professional | | Proprietary | | Clerical | | Skilled | | Semiskilled | | Unskilled | | Domestic | |
	Number	Percentage	Number	Percentage	Number	Percentage	Number	Percentage	Number	Percentage	Number	Percentage	Number	Percentage
Males														
Negroes	50	1.4	87	2.5	104	3.0	388	11.1	255	7.3	905	25.9	1,033	29.6
Native whites of native parentage	1,436	3.6	3,696	9.5	9,523	24.3	9,691	24.5	3,134	8.0	1,923	4.9	953	2.4
Native whites of foreign or mixed parentage	979	1.8	4,730	8.6	10,137	18.8	15,412	28.0	4,970	9.0	3,626	6.6	1,263	2.3
Foreign-born whites	611	0.6	8,349	8.7	4,438	4.6	25,125	26.1	7,848	8.2	19,792	20.6	1,546	1.6
All workers	3,077	1.6	16,877	8.7	24,218	12.5	50,818	26.2	16,209	8.4	26,345	13.6	4,858	2.5
Females														
Negroes	54	3.4	62	3.9	23	1.4	36	2.3	201	12.7	—	—	1,149	72.6
Native whites of native parentage	1,508	12.3	530	4.3	4,481	37.5	222	1.8	2,498	20.3	—	—	1,404	11.4
Native whites of foreign or mixed parentage	1,756	7.2	483	2.0	6,506	26.3	1,204	5.0	7,412	30.5	—	—	2,597	10.7
Foreign-born whites	529	3.2	943	5.7	1,337	8.0	561	3.7	4,219	25.3	—	—	6,832	41.0
All workers	3,847	7.0	2,018	3.7	12,347	22.6	2,023	3.7	13,732	25.1	—	—	11,987	21.9

SOURCE: U.S. *Thirteenth Census, 1910* (Washington, 1912), IV, 548–50.
NOTE: Totals include the category "Indians, Chinese, Japanese, and all others." In 1910, 26 percent of the male occupations and 16 percent of the female occupations in Cleveland were unspecified by the Census Bureau.

city noted that black union men were still able to "receive the same wages and work on the same jobs with the white men without any friction." Thus Cleveland's nineteenth-century heritage of equality continued, in these unions, to linger on until well into the twentieth century.[10]

The skilled trades were not the only "integrated" black occupations that receded in importance during the 1870–1915 period. Throughout most of the nineteenth century, Negro waiters (especially headwaiters) who worked in Cleveland's exclusive downtown establishments were often held in high esteem by both the Negro and white communities, and a few were considered members of the black leadership class. As early as the 1880s, however, some black waiters were discharged and replaced with whites, and this marked the beginning of the exodus of black waiters from the city's better hotels and restaurants. The decline was a gradual one, but by 1918 only two leading establishments continued to employ black waiters. A parallel trend occurred in the bar-

[10] Cleveland *Gazette*, February 20, 1886; Frank U. Quillin, *The Color Line in Ohio* (Ann Arbor, 1913), 155–56. A decline in numbers of blacks in the skilled trades was probably common throughout the North in the late nineteenth and early twentieth centuries; the pace of change varied considerably from city to city, however. Three factors appear to account for a slower decline in some cities: (1) a tradition of racial liberalism; (2) smaller size and consequently less advanced state of industrialization and economic specialization; (3) a smaller immigrant population. It was primarily the first factor which retarded the decline of black opportunity in Cleveland, New Haven, and perhaps a few other cities. In 1890 15.3 percent of Cleveland's Negro males were engaged in skilled work, and in New Haven the percentage in skilled jobs was 16.6. In most cities, however, the second and third factors (or, in many cases, a combination of the two) were much more important. Thus, despite the high level of racial discrimination evident in schools and public accommodations in medium-sized Midwest cities at the end of the nineteenth century, these communities often afforded blacks more opportunities in the skilled trades than did eastern cities, chiefly because they contained fewer immigrants to compete for these jobs. In 1890, for example, Columbus, Indianapolis, and Des Moines had higher proportions of black males in skilled work (13.8, 10.8, and 19.2 percent, respectively) than eastern cities like Boston (9.7 percent), New York (4.8 percent), and Paterson, N.J. (6.1 percent). Chicago was also below average, with 7.8 percent of its black males in skilled occupations in 1890. It is evident that blacks in New York suffered a much higher degree of economic discrimination at an earlier date than did their counterparts in most other cities. In 1908, one observer noted of New York that "even in the colored districts the cobblers are largely Italians, and the colored shoemakers drift into other things." See Helen A. Tucker, "Negro Craftsmen in New York," *Southern Workman*, 37 (January 1908), 99; Mary White Ovington, *Half a Man: The Status of the Negro in New York* (New York, 1911), 85–91, 94–98, 99n; Herman D. Bloch, *The Circle of Discrimination: An Economic and Social Study of the Black Man in New York* (New York, 1969), 89–96. The percentages listed above were calculated from data in U.S. *Eleventh Census, 1890*, II, 638, 650, 654, 662, 674, 700, 704, 708. The occupational classification system used is discussed in Appendix I.

bering trade. George Myers's large well-known barbershop in the Hollenden, which sometimes employed thirty barbers, continued to serve an exclusively white clientele until Myers's death in 1930—but this was exceptional. Although blacks continued, in ever-decreasing numbers, to enter the barbering trade during the prewar years, their proportionate share of this occupation fell off sharply. In 1870, 43 percent of the city's barbers were blacks; by 1890, this figure had slipped to 18 percent. In 1910 less than one of every ten barbers in Cleveland was black, and it is likely that many of these were serving Negroes rather than the more lucrative white clientele.[11]

The declining importance of black waiters and barbers and the gradual disappearance of black businesses that catered to a predominantly white clientele were common to all northern cities during the late nineteenth and early twentieth centuries. In smaller, less industrialized cities the process occurred at a much slower pace than the big centers of population, however. In Columbus, Evansville, Indianapolis, Des Moines, and Kansas City, Missouri, blacks were able to maintain their hold on the barbering trade much longer than elsewhere, because these cities did not attract the large immigrant work force that was responsible for driving blacks out of barbering in other cities. In the major urban centers the process occurred much more rapidly and in most cases was virtually completed by 1915. Surveying Negro businesses in New York in 1909, George Edmund Haynes found that only seven of fifty Negro barber shops in the city still served a predominantly white clientele, while only one Negro merchant in ten catered to a predominantly white trade. "The Negro barber is rapidly losing ground in this city," said W. E. B. Du Bois in analyzing Philadelphia's black community in the late 1890s; and although he found some black catering establishments "still prominent," Du Bois noted that "they do not by any means dominate the field, as [a generation ago]." Students of the race situation in Boston, Detroit, and elsewhere echoed these observations. Because of its integrationist traditions, Cleveland did not succumb to this trend as quickly as other cities its size; but there, as elsewhere, the process of occupational change was irreversible.[12]

---

[11] H. T. Eubanks to John P. Green, February 5, 1899, Green Papers; Cleveland Advocate, September 7, 1918; John Garraty, ed., The Barber and the Historian: The Correspondence of George A. Myers and James Ford Rhodes, 1910–1923 (Columbus, Ohio, 1956), xxii–xxiii; U.S. Ninth Census, 1870 (Washington, 1873), I, 784; Thomas Goliber, "Cuyahoga Blacks: A Social and Demographic Study, 1850–1880" (M.A. thesis, Kent State University, 1972), 78; U.S. Eleventh Census, 1890, II, 654; U.S. Thirteenth Census, 1910, IV, 549.

[12] George Edmund Haynes, The Negro at Work in New York City, Columbia

In discussing the class structure of black communities around 1900, August Meier has noted that a "growing antipathy on the part of whites toward trading with Negro businessmen and changes in technology and business organization" were chiefly responsible for the decline of black entrepreneurs who serve an elite white clientele. While this is true, it is important to add that the changing nature of urban society itself (not just the growth of the ghetto) and developments in the white upper class during the 1870–1920 period may also have facilitated the decline in number of these Negro entrepreneurs. At the end of the nineteenth century, white urban elites were beginning to set themselves apart from the rest of the society residentially (through suburbs or the development of areas within the city which served much the same function) and institutionally (through clubs, private schools, and other institutions). This self-segregation on the part of the white upper class helped break the paternalistic tie between themselves and the black elite, and it is likely that this break would have eventually occurred even if racial discrimination had not been on the rise at the time. Commenting on the deterioration of the Negro catering business in Philadelphia during the 1900–1930 period, two writers found the main cause to be the caterers' "loss of personal contact with the fashionable group whose first thought used to be for the Negro when 'service' of any kind was to be done. . . ." While racism contributed to this loss of contact, the self-consciousness of the white upper class and the increasing fragmentation of urban life also played an important role.[13]

University Studies in History, Economics and Public Law, vol. 49, no. 3 (New York, 1913), 125, 128–29; W. E. B. Du Bois, *The Philadelphia Negro: A Social Study* (Philadelphia, 1899), 115–16, 119; John Daniels, *In Freedom's Birthplace: A Study of the Boston Negroes* (Boston, 1914), 324; Allan Spear, *Black Chicago: The Making of a Negro Ghetto, 1890–1920* (Chicago, 1967), 111–12; Ovington, *Half a Man*, 107; David M. Katzman, *Before the Ghetto: Black Detroit in the Nineteenth Century* (Urbana, Ill., 1973), 116–17. In 1890, the percentage of the barbering trade controlled by blacks varied widely throughout the North. In some cities blacks had already been virtually eliminated from the trade. In New York, only 2.2 percent of all barbers were Afro-Americans, and in Paterson, N.J., Newark, Hartford, Chicago, and Boston, the figure ranged from 1.9 to 9.5 percent. In other cities (New Haven, Philadelphia, Pittsburgh, Cleveland, and Minneapolis) the position of black barbers was declining, but they still held between 12 and 18 percent of the trade. There were a number of communities, however, where black barbers still dominated the trade at the end of the nineteenth century. In 1890 blacks controlled between 30 and 40 percent of the barbering trade in Columbus, Ohio; Kansas City, Missouri; and Indianapolis and Evansville, Indiana. These figures were computed from data in U.S. *Eleventh Census, 1890*, II, *passim*.

[13] August Meier, "Negro Class Structure and Ideology in the Age of Booker T. Washington," *Phylon*, 23 (Fall 1963), 259; G. J. Fleming and Berenice D. Shelton, "Fine Foods of Philadelphia," *Crisis*, 45 (April 1938), 114; Clara A. Hardin, *The*

In addition, black entrepreneurs who served a predominantly white clientele were adversely affected by the status anxieties of nouveau riche whites who, around 1900, were challenging an older, more genteel group of wealthy individuals. In 1913, for example, blacks in Dayton complained of "the newly-rich and uncultured [white] families who were ready to take advantage of all artificial props to uphold their importance. To the negroes they could show no mercy." Thus urban change, the growth of special upper-class white institutions, and the nouveau riche character of a portion of the white elite all contributed to the decline of the older group of Negro entrepreneurs.[14]

As traditional areas of black employment receded in importance, Negroes who aspired to middle-class status increasingly found themselves limited to three options: they could become clerical workers, enter one of the professions, or start a small business that catered to a predominantly Negro clientele. Each of these paths had its pitfalls.

One of the most significant changes accompanying the growth of the American economy between the Civil War and World War I was the creation of a new, much enlarged group of clerical and managerial positions in business firms of all types. Much like the urban systems of which they formed so crucial a part, these businesses were becoming more specialized in function as well as larger in size, and they required not only an army of factory workers but a wide variety of white-collar employees as well. Few Negroes, however, were able to gain entrance to this new white-collar world. In Cleveland the number of black males employed in clerical positions increased from 1.7 percent in 1870 to 3.7 percent forty years later. During this same period, the proportion of black females in clerical work rose from zero to 1.4 percent. (see Table 9). These modest increases in white-collar employment, however, fell far short of those experienced by the city's white work force. The one substantial gain occurred in black male employment as clerks in offices; the proportionate share of blacks in this occupation (where 100 percent would equal parity) increased from 28 to 54 percent between 1890 and 1910. In other white-collar jobs improvement was negligible at best, and

Negroes of Philadelphia: The Cultural Adjustment of a Minority Group (Bryn Mawr, Pa., 1945), 26. On the development of the white urban elite, see E. Digby Balzell, Philadelphia Gentlemen: The Making of a National Upper Class (Glencoe, Ill., 1958); E. Digby Balzell, The Protestant Establishment: Aristocracy and Caste in America (New York, 1964), 109–42; Neil Harris, "Four Stages of Cultural Growth: The American City," in History and the Role of the City in American Life, Indiana Historical Society Lectures, 1971–72 (Indianapolis, Ind., 1972), 35–42.
14 Quillin, The Color Line in Ohio, 139.

the proportionate share of blacks ranged from 20 percent to an abysmally low 3 percent. (See Tables 26 and 27 in Appendix II.)

Perhaps because of the existence of standardized tests for some jobs in the federal or municipal government, blacks sometimes found more opportunity for white-collar employment in public service than in private enterprise. In 1915 several Cleveland Negroes were clerks in departments of the city government; two were government meat inspectors; and forty-two were postal clerks or carriers. These gains were significant for the black middle class, but even in public service blacks suffered the onus of racial discrimination. In some areas of municipal employment it was standard procedure to exclude Negroes. The fire department, for example, employed no blacks in 1910 and had probably always been totally white.The number of blacks serving on the police force was inadequate. Cleveland had employed black constables as early as the 1870s, but in 1910 blacks still had only one-half their rightful share of police positions. Nor did blacks in civil service jobs always rise in the ranks as rapidly as they should have. The case of Charles S. Smith, an Afro-American who placed fourth in the police examinations in 1897, is a good example. Because of his valued stenographic skills, Smith was immediately chosen to be the secretary to the chief of police. He had to remain in that position for twenty years, however, before his salary was raised from a patrolman's to that of a lieutenant. Despite the significant number of blacks who found employment in the post office, as late as 1930 few had risen to positions of authority. Finally, although Cleveland's black community could point with pride to those of the race who had obtained white-collar government employment, the fact was that most of the Negroes employed by the city were unskilled laborers, hired to do a variety of unappealing, low-paying tasks. As the editor of the *Gazette* caustically noted in 1916, most blacks in municipal employment were restricted to "spittoon cleaning, garbage hunting [hauling?], street-cleaning, truck driving, and other jobs of that kind," with little opportunity to rise to better positions.[15]

The status anxieties of those whites who had moved up from factory to clerical work undoubtedly played a major part in the difficulties

[15] Robert I. Drake, "The Negro in Cleveland," Cleveland *Advocate*, September 18, 1915; U.S. *Thirteenth Census, 1910*, IV, 549; Charles W. Chesnutt, "The Negro in Cleveland," *The Clevelander*, 5 (November 1930), 24; Cleveland *Leader*, March 8, 9, 1875; Cleveland *Gazette*, April 1, 1916, January 11, 1919; Cleveland *Press*, April 21, 1923, clipping in unnumbered Walter B. Wright Scrapbooks, Western Reserve Historical Society; interview with Russell and Rowena Jelliffe, September 1, 1971.

blacks encountered in entering white-collar employment. Another factor may have been related to the beginnings, during the Progressive era, of the preoccupation of American business with public relations and advertising techniques. The preponderance of native-born white women in department store jobs, one observer noted in 1909, was partially "due to the fact that many customers prefer to be served by [native-white] Americans. . . ." The mass market that the department stores catered to forced the stores to adopt a neutral image in dealing with the public, and this virtually eliminated Negroes (as well as many immigrants) from positions as sales clerks. The newer communications and transportation industries also tended to exclude blacks from jobs involving contact with the public. In 1905, there was only a single Negro telephone operator in New York, and other northern cities were no different in this regard. In 1900 Cleveland was one of three cities in the North that employed a few Afro-Americans as streetcar conductors, but within ten years the city's privately owned transportation companies had ended this policy of integration.[16]

For those Negroes who had the funds to obtain the necessary specialized training, the professions offered a surer path to success than did the clerical occupations. At the beginning of the twentieth century the increase in Negro populations in urban areas, combined with the refusal of most white professional men to accept Negro clients, led to a general increase in the number of black professionals. This trend was not uniform in all occupations. Blacks were over-represented in the poorly paid profession of the ministry, but they found the newer engineering fields completely closed to them; black journalists found little opportunity outside the small Negro weeklies that struggled to survive in many urban areas. In the traditional professions, black doctors did much better than black lawyers. Surveying Negro professionals as a whole, Kelly Miller noted that blacks were "crowding into" the medical profession, but were not entering the legal field nearly as fast; at the turn of the century there were two and one-half times as many blacks in medicine as in the law. In Philadelphia, W. E. B. Du Bois found black doctors successful.

16 Elizabeth Beardsley Butler, *Saleswomen in Mercantile Stores* (New York, 1912), 144; Haynes, *The Negro at Work in New York City*, 76; James S. Stemons, "The Industrial Color-Line in the North," *Century Magazine*, 60 (July 1900), 478; *Cleveland Journal*, June 3, 17, 1905; U.S. *Thirteenth Census, 1910*, 549. See also John Daniels, "Industrial Conditions among Negro Men in Boston," *Charities*, 15 (October 7, 1905), 37. The anti-immigrant and anti-Negro aspect of department stores at the turn of the century is ignored by Daniel Boorstin, who calls the stores examples of "the democratization of luxury." Boorstin, *The Americans: The Democratic Experience* (New York, 1973), 101–12.

Lawyers, however, were "a partial failure" because "Negroes furnish little lucrative law business, and a Negro lawyer will seldom be employed by whites." On the other hand, the number of blacks in the teaching profession grew rapidly during this period. Many cities established separate schools for Negroes, and when they did so they usually hired Negro teachers to preside over the classes; the result was a gain for the black middle class, if a loss for the principle of integration.[17]

Opportunities in the professions were unusually good for black Clevelanders. In 1915 the black community could claim eight doctors, three dentists, two professionally trained nurses, a dozen lawyers, and thirty school teachers. These numbers may seem small, but proportionately (with the exception of the nurses) blacks did not lag very far behind the rest of the population. The number of black lawyers in Cleveland was quite exceptional, given the relatively small size of the city's black community. In 1910, St. Louis and Philadelphia had black populations that were many times the size of Cleveland's; yet all three cities had about the same number of black lawyers. The success of these professionals in Cleveland was due primarily to their unusually integrated practices. Although most northern cities had some black lawyers serving an integrated clientele, all of Cleveland's black lawyers were able to draw clients from both races. A majority, in fact, had more white clients than Negro in 1915. At that time many of Cleveland's black doctors also had integrated practices.[18]

At the same time that the black professionals were making steady—if uneven—progress, a new group of black businessmen was on the rise. In the South as well as the North the Negro merchants and entrepreneurs whose clientele was primarily white were disappearing during the twenty years prior to the World War I migration. They were gradually replaced by a different group of entrepreneurs—real estate dealers, undertakers, newspaper editors, insurance agents, bankers, and a plethora of small businessmen—who were dependent mostly upon the Negro market. Ironically, the deterioration of race relations at the end of the nineteenth century, as evidenced by discrimination in housing, the trend

---

[17] Kelly Miller, "Professional and Skilled Occupations," *Annals of the American Academy of Political and Social Science,* 49 (September 1913), 13, 17; Du Bois, *The Philadelphia Negro,* 114; Meier, "Negro Class Structure and Ideology in the Age of Booker T. Washington," 259–60.

[18] Robert I. Drake, "The Negro in Cleveland;" U.S. *Thirteenth Census, 1910,* IV, 549; Jane Edna Hunter, *A Nickel and a Prayer* (Cleveland, 1940), 87; William A. Crossland, *Industrial Conditions among Negroes in St. Louis,* Washington University Studies in Social Economics, vol. 1, no. 1 (St. Louis, Mo., 1914), 38; interview with Dr. William P. Saunders, August 6, 1972.

toward residential concentration, the refusal of white insurance companies to grant policies to Negroes, and the discrimination of white banks in authorizing loans, made the development of this new class possible.[19]

This new group of black entrepreneurs did not gain ascendancy over the old as fast in Cleveland as elsewhere. The moderate size of the city's black community made it more difficult for black businessmen to acquire an economic base among their own race. On the other hand, the continued (though weakened) heritage of integration and the paternalistic support by a segment of the white upper class allowed a number of black businesses that dealt only with whites to survive and prosper longer than their counterparts in cities like Chicago and Philadelphia. On the eve of the Great Migration, a small group of Negro tailors, caterers, barbers, and merchants continued to serve a predominantly white clientele. One of the most successful of this older group was Jacob E. Reed, who for many years operated a well-known downtown markethouse that specialized in fish, oysters, and other seafood products. Reed's business may have declined somewhat with the passage of time, but as late as 1919 the aging merchant could still count "a number of the best families in the city" as well as "the leading hotels and restaurants" among his customers.[20]

If the older, white-oriented black businessmen were represented by Reed, the younger generation of entrepreneurs with roots in the black community was exemplified by S. Clayton Green. Green began his business career in 1902 when he patented a sofa bed and, together with several other Negroes, established the Leonard Sofa Bed Company. The energetic Green did not limit himself to this venture, however. He soon invested in a laundry company and purchased a restaurant on Central Avenue. Well aware of the fact that Negroes were often given unequal treatment in white theaters, Green opened the first Negro-owned and

[19] W. E. B. Du Bois, *The Negro in Business*, Atlanta University Publications, no. 4 (Atlanta, 1899), 10; Robert A. Warner, *New Haven Negroes: A Social History* (New Haven, Conn., 1940), 233–34; St. Clair Drake and Horace R. Cayton, *Black Metropolis: A Study of Negro Life in a Northern City* (New York, 1945), 462–63; Meier, "Negro Class Structure and Ideology in the Age of Booker T. Washington," 260 (see especially Meier's footnote 3 for additional sources on the development of black business). A useful overview is J. H. Harmon, Jr., "The Negro as a Local Business Man," *Journal of Negro History*, 14 (April 1929), 121–43, especially 140–41.

[20] Clement Richardson et al., eds., *The National Cyclopedia of the Colored Race* (Montgomery, Ala., 1919), I, 245. The slower development of elite suburbs in Cleveland (Shaker Heights was not established until after World War I) may also have helped businessmen like Reed retain their white clientele.

-operated theater in the city in 1911. The Alpha Theater, located at 32d and Central, was an excellent example of how the new breed of black businessmen could turn segregation and discrimination to their own advantage. A severe stroke in 1913 followed by his death less than two years later cut short Green's remarkable career; but he had succeeded in proving that blacks could be financially successful by relying upon the buying power of the black masses.[21]

Green and a fellow businessman with the intriguing name of Welcome T. Blue were the two most important black real-estate dealers in Cleveland before World War I. At the turn of the century Blue established the Acme Real Estate Company, an enterprise designed to build low-cost homes for blacks who were finding it increasingly difficult to purchase houses in the white real estate market. Within a few years, he and Green had organized the much larger Mohawk Realty Company; they purchased several homes and two apartment buildings and constructed the Clayton Building, a complex of stores, offices, and apartment suites located in the heart of the developing ghetto. Blue also attempted, with some success, to crack the suburban housing market for blacks. He purchased a good-sized tract of land at the end of one of the new streetcar lines, on the outskirts of the city, and by 1907 had managed to induce about one hundred Negroes to move into the development.[22]

These were not the only examples of black businesses that served the Negro market during the prewar years. Four black undertakers, including the very successful J. Walter Wills, established themselves during this period; and the increased size of the black population also made possible the existence of two black newspapers, the *Gazette* (founded in 1883) and the *Journal* (founded in 1903). These and other race enterprises instilled a feeling of race pride among the new group of black entrepreneurs. "Central Avenue," one black resident boasted in 1905, "has developed into a regular business street, and we are happy to state that many of those business houses are owned by colored people." "When one walks up Central Avenue with a visitor," the *Journal* noted the same

[21] Frank U. Quillin, "The Negro in Cleveland, Ohio," *Independent*, 72 (March 7, 1912), 518; "New Leonard Sofa Bed Company," *Colored American Magazine*, 7 (March 1904), 210–11; Cleveland *Journal*, March 24, 1906; Cleveland *Gazette*, December 30, 1911, May 1, 1915; Russell H. Davis, *Memorable Negroes in Cleveland's Past* (Cleveland, 1969), 43. Both Green and Reed are discussed in greater detail in Chapter 6.

[22] Cleveland *Gazette*, December 10, 1904; Cleveland *Journal*, April 28, 1906; Carrie W. Clifford, "Cleveland and Its Colored People," *Colored American Magazine*, 9 (July 1905), 372; Davis, *Memorable Negroes*, 43; David A. Gerber, "Ohio and the Color Line: Racial Discrimination and Negro Responses in a Northern State, 1860–1915" (Ph.D. dissertation, Princeton University, 1971), 409–10.

year, "it should make his heart glad to be able to point out the residence and office of four or five doctors, a dentist, several churches, three groceries, two funeral homes, one hotel, three restaurants, one jeweler, one shoemaker, several dressmakers, one milliner, one club house, bicycle manufacturer, one tailor, and other places of interest." The impressive variety of the black businesses mentioned, however, could not obscure the fact that they were small in number and frequently lacking in sufficient capital to make them profitable. S. Clayton Green's achievements were laudable, but they looked rather insignificant beside those of Chicago's Jesse Binga or any one of a number of black real-estate dealers in Harlem. No Negro insurance companies were active in Cleveland before the Great Migration, and it was not until 1921 that a black entrepreneur established the first Negro-owned bank in the city. That Negro-based businesses in Cleveland were increasing in number was incontestable; but it was also evident that this growth rate was considerably slower than that of larger black communities elsewhere in the North.[23]

Among black males, occupational declines in some areas during the prewar decades were frequently offset by gains in other areas. For black females, however, the period can only be described as one of sharp decline relative to the rest of the population. Between 1870 and 1910, the occupational structure of Cleveland's entire female work force underwent something of a revolution. The proportion of women in clerical work increased dramatically from 1.7 to 22.6 percent, and the number of women in the professions also rose substantially. At the same time the percentage of all working women engaged in domestic and personal service plunged drastically from 65.7 to 21.9 percent (see Tables 2 and 9). White women, especially the native-born, were escaping from domestic service employment in increasing numbers—and with good reason. The pay was low, averaging in 1900 only $3.23 per week plus room and board. For almost all domestics there was no hope of advancement to better-paying positions. The work was dull, repetitious, and seemingly endless, and many women especially disliked the irregular working hours, which often interfered with their personal independence. A workday of ten hours or more was by no means exceptional. Yet it was to these unrewarding, personal-service occupations that black women found themselves increasingly relegated. Between 1870 and 1910 there

---

[23] Clifford, "Cleveland and Its Colored People," 278–80; Cleveland *Journal*, May 6, 1905. From 1884 to 1896 the *Globe*, another Negro weekly, was also published in Cleveland. For discussions of black businessmen in Chicago and New York, see Spear, *Black Chicago*, 74–75, and Gilbert Osofsky, *Harlem: The Making of a Ghetto* (New York, 1966), 92–104.

No member of the black community opposed the home for the aged. A plan to counter the growing discrimination in the Cleveland YMCA by creating an all-Negro branch, however, stirred up considerable controversy. The idea for an all-Negro Y was first advanced by Nahum Brascher in 1906, but it was not until 1910 that a movement for such an institution got firmly under way. Most of the new elite endorsed Brascher's proposal as a useful example of race solidarity and self-help, while the Old Guard almost to a man (with the notable exceptions of John P. Green and Jere Brown) protested the establishment of such an institution as a step down the road to segregation. Harry C. Smith, as might be expected, was particularly vocal in his criticism; he attacked the proponents of the black YMCA for attempting to build an institution from which they and their friends would gain jobs and prestige. Blacks, the editor insisted, should "be trying to wipe out color-lines, rather than be trying to multiply them." As it turned out, Smith had little to fear: in 1911 the YMCA movement died out. But its defeat—the boasting rhetoric of the *Gazette* notwithstanding—signified less a triumph for integrationism and the old leadership than a pragmatic facing of economic realities. Cleveland's black community was barely large enough to support a home for the elderly; in 1910 the creation of a second secular community organization was only a pipe dream in the minds of the new elite. New York's first Negro YMCA (there were three by 1915) dated to 1899, and in 1911 black Chicagoans quickly raised $65,000 toward the construction of what became "the largest and finest [YMCA] building for colored men in the United States." It would not be until after the Great Migration, however, that Cleveland's Negroes were able to create a similar, smaller facility of their own.[60]

During the prewar era, the only major secular institution created solely for Negroes was the Phillis Wheatley Association, a residence and job-training center for girls who had come to the city on their own or who were separated from their families for some other reason. The association was founded in 1912 by Jane Edna Hunter, a black professional nurse who was determined to find "ways and means of ameliorating the hard lot of homeless girls." Hunter was an admirer of Booker T. Washington and felt that a more self-sufficient black community was the

[60] Cleveland *Journal*, October 6, 1906, March 5, 1910; Cleveland *Plain Dealer*, February 1, 1911; Cleveland *Gazette*, March 9, 1910, January 21, February 4, 1911, February 14, 1914; Gilbert Osofsky, *Harlem: The Making of a Ghetto* (New York, 1966), 15; Channing H. Tobias, "The Colored Y.M.C.A.," *Crisis*, 9 (November 1914), 33, quoted in Spear, *Black Chicago*, 101. In 1914 a movement to establish an all-Negro children's home in Cleveland also failed. Cleveland *Gazette*, August 8, 1914.

answer to increasing white hostility. She viewed the struggle for integration as misguided:

> Too often, alas, has the Negro been misled by leaders of his own race. There are those false prophets who would persuade us that some day the Negro will be absorbed by the white race. What the Negro really desires is a change of industrial and economic status so that he may enjoy the privileges and culture that other men possess. By thorough and complete miscegenation we should lose our richest heritage. The Negro must continue to make his distinct contribution to the world—as a Negro.

The Phillis Wheatley Association met with opposition from one segment of the black community, and the ensuing dispute was one of the chief examples of ideological conflict between the old and new elite. Harry C. Smith was a vociferous opponent of the PWA (he once labeled it a "jim-crow hotel" for black girls) and continued to denounce it for years as the first step down the road to institutional segregation. The main opposition, however, came from "a small group of club women who, blessed with prosperity, had risen from the servant class and now regarded themselves as the arbiters and guardians of colored society." The aloofness of these members of the old upper class from the city's black masses and their unawareness of the increasing discrimination which the average Negro faced was evidenced by the naïve criticism of one of the "club women": ". . . we will not permit you, a Southerner," she said to Jane Hunter, "to start segregation in this city." Another elite black woman remarked in a similar patronizing vein: "We call on the white people, and the white people call on us. Now that the more intelligent of us have broken down the barriers between the races, you are trying to build them up again with your absurd Southern ideas for working girls."[61]

The founders of Phillis Wheatley gradually overcame these critics, converted most of the Negro ministers of the city to their side, and launched their enterprise. Financing the new organization was another matter. The PWA started with literally "a nickel and a prayer," and by 1914 Jane Hunter realized that white philanthropy would be a necessity if her dream was to become a reality. Henry A. Sherwin, the head of the Sherwin-Williams Paint Company, agreed to help finance Phillis Wheatley, but only on the condition that certain prominent white women

[61] Hunter, A Nickel and a Prayer, 84, 90–91, 94, 189; Cleveland Gazette, January 17, 1914, November 13, 1926. The association was named after Phillis Wheatley (1753?–84), who was brought from Africa to Boston as a slave in 1761, began writing poetry at the age of thirteen, and gained fame in America and England for her published work.

be named to the Board of Trustees. Jane Hunter found herself faced with a dilemma, however, when these women refused to serve unless they were allowed the right of choosing the Negro officers of the organization as well. "This," said Hunter, "created a delicate situation. I was faced with a choice between offending members of my own race who had given far more than they could actually afford, and yielding to influences which could give our organization a sound financial basis." Hunter reluctantly chose the latter. "It seemed necessary," she later related, "to sacrifice personal feelings for the sake of the cause."[62]

By 1916 170 girls were being housed yearly in Phillis Wheatley, and many more were using its facilities. To achieve this, however, Hunter had been forced to jettison the principle of black control of a community institution. Though billed as such by its black supporters, Phillis Wheatley was hardly an example of black self-sufficiency during its early years. The organization was almost entirely financed by whites. But more important was the fact that the direction of the institution at the beginning was strongly influenced by a group of upper-class white women who knew little about the needs and interests of recent southern migrants. In addition, some of these women probably had ulterior reasons for backing the organization. There was a direct relationship between the creation of Phillis Wheatley and the movement to exclude black girls from Cleveland's YWCA. Harry C. Smith claimed that the whites who supported the PWA did so to head off a movement to keep the local Y integrated. George Myers, in a less conspiratorial explanation, asserted that Phillis Wheatley was "fostered by a few misguided whites endeavoring to relieve their consciences of the discrimination by the YWCA against our women." In either case, one of the latent functions of Phillis Wheatley, with its facilities for lodging, board, and recreation, was to keep blacks out of the YWCA. It was certainly no coincidence that Mrs. Levi T. Schofield, the white woman who became the first president of the Board of Trustees of the PWA, was also head of the city's YWCA at the time when that organization began its discriminatory policy.[63]

Unlike the Phillis Wheatley Association, the Cleveland Association of Colored Men was a racial advancement organization that caused no dispute in the black community. The CACM, founded in 1908, was primarily sponsored by the new elite, although a few of the city's older

[62] Hunter, *A Nickel and a Prayer*, 99–100.

[63] *Ibid.*, 93–94, 104; Harry C. Smith, "Some 'Phillis Wheatley' History," Cleveland *Gazette*, May 14, 1927; *ibid.*, March 28, 1928; George A. Myers to Booker T. Washington, July 20, 1914, Myers Papers; minutes of the Phillis Wheatley Association, February 13, 1917, December 8, 1921, Phillis Wheatley Association Papers.

Negro leaders also took part. The popularity of the organization derived from the breadth of its activities: the CACM sponsored social events, inaugurated a lecture series, and launched several modest charitable projects in the black community. In addition, one of the avowed purposes of the organization was to take up the question "of discrimination in public places. . . ." At no time, however, did the CACM take a strong civil rights stance; typically, the association "investigated" cases of blatant discrimination but took little concrete action. This accommodationism is not surprising, since William Green and Thomas Fleming were the most prominent leaders of the CACM during its early years and the organization contributed to several of Booker T. Washington's Tuskegee projects. The rather conservative nature of the association was revealed in its policy of holding the major black social event of the year (ironically dubbed the "Emancipation Celebration") at the usually whites-only Luna Park, a policy that Harry C. Smith repeatedly criticized to no avail.[64]

IV

In Cleveland, as in other northern black communities, the growth of the black population in the late nineteenth and early twentieth centuries promoted a shift in black leadership and led to the development of black institutions. But in several ways these developments did not duplicate patterns established elsewhere. On Chicago's South Side, for example, ideological conflict often developed when the rising new black leadership attempted to establish all-Negro institutions. In Cleveland, however, fewer separate institutions were proposed because the black population was too small to support them. The smaller size of the black community, combined with the absence (before 1915) of a clearly defined ghetto, made the business-oriented new black leadership less predominant in Cleveland than in Chicago. This, coupled with the growing conservatism of some black integrationists, kept the ideological differences between the two groups from breaking into the open too often. Nevertheless, hostility between the old and new elites was increasing during the decade before the Great Migration as more and more blacks began to support the idea of separate institutions.[65]

Regardless of their positions on purely racial questions, most black

---

[64] *Summary of the Work Done by the Cleveland Association of Colored Men,* n.p.; Cuban, "A Strategy for Racial Peace," 305; Cleveland *Gazette,* July 31, 1915.

[65] For a discussion of ideological conflict among black leaders in Chicago, see Spear, *Black Chicago,* 52–54, 84–89, and chs. 3 and 4, *passim.*

leaders adhered to a basically conservative view of social change. Whether they opposed or favored the creation of a separate, "group" economy, both the old elite and its challengers firmly believed that the "strive and succeed" ethic and the doctrine of economic individualism were applicable to the black experience in the United States. These black leaders—and, for that matter, blacks in general—did not participate very much in the new organizational, bureaucratic society that was beginning to emerge during the Progressive era. For that reason and, perhaps, because many of the black elite had through various means risen from poverty to middle-class respectability, they retained a faith in individualism and the free-enterprise system that sometimes bordered on naïvete; and their economic conservatism was bolstered by the growing racism of many labor unions.

Because of its smaller size, Cleveland's black community remained more dependent on white institutions and white financial support than did the black communities of cities such as New York, Chicago, and Philadelphia. There was no equivalent in Cleveland to Chicago's Provident Hospital, for example. Philadelphia's black community also had its own hospital (Douglass Memorial, founded in 1895); and as early as 1896 its Home for Aged Colored Persons had an annual income of $20,000 and property valued at $400,000. A survey of black life in New York in 1901 found "a successful building association, a hospital, an orphan asylum, and a home for the aged, all entirely conducted by Negroes, and mainly supported by them." The institutional development of Cleveland's black community lagged behind these larger metropolises.[66]

The experience of blacks in Cleveland was far from being unique, however. Early in the twentieth century there were many moderate-sized or small black communities in the North. In 1910, Detroit's black population was only 5,700; Newark's was 9,500; New Haven's only 3,600. Paterson, New Jersey; Albany and Buffalo, New York; and Gary, Indiana, all had black populations under 2,000. Although detailed studies of black leadership and institutional development in these cities during the Progressive era are lacking, it is highly probable that in many cases the tradition of black dependency that developed in Cleveland at this time found expression there as well. Actually, even in larger black com-

[66] W. E. B. Du Bois, *The Philadelphia Negro: A Social Study* (Philadelphia, 1899), 230, 231–32; Elliott Rudwick, "A Brief History of the Mercy-Douglass Hospital in Philadelphia," *Journal of Negro Education,* 20 (Winter 1951), 50–53; W. E. B. Du Bois, "The Black North," *New York Times Magazine,* November 24, 1901; Ovington, *Half a Man,* 171–80; Osofsky, *Harlem,* 67; Spear, *Black Chicago,* 91–105.

munities like Chicago and Philadelphia, blacks were frequently unable to establish separate race institutions without at least some white assistance, and this assistance sometimes entailed white paternalistic involvement and hence a degree of white control. (This was especially true of the branches of the National Urban League, established in 1911; since the League did not gain prominence until after the wartime migration, however, a discussion of its role is left to a later chapter.) In the political sphere also, the patron-client relationship that developed between Cleveland's Republican machine and black councilman Thomas Fleming was duplicated in many cities of the North.[67] Only in the wake of the Great Migration, with the consolidation of the ghetto and intensification of racism that accompanied it, would a more independent and assertive black leadership begin to emerge.

[67] Population data taken from U.S. Bureau of the Census, *Negroes in the United States, 1920–1932* (Washington, 1935), 55.

PART III

A Ghetto Takes Shape, 1915-30

CHAPTER 7

The Great Migration and the Consolidation of the Ghetto

Blacks had been coming north in a slow but steady stream since the Civil War. There was little precedent, however, for the huge exodus of southern migrants that accompanied the World War I era. While war raged in Europe, the inhabitants of northern black communities were undergoing their own traumatic experience as their numbers were swelled by the arrival of hundreds of thousands of newcomers. Between 1910 and 1920, Cleveland's black population increased 308 percent, Detroit's rose 611 percent, and Chicago's increased 148 percent; other cities experienced substantial, if smaller, gains. These cities were suddenly faced with the difficult task of assimilating a large number of individuals who were, in most cases, uneducated and completely unaccustomed to urban surroundings. The responses of both the Negro and white communities to this problem helped shape and delimit the lives of northern Negroes for decades afterward.[1]

Like most mass movements, the causes of the Great Migration were many and varied. Dissatisfaction with race relations in the South undoubtedly played a part in motivating many Negroes to move. The violence of lynch mobs and the sharp discrimination in housing, schools, and the court systems in many southern communities were constant sources of grievance to blacks. The desire to "go North," however, involved more than an aversion to the racial prejudices of white southerners. In his invaluable 1932 study of black migrants from the South Caro-

[1] U.S. Bureau of the Census, *Negroes in the United States, 1920–1932* (Washington, 1935), 55 (Table 10).

lina Sea Islands, Clyde Vernon Kiser indicated that one of the chief
underlying causes of black migration from the region was what we
would now call a "generation gap." Despite poor economic conditions,
few blacks left the Islands between 1865 and 1890. "The Islanders of
that time," Kiser explained, "had little besides their former slave condition by which to judge their economic status." After 1890, however,
younger black residents of the Islands who had been born after the
Civil War had a different perspective. They often viewed their condition
as one of social and economic stagnation rather than (as their fathers
had) one of improved circumstances. One migrant who left the Islands
in 1911 at the age of nineteen put it this way: "Young people grow up
now and say, 'I want to get 'way from heah. No diggin' in the sile fo'
me. Let other man do the diggin'. I'm through with farmin'.'" In a
similar vein, another migrant stated her distaste for the monotonous
routine of farm life: "Got tired living on Island. Too lonesome. Go to bed
at six o'clock. Everything dead. No dances, no moving picture show,
nothing to go to. . . . That's why people move more than anything else."
Said another migrant, "Young folks just ain't satisfied to see so little
and stay around on farm all their lives like old folks did."[2]

However important such underlying motivations were, it is unlikely
that they would have resulted in the extensive movement of population
that occurred between 1916 and 1919, had immediate and powerful
economic factors not intervened. Immigration to the United States,
which had reached a high point in 1914, fell off drastically during the
next four years and with it the supply of cheap labor which American
manufacturers depended upon. The labor shortage became particularly
acute because of the sudden demands placed upon industries for the
production of war materials. The need for workers in the North coincided with a period of economic depression in the South. Many southern
Negroes, of course, had been reduced to virtual peonage by the crop-
lien and tenant-farm system that was introduced during and after Reconstruction. But the spread of the boll weevil throughout the South,
ruining thousands of acres of cotton, and a series of floods in the Gulf
States in 1915 made the lot of black farmers particularly hard. It was
under these unusual circumstances that northern manufacturers began
to realize the value of the black labor force as an "industrial reserve."
Putting aside their doubts about the adaptability of black workers,
northern industrialists began to send labor agents south to induce Negroes to migrate. More than a few blacks accepted the inducement of

[2] Clyde Vernon Kiser, Sea Island to City: A Study of St. Helena Islanders in
Harlem and Other Urban Centers (New York, 1931), 117, 131, 144.

free train tickets and the promise of good jobs when they reached their destination.[3]

After a while, the migration became self-generating as news of the better life in the North circulated through southern black communities. "For the first time in American history," one contemporary historian noted, "opportunities, large in number, in skilled as well as unskilled labor, were offered to Negro workmen." Northern Negro editors, gleeful over the inability of the white South to stop the migration, urged southern blacks to take advantage of the unusual economic situation. "To ask the colored people to remain" in the South, the editor of the *Gazette* exclaimed, "depending upon the people who have destroyed them in the past to aid them in the future, is sheer folly." Recent arrivals in the North wrote home to relatives telling of the high wages they were receiving. "We are making good money here," one newcomer to Cleveland wrote in 1917. Although wages in the South averaged between $1.10 and $1.25 per day in many instances, in Cleveland he could earn three times that amount—or more. He explained (in the semiliterate style typical of many immigrants), "I have made as hight at 7.50 per day and my wife $4 Sundays my sun 7.50 and my 2 oldes girls 1.25 but my regler weges is 3.60 fore 8 hours work." In February, 1917, the city employment Bureau in Cleveland was receiving an average of fifty to sixty letters a day from southern blacks seeking jobs. By spring hundreds of migrants were arriving each week, and the *Gazette* reported that newcomers were "vainly 'running the streets' in the Central Avenue vicinity, seeking rooms last week worse than ever before, two carloads more having arrived from the South, Sunday evening. . . ." The Cleveland *Advocate* caught the drama of the situation. "There is no mistaking what is going on," the paper editorialized at the end of April, "it is a REGULAR EXODUS. It is without head, tail, or leadership. Its greatest factor is MOMENTUM, and this is increasing, despite amazing efforts on the part of white southerners to stop it. People are leaving their homes and

[3] Charles H. Wesley, *Negro Labor in the United States, 1850–1925: A Study in American Economic History* (New York, 1927), 290–92; Louise Venable Kennedy, *The Negro Peasant Turns Cityward* (New York, 1930), 42–48; Emmett J. Scott, *Negro Migration during the War* (New York, 1920), 13–15 and *passim*; U.S. Department of Labor, Division of Negro Economics, *Negro Migration in 1916–17* (Washington, 1919), 17–18, 86–87; George Edmund Haynes, "Negroes Move North," *Survey*, 40 (May 4, 1918), 115–22; Chicago Commission on Race Relations, *The Negro in Chicago: A Study of Race Relations and a Race Riot* (Chicago, 1922), 80–84, 357–65; Roi Ottley and William J. Weatherby, eds., *The Negro in New York: An Informal Social History* (New York, 1969), 188. See also the recent study by Florette Henri, *Black Migration: Movement North, 1900–1920* (New York, 1975), 47–62.

everything about them, under cover of night, as though they were going on a day's journey—leaving forever." The Great Migration was under way.[4]

The annual number of migrants to Cleveland prior to 1916 was small compared to other northern cities, but during and after the war the Forest City became one of the principal destinations of Negroes leaving the South. The city's black population increased from 8,448 in 1910 to 34,451 in 1920, a gain of 26,003. It is likely that about three-quarters of this increase was due to migration from the South between 1916 and 1919. Thus the black community, which numbered no more than 12,000 in 1916, had to accommodate an increase of over 20,000 during a single three-year period. By March, 1919, this wave of migrants had temporarily slackened. A railroad office in Cleveland reported that the number of newcomers from the South had fallen off sharply and that some of the recent arrivals, unable to find work because of the postwar business slump, were returning to their native states.[5]

With the return of prosperity after 1920, migration quickly resumed. During the 1920s, Cleveland's black population more than doubled; by 1930 there were almost 72,000 Negroes living in the city (see Table 1). It is likely that over one-half of this new increase occurred between 1921 and 1924; the acceleration of business activity during those years brought a new wave of seventeen to twenty thousand blacks to the city. It is fair to say, then, that the twenties—especially the first half of the decade—in many ways represented a continuation, rather than a curtailment, of the crisis engendered by the Great Migration of 1916–19. Population growth did gradually diminish between 1920 and 1930, but the influx of migrants during that period was still so large that the assimilation of newcomers into the urban setting remained a continuing problem.[6]

[4] Wesley, Negro Labor in the United States, 282; Cleveland Gazette, February 10, April 21, 1917; Scott, Negro Migration during the War, 17; Emmett J. Scott, comp., "Additional Letters of Negro Migrants of 1916–1918," Journal of Negro History, 4 (October 1919), 460–61; minutes of the Board of the Negro Welfare Association, March 19, 1918, Cleveland Urban League Papers, Western Reserve Historical Society; Cleveland Advocate, April 28, 1917.

[5] Cleveland Gazette, March 15, 1919. There is no way to ascertain the exact number of migrants who came to the city during and immediately after the war. Allan Spear estimates that 50,000 of the approximately 61,000 Negroes who migrated to Chicago between 1910 and 1920 came during the 1916–20 period, and I have followed his analysis in computing figures for Cleveland. See Spear, Black Chicago: The Making of a Negro Ghetto, 1890–1920 (Chicago, 1967), 140–41.

[6] This estimate is based on elementary school enrollment figures compiled in Howard W. Green, A Study of the Movement of the Negro Population of Cleveland (Cleveland, 1924), 1–5. In April, 1921, there were 5,078 Negro children in city

Before World War I a large minority of the city's black residents had been born and raised in Cleveland. This element of demographic stability was ruptured by the Great Migration, however, and between 1910 and 1920 the proportion of Cleveland Negroes born in Ohio fell precipitously from 35.7 to 16.9 percent. A shift in the origins of migrants was also evident. Before the war, most of the Afro-Americans who came to Ohio (no breakdown by city is available for 1920) from other states had been born in the Upper South or the border states, and less than 5 percent had listed the Deep South as their place of birth. During World War I, migrants from Kentucky and Tennessee continued to come to Ohio in substantial numbers, but over 50 percent of the increase in Ohio's Negro population between 1910 and 1920 was due to migration from the Deep South. (See Table 24 in Appendix II.) The data on migration into Ohio gives only a rough indication of the nativity of migrants to Cleveland between 1910 and 1920. The census statistics for 1930, however, which give a breakdown by city, indicate that the Ohio figures for 1920 accurately reflect the origins of black migrants to Cleveland during the war. In 1930, Cleveland had far more black migrants from Georgia and Alabama than from any other state outside Ohio.[7]

The new migration accelerated the process of residential segregation which had already begun in Cleveland before World War I. Between 1910 and 1920, the number of census tracts containing no Negroes at all rose from seventeen to thirty-eight. At the same time the migrants began to crowd into neighborhoods where Negroes had previously been only a minority of the population. In 1910 no census tract in the city was greater than 25 percent Negro, but ten years later ten tracts exceeded that figure, and two tracts had become more than 50 percent black (see Table 13). The pattern of increasing concentration of the

---

elementary schools; in October, 1923, there were 7,430, an increase of 2,352 during that two-and-one-half-year period. If these statistics reflect the growth of the Negro population as a whole, then it seems likely that the black community grew by about 50 percent during this period. Most of this growth can be attributed to migration into the city. The correlation between school statistics and the entire population, however, is of limited accuracy because there was some natural increase and, more important, because many of the migrants were single and hence did not bring children; it is probable, then, that the 50 percent figure is an underestimation of the amount of migration between 1921 and 1924. For a more detailed discussion of the use of such statistics, see Elliott M. Rudwick, *Race Riot at East St. Louis, July 2, 1917* (Carbondale, Ill., 1964), 163–65. On the general resurgence of migration in the early 1920s, see "Southern Negroes Again Moving," *Opportunity*, 1 (January 1923), 19, and "Negro Labor Moves Northward," *ibid.*, 1 (May 1923), 5–6.

[7] U.S. Bureau of the Census, *Negroes in the United States, 1920–1932*, 32, 34–37. (The title of this volume is somewhat misleading, since it contains some data for 1910 as well as later years.)

TABLE 13. *Distribution of Negroes by census tracts, Cleveland, 1910–30*

Percentage Negro[a]	Number of census tracts[b]		
	1910	1920	1930
None	17	38	47
1–2	114	92	100
2–5	9	11	11
5–10	8	10	7
10–20	5	6	6
20–30	1	6	5
30–50	0	5	4
Over 50	0	2	17

SOURCE: Howard W. Green, *Population Characteristics by Census Tracts, Cleveland, 1930* (Cleveland, 1931), 160–65.

[a] The percentages for several of the tracts are estimates, because the Census Bureau statistics for two or more tracts were sometimes combined.

[b] The number of tracts increased from 158 in 1910, to 185 in 1920, and to 208 in 1930.

black population in certain areas continued during the early 1920s. This is clearly revealed by enrollment figures for Cleveland elementary schools. Between April, 1921, and October, 1923, there was a gain in black enrollment of 2,352 students. Almost all of this increase (2,287 students, or 97.5 percent) occurred in schools which were already 5 percent or more black—in areas, in other words, where the black population had already gained a foothold. At the same time the number of all-white elementary schools increased from 17 to 30 (out of a total of 112), and several schools experienced substantial declines in black enrollment as Negro families moved out of predominantly white neighborhoods.[8]

During the Great Migration, the area west of East 55th Street between Euclid Avenue and the Cuyahoga River absorbed most of the newcomers; Census Tracts H-7, H-9, I-2 through I-8, J-1, and J-2 recorded the largest gains in Negro population between 1910 and 1920. At the same time, a smaller but still significant number of Negroes had crossed the East 55th Street boundary and were beginning to fill in areas where a few scattered black families (usually members of the elite) had settled before the war. The Negro enclaves to the north of Hough Avenue (Tract L-6) and to the east of East 105th Street (Tract S-2) grew slowly during the wartime migration. Few Afro-Americans moved into other parts of the city, despite the huge influx of migrants, and the West Side remained almost solidly white. Most significant, by 1917 a few all-Negro neighborhoods had begun to emerge in the Central Avenue district.

[8] Green, *A Study of the Movement of the Negro Population of Cleveland*, 1–5, 14.

Though only a few blocks in size at the time, these black areas were portents of future developments. Kelly Miller, visiting the city at the height of the wartime migration, observed that it was possible for an individual, by standing on the right street corner, to "imagine himself in the heart of Hayti or Liberia. The segregated sections are as sharply meted out as if cut by a knife." In the midst of a city that had once been proud of its integrationist tradition, a black ghetto was taking shape.[9]

The inexorable trend toward segregation continued throughout the 1920s as blacks moved into the area between Euclid and Woodland avenues in larger numbers. Enclaves of Russian immigrants (most of whom were probably Jewish) and Italians in that part of the city which had resisted Negro encroachment as late as 1920 now suddenly gave way. Tracts I-8 and I-9, for example, were almost 60 percent Russian in composition in 1920; ten years later Russian immigrants constituted less than 5 percent of both tracts. The Italian immigrants, who had shared the oldest sections of the city with Negroes for two decades, proved more tenacious; and as a result some neighborhoods near Central Avenue remained integrated even after 1920. Nevertheless, a significant exodus of Italians was also evident. In 1920 four tracts in the Central-Woodland area were, respectively, 61, 54, 48, and 41 percent Italian. By 1930 the proportion of Italian immigrants in these tracts ranged from 13 to 34 percent.[10]

Prior to World War I, the tendency toward residential segregation that was exhibited by Cleveland's black population was shared by several of the city's immigrant groups. Italian and Romanian immigrants were actually more segregated from the dominant native-white population than were Negroes in 1910, and Hungarians and Russians also tended to settle within fairly well restricted sections of the city. Although specific data on the population distribution of Polish, Czech,

[9] Kelly Miller, "Negro Migration," *Pittsburgh Courier*, July 7, 1917 (clipping in Brown Papers). See Tables 12 and 25 and maps between pp. 146 and 147.

[10] Howard W. Green, comp., *Population Characteristics by Census Tracts, Cleveland, 1930* (Cleveland, 1931), 23–27 (maps showing location of Russian and Italian immigrants, 1910–30), 216–23. As late as 1928, in surveying conditions in a number of northern cities, Thomas J. Woofter could state that "Almost without exception the groups which are most heavily mixed [residentially] with Negroes in the North are Jewish and Italian." Woofter et al., *Negro Problems in Cities* (Garden City, N.Y., 1928), 39. By that time, however, the physical separation of blacks from these white ethnic groups was already well under way. In 1930, in most northern cities, the segregation of Italian and Russian immigrants from blacks was almost as great as that of other ethnic groups. See the segregation indexes computed for nine cities by Stanley Lieberson in his *Ethnic Patterns in American Cities* (Glencoe, Ill., 1963), 209–18.

and Slavic immigrants do not exist for the period before 1920, it is likely
that these groups also had a rather high degree of spatial isolation.[11]

Between 1910 and 1920 this demographic pattern underwent a subtle
but significant change. The segregation of foreign-born whites from
native whites, which had been increasing for several decades before
World War I, now receded to some extent. The index of dissimilarity
for native whites v. all foreign-born whites declined during this period
from 36 to 31 (see Table 14). To be sure, several immigrant groups con-

TABLE 14. *Index of dissimilarity, selected immigrant groups with native whites and
Negroes, 1920; and change in index, 1910–20*

	Index, 1920		Change in index, 1910–20	
	Native whites	Negroes	Native whites	Negroes
Italians	52	50	−24	−16
Germans	19	78	− 2	+ 4
English	18	68	+ 1	+11
Hungarians	46	76	+ 1	+ 4
Irish	23	72	− 5	+ 5
Russians	45	46	− 7	−16
Romanians	54	48	−11	− 6
Swedes	35	72	− 5	+ 7
Poles	48	78	NA	NA
Czechoslovakians	45	81	NA	NA
Yugoslavians	56	84	NA	NA
All foreign-born whites	31	68	− 5	+ 2

SOURCE: U.S. Bureau of the Census, *Fourteenth Census, 1920, Population* (Washington, 1922), I, 801–2.
NOTE: NA indicates data not available.

tinued to have moderately high rates of segregation; and they would
continue, for several decades to come, to live for the most part within
fairly distinct (though not completely homogeneous) ethnic neighborhoods. But the declining segregation rates of the three ethnic groups
which had been most isolated geographically before the war—the Italians, Romanians, and Russians—was a clear indication that even the
poorer, more recent immigrant communities were beginning to undergo
the process of residential dispersion that had already affected the Irish,
German, and English populations of the city.

At the same time that the immigrant population of the city was becoming generally more dispersed, however, the black community was
becoming ever more concentrated. Between 1910 and 1920, the index of

[11] See Chapter 2.

dissimilarity between Negroes and native whites increased from 61 to 70; the index for Negroes v. all foreign-born whites rose from 66 to 68. Although comparable data on residential segregation is lacking for 1930, it is clear that no diminuation of the trend toward the concentration of the black population of Cleveland occurred during the intervening ten years. When the black community expanded during the twenties, it did so not by diffusing throughout the city (as did the native whites, the Germans, the Irish, and the English) or by moving out to newer, smaller ethnic areas in better sections of the city (as did many Italians), but by filling in areas contiguous to the already existing black neighborhoods along Central and Scovill. On the eve of the Great Depression, at least 90 percent of the city's Afro-Americans lived within a region bounded by Euclid Avenue on the north, East 105th Street on the east, and Woodland Avenue to the south.[12]

Prior to World War I, suburban growth in Cuyahoga County had been rather slow. In fact, during the last three decades of the nineteenth century, Cleveland had continued to grow in size by annexing nearby towns and unincorporated areas. When voters in several suburbs rejected annexation proposals in the early 1900s, however, it signaled the rise of a new feeling of independence among suburbanites. During the 1920s, the suburbs encircling Cleveland, though still small in size compared to what they would become after 1945, expanded at a dynamic pace compared to the central city. While Cleveland's population during that decade increased only 11 percent, Cleveland Heights grew by 234 percent and Garfield Heights by 511 percent. Shaker Heights, one of the most rigorously planned suburbs in the nation, had a phenomenal growth rate of 1,000 percent. Few blacks were able to join this exodus from the metropolis. White hostility and an economic barrier (most of the early suburbanites were upper middle class or above) kept over 97 percent of Cuyahoga County's black population within Cleveland. In 1930, Charles W. Chesnutt reported that "only a few families not obviously Negroid" had been able to establish themselves in Shaker, Garfield, or

---

[12] Unfortunately, the size of the areal units available for measuring the index of dissimilarity changes drastically from 1920 (wards) to 1930 (census tracts); this change has some effect on the index and thus makes any direct comparison between 1920 and 1930 impossible. (See Karl Taeuber and Alma Taeuber, *Negroes in Cities: Residential Segregation and Neighborhood Change*, Chicago, 1965, 220–31, for a theoretical discussion.) It is clear, however, from the data and maps in Green, comp., *Population Characteristics by Census Tracts, Cleveland, 1930*, that there was some tendency toward dispersal among major white ethnic groups in the city during the 1920s. For a discussion of the dispersal and regrouping of the Italian population of Chicago after World War I, see Humbert Nelli, *The Italians in Chicago, 1880–1930: A Study in Ethnic Mobility* (New York, 1970), 204–11.

Cleveland Heights. At that time only fifteen Negro families altogether lived in those three communities. Ten Negro families resided in East Cleveland and six in nearby Euclid. Western suburbs proved even less hospitable to blacks; in 1930 Lakewood had but three black families and the rapidly growing community of Parma none at all.[13]

The increasing concentration of the black population exacerbated the housing problem faced by black Clevelanders. Even before the war, blacks had encountered difficulties in obtaining suitable lodging. During the Great Migration, however, the housing shortage in the black community reached crisis proportions. In the spring of 1917 the arrival of thousands of migrants was already having its effect. Harry C. Smith noted that the "local boarding and rooming houses are packed" with migrants, and complained that it was "distressing to meet daily numbers of these people almost begging to stop and house their families, even temporarily." In August, 1917, the secretary of the Cleveland Real Estate Board reported the need for an additional ten thousand housing units to take care of the newcomers, and the Gazette stated that many migrants were "living in old railroad cars, abandoned buildings, shacks, under tents. . . ." Landlords openly took advantage of this situation by charging black tenants higher rents than whites. "Our people," charged Smith in 1918, "are being asked EIGHT AND TEN DOLLARS A MONTH more rent for rooms and houses than white people, or our people, paid for the same a year ago. . . ." The local Urban League affiliate reported that one black family was paying almost one-third more for rent than white tenants occupying similar suites in the same building, and the Advocate declared angrily that, in the face of increased demand, owners were "raising their rents all the way from 25 to 75 percent. . . ." It was all too easy to take advantage of the uninitiated newcomers, and one Negro complained that "some landlords raise rents in houses occupied by white people to get rid of them, and then make a higher charge to colored tenants." A survey conducted by a committee of the Cleveland Chamber of Commerce in 1918 verified these claims. Negroes, the committee discovered, paid 65 percent more for comparable housing than did whites. The average monthly rent for white workers in the city was $13.12; the average for Negroes $22.50.[14]

[13] Charles W. Rawlings and Lyle E. Schaller, Suburbanization of the Negro Population (Cleveland, 1963), 1–2; Charles W. Chesnutt, "The Negro in Cleveland," The Clevelander, 5 (November 1930), 3; Charles N. Glaab and A. Theodore Brown, A History of Urban America (New York, 1967), 281; U.S. Fifteenth Census, 1930, Population (Families) (Washington, 1932), VI, 1046–49; interview with Russell Jelliffe, September 1, 1971.

[14] Cleveland Gazette, May 5, 12, August 18, 1917, May 11, August 17, 1918;

Some whites in areas close to the expanding ghetto were torn between their desire to resist the "Negro invasion" and the opportunity to make money by dividing their homes into kitchenette apartments and renting the "suites" to black migrants clamoring for a place to live. As one famous Negro resident of the city, Langston Hughes, sardonically put it, "the white neighborhoods resented Negroes moving closer and closer—but when the whites did give way, they gave way at very profitable rentals." The promise of monetary gain, however, did not always prove sufficient as a deterrent to white hostility. Few whites objected to blacks filling in the older areas of settlement on Central and Scovill avenues—a phenomenon that had been taking place at a slower rate even before the Great Migration. But when blacks began to move into all-white neighborhoods, white resistance, now accompanied sometimes by intimidation and violence, began to harden. Whites tried, of course, to exclude Negroes from neighborhoods through mutual understandings or restrictive covenants that denied (in theory) the owner of the house the right to sell to Afro-Americans. But if these methods failed, some whites were willing to adopt more drastic means to maintain the racial "purity" of their section of the city. In 1917 and 1919 gangs of whites attacked the homes of blacks on several occasions. In one case "windows were smashed with large stones, fence pickets torn off and the front porch smashed," in an effort by a white mob to convince a black family that they should leave the previously all-white neighborhood into which they had moved.[15]

White reaction was particularly hostile to those blacks who tried to establish themselves in the suburbs or in outlying sections of the city. When a black family attempted to occupy a home in Garfield Heights in 1924, they soon found their house surrounded by a mob of two hundred whites. A spokesman for the mob informed the occupants that they would have ten days to vacate; he returned a few days later and repeated the threat. When the purchaser, Arthur Hill, asked the mayor of Garfield Heights for protection, he received the response that the village could not afford to pay for police guards and that, furthermore, "colored people had no right to purchase such a nice home." The Cleveland

---

Cleveland *Plain Dealer*, August 4, 1917; Cleveland *Advocate*, August 18, 1917; Report of the Executive Secretary [of the Negro Welfare Association], May to August, [1918], April 9 to May 6 [1919], Cleveland Urban League Papers; Committee on Housing and Sanitation of the Cleveland Chamber of Commerce, *An Investigation of Housing Conditions of War Workers in Cleveland* (Cleveland, 1918), 12–15, 21.

[15] Langston Hughes, *The Big Sea* (New York, 1940), 27; Chesnutt, "The Negro in Cleveland," 3; Cleveland *Gazette*, September 8, 1917, July 5, 1919. The near-riots of 1917 and 1919 are discussed at greater length in Chapter 8.

branch of the NAACP intervened on Hill's behalf and attempted, for several months, to pressure the governor to investigate the case and provide protection for the Hill family. When this appeal also failed to bring about the desired result, the Hills decided to abandon their new home rather than face the continued threats of white mobs.[16]

When Dr. E. A. Bailey, a black physician, moved into a white neighborhood in the much more exclusive suburb of Shaker Heights, he encountered similar threats. Unlike Hill, Bailey refused to flee in the face of this intimidation. As a result, whites threw stones at his house, fired shots into it, and set his garage on fire. The mayor of Shaker Heights was somewhat more helpful than his counterpart in Garfield; he provided police protection almost immediately after the first incident of violence occurred. The Shaker Heights police, however, proved less than model law-enforcement officers. While guarding the Bailey home, they insisted on searching the black doctor and his family, as well as any visitors, whenever they entered or left the premises. Dr. Bailey was able to endure these harassments as well as the threats of some of his neighbors, but it took considerable personal sacrifice on his part to gain even the grudging toleration of the community in which he lived.[17]

Perhaps the most serious example of interracial conflict over housing occurred when Dr. Charles Garvin, one of the city's most prominent Negro residents, built a home in a neighborhood close to the border of Cleveland Heights. When whites learned in the fall of 1925 that the house was being constructed by a black man, they immediately circulated a handbill which warned blacks to stay out of their community or suffer the consequences of violent resistance:

Be Sure to Read This.

Certain niggers have recently blackmailed certain residents of the Cleveland Heights and other sections of the city. They are now trying to erect a house at 11114 Wade Park Avenue to blackmail us. But they will not. The residents of the Neighborhood will not give one cent to those blackmailers.

[16] "Resumé of Facts in Case of Intimidation of Mr. and Mrs. Arthur Hill" (typescript); James Weldon Johnson to Harry E. Davis, September 29, 1924; Davis to Johnson, October 1, 1924; Johnson to Davis, October 3, 1924; "Ohio Governor Fails to Assure Protection for Negro against Mob" (NAACP press release, October 24, 1924); Harry C. Smith to Herbert Selligmann [*sic*], November 1, 1924, Papers of the National Association for the Advancement of Colored People, branch files (Container G157), Manuscript Division, Library of Congress; *Crisis*, 29 (November 1924), 20.

[17] Clayborne George to Robert W. Bagnall, October 13, 1925; Bagnall to George, October 20, 1925, branch files, NAACP Papers; Cleveland *Gazette*, October 17, 1925; interview with Russell and Rowena Jelliffe, September 1, 1971.

Appoint your committees to oppose and eradicate this group of black gold diggers. Let them know we can duplicate [the] riots [that took place] in Tulsa, St. Louis, Chicago, and Baltimore.

Whites in the Wade Park development used every conceivable tactic in their attempt to keep Garvin out of the neighborhood. While the house was being built, they harrassed and threatened the workmen. Once construction was completed and the Garvins had occupied their new home, whites dynamited the house twice in an effort to force the black doctor to leave. The first bomb, luckily, only shattered a window, but the second did considerable damage to one section of the house.[18]

Some of Garvin's friends, concerned for his own safety, urged him to move. "People are advising that he put up a 'For Sale' sign and *sell out*," Garvin's sister, Mabel Clark, wrote to James Weldon Johnson shortly after the second bombing. But Garvin was determined to fight it out. As his sister told Johnson, "he has made a home for himself and will stay there[;] all he wants is to be let alone." During the summer of 1926, Garvin was anything but alone. Police officers were usually stationed outside his house; and when at one point they were temporarily withdrawn, a number of Garvin's friends (whites as well as Negroes) took on the burden of providing protection for the black doctor. This determined effort had, by the fall of 1926, broken the back of white resistance to Garvin's occupying his new home, and in March, 1927, Mrs. Clark could inform Johnson that "He and his family are living in their home, peacefully, and we are happy. . . ." But while the tactics of intimidation and violence again failed to achieve their purpose, the traumatic experience which the black doctor and his family went through must have given many Negroes second thoughts about moving into predominantly white sections of the city.[19]

[18] Harry E. Davis [to Walter White], February 5, 1926; White to Davis, February 6, 1926; Davis to White, February 8, 1926, Container G157, NAACP Papers; Cleveland *Plain Dealer*, July 7, 1926; President's Conference on Home Ownership and Home Building, *Negro Housing* (Washington, D.C., 1931), 46; Russell H. Davis, *Memorable Negroes in Cleveland's Past* (Cleveland, 1969), 57.

[19] Mabel Clark to James Weldon Johnson, July 12, 1926; Johnson to Clark, July 13, 1926; Walter White to Clayborne George, July 12, 1926; Harry E. Davis to James Weldon Johnson, July 15, 1926; George to White, July 20, 1926; Johnson to Davis, August 13, 1926; Mabel Clark to Johnson, March 24, 1927, branch files, NAACP Papers; interview with Russell Jelliffe, September 1, 1971 (Jelliffe was one of the individuals who helped guard Garvin's home). Though less publicized, Garvin's situation was in many ways similar to that of Dr. Ossian Sweet, a Detroit Negro who shot and killed a white man while defending his home against a mob in 1925. See David A. Levine, " 'Expecting the Barbarians': Race Relations and Social Control, Detroit, 1915–1925" (Ph.D. dissertation, University of Chicago, 1970), 247–98.

The mob action precipitated by the movement of individuals like Garvin into upper-middle-class areas of the city or suburbs was a clear indication that the integrated residency pattern of the black elite, so noticeable at the beginning of the century, was becoming impossible for all but a handful. Middle- and upper-class blacks were increasingly forced to live in predominantly black sections of the city, even if they had the money to purchase better homes in other neighborhoods. The group that was largely responsible for this was that segment of the native white population which had forsaken the central city for the suburbs. Once the bulwark of egalitarianism, this group now became increasingly hostile to blacks (and, indeed, all non-WASP groups) when it abandoned the urban milieu for the purified islands of suburban culture.[20]

However hostile they were to integration, it was not suburbanites who were chiefly responsible for the shaping of the black ghetto during the postwar years. The suburban housing market was simply too expensive for the vast majority of black Clevelanders. A much more important factor in containing and channeling the black population was the staunch resistance of certain urban ethnic groups. During the 1920s, the primary area of black expansion was to the east of the original area of settlement. Lying between East 55th and East 105th streets and bounded on the north by Euclid and on the south by Woodland Avenue, this area of the city had been occupied mostly by native Americans, British immigrants, and Russian Jews prior to 1920. Possibly because they had reached an economic stage where they were ready to move to better neighborhoods, these groups did not offer much resistance to the black influx, and by 1930 the area was about two-thirds black (although in some census tracts the proportion of Negroes was lower than this). Dispersion of the black population to the south and southeast of this area and the Central district, however, was checked by the immigrant

[20] It should not be thought, however, that all of the "old American" types in Cleveland became violently Negrophobic during the twenties. In fact, most of the enclaves of elite Negroes that continued to exist outside of the main ghetto at this time were located in sections of the city inhabited predominantly by native whites. It is clear that native whites became most hostile to blacks when they moved farthest away from the main black district. For an explanation of this seeming incongruity, see the informative discussion in Richard Sennett, *The Uses of Disorder* (New York, 1970), 3–84.

In some of the eastern suburbs during the post-World War I era there was a good deal of hostility to Jews as well as to blacks. Although anti-Semitism never resulted in violence, there was a concerted effort to keep Jews out of Shaker and Cleveland Heights. Throughout most of the twenties there was only one Jewish family in the entire city of Shaker Heights. Interview with Melvin Jay, September, 1974.

groups who resided there. To the south of the original black residential area, along Broadway, ethnic communities composed mostly of Poles and other Slavic-Americans halted the black population advance; to the southeast, Hungarians, Italians who had moved out from the Central district, and other ethnic groups put up resistance. When blacks tried to integrate the facilities at Woodland Hills Park, located slightly to the southeast of the principal black section of the city, it was members of these immigrant groups who fought against this change. Throughout the twenties the park remained a smouldering racial trouble spot.[21]

These resistant white groups were not the poorest of the ethnic population. A breakdown of the census tracts of Cleveland and four nearby suburbs by economic-tenths shows that, in 1930, these groups generally ranked from the 10th to the 30th percentile in yearly income—a few cuts above the most impoverished residents of the city. For the most part artisans, factory operatives, and small entrepreneurs, the inhabitants of these areas had acquired a modest level of middle-class respectability, as is evidenced by the moderate or high incidence of home ownership in the census tracts in question. It seems likely that these ethnic communities were composed of individuals highly prone to what social scientists have called "status anxieties." Having raised themselves above poverty, acquired a small home (with perhaps a large mortgage as well), and attained a modest level of income, they were fearful of association with any group bearing the stigma of low status. They naturally resisted the encroachment of a racial group that American society had designated as inferior. In so doing, they unthinkingly helped create a black ghetto.[22]

Prior to World War I, clearly defined black ghettos existed in only a few large northern cities—notably New York, Chicago, and Philadelphia.

[21] Cleveland Branch, NAACP, "Statement of Activities of the Branch for the Year ending Dec. 31 [1927]," Container G157, NAACP Papers; Green, comp., *Population Characteristics by Census Tracts, Cleveland, 1930,* 20–33 (maps); George A. Myers to Frank S. Harmon, August 23, 1923; Myers to Harmon, August 25, 1927; Myers to William R. Hopkins, August 9, 1927, George A. Myers Papers, Ohio Historical Society; interview with Dr. William P. Saunders, August 6, 1972. On ethnic hostility to black expansion in other cities, see Gilbert Osofsky, *Harlem: The Making of a Ghetto* (New York, 1966), 45–46, 81; St. Clair Drake and Horace R. Cayton, *Black Metropolis: A Study of Negro Life in a Northern City* (New York, 1945), 61–64, 180–82; Spear, *Black Chicago,* 201, 206, David M. Katzman, *Before the Ghetto: Black Detroit in the Nineteenth Century* (Urbana, Ill., 1973), 78, 101. Particularly valuable is the discussion in William M. Tuttle, Jr., *Race Riot: Chicago in the Red Summer of 1919* (New York, 1970), 156–83.

[22] Howard W. Green, *Nine Years of Relief, 1928–1937* (Cleveland, 1937), 45 (map showing economic divisions of Cleveland).

In Cleveland, Boston, and many other cities, there had been a definite trend of increasing segregation of the black population, but the process of ghetto development had not yet reached the point where all-black areas of significant size had emerged. In the wake of the Great Migration this diversity among black communities rapidly declined. The sudden influx of migrants accelerated trends that had been gathering force for several decades and caused the black ghetto in cities like Cleveland to consolidate sooner than would otherwise have been the case. By the eve of the Depression, the vast majority of urban centers outside the South had clearly defined black ghettos. Even Los Angeles, which in 1910 had had an extraordinarily low degree of residential segregation, now began to witness the beginnings of the Watts ghetto. The newer, more industrialized cities in the South also shared in this trend. Black sections in Birmingham, Tulsa, and Durham tended to develop on the outskirts of the city, rather than (as in the North) in the older central core. But they were no less segregated as a result.[23]

There were two exceptions to this trend. First, in a distinct minority of northern communities (mostly small or medium-sized cities), egalitarian traditions, slow population growth, the lack of urban transportation systems to facilitate geographic separation, or unstable housing patterns (due to a city's youthfulness) retarded the growth of ghettos. In Minneapolis in 1926, for example, not one but four general areas of

[23] Many of the conclusions presented here are based upon a study being made by the author of the growth of residential segregation in thirty cities for the period 1870–1930. For information on the consolidation and expansion of ghettos in specific cities after 1915, see J. S. Himes, "'Forty Years of Negro Life in Columbus, Ohio,'" *Journal of Negro History*, 27 (April 1942), 141–42; George Edmund Haynes, *Negro New-Comers in Detroit, Michigan: A Challenge to Christian Statesmanship* (New York, 1918), 8–10; A. L. Manley, "Where Negroes Live in Philadelphia," *Opportunity*, 1 (May 1923), 10–15; George W. Buckner, "'St. Louis Revives the Segregation Issue,'" *ibid.*, 1 (August 1923), 239; Woofter et al., *Negro Problems in Cities*, 37–111; Scott Nearing, *Black America* (New York, 1929), 107–26; E. Franklin Frazier, *The Negro Family in Chicago* (Chicago, 1932), 91–97; Drake and Cayton, *Black Metropolis*, 61–64, 77–83, 174–213; Emma Lou Thornbrough, "Segregation in Indiana during the Klan Era of the 1920's," *Mississippi Valley Historical Review*, 47 (March 1961), 595–97; Osofsky, *Harlem*, 127–49; Lawrence B. De Graaf, "The City of Black Angels: Emergence of the Los Angeles Ghetto, 1890–1930," *Pacific Historical Review*, 39 (August 1970), 345–50; Jerome Dowd, *The Negro in American Life* (New York, 1926), 96–97; Charles S. Johnson, *Patterns of Negro Segregation* (New York, 1943), ch. 1.

In the industrial cities of the South, it should be pointed out, the ghettos were less unified than in the North. In Birmingham in the 1920s, for example, most of the black population lived in residentially distinct neighborhoods, but these districts tended to be scattered over a much wider portion of the city than in the North. See Blaine A. Brownell, "Birmingham, Alabama: New South City in the 1920's,'" *Journal of Southern History*, 38 (February 1972), 28–29.

black settlement existed. Even those sections were not clearly defined, however, and blacks lived in many parts of the city. As late as 1940 Robert Warner could describe the residential pattern of New Haven blacks as "not distinct and clear cut. . . . There is no section, perhaps no street block, where white people do not also dwell; and every ward in the city has at least one Negro resident." The development of the ghetto in cities like Minneapolis and New Haven would be as much a product of the migration after World War II as that of earlier years.[24]

The growth of ghettos was also retarded in a number of older southern cities. For example, while there was some increase in residential segregation in Charleston, South Carolina, and Savannah, Georgia, during the period between the wars, both of these cities failed to develop well-defined ghettos. Slow population growth, coupled with an extreme separation of the races in all other aspects of life, allowed the traditional pattern of white and black residential intermingling in Charleston, Savannah, New Orleans, Little Rock, and some other cities in the South to remain in effect until as late as the 1950s.[25]

These exceptions aside, black ghettos had become a permanent feature of the urban landscape by the eve of the Great Depression. By today's standards, of course, these ghettos appear rather moderate in size; since 1945, continued black migration to the cities has led to an enormous increase in the size of black districts in urban areas. Yet for the most part, this second phase of ghetto expansion simply repeated on a larger scale what had already ocurred prior to 1930. During the period since 1930 there have been significant changes in many areas of black life, including black occupational structure and access to public accommodations. There had been little change, however, in the degree of residential segregation that urban blacks have experienced.[26] Even before the post–World War II migration began, the physical isolation of black people in most cities had reached a high level.

[24] Abram L. Harris, *The Negro Population in Minneapolis: A Study of Race Relations* (Minneapolis, Minn. [1927]), 13–14; Robert Austin Warner, *New Haven Negroes: A Social History* (New Haven, 1940), 195. See also Charles S. Johnson, "The Negro Population of Waterbury, Connecticut," *Opportunity*, 1 (October 1923), 299, and Frank F. Lee, *Negro and White in Connecticut Town* (New York, 1961), 28–30.

[25] Charles L. Knight, *Negro Housing in Certain Virginia Cities* (Richmond, Va., 1927), 36; Taeuber and Taeuber, *Negroes in Cities*, 189–92; Johnson, *Patterns of Negro Segregation*, ch. 1; E. Franklin Frazier, *The Negro in the United States*, rev. ed. (New York, 1957), 237.

[26] See the segregation indexes computed for 1940, 1950, and 1960 in Taeuber and Taeuber, *Negroes in Cities*, 39–41.

CHAPTER 8

Racism at High Tide

The increasing residential segregation of urban blacks after 1915 was accompanied by an intensification of white hostility and a crystallization of the pattern of discrimination that had begun to take shape before the war. Both were in large part the result of what one historian has called the "flowering of racism" that occurred during the 1920s. To be sure, a few scholars were beginning to build a scientific critique of the racist theories that had been formulated at the turn of the century. But the average white person continued to believe in Negro inferiority; and as black sociologist Charles S. Johnson lamented in 1923, "False notions, if believed, . . . may control conduct as effectively as true ones." During and immediately after World War I, whites vented their fears and frustrations in a series of vicious race riots; the two worst riots alone, in East St. Louis and Chicago, were responsible for eighty-five deaths and over a thousand injuries. Although this type of extreme violence fell off sharply after 1919, lesser forms of white hostility did not. The white quest for racial purity found its embodiment in a rejuvenated Ku Klux Klan, an organization which directed its propaganda at Catholics and Jews as well as blacks. Founded in 1915, the new Klan was as much a northern as a southern phenomenon, and at least one-third of all Klansmen could be found in urban areas. By 1924 at least one million whites had joined the organization, and in several localities the Ku Klux Klan became a force to be reckoned with.[1]

[1] John Higham, *Strangers in the Land: Patterns of American Nativism, 1860–1925* (New York, 1963 ed.), 264–99; Herbert Adulphus Miller, "The Myth of Superiority," *Opportunity*, 1 (August 1923), 228–29; Charles S. Johnson, "Public Opinion and the Negro," *ibid.*, 1 (July 1923), 202; Kenneth T. Jackson, *The Ku Klux Klan in the City, 1915–1930* (New York, 1967), 236 and *passim*; William M.

Cleveland, a city more liberal than most, managed to avoid the racist excesses that plagued other communities. During the tense summers of 1917 and 1919, interracial violence did break out on several occasions, but these encounters did not, luckily, escalate into racial warfare. Nor was the Ku Klux Klan an important factor in Cleveland's racial scene. During the 1920s, a small local chapter was organized, but Klan membership in the city never exceeded two thousand (Chicago may have had fifty thousand Klansmen at one time), and local authorities remained hostile to the secret organization. But there was still a noticeable increase in race prejudice in the city after 1915. Before the war the Negro population of Cleveland was small and easily overlooked. By 1920 it could no longer be ignored. As black migrants entered the mills and foundries of the city, whites sometimes felt that their jobs were threatened. At the same time, the expansion of the ghetto made white home owners fearful for the value of their property and the stability of their neighborhoods. The result was a sharp rise in racial tension and an increase in institutional discrimination.[2]

The initial response of many whites to the Great Migration was one of fear. White journalists, who previously had for the most part avoided any discussion of the city's black community, now took a more hostile view of the race. In the spring of 1917 one white newspaper printed a scare article which warned Clevelanders of the "danger of the spread of small pox, hookworm, and other diseases prevalent in the South, as a result of the Negro influx." Throughout the year, two Cleveland newspapers, the *News* and the *Leader*, continued to stir dangerous emotions by allowing the terms "nigger" and "darkey" to appear in print. In 1919, a year of anti-Negro violence throughout the nation, these two papers fanned the flames of racial discord by publishing blatantly prejudiced articles. Both papers made derogatory remarks about the all-Negro 372d Regiment when it returned to Cleveland after the signing of the peace treaty. During the "red summer" of 1919, the *News*, a leading daily, printed a sensationalistic article on lynchings on the front page and blamed the racial disturbances that were spreading across the country on "the active and systematic proselyting [*sic*] done among the colored workers of the South by Bolshevists." Such copy was hardly designed to promote racial harmony.[3]

Tuttle, Jr., *Race Riot: Chicago in the Red Summer of 1919* (New York, 1970), 64; Elliott M. Rudwick, *Race Riot at East St. Louis, July 2, 1917* (Carbondale, Ill., 1964), 50, 52.

[2] On Klan membership in cities, see Jackson, *Ku Klux Klan in the City*, 236.

[3] Cleveland *Advocate*, December 30, 1916 (quoting the *News*); Cleveland *Lead-*

Mass circulation newspapers were not the only media that reflected (and influenced) the deepening antagonism toward blacks that surfaced during the war. The popularity of the racist films *The Nigger* and *The Birth of a Nation*, both of which came to the city in 1917, were signs of a growing anti-Negro sentiment among the white population. *The Nigger*, as described by the *Advocate*, contained "huge mob scenes and race riots" and was filled "with the crack of the white man's whip and the scream of the blacks. . . ." A cheap but gaudy production, it was the less popular of the two motion pictures. *The Birth of a Nation* was more invidious because of its high technical—if not moral—qualities. Produced by D. W. Griffith, *The Birth of a Nation* was quickly recognized as an outstanding example of the art of film-making. The subject matter of the film, however, was volatile; based on a caustically racist novel by Thomas Dixon, it portrayed Negroes as ignorant brutes and glorified the original Ku Klux Klan as the righteous upholders of white civilization in the South. *The Birth of a Nation* was eventually banned from Cleveland, but not before it had become a box-office hit in several theaters.[4]

White politicians, sensitive to the changing temperament of the electorate, equivocated on the issue of civil rights or dangerously played upon the racist emotions of voters for their own political advantage. In 1917 William Finley, the state chairman of the Democratic party in Ohio, attempted to gain support for the Democratic ticket by associating Republicans with the migration of southern Negroes that was then under way. Negroes were traditionally Republican, and Finley claimed that the Ohio GOP was assisting in the "colonization" of thousands of poor black migrants for the purpose of increasing the Republican vote. A similar claim, made against the Republicans of East St. Louis in 1916, was one of the underlying causes of the bloody race riot that occurred there the following year. Such racist propaganda was not limited to the party of Woodrow Wilson. In Cleveland the Republican successor to Mayor Newton D. Baker, Harry L. Davis, implied in a speech in 1917 that the Central Avenue area had developed into a vice district because Negroes were naturally degenerate. Davis steadfastly refused to appoint

---

er, April 17, 1917, March 2, 1919; Cleveland *Gazette*, January 20, June 2, 1917; March 8, 1919 (quoting the *News*).

4 Cleveland *Advocate*, April 14, 1917; Cleveland *Leader*, April 18, 1917; Cleveland *Plain Dealer*, April 8, 1917; Cleveland *Gazette*, April 14, 21, May 12, 1917. See also Thomas R. Cripps, "The Reaction of the Negro to the Motion Picture *Birth of a Nation*," *The Historian*, 25 (May 1963), 344–62, and Everett Carter, "Cultural History Written with Lightning: The Significance of *The Birth of a Nation*," *American Quarterly*, 12 (Fall 1960), 347–57.

Negro clerks to City Hall during his administration or to choose a Negro as an assistant police prosecutor or member of the mayor's Advisory War Board—despite the fact that one of the board's functions was to deal with the immediate problems resulting from the influx of black migrants during the war. In 1920, race once again became an election issue when several candidates for local office distributed racist literature claiming that blacks would not be satisfied until they could "dominate" Cleveland.[5]

Fears of black "domination" were more than simply false; they actually amounted to an inverted view of race relations in the city. Politically, blacks had gained little as a result of their consistent support of the Republican party. From 1915 to 1930 a string of Republican administrations in Cleveland refused, with few exceptions, to appoint Afro-Americans to anything but minor positions. In the area of municipal services, black neighborhoods were consistently shortchanged. In the Central and lower Woodland Avenue districts, recreational facilities were scarce, garbage and rubbish removal were often irregular, and the streetcars were notorious for their poor service and shoddy conditions— despite the fact that the Central line was one of the most profitable in the city. During the twenties, Cleveland adopted the city manager form of government (it was the largest metropolis to do so), yet the vaunted "efficiency" of this system of administration did not seem to work to the benefit of the black community.[6]

As far as police protection was concerned, black people could without contradiction say that they received both too little and too much. Throughout the postwar period no effort was made by City Hall to clean up the gambling and prostitution rackets on Central Avenue. The

[5] Cleveland *Gazette*, May 5, 19, 26, November 10, 1917, October 23, November 13, 20, 1920; Rudwick, *Race Riot at East St. Louis*, ch. 2. Not all white politicians lapsed into racist demagoguery, of course, and there were a few who remained consistent supporters of equal rights. Two racial liberals on the City Council in the 1920s were Peter Witt and F. W. Walz; both supported the integration of City Hospital when that issue arose at the end of the decade. Congressman Henry I. Emerson, of the East Side 22d Congressional District, was also a strong advocate of equality. Emerson was a firm supporter of the National Association for the Advancement of Colored People. "He has stood 'right' and voted 'right,'" the Cleveland NAACP Branch *Bulletin* stated in 1920, "on every race issue which was presented to congress during his first three terms." Among other actions, Emerson endorsed the federal anti-lynching bill and entered a resolution condemning the Washington race riot of 1919. Francis Young to Mary White Ovington, February 26, 1919, Container B-1, Papers of the National Association for the Advancement of Colored People, Manuscript Division, Library of Congress; Cleveland Branch *Bulletin*, 1 (August 1920), 1.

[6] Cleveland *Gazette*, January 13, February 24, March 17, 1917, October 12, 1918, October 15, 1927, March 31, 1928.

number of police assigned to black sections of the city was inadequate, and when the police received reports of crimes they were often slow to arrive on the scene. "It is only on rare occasions," complained Harry C. Smith, that "policemen are seen in 'the roaring third' [as whites called the Central area] and then as a rule, after some crime has already been committed." On the other hand, when police did enter the ghetto to make an arrest or to patrol the area, they often seemed unnecessarily brutal. In 1917 Smith noted that "flagrant and barbarous beating-up of Negroes" was an all too common occurrence with white officers. ". . . since the influx from the South," Smith reported a few years later, "there has been a growing tendency upon the part of the police, both public and private, to kill members of the race sought for committing crimes and misdemeanors." Police were "too quick to shoot" if the suspect was a Negro and were not overly concerned about harming bystanders if they had the misfortune of being black. Undoubtedly, part of the problem was the small number of black patrolmen; in 1919 only seven of the city's thirteen hundred police officers were Negroes, and eleven years later there were still only twelve blacks on the force.[7]

In 1919 a small incident symbolized the state of race relations in Cleveland in the wake of the Great Migration. With the city's tradition of fairness to blacks in mind, the NAACP in that year chose Cleveland as the site of its annual convention. "We were not in the cotton fields of Louisiana," Mary White Ovington wrote in retrospect, "but in the City of Cleveland of the State of Ohio, that had bred abolitionists, and started Oberlin." At the same time that Miss Ovington was exulting over the heritage of northern freedom, however, James Weldon Johnson, field secretary for the NAACP, was being refused service in a Cleveland restaurant because he was black. The irony of the situation was symptomatic of the continuing deterioration of the city's liberal racial climate during the postwar era: the abolitionist heritage of Cleveland's past was rapidly being supplanted by the reality of its discriminatory present.[8]

Nowhere was this increasing discrimination more evident than in the unequal treatment Negroes received in the city's restaurants, theaters,

[7] *Ibid.*, November 24, 1917, March 2, 1918, October 11, 1919, June 12, 1920; U.S. *Fifteenth Census, 1930, Population (Occupations)* (Washington, 1932), IV, 1286. For several years during the 1920s, black prisoners were segregated in the county jail. This policy ended in 1927, however, when racially liberal Edward J. Hanratty was elected sheriff. *Ibid.*, October 30, 1926, April 30, 1927. There was a sharp decline in the relative concentration of blacks in the police force between 1910 and 1930; see Table 26 in Appendix II.

[8] Mary White Ovington, *The Walls Came Tumbling Down* (New York, 1948), 171–72; Cleveland *Gazette*, April 27, 1919. Oberlin was not founded by Ohioans, as Ovington suggested, but by settlers from New England.

and other places of public accommodation. As the black population expanded out of its original area of settlement, white restaurant owners, like some white property owners, often tried to "hold the line" against the advancing black tide. They used a variety of tactics. Some simply refused Negroes altogether, and a few of these had the effrontery to place "white only" signs in their windows. Others discouraged black patrons by giving them poor service. Still others served Negroes but charged them higher prices; one Greek restaurant owner blandly informed a Negro customer that he would be glad to serve him but would have to charge him four times the regular price of a meal. Previously liberal downtown restaurants and hotels also began to exclude Afro-Americans more frequently, although they faced no threat of "invasion." Even prominent black visitors were not always able to find adequate hotel accommodations. When Robert R. Moton, Booker T. Washington's successor as head of the Tuskegee Institute, came to Cleveland in 1923 to address the Chamber of Commerce, officials at the Statler Hotel told him that they would be able to accommodate him only if he agreed to take his meals in his room. In a number of exclusive establishments, however, skin color remained an important factor in determining who would be admitted. Light-skinned Negroes could still eat at many of the city's better restaurants during the twenties, but Charles W. Chesnutt (who himself had a very fair complexion) noted in 1930 that he did not "know more than one place downtown where [he] could take for luncheon a dark-colored man." Not all of the increase in restaurant discrimination, it should be noted, was the result of a conscious policy of management. In many cases waiters and waitresses acted on their own initiative in refusing to serve Afro-Americans. The white Waiters' Union was one of Cleveland's most intensely racist labor organizations.[9]

Discriminatory practices were not limited to hotels and restaurants. Theaters often refused to admit Negroes, segregated them within the theater, seated them in the balcony, or charged them higher prices. Blacks could, of course, ride the city streetcars. But a local taxi company attempted to restrict its service to whites only, and by the end of the

[9] Cleveland *Gazette*, May 12, June 23, 1917, March 16, May 4, 1918, March 3, 1923, February 18 March 24 May 5, 26, 1928, August 31, 1929; Langston Hughes, *The Big Sea* (New York, 1940), 51; Cleveland *Herald*, September 11, 1926 (clipping in Scrapbook 1, Chester K. Gillespie Papers, Western Reserve Historical Society); [Charles White,] "Cleveland Branch of the N.A.A.C.P., Communication to Executive Committee, February 14, 1927," 1; "Brings Action against Two Restaurants for Segregation" (in 1929 folder); Harry E. Davis to Walter White, September 29, 1929, all in branch files (Containers G157 and G158), NAACP Papers; Charles W. Chesnutt, "The Negro in Cleveland," *The Clevelander*, 5 (November 1930), 24. For additional examples, see the discussion of NAACP activities in Chapter 11.

twenties the Greyhound Bus Company was making blacks sit in the back of buses traveling to the South.[10]

Racial lines also hardened in recreational facilities. Cleveland's two main amusement parks, Luna Park and Euclid Beach Park, continued their established policy of restricting the use of their facilities by blacks to a small number of days each summer. Social agencies involved in recreation frequently introduced a policy of segregation where none had existed before the war. "Some of the settlement houses," Jane Edna Hunter remarked, "alternate their camp periods, sending the Negro children out to the camp for one period and the white children for another." The YMCA restricted Negro participation in its activities to one branch on Cedar Avenue in the 1920s, and the YWCA continued its policy of excluding blacks altogether. Blacks also encountered a considerable amount of discrimination in public facilities. At the city beach nearest to the ghetto, Gordon Park, blacks were segregated, while they were excluded altogether from some other beaches. At the instigation of Thomas Fleming, the Negro councilman, the city did construct a bathhouse on Central in 1919 at a cost of $45,000. It was apparent, however, that the black community was being shortchanged when the city announced construction of a similar facility in the ethnic St. Clair Avenue area with a price tag of $125,000. Surveying the Central Avenue bathhouse shortly after it opened, the editor of the *Gazette* pronounced it "cheaply constructed." "*Anything*," he concluded, "seems good enough for *colored* people, as far as Fleming and the Davis Administration goes. . . ."[11]

As before the war, black Clevelanders achieved only partial success in forcing white establishments to end discriminatory practices. Negroes actually brought more civil rights suits in the 1920s than ever before, and they did force a number of white restaurants and downtown theaters to open their doors to black people. Those of the race who sought redress in the courts, however, were hindered in a number of ways. They continued to be stymied by narrow interpretations of the Ohio Civil Rights Law. In 1918, for example, a black man brought suit against an

[10] Cleveland *Call*, February 12, 1927 (clipping in Scrapbook 1, Gillespie Papers); Cleveland *Gazette*, May 5, 12, 1917, July 25, 1929; Julian Krawcheck, "Society Barred Negroes—They Formed Own Groups," Cleveland *Press*, May 30, 1963. A Negro who was refused service by the taxi company, however, brought suit against the firm in 1917 and won the case.

[11] Cleveland *Gazette*, March 10, 1917, August 17, 31, 1918, March 1, September 13, 1919, September 12, 1925, May 31, 1927, March 10, 1928, January 19, 1929, July 9, 1930; Chesnutt, "The Negro in Cleveland," 4; Jane Edna Hunter, "Negroes in Cleveland" (undated manuscript, Jane Edna Hunter Papers, Western Reserve Historical Society), 2.

Euclid Avenue restaurant owner who refused him service. The jury, however, ruled in favor of the proprietor, apparently on the ground that the black man "was not a bona fide patron but was merely there for the purpose of stirring up trouble." Such circuitous reasoning made "test cases" against discriminatory establishments difficult and in some instances rendered the Civil Rights Law null. Blacks encountered less hostility and prejudice from white judges and lawyers than from juries. "Juries are prejudiced," one black lawyer reported, "and if a personal injury case is worth $5,000 the jury would give a colored man, in my opinion, $2,000 or possible $2,500." One of the hindrances to equal justice in Cleveland was the fact that fewer Negroes served on juries than their percentage of the population would seem to warrant. Negroes complained that—whether by design or accident—too few of their race were called to jury duty and that many who were called were "excused." "Only ceaseless insistence on the enforcement of law," the black *Call and Post* editorialized in 1928, "will prevent the Ohio Civil Rights Statute from becoming a dead letter. . . ." Such continual vigilance, however, was bothersome, difficult, and often expensive; few blacks had sufficient time, funds, and tenacity to indulge in such tactics. As Charles Chesnutt laconically put it, "One does not care to have to bring a lawsuit or swear out a warrant every time one wants a sandwich or a cup of coffee."[12]

Cleveland's hospitals and schools also mirrored the rising tide of discrimination after 1915. Before the war, little noticeable discrimination was seen in hospital policies. During the Great Migration several hospitals adopted the procedure of segregating Negro and white patients in separate wards; during the next decade many other hospitals in the area followed suit. In addition, some medical institutions reserved only a designated number of beds for black patients. The number of spaces reserved was sometimes woefully inadequate. "These hospitals," a group of Negroes complained in 1927, "ask doctors on requesting admission of patients whether the patient is white or colored, and frequently the answer is: 'there are no colored beds vacant.'" At the peak of the wartime migration, one institution, Charity Hospital, belied its name by refusing to accept black patients who could not pay for their treatment

[12] Cleveland *Gazette*, April 21, May 12, 1917, July 27, 1918, July 26, 1919, February 18, May 26, 1928, March 9, 1929; Cleveland *Call and Post* [February, 1928], (clipping in Scrapbook 1, Gillespie Papers); Chesnutt, "The Negro in Cleveland," 4, 26. "Recently [civil rights cases] have met with poor results," the Cleveland *Herald* complained in 1926, "juries in most instances voting verdicts of 'Not Guilty' against white proprietors of restaurants." Cleveland *Herald*, September 11, 1926 (clipping in Scrapbook 1, Gillespie Papers).

in advance. Although there is no evidence that this policy became standard procedure in later years, while in force it was most disconcerting to black Clevelanders.[13]

The color bar against Negro doctors and nurses remained as firm in Cleveland hospitals as it had been before the war. Most Cleveland hospitals refused to allow Negro physicians on their staffs or to provide training programs for black interns. This eventually led to an unsuccessful attempt, by a group of black doctors, politicians, and businessmen, to establish an all-Negro hospital. But at the end of the twenties, there was still no hospital in the city which would accept Negro interns or nurse trainees. Only two hospitals had black doctors attached to their staffs.[14]

The changes that occurred in the policies of Cleveland's educational institutions as a result of the migration were more subtle. The city's public schools had been integrated for many decades and to a large extent they remained this way during and after the war. With the exception of the city's trade schools, which discouraged black attendance because of the exclusionary policies of many union apprenticeship programs, the schools and colleges of Cleveland remained open to both races on a nondiscriminatory basis.[15] During the peak month of the wartime migration, however, several school principals sought to establish segregated classes *within* their schools, and one head of an all-white school refused to accept a black teacher who had been assigned to his district. Yet there is no indication that either of these policies became accepted practice or amounted to anything more than a temporary aber-

[13] Cleveland *Gazette*, November 10, 1917, December 21, 1918, November 26, 1926, January 12, 1929; George A. Myers to Msg. Joseph F. Smith, September 21, 1927; Joseph Smith to Myers, February 4, 1929; Harry C. Smith to Myers, August 17, 1929, George A. Myers Papers, Ohio Historical Society; Mercy Hospital Association of Cleveland, *Does Cleveland Need a Negro-Manned Hospital?* (n.p. [1927], pamphlet).

[14] Cleveland *Gazette*, October 22, 1927; Chesnutt, "The Negro in Cleveland," 4; Henry C. Smith to George A. Myers, August 17, 1929; Smith to Myers, September 4, 1929 (two letters); Smith to Myers, September 11, 1929, Myers Papers; Mercy Hospital Association of Cleveland, *Does Cleveland Need a Negro-Manned Hospital?* On the controversy over the proposal to establish a black hospital, see Chapter 11.

[15] Chesnutt, "The Negro in Cleveland," 3–4. Another partial exception was the city's business colleges, which, according to George Myers, only allowed Negroes to attend evening classes. George A. Myers, "Answer to Questionnaire from Chamber of Commerce Committee on Immigration and Emigration" (in 1926 correspondence, Myers Papers). In addition, Carter G. Woodson reported in 1934 that Western Reserve University was one of a number of northern institutions that "restrict the number of Negro nurses that might be admitted because of the racial difficulties encountered in providing for their field experience." Carter G. Woodson, *The Negro Professional Man and the Community* (n.p., 1934), 144.

ration. During the twenties black teachers not only increased steadily in numbers but remained fairly well integrated in the system. In 1929 eighty-four black instructors taught in forty-one different schools, most of them in predominantly white neighborhoods.[16]

Nevertheless, a subtle process of discrimination did begin to affect the public schools. Two of the city's technical high schools—Jane Addams Vocational School and the Cleveland Trade School—had no black students at all. The third, East Technical High School, although located in the heart of the ghetto, was only 4 percent black in 1929. As the ghetto consolidated and expanded during the twenties, some schools became predominantly Negro. On the eve of the Great Depression, 89 percent of Cleveland's black junior high school students were enrolled in only four (out of a total of twenty-three) schools; and fully 61 percent of all black senior high school students attended a single institution, Central High. In 1931 whites made up only about 3 percent of the student body at Central. The gradual development of segregation in the schools after World War I was, initially, a by-product of the shifting demographic patterns of the city; as blacks moved into neighborhoods in larger numbers, nearby schools naturally gained in black enrollment. By the early 1930s (it is difficult to determine exactly when the policy began), however, the Board of Education was beginning to reinforce and accelerate this trend through artificial means. In 1933 blacks complained that most black children on the East Side were being forced to attend Central High, even though many lived much nearer to other schools. A few years later, it was charged that white students who lived in the Central High district were permitted to transfer to other schools. This policy of selective transfers, which would continue

---

[16] Cleveland *Gazette*, April 21, May 5, September 22, 1917; Alonzo Gatskell Grace, "The Effect of Negro Migration on the Cleveland Public School System" (Ph.D. dissertation, Western Reserve University, 1932), 64–66. It should be noted, however, that Grace found that almost all of these black teachers (seventy-eight of eighty-four) were elementary school instructors. Despite this, the large number of black teachers and their relative integration within the school system made Cleveland truly exceptional compared to other northern cities at the end of the 1920s. In Pittsburgh and Omaha, for example, black students were integrated to about the same extent as in Cleveland, but school boards in both cities refused to hire *any* black teachers. Most northern cities hired black teachers, but they usually placed black instructors in charge of classes composed entirely or predominantly of Negro students. See Ira De A. Reid, *Social Conditions of the Negro in the Hill District of Pittsburgh* ([Pittsburgh,] 1930), 16; T. Earl Sullenger and J. Harvey Kerns, *The Negro in Omaha: A Social Study of Negro Development* (Omaha, Neb., 1931), 19; Hannibal G. Duncan, *The Changing Race Relationship in the Border and Northern States* (Philadelphia, 1922), 37–39; Emma Lou Thornbrough, "Segregation in Indiana during the Klan Era of the 1920's," *Mississippi Valley Historical Review*, 47 (March 1961), 600.

for several decades, often placed a considerable hardship on students, since it sometimes forced them to attend a school that was several streetcar lines away from their home. Ironically, in the 1960s and 1970s, whites would vigorously oppose the busing of children for the purpose of creating racial balance in the schools, whereas over thirty years earlier, the Board of Education had already established a program of busing (or its equivalent), not for the purpose of ending segregation but as a means of furthering it.[17]

As schools became predominantly Negro, their curricula often changed from an emphasis on liberal arts to a stressing of skills of a more mundane nature. The changes that occurred at Kennard Junior High School during the twenties are a good example of this process. In 1924 the school's student body was 31 percent Negro in composition; in 1930, as a result of the white exodus from neighborhoods near the school, Negroes constituted 60 percent of the students. As the racial balance of the school shifted, administrators gradually altered the curriculum. They dropped foreign languages altogether; intensified course offerings in certain types of industrial work; cut back on the number of available electives, and placed more emphasis on "sewing, cooking, manual training, foundry work, and sheet metal [work]." In Central High School the same transformation was occurring. In 1933 the Cleveland branch of the NAACP discovered that over half the tenth-grade students at Central were receiving no training in mathematics at all. Most of the home economics courses at the school emphasized laundry work, and such electives as Spanish, German, bookkeeping, and stenography (standard fare in other high schools) had been dropped from the curriculum. These changes in course offerings undoubtedly lowered the expectations of black students and oriented them, at an early age, toward lower-paying, less prestigious occupations. Once a powerful force for equality and integration, the public schools had by 1935 become yet another factor leading to two separate but unequal worlds of race.[18]

With the growth of prejudice evident in so many aspects of life in

[17] Grace, "The Effect of Negro Migration on the Cleveland Public School System," 20–23; Willard C. Richan, Racial Isolation in the Cleveland Public Schools (Cleveland, 1967), 33; interview with Russell and Rowena Jelliffe, September 1, 1971. It was also during the 1930s that the policy of placing black teachers in predominantly white schools came to an end. By 1944 most black teachers in Cleveland taught in the ghetto. Christopher G. Wye, "Midwest Ghetto: Patterns of Negro Life and Thought in Cleveland, Ohio, 1929–1945" (Ph.D. dissertation, Kent State University, 1973), 56–57.

[18] Grace, "The Effect of Negro Migration on the Cleveland Public School System," 84–86; Richan, Racial Isolation in the Cleveland Public Schools, 33–36.

Cleveland after 1915, it was almost inevitable that violent encounters between blacks and whites would occur. Before the war, the city had been relatively free of interracial violence; but now whites were more willing to use intimidation, mob action, and even terrorism in the face of an assumed threat to their homes and jobs.

It was during the tense summers of 1917 and 1919 that anti-Negro violence in Cleveland reached a peak. Several times lynchings or a race riot seemed imminent but miraculously failed to materialize. In June, 1917, two incidents occurred within the span of a single week. The first took place in the predominantly white neighborhood near East 71st Street, far from the main area of black settlement. The trouble began when a white woman began to complain loudly that a Negro had insulted her. A crowd of whites soon gathered and started to harass and then to chase the black man, who sought refuge in a nearby house. By the time a patrol wagon arrived on the scene, a menacing crowd of two hundred whites had gathered and were preparing to storm the house, capture its black occupant, and lynch him. Only the somewhat belated appearance of the police prevented bloodshed. Less than a week later, a near riot occurred in the lower Central Avenue district. No one seemed to know how the trouble began, but by the time the police were summoned "scores of Negroes and foreigners were fighting with fists, clubs, and stones." After these two outbursts of racial hostility, Harry C. Smith feared that a major clash between blacks and whites was imminent. Not one to mince words, he urged his readers to "purchase a regular army riot gun and plenty of ammunition" for self-defense.[19]

In the summer of 1919, anti-Negro violence again flared up in Cleveland. This time the attackers directed their fury at children rather than adults. On three separate occasions mobs of white men and boys stoned groups of black youngsters. The first incident occurred when a group of black children were riding a streetcar through a white neighborhood; the second and third while parties of black youths were swimming in one of the local park lakes, a recreation spot some distance from the ghetto and usually not frequented by Negroes. Luckily, in none of the incidents were there any serious injuries. For many weeks afterward, however, the racial atmosphere of the city was taut with fear. Commenting on the two occurrences at the park lakes, the editor of the *Gazette* cautioned his readers that "this is just what started the Chicago riot" and again urged black Clevelanders to prepare to defend themselves. Fortunately, Smith's premonition proved to be without founda-

[19] Cleveland *Gazette*, June 9, 16, 1917.

tion, and the "red summer" of 1919 ended without a major racial confrontation in Cleveland.[20]

Given the intensification of racial prejudice and the propensity of some whites to resort to violence against Negroes, why did no race riot take place in Cleveland during the migration years? A comparison with Chicago—which did experience a violent race riot in 1919—shows that a number of factors must be taken into account. First, Cleveland's industries were far more diversified than Chicago's. In Chicago the stockyards served as a focal point of racial hostility between black and white workers; in the Lake Erie metropolis no such focal point existed. In addition, Cleveland was fortunate in that its black steel workers were almost completely unionized during the crucial year 1919. By refusing to act as strikebreakers, blacks in Cleveland temporarily undercut a major source of racial strife. The residential pattern of black settlement in the city also was important in preventing a riot. In Chicago, black workers found it necessary to pass through hostile ethnic neighborhoods on their way to work; this made them easy prey for white mobs. In Cleveland, however, as the black ghetto consolidated after 1915 it abutted the main industrial district, and most blacks could go to and from work without straying very far from the predominantly black (or at least integrated) sections of the city. Despite the hostility of white ethnic groups, blacks in Cleveland had considerably more opportunity for expansion than the hemmed-in South Side black belt of Chicago. The streets directly to the east of the original area of Negro settlement were occupied primarily by Russian Jews, British immigrants, and native white Americans. Though far from unprejudiced, most of these whites were not anti-Negro in the violent, defensive manner of suburbanites and those ethnic groups living to the south and southeast of the ghetto; and when black expansion became a necessity after 1915, they were willing to allow the peaceful movement of Negroes into their neighborhoods. The existence of this "escape valve" reduced the possibility of contested neighborhoods and lessened tensions in the city during a critical period of race relations.[21]

Finally, in assessing the differences between the two cities one cannot underestimate the effects of the slower development of the ghetto in Cleveland. In Chicago, the black belt had taken shape by 1910 (perhaps earlier), and on the eve of the wartime migration a gulf had opened

[20] Ibid., July 5, August 2, 16, 1919.
[21] On Chicago, see Chicago Commission on Race Relations, The Negro in Chicago: A Study of Race Relations and a Race Riot (Chicago, 1922), passim; Allan H. Spear, Black Chicago: The Making of a Negro Ghetto, 1890–1920 (Chicago, 1967), 159–64, 208–22; Tuttle, Race Riot, passim.

between the two races that has not yet, to this day, been bridged. Sociologists have noted that personal experience with Negroes is an important factor in shaping white racial attitudes, and that those who have the least contact with members of the opposite race often harbor the most intense prejudice. Conditions in Chicago before the riot nurtured such intolerance. There, says historian William Tuttle, Jr., "because of extreme residential segregation, there was a paucity of social interchange between the races. Consequently, there was a decided lack of interracial understanding. . . ." In spite of increasing evidences of racism in Cleveland during the prewar years, the city's black community was not nearly as isolated as was Chicago's in 1915; the existence of integrated schools and neighborhoods kept open crucial lines of communication between the races and helped check the racial paranoia that resulted in a bloodbath in Chicago.[22]

By the end of the 1920s, however, most of these lines of communication had been effectively closed. With the new racism in public facilities and the increasing ghettoization of the black population more evident with each passing year, Cleveland was coming to resemble other metropolises in its prejudicial treatment of black citizens. This fact was a painful one for older black residents of the city to accept. "Time was," said George Myers despairingly in 1928, "that Cleveland was the freest from race prejudice and the fairest city in the United States not excepting Freedom's birthplace Boston. Today we have only two unrestricted privileges left, the Ballot and the Public Schools." The same year, the Negro *Call and Post* editorialized: "Daily it becomes more apparent that the virus of southern race prejudice is bearing its malignant fruit in this cosmopolitan city of Cleveland. With amazing rapidity it is spreading through the very arteries of this city—once famous for its liberality to minority groups."[23]

The comparison of Cleveland with the South was apt, and it pinpointed an important national trend. Among whites, something of a consensus in favor of racial separation emerged in the postwar era. "There seems to be a concerted effort," Robert W. Bagnall, the NAACP's director of branches, wrote in 1925, "to force segregation on Negroes

---

[22] Tuttle, Jr., *Race Riot*, 103. On the importance of personal experience with members of the opposite race in shaping personal attitudes and attenuating racial antagonisms, see Morris L. Haimowitz, "The Development and Change of Ethnic Hostility" (Ph.D. dissertation, University of Chicago, 1951), 110–24.

[23] George A. Myers to William R. Hopkins, February 6, 1928, Myers Papers; Cleveland *Call and Post* [February, 1928] (clipping in Scrapbook 1, Gillespie Papers).

all over [the United States]. . . ." The "Southern Way," remarks C. Vann Woodward in his discussion of racial discrimination in the twenties, "was spreading as the American Way in race relations." Nevertheless, while the distance between North and South on the race question had narrowed, essential differences still remained. Blacks, as George Myers pointed out, retained the right to vote in the northern states, and in Cleveland they would soon use their increased numbers as a political tool to gain concessions from city government. Furthermore, the separation of the races never became as complete in Cleveland as it did in many of the southern states. No system of "racial etiquette" took root in the North in the twenties—there were no Jim Crow streetcars, Jim Crow drinking fountains, or Jim Crow bibles for witnesses in court, and northern blacks were not required by custom to constantly show deference to whites in day-to-day contacts between the races.[24]

Why did Cleveland not become like Atlanta, Charleston, and Mobile, where the principle of segregation was applied rigidly, dogmatically, to almost every facet of life? The question is not one that can be answered with absolute certainty, but two important factors, at least, must be taken into account. First, a portion of the white community continued to adhere to the tradition of tolerance and egalitarianism that at one time had been dominant. Influential white liberals included Russell Jelliffe, codirector of the interracial settlement house that would later become known as Karamu House, and Charles F. Thwing, president of Western Reserve University. Both were active in the NAACP, and Jelliffe served on a number of interracial committees during the 1920s. Although it is clear that Thwing and Jelliffe were not representative of most whites, they did speak for a constituency that was able to exercise some restraint on the growth of segregation and intolerance in the city.[25]

Perhaps a more important factor that has been neglected was the nature of urban life in the North. The intricate subtleties of the race system common throughout most of the South simply could not be adapted to life in huge, industrialized, impersonal northern cities such as Cleveland. Beyond a certain point in urban development, the separa-

[24] Robert W. Bagnall to Clayborne George [President of Cleveland NAACP], October 20, 1925, branch files (Container G157), NAACP Papers, Manuscript Division, Library of Congress; C. Vann Woodward, *The Strange Career of Jim Crow*, 2d rev. ed. (New York, 1966), 115 and 111–18 *passim*; Bertram W. Doyle, *The Etiquette of Race Relations in the South* (Chicago, 1937), 136–59; Jerome Dowd, *The Negro in American Life* (New York, 1926), 41.

[25] Information from interviews. On Thwing's active support of the NAACP, see also Senator Harold Burton to Charles F. Thwing, September 1, 1913; Oswald Garrison Villard to Thwing, September 13, 1913, Container C403, NAACP Papers; and Cleveland *Gazette*, April 14, 1917.

tion of the races in public and private facilities becomes inefficient, expensive, and dysfunctional to the operation of a modern industrial metropolis; by 1920, Cleveland, Chicago, and other large northern cities had long since passed that point. Paradoxically, however, the same dynamic urban growth that made segregated streetcars and certain aspects of racial etiquette almost impossible also rendered them largely unnecessary. In contrast to the South, where in many cities the growth of ghettos was retarded, in the North blacks were rapidly becoming residentially isolated from the rest of the population. Thus in northern cities informal contacts between the races in daily life were becoming less and less frequent. Because most blacks now lived in a circumscribed section of the city, there was less need for the formal establishment of separate streetcars, schools, and so on: de facto segregation, resulting from the growth of the black ghetto, was accomplishing in many instances the same end.

CHAPTER 9

Occupations in Flux:
The Industrial Breakthrough

Despite the increasing segregation and discrimination that confronted blacks in Cleveland after 1915, thousands of migrants came to the city and became permanent residents. They were drawn there—as they were to other northern cities—by the lure of economic opportunity. Before World War I, almost a third of the city's employed Negro men were engaged in domestic or personal service occupations and only 22 percent worked in manufacturing. During the Great Migration the occupational status of Cleveland's Negro workers underwent a considerable transformation. By 1920, almost two-thirds of the city's black males worked in industrial occupations, while only 12 percent were now engaged in domestic or personal service. During the next ten years, the percentage in industrial work fell off slightly, and the proportion in service occupations rose to 16 percent; but this reversal was quite moderate compared to the gains that had been made during the war years.[1]

Most of the new job openings were in the area of unskilled labor (over half of all black males were in this category in 1920), but blacks made significant gains in semiskilled and skilled factory work as well. The pressing needs of manufacturers during the wartime crisis broke down the color barrier in Cleveland's heavy industries. In 1923 an official of the city's National Malleable Casting Company stated his approval of the performance of black employees in a wide variety of positions. "We have [black] molders, core makers, chippers, fitters, locomotive crane

[1] Louise Venable Kennedy, *The Negro Peasant Turns Cityward* (New York, 1930), 75; U.S. *Fourteenth Census, 1920* (Washington, 1922), IV, 1084–86; U.S. *Fifteenth Census, 1930* (Washington, 1932), IV, 1285–87.

operators, melting furnace operators, general foremen, foremen, assistant foremen, clerks, timekeepers[;] in fact, there is no work in our shop that they cannot do and do well, if properly supervised." A survey of local firms the following year revealed that twelve large foundries employed labor that ranged from 10 to 60 percent Negro in composition. In all but one of the plants some Afro-Americans had advanced to semiskilled and skilled positions, and a few had become foremen. Many of the migrants earned double or triple the wages they had received in the South. A 1918 study of over one thousand Cleveland workers revealed that the growing discrimination in other areas of life was not reflected in wage scales; white and black workers in similar industries received essentially the same pay, which averaged about $20 a week.[2]

At the opposite end of the occupational scale, the increase in black population after 1915 created a larger clientele for some Negroes in the professions and stimulated the further development of black business. "For the first time in the history of the city," the *Advocate* proclaimed in 1917, "the Average Business and Professional Man is making real money. He is able to meet his obligations promptly and to lay something aside for the proverbial 'rainy day.'" With a few exceptions, the increase in black professionals kept pace with the growth rate of the black community. The largest gains were in the teaching field; the number of black public school teachers increased eightfold between 1910 and 1930. The number of black clergymen and dentists expanded equally as fast during these years. The number of Negro physicians increased at a more moderate rate, and movement of blacks into the legal profession slowed considerably. The less dramatic expansion in law and medicine was probably due to the changing racial climate of the city. Prior to World War I, both black doctors and, especially, black lawyers often were able to draw clients from both races. In the wake of the Great Migration this situation gradually changed. For several years after his arrival in Cleveland in 1917, Dr. William P. Saunders, a Negro physician, had as many white patients as Negro; by the end of the 1920s, however, his clientele was becoming almost exclusively Negro. Although as late as the early 1930s a few black lawyers and physicians still had integrated practices, the consolidation of the ghetto and the intensification of racial prejudice that accompanied the postwar era made this much less likely

[2] John B. Abell, "The Negro in Industry," *Trade Winds* (March 1924), 20; J. O. Houze, "Negro Labor and the Industries," *Opportunity*, 1 (January 1923), 21; Committee on Housing and Sanitation of the Cleveland Chamber of Commerce, *An Investigation of Housing Conditions of War Workers in Cleveland* (Cleveland, 1918), 28.

than before. Increasingly, the clientele of these professionals was limited to members of their own race.[3]

The trend toward increasing reliance on black patronage was also evident among Negro businessmen. Between 1910 and 1930, the number of black retail dealers in Cleveland increased almost tenfold. Most of these enterprises were relatively small, ghetto-based enterprises; the Negro tailors, barbers, and caterers who serviced an all-white, elite clientele were rapidly becoming obsolete. A survey of black businesses made in 1929 found 215 stores in the black community. Each was usually owned by a single proprietor, and altogether they employed only 161 full-time and 34 part-time employees. Food stores, restaurants, and lunch counters accounted for over one half of all black businesses; a variety of drug stores, cigar stands, candy shops, clothing and jewelry stores, ice houses, coal yards, and automotive repair shops and parts dealerships made up the remainder. Black businesses had increased dramatically in number as a result of the migration, but they continued to be inadequately financed. Unable to compete with the lower prices, wider selection of goods, and expensive advertising campaigns of the large white firms and chain stores, black businessmen depended almost exclusively on the ghetto trade for their livelihood.[4]

In spite of these handicaps, a number of black businessmen managed to establish profitable enterprises. The tightening housing market for blacks proved a boon for real estate dealers. During the severe housing shortage of the Great Migration period, Thomas Fleming, Welcome Blue, Nahum Brascher, and several other prominent blacks formed the Cleveland Realty, Housing, and Investment Company for the purpose of buying up Central Avenue properties. By the winter of 1917–18, the company owned almost every apartment building on East 40th Street between Central and Scovill, and was still expanding. These black real

[3] Cleveland Advocate, January 13, 1917; U.S. Census Bureau occupational data, 1910–30; interview with Dr. William P. Saunders, August 6, 1972. It should be noted, however, that while there was strong tendency for black professionals to rely upon the patronage of their own race to a great extent, many black doctors, lawyers, and dentists managed to retain some white clients. This was especially true of the lawyers. At the beginning of the 1930s, there was still one Negro lawyer in Cleveland whose practice was 50 percent white, and some others had a "considerable" number of white clients. This state of affairs also prevailed in New York, Chicago, Detroit, and throughout New England, and Negro lawyers in these areas were perhaps the members of their race most integrated in society at this time. For a discussion of the clientele of black professionals in different parts of the country, see Carter G. Woodson, The Negro Professional Man and the Community (n.p., 1934), 98–103, 171–73, 237–39.

[4] U.S. Bureau of the Census, Negroes in the United States, 1920–1932 (Washington, 1935), 522.

estate dealers, like their white counterparts, attempted to squeeze the most economic gain out of the wartime emergency. The *Gazette* complained that after the company gained control of properties, it proceeded to overcharge the new black tenants, "boosting the rents from three to seven and ten dollars a month above what the 'rooms' were renting for up to the time they secured control of them." Such activities among black entrepreneurs were not, of course, unique to Cleveland. In New York at the turn of the century Philip A. Payton, Jr. organized the Afro-American Realty Company and was responsible for opening up a number of apartment buidings in Harlem to Negro tenants for the first time; and although the Afro-American Realty Company folded in 1908, Payton and other black entrepreneurs who succeeded him reaped small fortunes as a by-product of housing discrimination against blacks. For Payton, as for black real estate men in Cleveland, segregation sometimes could be profitable.[5]

Other black businessmen capitalized on the existence of the ghetto in non-exploitative ways. By the end of the 1920s there were ten Negro undertaking establishments in the city. Of these, J. Walter Wills's "House of Wills" remained by far the most prominent. Aware that the shift of the black population eastward could mean losing clientele to his competitors, Wills sold his Central Avenue funeral home in 1925 and invested in a much larger building on East 55th Street. By then Wills was well on his way to becoming one of the richest Negro funeral directors in Ohio, and he enjoyed the respect of both the black community and white leaders in the city.[6]

Less well known among whites, but equally successful, was the young black entrepreneur Alonzo Wright. Born in Tennessee, Wright had only an eighth-grade education when he came to Cleveland in 1917. After working for a while in a downtown garage as a parking attendant, Wright was befriended by a Standard Oil Company executive who helped him obtain the franchise for the first Standard service station located in a predominantly black neighborhood. Through innovations in customer service (Wright was among the first to institute free tire and radiator checks and windshield cleaning as a regular procedure), he made this station a success; and when Standard built gas stations in other black neighborhoods during the following decade, the company

[5] Cleveland *Gazette*, April 28, 1917, September 7, 1918; Cleveland *Advocate*, March 31, April 21, December 8, 1917; Gilbert Osofsky, *Harlem: The Making of a Ghetto* (New York, 1966), ch. 7.

[6] Charles W. Chesnutt, "The Negro in Cleveland," *The Clevelander*, 5 (November 1930), 4; Russell H. Davis, *Memorable Negroes in Cleveland's Past* (Cleveland, 1969), 45.

found it both natural and profitable to lease the new franchises to Wright. By the early 1930s, the black entrepreneur had acquired a chain of seven service stations.[7]

If the expanding ghetto created an economic base for a businessman like Wright, it also enlarged the opportunities for black journalists. Although a number of black newspapers were founded in Cleveland before World War I, only the *Journal*, which published continuously for nine years, managed to compete successfully against the *Gazette*, the city's oldest race paper. After the *Journal* folded in 1912, its place was taken two years later by the *Advocate*, a moderate weekly edited by an articulate West Indian immigrant, Ormand Forte. For several years the *Advocate* appeared quite successful, but by 1922 it too had folded. Undoubtedly this failure was the result of competition from two additional race papers, the *Call* (founded in 1920 by Garrett Morgan) and the *Post* (published by Norman McGhee and Herbert S. Chauncey). Undaunted, Forte established in 1924 yet another black weekly, the *Herald*. The black population of the city, however, was simply not large enough to support three or four newspapers. By the end of the decade, the *Herald* had ceased publication, and the two remaining competitors of the *Gazette* had wisely merged to form the *Call and Post*. The *Call and Post* would soon outdistance its older rival and become, during the following decade, the leading race paper in Cleveland.[8]

The most successful businessman in Cleveland's postwar black community was Herbert Chauncey. Born in Georgia, Chauncey migrated to Cleveland before the war. While working in the postal service, he studied law and soon was able to pass the bar exam and open his own law office. In 1921 with the assistance of George Hinton and several other black entrepreneurs, Chauncey opened the first Negro-owned and -operated bank in the city, the Empire Savings and Loan Company. "The company grew," a Negro resident later recalled, "because it was the one banking institution that was willing to finance home buying for Negroes without discrimination." By 1926 Empire Savings had succeeded to the point where it was able to open a branch office. Chauncey

[7] Chesnutt, "The Negro in Cleveland," 4; interview with Dr. William P. Saunders, August 6, 1972.
[8] Biographical statement and newspaper clipping relating to Ormand Forte, Western Reserve Historical Society; interview with Norman McGhee, September 3, 1971. According to Harry C. Smith (Cleveland *Gazette*, May 29, 1920), at one time or another prior to 1920, sixteen black newspapers had competed with the *Gazette*. If this was true—Smith was given to exaggeration in comparing his newspaper to others—then most of the *Gazette*'s competitors must have been very short-lived, for no clippings or record of their existence seems to have survived.

was similar to his predecessor, S. Clayton Green, in the diversity of his activities. Besides the *Post* and Empire Savings, the black entrepreneur also established a real estate company and one of the first black life insurance companies in Cleveland. Unfortunately, like Green, Chauncey did not live to see his many projects come to fruition. After his untimely death in 1930, Chauncey's enterprises quickly collapsed in the wake of the Great Depression.[9]

The chief difference between Chauncey and S. Clayton Green was the degree of white involvement in, and patronage of, their business enterprises. Green found it necessary to widen his financial base by appealing, in some of his entrepreneurial schemes, to white customers. The increased size of Cleveland's black population after 1915, however, made it possible for Chauncey to build up successful businesses without relying even partially upon white patronage. With the exception of Empire Savings, in which a few whites had savings accounts, *all* of Chauncey's projects were committed exclusively to the Negro market.

Despite notable advances in industrial work and moderate gains for some blacks in business and the professions, the postwar economic achievement of Cleveland's black community was still deficient in a number of respects. Perhaps the most notable failure was the small change which occurred in the economic status of black women. As a result of the wartime labor shortage, black women in cities throughout the North were able, for the first time in many instances, to obtain jobs as semiskilled operatives in manufacturing. Blacks who optimistically saw this as the beginning of "a new day for the colored woman worker," however, were mistaken. After 1918, most of the black women in manufacturing lost their jobs to returning soldiers; and by 1930 the overwhelming majority of employed Negro women were still engaged in domestic or personal service. As charwomen, laundresses, and house servants, these women continued to occupy the lowest rungs of the occupational ladder.[10]

[9] Cleveland *Gazette*, January 15, 1921, November 10, 1923, September 18, 1926, November 5, 1927; Davis, *Memorable Negroes in Cleveland's Past*, 53. In addition to banking and insurance, another area of black entrepreneurial involvement in the 1920s was sports promotion. A number of black businessmen were responsible for organizing a black baseball team in Cleveland early in the decade. The Cleveland Stars were managed by George Tate, a black baseball star who had attended Oberlin College. Interview with Dr. William Saunders, August 6, 1972; Cleveland *Gazette*, March 18, 1922.

[10] For an example of the ill-founded optimism over wartime employment of black women in industry, see [Joint Committee on Employment of Colored Women in New York and Brooklyn,] *A New Day for the Colored Woman Worker: A Study of Colored Women in Industry in New York City* (n.p., 1919), *passim.*

Another deficiency in the black economic structure was the lack of improvement in white-collar employment. The percentage of the black work force engaged in clerical work changed very little between 1910 and 1930. In most cases white businesses steadfastly refused to hire Negro clerks. When a Euclid Avenue department store hired two Negro saleswomen in 1919 and placed them "conspicuously" at the front of the store, it was an item worthy of mention in the Negro press. As during the prewar era, only a handful of blacks gained positions as bookkeepers, cashiers, or stenographers. Throughout the 1920s, the East Ohio Gas Company and the Ohio Bell Telephone Company refused to employ Negroes "in anything but the humblest positions," and the small number of clerical jobs opening up in black businesses could not possibly counter the effects of the exclusionary policies of such giant firms.[11]

In the area of public service, Negroes did register some gains. The dramatic increase in black population after 1915, coupled with the consolidation of the ghetto, made the election of a Negro to the state legislature once again possible. Councilman Thomas Fleming helped a number of blacks acquire positions as clerks or assistants to department heads in city government.. However, most Afro-Americans employed by the city or county occupied low-level positions. The highest Negro appointments before 1928 were those of assistant county prosecutor in 1918 and assistant city police prosecutor six years later. Some city agencies, such as the fire department, continued to exclude blacks after the Great Migration, and it was small consolation that the city's garbage collection unit was manned and supervised mostly by blacks by 1930.[12]

Animosity between black workers and white labor unions continued to hinder black economic progress after 1915. At the annual convention of the American Federation of Labor in 1916 the Cleveland Federation expressed the fear, shared by many unionists, that a large-scale migration of southern Negroes to the North might seriously threaten the labor movement there. By then, the fears of white laborers that blacks were antilabor had almost become (like so many other racial fears) a self-fulfilling prophecy. Many Afro-Americans had come to associate the labor movement with discrimination and mob violence, and more than a few looked to their employers, rather than their white fellow workers, for protection and an equal opportunity to work. To be sure, an important exception to this pattern of interracial hostility between black and

[11] Cleveland *Gazette*, February 1, 1919; Chesnutt, "The Negro in Cleveland," 4. For occupational data, see Tables 15 and 16.

[12] Thomas W. Fleming, "My Rise and Persecution" (manuscript autobiography [1932] in Western Reserve Historical Society), 54–55; Chesnutt, "The Negro in Cleveland," 4.

white workers occurred in the Cleveland steel industries during World War I. The Amalgamated Association of Iron and Steel Workers local actively recruited black workers during the war, and one result was that Cleveland became one of the very few cities where black workers solidly backed the Great Steel Strike of 1919. After 1920, however, the Amalgamated rapidly declined as an organization, and the general conservatism and racism of the AFL led to a neglect of the black worker. This, coupled with the immigrant steelworkers' increasing "feeling of antagonism and dislike" toward blacks, fueled black hostility to unions. A survey conducted among seventy-five Cleveland firms in 1924 reported that black workers were "loyal to their northern employers to the best of their ability. Scarcely has there been a complaint against these people," the study noted, "on the ground of their being trouble makers. . . . They come here understanding the American Language and having a knowledge of our basic ideals. They do not bring with them any of the communistic or socialistic spirit to be found among some immigrants from certain portions of Europe."[13]

Ironically, evidences of interracial solidarity during the steel strike of 1919 did not lead unionists in other industries or trades to change their attitude toward blacks. During the Great Migration, one Ohio AFL spokesman bluntly stated that integrated locals were not in the best interests of labor. Southern black migrants, he claimed, did not make good union men because they did not understand the necessity for a "sustained effort" by labor organizations against manufacturers. Black workers rarely had an opportunity to vindicate themselves of this charge. The policy of excluding blacks from union membership, widespread before 1916, came close to being universal in the craft unions during the 1920s. Only in a few of the more traditional skilled trades, such as masonry, did a small group of older black workers continue to maintain union ties. Younger blacks were kept out of the unions by being denied the opportunity to gain the skills requisite for union membership. "The trade schools conducted by the Board of Education," Charles Chesnutt explained in 1930, "are so tied up by rules and regulations, largely dictated by the labor unions, that it is difficult for a Negro boy to acquire a trade in them." The Negro youth, Chesnutt continued,

> cannot study unless he secures in advance the promise of a job where he can do practical work on part time during his studies, or where he

[13] Sterling D. Spero and Abram L. Harris, *The Black Worker: The Negro and the Labor Movement* (New York, 1931), 102, 257–61; Abell, "The Negro in Industry," 17; Houze, "Negro Labor and the Industries," 21, 22; David Brody, *Labor in Crisis: The Steel Strike of 1919* (Philadelphia, 1965), 162.

will be permanently employed at the end of his course. The difficulty in placing them has caused the officials to discourage the attendance of Negro students. A colored youth can take elementary training in the East Technical High School, but practical training in many trades can only be acquired in factories which discourage or limit the number of apprentices and especially Negro apprenticeships.

By such devious means blacks were effectively excluded from the skilled trades for decades to come.[14]

Perhaps the most severe example of white antagonism toward black workers was that of the Waiters' Union. In 1917 white waiters, many of whom were Greek immigrants, went on strike in an attempt to force black waiters out of their jobs. Violence erupted between the two groups and one Negro was severely beaten. Within a year, these tactics proved partially successful; white waiters forced the managers of three Cleveland hotels to fire their black waiters and replace them with whites. By 1929, "jobs as hotel help had practically vanished" for blacks. Black waiters gained partial revenge in 1930 when they served as strikebreakers against the now completely white Waiters' Union. Once again violence broke out between the two groups, and for a while the police found it necessary to place an armed guard at the home of the leader of the strikebreakers. The black waiters gained no lasting benefit from their retaliation, however. When the strike was finally settled in 1931, the whites were allowed to return to the jobs, and the black waiters were once again dismissed from their positions in the hotels. Nothing had changed.[15]

In the face of such blatant racism, it is not surprising that black leaders had small regard for labor unions. The opposition of prominent Negroes, in 1928, to the Shipstead anti-injunction bill was indicative of a long-standing distrust of organized labor. Two influential Cleveland Negroes, Charles Chesnutt and Harry E. Davis, appeared before the Senate Judiciary Committee to oppose the bill, claiming that any restriction on the power of the courts to limit union activities would have a damaging effect on the black labor force. If black workers were going

[14] Cleveland *Gazette,* March 24, May 12, 1917, February 22, 1919; George A. Myers, "Answer to Questionnaire from Chamber of Commerce Committee on Immigration and Emigration," in 1926 correspondence; George A. Myers to Clayborne George, November 29, 1926, George A. Myers Papers, Ohio Historical Society; Chesnutt, "The Negro in Cleveland," 3–4. See also F. Ray Marshall and Vernon M. Briggs, Jr., *The Negro and Apprenticeship* (Baltimore, Md., 1967), 102.

[15] Chesnutt, "The Negro in Cleveland," 27; Cleveland *Gazette,* November 3, 1917, September 21, 28, 1918, August 16, 30, 1930; interview with Russell and Rowena Jelliffe, September 1, 1971.

to be denied the protection of union membership, Davis told the Committee, there was only one place where they could have their "employment rights" protected: the courts. "For all practical purposes the proposed bill would take away this right from the group of independent workers for whom I am speaking and it would mean their subjection to a state of economic serfdom." When white unionists simultaneously denied Negroes membership and vilified them for becoming strike-breakers, black citizens had ample reason to question the utility of the labor movement. They had little to lose by favoring the open shop.[16]

How did the changes in black occupational structure wrought by the Great Migration compare to the pattern of job-holding of other groups? To answer this question, occupational data for native whites and foreign-born whites for 1920 and 1930 were tabulated and transformed into occupational indexes, using the same procedure followed in analyzing the 1870, 1890, and 1910 census data. Unfortunately, no data on specific immigrant groups are available after 1890, and for 1930 the category "native whites" is not broken down into second-generation immigrants and native whites of native parentage. As a result, the comparative analysis must be somewhat less detailed than for other years.

Considering first the male work force, it is evident that the 1910–20 decade was one of moderate occupational improvement for Cleveland Negroes. These changes occurred mostly at the lower levels of the occupational hierarchy, but this does not make them less significant as a result. The percentage of blacks employed in domestic or personal service fell sharply from 29.6 to 12.2; the proportion in unskilled labor rose dramatically, and the percentage in semiskilled and skilled work also improved. The overall occupational index for black males moved up from 568 to 549.[17] (See Tables 15 and 17.)

The increased wartime demand for unskilled and semiskilled factory labor also affected native whites and the foreign-born. Between 1910 and 1920, the percentage of all male workers engaged in unskilled labor rose from 13.6 to 20.2; the percentage in semiskilled labor increased from 8.4 to 16.6. Unlike the employment impact on blacks, however, the impact of this trend on the overall occupational status of white groups in the economy was negative. Because their occupational status in 1910 was fairly high, the movement of some native whites and immigrants

---

[16] Spero and Harris, *The Black Worker*, 139; *A Bill to Amend the Judicial Code* . . . , Hearings before the Senate Subcommittee of the Committee on the Judiciary on S. 1482, 70th Cong., 1st sess. (1928), 603–14. For a general survey of the strained relationship between organized labor and black workers in the 1920s, see Spero and Harris, *The Black Worker*, 87–315 *passim*.

[17] The occupational index is discussed in Appendix I.

TABLE 15. *Occupational structure of Cleveland, by racial and ethnic group, 1920*

| | Occupational category | | | | | | | | | | | | |
| | Professional | | Proprietary | | Clerical | | Skilled | | Semiskilled | | Unskilled | | Domestic | |
	Number	Percentage	Number	Percentage	Number	Percentage	Number	Percentage	Number	Percentage	Number	Percentage	Number	Percentage
Males														
Negroes	212	1.3	217	1.4	406	2.7	2,194	14.6	1,785	11.9	7,953	53.0	1,830	12.2
Native whites of native parentage	4,629	7.0	5,636	8.5	16,047	24.3	20,998	31.8	9,629	14.6	4,656	7.1	1,196	1.8
Native whites of foreign or mixed parentage	3,115	4.3	5,726	8.0	15,027	20.9	24,278	33.8	12,958	18.0	6,603	9.2	1,222	1.7
Foreign-born whites	2,103	1.7	9,416	7.8	7,251	6.0	38,404	31.8	20,878	17.3	36,009	29.8	2,541	2.1
All workers	10,065	3.7	21,014	7.7	38,760	14.2	86,164	31.5	45,377	16.6	55,230	20.2	6,854	2.5
Females														
Negroes	150	2.9	164	3.2	191	3.7	151	2.9	888	17.4	176	3.5	3,223	63.0
Native whites of native parentage	3,585	15.8	718	3.2	11,958	53.0	350	1.5	3,846	17.0	153	0.7	1,458	6.4
Native whites of foreign or mixed parentage	2,574	9.2	625	2.2	13,852	49.3	767	2.7	7,434	26.5	302	1.1	1,963	7.0
Foreign-born whites	733	4.1	915	5.2	3,551	20.1	470	2.7	6,253	35.3	667	3.8	4,531	25.6
All workers	7,042	9.6	2,422	3.3	29,552	40.2	1,738	2.4	18,421	25.0	1,298	1.8	11,178	14.8

SOURCE: U.S. *Fourteenth Census, 1920* (Washington, 1922), IV, 1084–87.
NOTE: Totals include the additional category "Indians, Chinese, Japanese, and all others." In 1920, 3.6 percent of the male occupations and 2.9 percent of the female occupations in Cleveland were unspecified by the Census Bureau.

TABLE 16. *Occupational structure of Cleveland, by racial and ethnic group, 1930*

| | Occupational category | | | | | | | | | | | | |
| | Professional | | Proprietary | | Clerical | | Skilled | | Semiskilled | | Unskilled | | Domestic | |
	Number	Percentage	Number	Percentage	Number	Percentage	Number	Percentage	Number	Percentage	Number	Percentage	Number	Percentage
Males														
Negroes	630	2.5	537	2.1	899	3.6	2,783	11.1	3,848	15.3	11,255	44.7	4,108	16.3
Native whites	9,949	6.2	11,654	7.3	36,807	23.0	42,609	26.6	33,749	21.1	14,394	9.0	3,832	2.4
Foreign-born whites	2,774	2.5	9,263	8.4	8,206	7.4	31,870	29.0	21,354	19.4	27,285	24.9	4,221	3.8
All workers	13,365	4.5	21,626	7.3	45,947	15.5	77,624	26.2	59,035	20.0	53,469	18.1	12,369	4.2
Females														
Negroes	297	2.7	291	2.7	282	2.6	292	2.7	1,714	15.6	99	0.9	7,665	69.8
Native whites	10,285	15.0	1,360	2.0	31,288	45.5	1,319	1.9	14,797	21.5	553	0.8	6,639	9.7
Foreign-born whites	1,215	6.3	849	4.4	3,927	20.4	277	1.4	6,135	31.9	283	1.5	5,785	30.1
All workers	11,801	11.9	2,514	2.5	35,499	35.9	1,888	1.9	22,662	22.9	935	0.9	20,094	20.3

SOURCE: U.S. *Fifteenth Census, 1930* (Washington, 1932), IV, 1285–88.
NOTE: Totals include the additional category "other races." "Native whites" includes all whites born in the United States, whether of native, foreign, or mixed parentage. In 1930, 4.2 percent of the male occupations and 3.7 percent of the female occupations in Cleveland were unspecified by the Census Bureau.

TABLE 17. *Occupational indexes, Cleveland, 1920–30*

	1920	Change, 1910–20	1930	Change, 1920–30
Males				
Negroes	549	+19	546	+ 3
Native whites of native parentage	371	− 9	NA	NA
Native whites of foreign or mixed parentage	392	− 9	NA	NA
All native whites	383	− 9	386	− 3
Foreign-born whites	459	−16	451	+ 8
All workers	425	−13	426	− 1
Females				
Negroes	601	+ 8	618	−17
Native whites of native parentage	330	+37	NA	NA
Native whites of foreign or mixed parentage	368	+45	NA	NA
All native whites	351	+47	356	− 5
Foreign-born whites	479	+61	479	NC
All workers	397	+50	410	−13

SOURCE: Tables 10, 15, and 16.
NOTE: As discussed in Appendix I, the occupational categories upon which the occupational index is based are ranked from 1 (high) to 7 (low). Thus a change in the index for a given group from a higher to a lower number indicates an improvement in occupational status, and is denoted with a plus (+) sign. NA indicates data not available. NC indicates no change.

into semiskilled and unskilled work tended to depress the white occupational index. The index for all native whites dropped from 374 to 383; for foreign-born whites it fell from 443 to 459; for all male workers, from 412 to 425. Thus between 1910 and 1920, black males gained occupationally in both an absolute *and* a relative sense, when their progress is compared with the moderate downward trends of other groups. The steady occupational decline that blacks experienced in the late nineteenth and early twentieth centuries had finally been halted, and the large economic gap between white and black workers had been shortened to some extent.[18]

[18] It must be emphasized again that changes in the occupational index measure *group* mobility and tell us nothing at all about the mobility of particular individuals within a given group. Thus we cannot know, on the basis of the occupational index, whether certain elements of the black, native white, or immigrant populations were advancing (or declining) occupationally faster than others. Despite this limitation,

During the 1920s, the occupational index for black males improved only to a negligible degree. The proportion of blacks in domestic service increased slightly, but this was offset by gains in the semiskilled, proprietary, and professional categories. (See Table 16.) The occupational index for native whites continued to decline during this period (probably because of the migration of unskilled southern whites to the city after World War I), while the index for foreign-born whites improved. In neither case, however, was the change very significant, and in general the postwar decade was marked by exceptional occupational stability for all groups in the economy.[19]

As in the decades before 1910, the trend in female occupations during the 1910–30 period did not parallel that of the male half of the population. During the war there was some upgrading of the occupations of black women. About one out of every seven Negro domestics took factory jobs, and the percentage of black clerical workers advanced from 1.4 to 3.7 percent. The occupational index for black women advanced from 609 to 601. Relative to other racial and ethnic groups, however, the position of Negroes continued the precipitous decline that had begun in the 1870s. White women continued, in even greater numbers than before the war, to move into clerical and professional work. Between 1910 and 1920 the proportion of all employed women in clerical work increased from 22.6 to 40.2 percent; fully one-half of native white women held white-collar jobs at the close of the decade. The occupational index for all employed women rose from 447 to 397. Equally significant was the gap in occupational status which began to open up between Negroes and the foreign-born. Prior to World War I, the position of black women was not unique, since a large proportion of immigrant women were also mired in low-paying domestic work. But between 1910 and 1920 foreign-born women began for the first time to obtain white-collar employment in sizable numbers, and at the same time the proportion of immigrant females working as domestics fell from 41 to 25.6 percent. While the occupational status of Negro women moved slowly upward, the index for foreign-born women jumped from 540 to 479.

---

the index is still a useful index of changes in the job structure—especially for the period after 1900, for which there is insufficient information to draw conclusions on the occupational mobility of specific individuals or families.

[19] It is likely, of course, that the occupational standing of native whites of New England stock was much higher than that of southern white migrants who had recently moved to the city. The anomalous rise in the occupational index of the foreign-born during the 1920–30 period may have been caused by the implementation of the Quota Act of 1924, which sharply reduced the influx of impoverished, occupationally depressed immigrants from southern and eastern Europe.

For women as well as men the 1920s was a period of occupational stability. The gradual upgrading of women's occupations that had occurred during the previous half-century now came to an end, and a slight trend in the opposite direction set in. The proportion of the total female work force in clerical positions slipped to 35.9 percent, and their overall occupational index dropped from 397 to 410. Black women also experienced a postwar occupational slump, but its significance was much more profound. The minor gains that they had made during and before the war were now completely wiped out, and the percentage of black women in domestic service returned to the high level it had reached in 1910. In 1930, the occupational status of Negro women was not much different from what it had been in 1870.[20]

In spite of all this, the economic status of Cleveland's black community in the postwar period cannot be summarized in negative terms. In 1930, males comprised approximately seven-tenths of all Negro workers in the city, and *their* occupational status had measurably improved since the Great Migration, even if that of Negro women had not.

Unfortunately, as blacks would all too soon discover, improvements in occupational status did not always entail job security. Accurate unemployment figures for the 1920s are not available, but it would appear that, in Cleveland, black workers—despite their loyalty to their employers and incipient distrust of labor unions—were too often "the last to be hired and the first to be fired." The problem of unemployment was not very serious during the early 1920s, when the mills and factories of the city were reaching new heights of productivity and were constantly in need of new workers. In 1924 the Cleveland Urban League affiliate was able

[20] The slight improvement in occupational opportunity for black women during the war masked the important fact that, in 1920, blacks made up a much higher *proportion* of all domestic service workers than they had in 1910. In 1910 only 9 percent of Cleveland's female domestic servants were Negro, but a decade later this figure had risen to 30 percent. This change was also common to other cities in the North, and in cities like Philadelphia, Indianapolis, and Kansas City, Missouri, the proportion of blacks in domestic service jobs rose to over 50 percent. This change was due less to the influx of blacks into these jobs than to an exodus of whites out of them. A study of eleven northern cities (using only slightly different occupational criteria than I have adopted) by the Census Bureau in 1929 showed that the total number of female servants actually declined between 1910 and 1920 from 238,002 to 187,894, while the number of black servants increased from 43,778 to 57,807. Given the large influx of migrants from the South, this black increase was rather moderate; nevertheless, the proportion of all servants who were black rose from 18.4 to 30.8 percent. Joseph A. Hill, *Women in Gainful Occupations, 1870–1920*, Census Monographs no. 9 (Washington, 1929), 115. The restriction on immigration from abroad after 1924 accelerated the black domination of the domestic occupations, gradually making northern cities, in this respect, more and more similar to the South.

to place almost three-fourths of its job applicants; three years later, it was still able to find employment for 60 percent of the blacks who came to its agency. Beginning in 1928, however, a serious black unemployment problem began to emerge. The Urban League reported that only 30 percent of its job applicants obtained employment; more ominous, one League official noted that in some factories "the colored worker was the first to go" when a layoff occurred. In 1930, as the city began to feel the effects of the Depression, the heaviest concentration of the jobless was in the Negro district west of East 55th Street. It was no coincidence that, five years later, the greatest concentration of relief cases would be located in this same area.[21]

[21] Annual Report of the Negro Welfare Association for 1924; Annual Report, June–October 1927; minutes of the Board of Trustees of the Negro Welfare Association, December 8, 1927, February 9, November 30, 1928, all in Cleveland Urban League Papers; Department of Industrial Relations of the National Urban League, *Unemployment Status of Negroes: A Compilation of Facts and Figures Respecting Unemployment among Negroes in One Hundred and Six Cities* (New York, 1931), 36; Howard W. Green, *Nine Years of Relief in Cleveland, 1928–1937* (Cleveland, 1937), 26–27, 59. The problems of black employment in Cleveland during the Great Depression are surveyed thoroughly by Christopher G. Wye in "The New Deal and the Negro Community: Toward a Broader Conceptualization," *Journal of American History*, 59 (December 1972), 621–39.

CHAPTER 10

Progress and Poverty
in the Black Community

The consolidation and expansion of the black ghetto in Cleveland had contradictory effects on the social and cultural life of the black community. On the one hand, it intensified the stratification of the black population along class lines that had begun before the Great Migration. More than ever, the particular church that a black family attended and the neighborhood they lived in indicated their socioeconomic status in the community, and after 1915 the divisions between upper, middle, and lower strata generally became more clear cut. On the other hand, the growth of the ghetto and the increase in white prejudice that followed in the wake of the migration fostered a growing sense of unity among Negroes, while a new middle-class interest in African and Afro-American folk traditions helped bridge the cultural gap between the average Negro and the black bourgeoisie to some extent.

After World War I, the fraternal orders that had played so important a part in the social life of the black community declined in both numbers and significance. The gradual decline of the lodges, which would continue during and after the Depression of the 1930s, has not been studied much by historians, but it is likely that the factors involved were mostly nonracial in character and affected white fraternal orders as much as black. At the end of the nineteenth century, lodges served a number of social and economic purposes: they offered members a convenient place for entertainment and socializing and at the same time provided valuable life insurance and health benefits. Between roughly 1915 and 1945, however, the development of radio, motion pictures, and the automobile helped undermine many of the social functions of the lodges, while the growth of insurance firms rendered the fraternal benefit programs less valuable. It is probable that the black lodges declined less rapidly than the white orders. Because they had less economic and geographic mobility than their white counterparts, working-class blacks in particular continued to find the lodges useful as all-purpose social and recreational centers. But even for the black working class, the fraternal orders were no longer the central institutions they once had been.[1]

In contrast to the lodges, the black church entered a period of dynamic change as a result of the Great Migration. The prewar trend toward an increasing number and diversity of black religious institutions accelerated rapidly during the two decades after 1915. A few years before the onset of the migration, there were only 17 black churches in Cleveland. By the winter of 1918, there were 44; by 1921, 78; by 1933, over 140. The Baptists remained the largest single denomination, claiming fourteen thousand of the city's twenty-two thousand Negro church members in 1921. Antioch Baptist Church grew steadily during the migration and remained the largest black congregation in the city; by 1925 its membership reached one thousand.[2]

Conspicuous among the new churches were the numerous storefront congregations of the Holiness and Spiritualist sects and the poorer Baptists. In the 1920s, lower Central and Scovill avenues were dotted with the makeshift edifices of these congregations. These churches, with their personalized, informal services and fervid religious emotionalism, appealed to many of the lower-class Negro migrants from the South. Some

[1] For a useful discussion of the decline of the fraternal orders in the new urban environment of the 1920s, see Robert S. Lynd and Helen M. Lynd, *Middletown: A Study in Modern American Culture* (New York, 1929), 277, 304–8. On the growth of Negro insurance companies, which dated to the turn of the century, see August Meier, *Negro Thought in America, 1880–1915: Racial Ideologies in the Age of Booker T. Washington* (Ann Arbor, Mich., 1963), 141–46, and Walter B. Weare, *Black Business in the New South: A Social History of the North Carolina Mutual Life Insurance Company* (Urbana, Ill., 1973).

[2] Report of the Executive Secretary [of the Negro Welfare Association for the period September–October, 1918], Cleveland Urban League Papers, Western Reserve Historical Society; The Cleveland Foundation, *The Cleveland Year Book, 1921* (Cleveland, 1921), 294; *The Baptist Answer in 1924–25: Being the 95th Annual Report of the Cleveland Baptist Association* (Cleveland, 1925), 26; Julian Krawcheck, "Negro Tide from South Swelled City's Problems," Cleveland *Press*, May 31, 1963. Useful studies of the religious life of black Americans in general include Benjamin E. Mays and Joseph W. Nicholson, *The Negro's Church* (New York, 1933); Arthur H. Fauset, *Black Gods of the Metropolis: Negro Religious Cults of the Urban North* (Philadelphia, 1944); and Seth M. Scheiner, "The Negro Church and the Northern City, 1890–1930," in William G. Shade and Roy C. Herrenkohl, eds., *Seven on Black: Reflections on the Negro Experience in America* (Philadelphia, 1969), 92–116.

of these new churches were able to preserve the congregations of southern communities almost intact. For example, one black minister, Charles C. Ailer, came to Cleveland from Alabama with his congregation and founded Zion Hill Baptist Church. This type of institutional "transplanting" gave a measure of continuity to the lives of southern migrants, and helped smooth the path of their adjustment to urban society.[3]

At first, many of the new black churches were unable to find permanent quarters. An Urban League survey of 1918 showed that all but one of the black churches founded between 1916 and 1918 were holding services in rented buildings. For the larger congregations, however, this problem was solved with the passage of time. As the Afro-American population gradually moved eastward, it often engulfed areas where white congregations had, many years before, erected churches. White churches usually held out for a while, but when most of their membership had moved to the suburbs or to outlying districts of the city they invariably sold the church edifices and relocated far from the ghetto. In 1927 the white First Baptist Church, an institution which had at one time personified the spirit of integrationism in Cleveland, symbolized the changing pattern of race relations in the city when it sold its Prospect Avenue building to a black church and moved out of the city. A member noted later that the Prospect Avenue location "was suited neither to a mission church nor to a membership who were gradually moving eastward to Cleveland Heights." In most cases it was unnecessary for Negro congregations to construct new churches; they usually bought the buildings of white congregations who were only too willing to sell at a reasonable price. In 1920 alone thirteen white congregations sold their buildings to black churches.[4]

[3] Krawcheck, "Negro Tide from South Swelled City's Problems." The growth of black churches during the postwar era probably obscures a gradual decline in church attendance among some of the migrants—notably younger black males. Though conducted during a later period, Frank T. Cherry's study of black migrants in Chicago after 1945 is probably indicative of the changing pattern of religious behavior that an earlier generation of newcomers underwent. Surveying a selected group of migrants, Cherry found that 98 percent had attended church in the South, but only 76 percent did so after having lived in Chicago for several years. This decline was due almost solely to the changing attitudes of young blacks; only 59 percent of the young males interviewed reported that they still attended church. Frank T. Cherry, "Southern In-Migrant Negroes in North Lawndale, Chicago, 1949–59: A Study of Internal Migration and Adjustment" (Ph.D. dissertation, University of Chicago, 1965), 121. For suggestive earlier comments on this phenomenon, see Charles S. Johnson, "The New Frontage on American Life," in Alain Locke, ed., *The New Negro* (New York, 1925), 286, and St. Clair Drake and Horace R. Cayton, *Black Metropolis: A Study of Negro Life in a Northern City* (New York, 1945), 650–53.

[4] Report of the Executive Secretary, 1918, Cleveland Urban League Papers; *His-*

The expansion of black religious activity during the migration years was primarily a lower- and middle-class phenomenon. Before World War I, there had been only two elite churches, Mt. Zion Congregational and St. Andrew's Episcopal; both were moderate in size compared to the larger Baptist churches, and St. Andrew's was quite select in its membership, which consisted of old-elite, light-skinned Negroes. After 1915 both of these churches expanded in size, and a third elite church, St. Mark's Presbyterian, was founded in 1918. Neither Mt. Zion nor St. Mark's was limited to old-elite families, and in the face of their competition St. Andrew's was also forced to open its doors to respectable members of the new business and professional classes in the black community. By 1922 St. Andrew's had almost four hundred communicants, and it remained the most prestigious black church in the city.[5]

Even more so than before the war, there were few integrated congregations in Cleveland. Most white Protestant churches took little interest in the city's enlarged black population and discouraged even the most respectable Negroes from joining their congregations. The Chesnutt family, which continued to attend a white Episcopal church, was virtually the only exception to this rule. In addition, the Catholic Church, which had previously made an effort to assimilate blacks into the activities of the Church, now reversed its policy in 1922 and set up a separate parish for blacks, Our Lady of the Blessed Sacrament.[6]

Prior to the Great Migration, there was a good deal of residential intermixing among classes in the black community. The average black family lived on or near Central Avenue; but many middle-class and even elite Negroes also resided close to that thoroughfare. Only the completely integrated old elite of the black community lived in neighborhoods far removed from the main area of black settlement. After 1915, this changed. The expansion of the black community and the tightening of the housing market altered this pattern to a considerable extent, and one's place of residency became a more accurate indicator of an individual's status in the black community.

In the wake of the Great Migration, as E. Franklin Frazier pointed out

---

tory of the First Baptist Church of Greater Cleveland, 1833–1933 (Cleveland [1935]), 62; The Cleveland Foundation, *The Cleveland Year Book, 1921*, 294; George A. Myers to Bishop J. H. Jones, September 8, 1922, George A. Myers Papers, Ohio Historical Society.

[5] George F. Bragg, *History of the Afro-American Group of the Episcopal Church* (Baltimore, Md., 1922), 239; interview with Dr. William P. Saunders, August 6, 1972.

[6] Cleveland *Gazette*, April 15, 1922; John T. Gillard, *The Catholic Church and the American Negro* (Baltimore, Md., 1929), 74–75.

in his classic study, *The Negro Family in Chicago*, upper- and middle-class blacks, as well as the more successful whites, fled the inner city and its impoverished masses. The result was "segregation by class" within the black community. In Chicago at the end of the 1920s, the economic status of residents of the Black Belt rose as one traversed from north to south. The poorest Negroes lived in the northernmost, oldest section of the ghetto, while the elite resided in the extreme southern part of the Black Belt. Frazier divided Chicago's South Side into seven socioeconomic "zones," which he differentiated by employing a number of variables for the measurement of income and status. Unfortunately, not all of the kinds of data which Frazier had at his command are available for Cleveland, but enough information exists to show that Cleveland's black community was also segregated residentially by economic class. I have used four variables to determine the economic status of different sections of the black community: home ownership, ownership of radios,[7] Negro illiteracy, and the percentage of individuals engaged in selected middle- and upper-class occupations. In each case, since there are no data available for earlier years, census-tract figures for 1930 were used. An area of high economic status would tend to have a low illiteracy rate but would register higher (relative to other predominantly Negro tracts) in the other three categories. Higher illiteracy rates would also indicate a greater concentration of recent arrivals from the South.[8]

These four measurements of economic status reveal that Cleveland's Afro-American population was stratified along an east-west axis at the end of the 1920s. It was possible to identify four zones in the black belt. (See Tables 18 and 19.) The zones, which correspond roughly to a series of concentric rings, contained neighborhoods of progressively higher economic status as one moved outward (primarily eastward) from the lower Central district. Zone 1, consisting of the area west of East 40th Street, was the oldest residential section of the Negro community. This

[7] In the 1920s, radios were usually fairly expensive items, and thus the ownership of radios can be used as a rough measure of economic status. In Cleveland in 1930, 22.8 percent of all black families, 37.9 percent of the foreign-born white families, and 62.5 percent of the native-white families owned radios. U.S. *Fifteenth Census, 1930, Population* (*Families*) (Washington, 1932), VI, 70.

[8] See E. Franklin Frazier, *The Negro Family in Chicago* (Chicago, 1932), ch. 6; for class differentiation in Harlem, see E. Franklin Frazier, "Negro Harlem: An Ecological Study," *American Journal of Sociology*, 43 (July 1937), 72–88. In analyzing class differentiation within the Cleveland ghetto, the most accurate indicator is the rate of illiteracy. The other three indicators are not broken down by race for each tract and hence are most useful, for the present purpose, in evaluating tracts where the black population constituted a high proportion of the total population.

area was filled with crowded and deteriorating lodging houses, had a high incidence of crime, and was close to the soot and noise of the industrial district and the docks. It contained the highest illiteracy rates and the lowest percentage of home ownership of any black section. Most blacks living in this area had recently migrated from the South, and few

TABLE 18. *Economic status of Cleveland Negroes by selected census tracts, 1930*

Census tract	Percentage Negro	Percentage of total families owning homes	Percentage of total families owning radios	Percentage of Negroes illiterate
Zone 1				
G-2	9	4	12	10.8
G-5	6	13	12	9.2
I-2	37	12	12	7.9
I-4	29	6	3	15.7
I-5	26	14	9	8.4
I-6	53	13	6	9.5
I-7	76	6	9	8.5
J-2	49	12	7	12.7
J-3	49	10	11	11.2
Zone 2				
H-9	89	6	19	5.6
I-8	76	6	17	7.3
I-9	82	10	10	6.7
Zone 3				
L-9	71	6	33	2.5
M-3	81	20	35	2.0
M-7	91	4	17	1.3
M-8	78	26	19	6.9
M-9	33	12	28	6.1
N-2	57	19	26	3.9
N-7	31	22	35	1.9
Zone 4				
L-6	9	21	60	3.9
M-4	76	26	44	0.9
M-5	70	34	40	1.3
M-6	81	26	31	0.9
S-2	19	28	41	1.2
S-8	14	28	43	0.7

SOURCE: Green, *Population Characteristics by Census Tracts, Cleveland, 1930* (Cleveland, 1931), 58, 60, 160–62.

NOTE: The figures in the second and third columns must be used with caution if the census tract in question contains less than about 70 percent Negro residents. It is probable, however, that whites and blacks in most tracts were of comparable economic status.

TABLE 19. *Percentage of residents of predominantly Negro census tracts engaged in selected occupations, 1930*

Census tract	Percentage Negro	Percentage engaged in professional, semiprofessional, or postal service
Zone 1		
I-7	76	0.6
Zone 2		
H-9	89	2.2
I-8	76	2.2
I-9	82	1.4
Zone 3		
L-9	71	3.0
M-3	81	3.8
M-7	91	1.9
M-8	78	1.8
Zone 4		
M-4	76	6.8
M-5	70	5.2
M-6	81	6.0

SOURCE: Green, *Population Characteristics By Census Tracts, Cleveland, 1930,* 189–92.

were engaged in professional, semiprofessional, or postal service occupations.[9]

As one moved eastward, illiteracy rates dropped and the number of residents owning their own homes and employed in middle- or upper-class professions increased. Zone 2 stretched approximately from East 40th to East 55th streets; as late as 1920 it was populated mostly by immigrants, but by 1930 it had become overwhelmingly Negro. Although less crowded and further removed from the industrial section than the lower Central area, this section was also deteriorating rapidly and beginning to take on the characteristics of a slum. Very few members of the black middle or upper classes lived in this area. One of the few who did so was Thomas Fleming, who was compelled to live there because of the residency requirement for his councilmanic seat. But even Fleming tried

[9] The census-tract data for 1930 do not give a further breakdown for the "professional and semi-professional service" category. On the characteristics of Zone 1, see also R. B. Navin, William D. Peattie, et al., *An Analysis of a Slum Area in Cleveland, Prepared for the Cleveland Metropolitan Housing Authority* (Cleveland, 1934), *passim,* and Gordon H. Simpson, comp., *Economic Survey of Housing in Districts of the City of Cleveland Occupied Largely by Colored People* (Cleveland [1931]), 20–50.

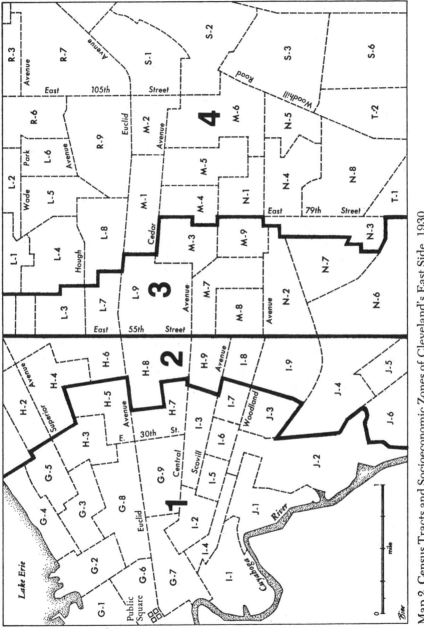

Map 2. Census Tracts and Socioeconomic Zones of Cleveland's East Side, 1930

to keep as far away from his constituency as possible, and in 1918 he moved into a new home on East 55th Street, on the very edge of the Eleventh Ward. Zone 3, from East 55th to East 79th streets, had a much higher incidence of home ownership and a substantially lower illiteracy than neighborhoods to the west. In 1930, the area between East 55th and East 65th (Tracts L-9 through M-8) was already making the transition to a working-class neighborhood, but the part of the zone stretching from East 65th to East 79th was solidly middle class.[10]

Only middle-class or elite Negroes lived in Zone 4, the area beyond East 79th Street. A pleasant residential section, it had only one-tenth of the illiteracy rate, and ten times the number of professionals, as Zone 1. Its population density was less than one-third that of the lower Central district. Included in Zone 4 were three small enclaves of elite Negroes outside of the main black belt. The two enclaves to the north of Hough Avenue near East 84th Street and to the east of East 105th Street had existed for several decades. The third lay along Kinsman Road (Tract S-8), well to the southeast of the central ghetto, and had come into being sometime prior to World War I. Residency in Zone 4 had once been limited almost exclusively to old-elite families who had close ties to the white community. After 1920, however, many businessmen and professionals who had offices or stores on Central Avenue now also resided far from the heart of the ghetto.[11]

The increasing "integration" of the new and old elites in patterns of residency and church affiliation signaled the decline of the once dominant group of light-skinned Negro entrepreneurs, barbers, and professionals who had catered to a predominantly white clientele. Although many teachers and professionals and a very small number of businessmen continued to maintain some social relationships with whites, this phenomenon was uncommon by 1930. Among the newer black businessmen there was no inclination to associate with whites, and as black lawyers and doctors found themselves increasingly restricted to a black clientele, they also had less occasion to socialize with the opposite race on an informal basis. Changing career ambitions among the children of the old elite and their propensity to intermarry with successful members

---

[10] Cleveland *Advocate*, October 19, 1918 (letter to the editor).

[11] Howard W. Green, comp., *Population by Census Tracts, Cleveland and Vicinity, with Street Index* (Cleveland, 1931), 7–9; Charles W. Chesnutt, "The Negro in Cleveland," *The Clevelander*, 5 (November 1930), 3; Simpson, comp., *Economic Survey of Housing*, 98–120, 157–70; interview with Dr. William P. Saunders, August 6, 1972. Much of the information on the residency of businessmen and professionals was obtained from newspaper reports and from the Cleveland *City Directory*.

of the new elite also helped undermine divisions between the two groups. Edwin Chesnutt, the son of Charles Chesnutt, took up the new-elite occupation of dentistry; Chesnutt's daughter Ethel married the principal of a Negro high school in Washington, D.C., while John P. Green's daughter, Clara, married a Cleveland pharmacist. This process of amalgamation and transformation of the black elite, of course, was a gradual one, and it would be many years before the old elite was completely eliminated as a distinct social group. But by the eve of the Depression, the transition was virtually complete.[12]

Despite their increasing geographic separation from the black masses, middle- and upper-class blacks took a new interest in the social condition and cultural traditions of the southern migrants after 1915. Part of this concern was reflected in an increased black participation in social welfare organizations, a subject which will be dealt with in the following chapter. The new interest in southern Negro and African folk culture, however, deserves mention in the present context. As August Meier has shown, the origins of these new cultural concerns antedated the Harlem Renaissance by several decades and were ultimately rooted in the changing social and economic organization of black life in the country as a whole, especially in its large cities. The increasing segregation and ghettoization of blacks at the end of the nineteenth and beginning of the twentieth century gradually nurtured a new racial consciousness in blacks, and fostered a philosophy of self-help, race pride, and group solidarity. An incipient interest in folk materials and race history was a natural outgrowth of this new climate of opinion, and a number of black scholars, folklorists, and literary societies began to explore these topics as early as the 1890s.[13]

In Cleveland, however, the ghetto developed later than in Chicago or New York, and the formation of the self-help ideology and group economy was retarded or adulterated in practice. Under these circumstances, it is not surprising that, prior to World War I, educated Negroes in Cleveland were either indifferent or openly hostile to black cultural traditions. At the turn of the century, for example, a delegate to the Cleveland convention of the Ohio branch of the National Association of Colored Women criticized ragtime—a musical form that had originated among black musicians in the South—for its supposed "evil" and "de-

[12] This information was obtained from widely scattered sources and from interviews. Despite their changing occupational interests, most of the children of the old elite remained in recognizably elite positions. Quite exceptional was the case of Herbert D. Myers, George Myers's son, who became a mechanic with the White Automobile and Truck Company.

[13] Meier, *Negro Thought in America,* 256–78.

under consideration, and it failed to organize the black community against the racist films *The Nigger* and *The Birth of a Nation* in 1915 and 1917. During the Great Migration, the branch was headed by Horace C. Bailey, the amicable and moderate pastor of Antioch Baptist Church, and under his leadership the NAACP appeared more interested in holding discussion meetings and organizing social and cultural events than in taking action to oppose discrimination.[40]

Early in the 1920s this situation changed. Through a concerted effort, the branch was able to increase its membership substantially, and at the end of 1922 had sixteen hundred members. The branch collected more money during the first six months of 1922 than it had during the entire preceding year, and within two years was able to exceed its annual quota by 21 percent. Through quarterly membership drives (often assisted by speakers sent by the national office) and the creation of a women's auxiliary and a college chapter, the Cleveland branch was able to promote greater interest in the organization and place itself on a firmer financial footing.[41]

Although part of this increased vitality can be laid to the population increase of the Great Migration, another important factor was the infusion of new leadership into the local branch in the early twenties. About two-thirds of the members of the branch's executive committee during the postwar decade were professionals, and most of these were young lawyers. Of the remainder, most were white-collar workers of one type or another; one of the most influential of this group was R. K. Moon, a government meat inspector. Only a handful of businessmen took any active part in the Cleveland NAACP; quite exceptional was Edward Jackson, a real estate dealer who served for a number of years as treasurer to the organization. There was a good deal of continuity among this leadership group during the twenties, and the cohesiveness of these individuals was often aided by close professional ties. A number of the attorneys on the executive board, for example, shared law offices.[42]

40 Cleveland Branch *Bulletin*, 1 (October 1920), 1; Cleveland *Gazette*, January 10, 1914, July 31, 1915, March 31, April 14, 21, May 12, 1917, October 12, December 7, 28, 1918; Larry Cuban, "A Strategy for Racial Peace: Negro Leadership in Cleveland, 1900–1919," *Phylon*, 28 (Fall 1967), 305.

41 Assistant Director of Branches to Addie Hunton, October 19, 1920; Addie Hunton to James Weldon Johnson, November 20, 1920; "Report of A. W. Hunton, October 6 to November 8, 1922," administrative files (Container C65); Thelma Taylor to Robert W. Bagnall, March 22, 1923; Bagnall to Taylor, April 10, 1923; Charles White to Bagnall, April 13, 1927, branch files (Container G157), NAACP Papers; *Annual Report of the Cleveland Branch . . . for the Year ending December 1st, 1924*, 4.

42 Information from NAACP Papers.

The persons most responsible for building up the Cleveland NAACP were Harry E. Davis, Clayborne George, and Charles W. White. Davis, whose career has already been discussed, served for many years as legal advisor to the local organization and often acted as liaison with the national office of the association. Davis was from an old Cleveland family, but both George and White were newcomers to the city. Born in 1888 in Surry, Virginia, George attended Howard University as an undergraduate and received law degrees from Howard and Boston universities. He came to Cleveland in the early twenties and soon made a name for himself as an excellent attorney and a vigorous advocate of equal rights. In 1922 George was named to the NAACP's executive committee, and at the end of the following year he was elected president of the branch. Charles White was born in Nashville and attended Fisk University and Harvard Law School. After graduating from the latter in 1924, White came to Cleveland. Described by Robert Bagnall as "capable, efficient, unselfish and earnest," White soon earned a reputation as one of the most independent-minded black leaders in the city. In December, 1926, he was elected president of the Cleveland NAACP, succeeding George, and remained in that capacity for the next three years.[43]

It is clear that, at least during the postwar era, the Cleveland NAACP was guided by New Negroes, and these individuals sought to avoid both the accommodationism of Thomas Fleming and Jane Hunter as well as the overbearing and sometimes counterproductive stridancy of Harry C. Smith. Though militant, the NAACP stressed the need for flexibility and cooperation among different groups and organizations in the struggle against racism. "Every organization," one issue of the *Branch Bulletin* stated, "rightfully aims at the same ultimate end, the advancement of the Negro or the breaking down of race prejudice." This problem, however, has "many sides, all of which are important and must be looked after." The editorial continued:

> This fact is often overlooked by those who insist that our salvation lay in our educating ourselves, or in acquiring wealth, or in battering down the bar of race prejudice with brute force. It is readily admitted that every one of these factors must enter into any program launched for the solution of this perplexing problem, but as important as every one of them is, none is capable of solving the problem alone. We must do, not one of these

[43] *Annual Report of the Cleveland Branch . . . for the Year ending December 1st, 1924*, 2; *Who's Who in Colored America*, 6th ed. (New York, 1942), 202; Selby, *Beyond Civil Rights*, 53, 55; Harry E. Davis to Robert W. Bagnall, December 9, 1926; Bagnall to Davis, December 27, 1926; Bagnall to Daisy Lampkin, July 23, 1930; Charles White to Bagnall, November 26, 1929, branch files (Containers G157 and G158), NAACP Papers.

things, but all of them. We cannot progress far as a race without education, nor can we progress without wealth, nor without courage enough to stand up and fight for our rights. Our progress, to be lasting, must be made along many lines, all developing at the same time, not at the expense of each other, but through a close co-operation of all the forces we can muster along each particular line. The aim of the branch is to bring about just such a co-operation in Cleveland.[44]

To a significant degree, the NAACP was able to realize this goal. The association became the most successful and effective racial advancement organization in Cleveland largely because it avoided the divisiveness that had plagued some previous black efforts at fighting discrimination. At both the national and the local level, the NAACP institutionalized protest. Whereas its predecessors, the Afro-American League and the Niagara movement, were more often than not disparate collections of individuals with an insufficient local base of support, the NAACP was truly an *organization*, functioning from year to year regardless of the personalities involved.

The NAACP struggled against discrimination on many fronts. The activities of the organization in 1924 were typical of the postwar era. In that year the branch brought five suits against discriminatory restaurant proprietors. The racism of some juries at that time was reflected in the fact that the association was able to win only two of these. The threat of legal action, however, was often sufficient to bring proprietors into compliance. The exclusionary policy of the Loew's Ohio Theater was ended when the branch protested to the theater manager. When a case of discrimination at Brookside Park's swimming pool was brought to the attention of the appropriate official, he issued an order to prevent a recurrence of the incident. After an investigation, the branch intervened with the manager of the Higbee Company department store to end that firm's policy of refusing to allow black women to try on articles of clothing. When the association learned that one of the tenants operating a restaurant in a market near East 46th and Euclid was encouraging his help to "doctor" the food served to Negroes, it brought the matter to the attention of the market master, who then informed all the tenants under his jurisdiction that henceforth such discriminatory practices would not be allowed. Finally, upon receipt of a complaint that the Erie Railroad shops on East 55th Street were constructing separate toilet facilities for

[44] Cleveland Branch *Bulletin*, 1 (October 1920), 3. See also *ibid.*, 1 (November 1920), 1–2; [Charles White,] "'Cleveland Branch of the N.A.A.C.P., Communication to the Executive Committee, February 14, 1927," branch files (Container G157), NAACP Papers.

blacks, both the local and New York offices of the association filed protests with the company's president in New York. After a conference with
two of the railroad's representatives in Cleveland, the NAACP persuaded
the company to drop the project.[45]

The NAACP did not limit itself to fighting discrimination and segregation in theaters, restaurants, and other facilities, however. It investigated, for example, the occasionally fraudulent claims of real estate and
insurance firms doing business in the ghetto, and warned blacks about
them. From 1924 to 1926 the local branch actively assisted several black
families who, upon moving into all-white neighborhoods, encountered
hostility and mob action. In an act of reprisal against Dr. E. A. Bailey,
who refused to vacate his home in Shaker Heights, the school board of
that community attempted to prohibit the use of its facilities by seventy
children—twelve of them black—from nearby Beechwood Village, despite the fact that Beechwood had made an agreement with Shaker that
allowed its children to use the Shaker schools. Acting on behalf of the
NAACP, Harry E. Davis promptly brought suit against the Shaker officials, and the Court of Common Pleas issued a writ of mandamus requiring the city to carry out the terms of its agreement with Beechwood.[46]

Critics of the NAACP, especially in the 1930s, frequently attacked the
association as an elitist organization unconcerned with issues that affected the broad mass of ghetto dwellers. While it is true that, prior to
the Depression, the NAACP seldom concerned itself with economic issues, an analysis of activities at the local level shows that the general
charge of aloofness from the masses is overstated. After 1920, the Cleveland branch made a special effort to keep working class blacks informed
of the activities of the association. From time to time NAACP officials
held special meetings with workers in the city's mills and foundries to
explain the purposes and objects of the organization, and the branch
established an auxiliary composed of a dozen "key men" in Cleveland
factories. In addition, the branch intervened in several instances to prevent lower-class blacks from being extradited to the South on trumped-
up charges. In one notable case, James Robertson, an iron worker at the
Cleveland Hardware Company, through ignorance of his rights signed

[45] Annual Report of the Cleveland Branch . . . for the Year ending December 1st,
1924, 1–2; Clayborne George to Robert W. Bagnall, June 10, 1924; George to Walter
White, April 21, 1924; "N.A.A.C.P. has Lunch Room Proprietor fined $50 for Dis-
crimination in Cleveland" (press release, June 13, 1924), branch files (Container
G157), NAACP Papers.

[46] Cleveland Branch Bulletin, 1 (November 1920), 2; "Cleveland Segregators Try
to Oust Colored Children from School" (press release, November 6, 1925), branch
files (Container G157), NAACP Papers.

an extradition waiver in 1922 allowing his return to South Carolina. When Harry E. Davis learned that the charges against Robertson were of dubious legality, he immediately wired the governor of Ohio, demanding a hearing on the extradition. NAACP attorneys gained a temporary stay of the extradition order, and after a hearing in a Cleveland court the defendant was discharged. (The local branch was particularly proud of its success in this case, since Robertson was a member of Marcus Garvey's Universal Negro Improvement Association but had received no assistance from his fellow Garveyites. "We took pains," Harry Davis wrote to Walter White, "to emphasize the fact that his connection with the Garvey Movement did not assist him, and that the organization which Garvey was attacking had come to his aid, and in all probability saved him from a long prison or debt sentence in South Carolina.") Apparently at least a portion of the working class viewed the activities of the NAACP as directly related to their own interests. In 1922 almost 40 percent of the local funds for the NAACP came from one-dollar memberships, and it is safe to presume that most of these contributions were from laborers.[47]

V

Before World War I, some Cleveland Negroes had agitated for a separate black YMCA, but they had been unsuccessful. During the Great Migration, however, the need for such an institution became more pressing. Old-line integrationists like Harry C. Smith again opposed the creation of a black YMCA; but when the institution finally came into existence in 1921 it attracted little attention, largely because a facility similar to a "Y" branch—the Negro Welfare Association's Community House—had already been in operation for two years. As early as April, 1920, the NWA proposed to transfer the activities of the Community House to the YMCA, but the NWA board decided to put off the change "until the question of segregation would not loom so large as to prevent success to the movement." Eighteen months later the issue had died down, however, and the changeover was quietly made. In 1923 the "Y"

[47] Cleveland Branch *Bulletin*, 1 (October 1920), 1; Harry E. Davis to James Weldon Johnson, September 15, 1920; George A. Mundy to Mary White Ovington, October 14, 1922; Thelma Taylor to Robert Bagnall, March 22, 1923; "Report of Cleveland, Ohio, Branch of N.A.A.C.P. for the Month of November, 1922"; Harry E. Davis to Walter White, November 15, 1922; "Memorandum for Mr. [James Weldon] Johnson . . . September, 1929"; James Weldon Johnson to Gov. Meyers Y. Cooper, September 5, 1929 (telegram); "Cleve., O., Branch, N.A.A.C.P., Spring Drive for Memberships, 1922," branch files (Containers G157 and G158), NAACP Papers.

branch was moved to a larger, permanent location on Cedar Avenue.[48]

Because of the unusual circumstances which brought it into existence, the creation of a black YMCA caused only a ripple of dissent. The movement to establish a Negro hospital in Cleveland, however, set off a major controversy in the black community that lasted for several years. As early as 1915 Dr. E. A. Dale, a black physician, had proposed the creation of a separate facility, but at that time the black community was far too small to consider financing such an institution; a decade later the idea seemed more feasible. The main proponents of Mercy Hospital (as the institution was to be called) were William R. Green, Herbert S. Chauncey, Thomas Fleming, Jane Hunter, and several black physicians. A number of New Negroes also lent their support, however, and in fact most of the city's black leadership either favored the institution or were noncommittal. In 1927 a campaign was begun to raise $220,000 for the construction of the hospital.[49]

The proponents of the hospital stated that the institution was necessary because of the discrimination in the city's white hospitals; in particular, they cited the fact that no hospital admitted blacks to nurses' training or internship programs. A vocal opposition to the hospital immediately arose, led by Harry C. Smith, George Myers, and a few physicians and ministers. Smith ridiculed the movement for the hospital in terms similar to those used in the debate over the creation of a black YMCA two decades before. Speaking for the die-hard element of the old elite, he perceived the backers of Mercy Hospital as selfish accommodationists, eager for the jobs and titles that the new institution would bring. Noting that one of the doctors supporting the project had recently migrated from Alabama, Smith urged him to "go back South! . . . And . . . *stay there* until you can 'take that red bandanna off your head.'" Some black doctors, the editor fumed, "would harm all of our people in this community almost beyond repair to attain their selfish desires." An elderly black physician agreed: "The men back of this project are *deceivers.* What they want is a job; that is all." Myers, too, condemned those Negroes who would accept segregated facilities if "there is a possible chance for individual profit." He and Smith both felt that the creation

[48] Harry C. Smith to George A. Myers, April 14, 1919, Myers Papers; Minutes of the Board of Trustees of the Negro Welfare Association, April 29, 1920, November 22, 1921, Cleveland Urban League Papers; Cleveland *Gazette*, March 24, 1923.

[49] E. A. Dale and P. H. Green to George A. Myers, June 3, 1915, Myers Papers; Cleveland *Gazette*, November 15, 1919, November 26, 1926, May 21, November 5, 1927; Mercy Hospital Association of Cleveland, *Does Cleveland Need a Negro-Manned Hospital?* (n.p. [1927], pamphlet).

of Mercy Hospital would only lead to further discrimination and "would close the doors of all other Cleveland hospitals to our people. . . ."[50]

Smith and Myers saw the Mercy Hospital issue as a clear-cut case of integration and equal rights versus separatism and self-help. But they were mistaken, for—unlike the 1911 YMCA incident—the black community did not generally divide along these lines. It is probable, of course, that some individuals did favor the proposed institution for the patronage it would bring. It is also true that a few Negroes like Jane Hunter lent their support because they favored separate institutions of any kind. But such accommodationist separatism was not a major force behind the Mercy Hospital movement. The sponsors of the hospital clearly stated that they opposed segregation "that restricts the social, economic, or political life of any group." They conceived of the hospital as a facility which would benefit the entire black community—a place where black patients would be assured admission and where black doctors and nurses could develop the skills that would eventually enable them to be accepted as equals by the white medical profession. Such an attitude more closely resembled that of the "New Negro" than the older, Tuskegee version of racial solidarity.[51]

That this was so was proven by the pragmatic response of the city's black leadership when, in 1929, the black community proved unable to raise the necessary funds for the hospital and the city council vetoed the use of public funds to finance a similar project. Several of those who had originally supported the drive for a black hospital now began a movement—this time fully supported by Smith and Myers—aimed at breaking down the discriminatory policies of tax-supported City Hospital. This new effort elicited a widespread positive response from the city's black population. Charles Garvin, Harry E. Davis, and other prominent blacks entered the fray, and in November, 1929, three Negroes won election to city council by vowing to fight for a change in the city's hospital program. The black population also showed their disapproval of the discriminatory policy of the municipal hospital by voting in large numbers against new hospital bonds. The new city manager, Daniel E. Morgan, soon yielded to the pressure of the black community. In September, 1930, five black women were admitted to the hospital's nurses' training program. The fol-

---

[50] *Ibid.*; Cleveland *Gazette*, April 19, 1927, February 25, 1928, April 13, October 26, 1929; George A. Myers to William R. Hopkins, February 6, 1928; Smith-Myers correspondence, 1927, Myers Papers.

[51] Cleveland *Gazette*, November 26, 1926, quoting Jane Edna Hunter's Phillis Wheatley Association journal, *The Open Door*; Mercy Hospital Association, *Does Cleveland Need a Negro-Manned Hospital?*

lowing year, the first black intern was admitted to the staff. The hospital's policy of segregating Negro patients also came to an end at this time.[52]

The role of the Cleveland NAACP in the dispute over Mercy Hospital was illustrative of that organization's desire to avoid ideological divisiveness without adopting an accommodationist posture. When the hospital movement began getting under way in 1927, the branch found itself "rather hopelessly separated" into two camps. "On the one hand," wrote Charles White of the planned hospital, "it is being bitterly opposed as a self-inflicted bit of jim-crowism. On the other hand, it is being espoused as a very much needed institution for the training of Negro physicians and nurses. . . ." White, seeking a policy that would unite the branch, rejected the "simple assertions" of some opponents that black YMCAs and hospitals should be dismissed simply as "instances of self-segregation." After consulting with the national office of the NAACP, the branch received a ruling from Robert Bagnall that if "the proposed Mercy Hospital is to be a private hospital, serving all groups and appealing to the general public for funds . . . its existence does not run counter to the principles of the National Association." Shortly thereafter, the branch decided to remain neutral on the issue.[53]

The board changed its mind in 1929, however, when black Councilman E. J. Gregg and several other backers of the hospital began to urge the use of *public* funds to create a black medical facility on the East Side. The NAACP came out strongly against this latest plan. In his 1929 *Annual Report*, Charles White made it clear that "our opposition is not to a Negro Hospital privately supported, nor to an East side branch of City Hospital with a mixed staff, designed to . . . serve the whole East

---

[52] Cleveland Gazette, July 28, 1928, January 12, 1929; George A. Myers to William R. Hopkins, December 13, 1927; Myers to Hopkins, December 27, 1927; Myers to Hopkins, February 6, 1928, Myers Papers; "Local N.A.A.C.P. Head Urges Defeat of Hospital Bonds," Cleveland *Call and Post*, October 27, 1928 (clipping in NAACP Papers); Charles White, "'Cleveland Branch, N.A.A.C.P., Annual Report of President, November 21, 1929," [5–6]; Charles White to Walter White, January 14, 1930, branch files (Containers G157 and G158), NAACP Papers; Charles H. Garvin, "Pioneering in Cleveland," *The Woman's Voice*, 1 (September 1939), 14–16 (copy in Garvin Papers); Thomas F. Campbell, *Daniel E. Morgan, 1877–1949: The Good Citizen in Politics* (Cleveland, 1966), 115–17. The first small breakthrough in the struggle to integrate City Hospital occurred in July, 1928, with the appointment of Dr. John McMorries to the surgical out-patient staff of the hospital. Dr. McMorries, who had practiced in Cleveland since 1916, was the first black doctor ever named to a post at City Hospital. Charles White to James Weldon Johnson, June 23, 1928, branch files (Container G158), NAACP Papers.

[53] [Charles White,] "Cleveland Branch of the N.A.A.C.P., Communication to the Executive Committee, February 14, 1927," 2; Charles White to Robert W. Bagnall, March 28, 1927; Bagnall to White, March 31, 1927, branch files (container G157), NAACP Papers.

side and to which all patients on the east side shall be required to go." Most people, White stated, failed to understand the distinction on which their opposition to the plan was based. "We stand against a branch of the City Hospital which, whether intended or not, will eventuate in a short while into what to all intents and purposes is a Negro branch of City Hospital." While the branch sympathized with the plight of blacks who desired to become nurses or doctors, it "'was not willing to compromise such a fundamental [principle] by acquiescing to the introduction of a pernicious double system of municipality owned and operated hospitals." Once the City Council had rejected Gregg's proposal, the NAACP quickly joined with other groups to successfully eliminate discriminatory practices from City Hospital. Throughout the entire controversy the branch had acted responsibly and with a good deal of flexibility to advance the best interests of the black community.[54]

VI

The reaction of the NAACP to the hospital dispute was indicative of the changing political and ideological temperament of black Cleveland at the end of the 1920s, and the successful conclusion of the controversy coincided with the rise to power of the New Negroes. Although Thomas Fleming was, throughout the decade, the most influential black politician in the city, it is clear that his conservative brand of leadership was becoming less and less representative of the views of the black community. One indication of this was the changing editorial stance of black newspapers in the city. After the Cleveland *Journal* folded in 1912, there would never again be an organ in Cleveland that represented the Booker T. Washington self-help philosophy in its pristine form. The *Advocate*, which published from 1914 to 1922, was in many ways the logical successor to the *Journal*. During its early years, especially, the paper preached race pride and "the doctrine of perseverance and stick-to-it-iveness." The *Advocate's* editor, Ormand Forte, supported Fleming, gave a nodding approval to the concept of a black YMCA, and generally refused to criticize Booker T. Washington or his successor, Robert R. Moton.[55]

The editorial stance of the *Advocate*, however, was never as conserva-

[54] Charles White, "Cleveland Branch, N.A.A.C.P., Annual Report of President, November 21, 1929" [5], branch files (Container G158), NAACP Papers.

[55] Cleveland *Advocate*, September 11, October 30, 1915, March 8, October 21, 1916. For editorials praising either Tuskegee or its headmaster, see *ibid.*, June 12, July 24, November 6, 1915.

tive as that of the *Journal*. Unlike its predecessor, its tone was not uniformly accommodationist. The paper attacked the racial injustice of the South and called for federal intervention to control what editor Forte called the southern white's "lust for blood." And while refusing to attack Washington, the *Advocate* was also lenient toward Washington's critics. "In spite of everything that might be said against Mr. [William Monroe] Trotter by his bitterest enemies," an editorial proclaimed in 1916, "the fact stands out clearly and unmistakably that he has fought 'in season' and 'out of season' for equal rights for his race." Although it was never a militant paper, the *Advocate* became more favorable to black protest during the Great Migration. Its editorials frequently charged the War Department with racism and in 1917 protested the segregation of black soldiers in separate training camps. By 1918 the *Advocate's* editor revealed the limitations of his support for Washingtonian principles when he vigorously attacked Governor James Cox's proposal to enlarge the facilities at Wilberforce University. Previously Forte had seen nothing wrong with a black YMCA, but he now feared an enlarged Wilberforce would be an "entering wedge for *Separate Education*" in Ohio. "Tuskegee Institute," said Forte, "is all right for Alabama, for it is needed there, but a 'Tuskegee' is not desired in Ohio."[56]

The *Advocate's* flexibility on race issues signaled the beginning of a movement away from the ideological dogmatism that had characterized some elements of the black community on the eve of the wartime migration. During the twenties, the successors to the *Advocate*—the *Call*, the *Herald*, and (after 1928) the *Call and Post* would be much more insistent than the *Advocate* had been in protesting discrimination in restaurants, theaters, and other public accommodations in Cleveland. Unlike the *Gazette*, however, which never ceased its militant agitation for civil rights, these newspapers did not make a fetish of integration. The increasingly attractive approach that they reflected in their editorials was that members of the black community should strive for integration wherever segregation restricted their social freedom or economic opportunity. But neither the *Advocate* nor its successors criticized the Phillis Wheatley Association or other black social-welfare organizations simply because they were institutions designed solely for Negroes.[57]

It was not until the end of the twenties that this view was translated

[56] *Ibid.*, June 24, July 1, August 26, October 21, 1916, September 8, November 24, December 1, 1917, January 12, 1918.
[57] Unfortunately, copies of most black newspapers (with the exception of the *Gazette*) published in Cleveland during the 1920s have not survived. The conclusions in this paragraph are based upon the scattered clippings that have been preserved in a number of manuscript collections.

into political power. Thomas Fleming, the sole black representative on the City Council until 1927, had no desire to use the black vote as a tool to force concessions from the dominant Republican machine. Although Fleming controlled patronage in his Eleventh Ward, he was never able to obtain significant appointments for blacks, and most of the jobs at his disposal were rather minor positions. Within a few years, all this would change, and the political subsystem of the black ghetto would be transformed from a neglected stepchild of the local GOP to a formidable power within the party, able to make its voice heard and to wrest important concessions from the city's white leadership. How did this happen?

As in so many other respects, the underlying cause was the growth of the ghetto. As the black population expanded eastward, it gradually engulfed the Seventeenth and Eighteenth wards, and in 1927 this enabled two new black members, E. J. Gregg and Clayborne George, to join Fleming on City Council. The election of Gregg and George was evidence of an increasing dissatisfaction with the regular Republican organization. Both had run for council as "independent Republicans" in 1925 but had lost, despite credible showings. They then set about building up separate political organizations outside the regular party caucuses. George established the East End Political Club in the area just beyond East 79th Street in which middle-class Negroes were settling in increasing numbers. He founded his organization "on those principles which the N.A.A.C.P. has advocated for some years, namely, that the Negro should use his ballot effectively for men and measures without respect to party label." In 1927 both George and Gregg ran as independents again, and Gregg was elected with Democratic support. "The whole of Cleveland," Charles White proclaimed in the wake of election, "is now awake to the fact that the Negro's vote can no longer be classed as solidly for the Republican party or for any party. These gratifying results were achieved by a unity that was outstanding and by an independence that has given rise to a new respect for the Negro vote."[58]

During the next year Gregg and George caucused with the Democratic minority in the council, and Democratic leaders made an effort to sway them to their side of the aisle permanently. W. Burr Gongwer, the local Democratic boss, appointed forty-two blacks as precinct committeemen

[58] Cleveland *Gazette*, November 19, 1927; Charles White to Robert W. Bagnall, November 15, 1927, branch files (Container G158), NAACP Papers. After 1924, Cleveland councilmen were elected from four large districts on the basis of proportional representation. Party organizations at the ward level remained intact, however, and in many respects the old ward boundaries continued to function as the basic political units.

in wards 11, 12, and 18, an arrangement more generous than that offered by the Republican machine. Whether Gregg and George actually considered joining the Democratic fold permanently, however, is doubtful; it is likely that they were using their relationship with the Democrats as a threat to force concessions from the GOP. In January, 1928, Republican council votes elected Harry E. Davis to the Civil Service Commission, and a year later the Republicans backed a known independent, Dr. Russell S. Brown, minister of Mt. Zion Congregational Church, for the council seat vacated by recently indicted Thomas Fleming. Shortly thereafter the rebellious black councilmen rejoined the Republican caucus.[59]

This episode marked the beginning rather than the end of black political independence in Cleveland, however. Fleming was soon convicted and imprisoned on bribery charges, which eliminated him once and for all from the political scene. The path for new black political leadership was now completely unencumbered. In the councilmanic elections of November, 1928, George was reelected, lawyer Lawrence O. Payne succeeded to the seat held briefly by Dr. Brown, and LeRoy Bundy, a black dentist and sometime-entrepreneur, replaced E. J. Gregg. In this same election Mary B. Martin became the first Negro to gain a seat on the Cleveland Board of Education; the previous year, lawyer Perry B. Jackson had won election to the state legislature.[60]

Under the leadership of Bundy, a militant advocate of equal rights who had played a controversial role in the black community of East St. Louis over a decade before, the three black councilmen now moved quickly to transform their votes into an effective political instrument.[61]

59 Cleveland *Plain Dealer*, January 3, 1928; Cleveland *Gazette*, February 16, 23, March 9, October 19, 1929; Giffin, "Black Insurgency in the Republican Party of Ohio," 36–37.

60 Thomas W. Fleming, "My Rise and Persecution" (manuscript autobiography [1932], Western Reserve Historical Society), 89–100; R. O. Huus and D. I. Cline, "Election Fraud and Councilmanic Scandals Stir Cleveland," *National Civic Review*, 18 (May 1929), 289–94; Cleveland *Gazette*, November 9, 1928, February 23, November 9, 16, 1929; Davis, *Memorable Negroes in Cleveland's Past*, 47.

61 Of the New Negro leaders who rose to power at the end of the 1920s, Bundy was clearly the most dynamic. He grew up in Cleveland (his father, Rev. Charles Bundy, was a prominent minister) and received a degree in dentistry from Western Reserve University. Before World War I, Bundy moved to East St. Louis, Illinois, where he set up his dental practice, became engaged in a number of entrepreneurial schemes, and rose to prominence in the local black community. Bundy soon became involved in politics and allied himself with the local Republican boss, Mayor Fred Mollman. Described as an "aggressive political agitator," Bundy managed to win favorable patronage concessions for the black community while simultaneously incurring the hatred of many East St. Louis whites. In the aftermath of the bloody race riot of July, 1917, many whites attempted to make Bundy the scapegoat.

They were greatly aided in this task by their strategic position in the new council: only fourteen of the twenty-five seats were held by Republicans, and this gave the black councilmen a balance of power in that body.

The integration of City Hospital was only the first of a series of victories that flowed from the enhanced political power of the black vote. In 1930, the black "triumvirate" (as Payne, George, and Bundy were labeled by the press), effectively marshaling the black vote, brought about a stunning primary-election defeat of an organization candidate for county prosecutor who had threatened to crack down on the East Side policy rackets, a "business" that had become an especially important source of black employment with the onset of the Depression. At the same time, all three councilmen won election as ward leaders, thereby significantly increasing the amount of patronage available in the black community. Winning reelection in 1931, the black councilmen once again put their balance of power to good use, refusing to support the Republican machine's candidate for council president until all three black representatives were given committee chairmanships. In 1932, at a time when the GOP suffered massive defeats at the local and state level as well as in the national elections, the black political leadership of Cleveland still managed to engineer the election of Chester Gillespie to the state legislature. And during the next three years the blacks who served on City Council continued to use their voting leverage to wring concessions from city hall and to enhance their own power within the party.[62]

Charged with murder and conspiracy, the black dentist eventually won acquittal and returned to Cleveland, where he became involved in the Garvey movement. It appears, however, that Bundy's interest in Garveyism was temporary and perhaps opportunistic. His militant agitation for equal rights and enhanced black political power in East St. Louis (and his support of labor unions there) was hardly typical of most of Garvey's followers, and in 1929 he was elected to the Cleveland City Council on a platform pledging to fight for the integration of City Hospital. Tremendously ambitious, Bundy was nevertheless a master political strategist; he was probably one of the most successful black politicians of his day. Cleveland *Journal*, May 20, 1905; Elliott M. Rudwick, *Race Riot at East St. Louis, July 2, 1917* (Carbondale, Ill., 1964), 119–32, 147, 185–90, 216n; interview with Dr. William P. Saunders, August 6, 1972.

[62] Cleveland *Gazette*, April 19, June 19, July 26, 1930, November 14, 1931, January 23, November 12, 1932, November 11, 18, 25, 1933, January 6, 1934; Maurice Maschke, "The Memoirs of Maurice Maschke," Cleveland *Plain Dealer*, September 5, 1934; Russell H. Davis, "The Negro in Cleveland Politics," Cleveland *Call and Post*, October 29, 1966. For a detailed discussion of black politics in Cleveland during the 1929–45 period, see Christopher G. Wye, "Midwest Ghetto: Patterns of Negro Life and Thought in Cleveland, Ohio, 1929–45" (Ph.D. dissertation, Kent State University, 1973), ch. 8.

VII

The triumph of the New Negroes did not, of course, culminate in the destruction of racial inequality in Cleveland, nor did it lead to an appreciable diminution of the slum conditions which continued to mar the quality of black life in the city and which would lead to increasing discontent in the years ahead. These aspects of what Gunnar Myrdal called "an American dilemma" were far beyond the capability of a few black councilmen—however strategically powerful—to solve. In fact it was becoming more and more apparent that these problems were beyond the ability of local government in general to solve, and the next generation of concerned citizens would look increasingly to the federal government and national protest organizations as a means of altering the racial status quo.

Nevertheless, a watershed had been reached; the first years of the Depression marked the conclusion of an important phase in the history of black Cleveland. The consolidation of the ghetto as a physical entity was complete. A process at least fifty years in the making had finally run its course, and in innumerable ways the average black citizen was more isolated from the general life of the urban community than he had ever been since the founding of the city. Yet it was this very isolation, and the sense of unique goals and needs that it fostered, that helped unify the black community and provided the practical basis for the future struggle against racism in all its manifestations. During the next half-century, the black ghetto would undergo many changes—but this paradox would endure.

A Note on the Analysis
of Occupational Data

With few exceptions, historians have generally failed to follow the
early lead of sociologists such as W. E. B. Du Bois and St. Clair Drake, who
urged the systematic study of black occupational structure. The position of
blacks in the economy has usually been studied in isolation, without relating
or comparing Afro-Americans with other groups. Scholars have also too readily
accepted the Census Bureau's classification of jobs. One traditional Census
Bureau category, "manufacturing," is too broad for all but the most general
purposes, while two other, "trade" and "transportation," are utterly useless
because they include everything from the most menial laborers to the highest
paid managers of large industrial firms. Finally, although some historians
have noted the changes in black occupational structure produced by such
dramatic events as the "Great Migration" of 1916–19, there has been little
attempt to systematically trace changes over a more prolonged period of time.[1]

[1] W. E. B. Du Bois, *The Philadelphia Negro* (Philadelphia, 1899), 97–146, and
St. Clair Drake and Horace R. Cayton, *Black Metropolis: A Study of Negro Life in
a Northern City* (New York, 1945), 214–62, both survey black occupations in great
detail. Since these studies of black urban life were chiefly sociological rather than
historical in nature, however, neither concerned itself much with the changes that
occurred in black occupations over the long run. The same can also be said for
other early ghetto studies, such as Mary White Ovington's *Half a Man: The Status
of the Negro in New York* (New York, 1911), John Daniels's *In Freedom's Birthplace: A Study of the Boston Negroes* (Boston, 1914), and William A. Crossland's
Industrial Conditions among Negroes in St. Louis (St. Louis, Mo., 1914). In *Harlem:
The Making of a Ghetto* (New York, 1966), Gilbert Osofsky mentions the depressed
state of black occupations in New York City in 1890, but he fails to follow this up
by discussing any changes in this pattern that may have occurred during the following forty years. Allan Spear's *Black Chicago: The Making of a Negro Ghetto, 1890–*

In this book I have attempted to rectify these deficiencies by systematically surveying male and female occupations in Cleveland's black community over a sixty-year period; by comparing blacks with immigrants and native whites (and, in some instances, comparing conditions in Cleveland with other cities); and by utilizing a more functional occupational classification system than that used by the Census Bureau.

The classification system used throughout this book is based upon that developed by Alba M. Edwards.[2] In 1937 Edwards compiled an *Alphabetical Index of Occupations by Industries and Social-Economic Groups* that exhaustively categorized every occupation tabulated by the Census under nine subheads ranked from 0 (the highest category) to 8 (the lowest):

0. Professional persons
1. Farmers (owners and tenants)
2. Proprietors, managers, and officials (except farmers)
3. Clerks and kindred workers
4. Skilled workers and foremen
5. Semiskilled workers
6. Farm laborers
7. Other laborers
8. Servant classes

In adapting it to the present purposes, I have made several modifications in Edwards's classification system. While retaining his general rank order of occupations, I have combined several of the categories. Since after 1870 there were fewer and fewer farm owners, tenants, or farm laborers in Cleveland, categories 1 and 6 were eliminated as separate groupings. Categories 1 and 2 were combined, as were 6 and 7. The result is the following ranking of

---

1920 (Chicago, 1967), represents a considerable methodological advance over Osofsky's treatment of the job structure. Spear systematically (rather than impressionistically) analyzes both male and female occupations during the first two decades of the twentieth century. Unfortunately, however, his discussion is rendered less valuable by his use of the Census Bureau's unwieldy classification system; and, unlike Drake and Cayton, Spear does not compare the job status of blacks with that of the foreign-born or native white populations of Chicago.

Although it is not primarily a study in black history, a recent outstanding exception to the lack of historically oriented studies of black occupations is Stephan Thernstrom, *The Other Bostonians: Poverty and Progress in the American Metropolis, 1880–1970* (Cambridge, 1973), 176–219. Thernstrom surveys black occupations in greater detail and over a longer period of time (ninety years) than any other scholar. I would question, however, his conclusion that there "was virtually no improvement in the occupational position of black men in Boston between the late nineteenth century and the beginning of World War II." By skipping from 1900 to 1940 in his analysis of occupational data, Thernstrom may have inadvertently overlooked a significant—if temporary—upward trend in black occupations during the 1916–30 period.

[2] Alba M. Edwards, *An Alphabetical Index of Occupations by Industries and Social-Economic Groups* (Washington, 1937), 5–7 and *passim*.

occupations, as used in this book (with some changes in the titles of categories):

Occupational category	Rank	Edwards's rank
Professionals	1	0
Proprietors, managers, and officials	2	1, 2
Clerical workers	3	3
Skilled workers	4	4
Semiskilled workers	5	5
Unskilled workers	6	6, 7
Personal and domestic servants	7	8

In a handful of cases I have placed a given ocupation in a category different from that adopted by Edwards. It seemed more appropriate, for example, to categorize newsboys as unskilled laborers than (as Edwards does) as clerical workers. I do not think that the mere fact that newsboys handle newsprint in the course of their work justifies their being grouped under the clerical category! Likewise, apprentices to skilled trades are listed as skilled workers rather than semiskilled workers. Apprentices do not, of course, earn the same pay as journeyman artisans; but they should still be ranked, I believe, with the occupational grouping that they will enter upon the completion of their training. Other deviations from Edwards's ranking system include boarding and lodging house keepers (listed as proprietors rather than semiskilled workers), bakers (skilled workers rather than semiskilled workers), whitewashers (semiskilled rather than unskilled), chauffeurs (personal service rather than semiskilled), deliverymen (unskilled instead of semiskilled workers), messenger, office, and bundle boys (personal service instead of clerical workers), and barbers, hairdressers, and manicurists (skilled instead of semiskilled). This last category may seem somewhat arbitrary, but it is defensible, I think, when one considers that prior to about 1910 the barbering trade offered one of the more visible routes of upward mobility in the black community. A number of black barbers owned their own shops, many gained prestige from their association with wealthy whites, and a few became—by the standards of the black community—well-to-do. In 1903 one Negro barber in Cleveland was even elected to the state legislature. After 1910 the prestige of barbering began to fall off rapidly as black barbers turned more and more to the less lucrative Negro trade of the ghetto. Still, quite a few of these individuals actually ran their own shops and might more properly be considered proprietors than either semiskilled or skilled workers. But since it is necessary, in this analysis, to lump all barbers together in one category, I have chosen the middle course and listed them as skilled tradesmen.

The following list of occupations by socioeconomic category is selective and includes only the most common job designations; for the categorization of all other jobs, the reader should consult Edwards's *Alphabetical Index of Occupations*.

Professionals
clergymen
dentists
lawyers
musicians and teachers of music

nurses (trained)
physicians and surgeons
teachers

Proprietors, managers, and officials
building contractors
garage keepers and managers
merchants and peddlers
retail dealers
undertakers

boarding- and lodging-house keepers
hotel keepers and managers
restaurant, cafe, and lunchroom
    keepers
saloon keepers

Clerical workers
clerks (including clerks in stores)
commercial travelers
insurance agents and officials
real estate agents and officials

salesmen
agents
bookkeepers, cashiers, and accountants
stenographers and typists

Skilled workers
apprentices to trades (before
    1910, all apprentices)
bakers
butchers
blacksmiths
brick and stone masons
carpenters
stationary engineers
foremen and overseers
machinists
milliners
molders

painters, glaziers, and varnishers
    (except those in factories)[a]
plasterers
plumbers
shoemakers and cobblers
tailors
tinsmiths
wheelwrights
locomotive engineers and firemen
barbers, hairdressers, and manicurists
policemen

Semiskilled workers
semiskilled operatives (all)
bartenders
laundry operatives
brakemen
undifferentiated iron and
    steel workers (as listed in 1870
    and 1890 censuses)

housekeepers
whitewashers
dressmakers and seamstresses
nurses and midwives (as listed
    in 1870 and 1890 censuses)
saw mill employees

[a] In the 1870 and 1890 censuses, the undifferentiated category "painters, glaziers, and varnishers" is counted as skilled work.

Unskilled workers

laborers (all, except those listed
   under domestic and personal
   service)
longshoremen and stevedores
porters in stores

newsboys
messengers, packers, and
   porters (as listed in 1890 census)
draymen and hackmen

Personal and domestic servants

chauffeurs
livery-stable keepers and
   hostlers (as listed in 1870 and
   1890 censuses)
charwomen
elevator tenders
janitors and sextons
laborers (domestic and
   personal service only)

launderers and laundresses
   (except those in laundries)
porters (except those in stores)
servants
messenger, office, and bundle boys
waiters

In a few instances, in compiling occupational data from the 1870 and 1890 censuses, it was necessary to omit certain job categories altogether. The following occupations were either too vague or too general to be of use:

1870 census
officials and employees of government
billiard- and bowling-saloon keepers and employees
hotel or restaurant keepers and employees
officials and employees of express companies
officials and employees of railroad companies
officials and employees of street-railroad companies
officials and employees of telegraph companies
1890 census
steam railroad employees
street railroad employees

The occupational index. By means of a proportionate weighting of the percentages of a given segment of the work force (blacks, native whites, etc.) employed in different occupational categories, it is possible to calculate a single number, the occupational index, which measures the average occupational standing of a group in a particular year. In this study the occupational index is used to compare the relative position of blacks in the economy at any given point and to trace changes in black occupational structure and status over a period of decades. It must be emphasized that the occupational index measures the mean occupational status of the *entire group* (blacks, for example) in a given year and that changes in the index over a period of time indicate alterations in this mean. The occupational index, traced over time, is not a measure of *individual* mobility. It does not tell us what *proportion* of blacks in the community at any given point were advancing or declining occupationally or whether intergenerational mobility was high or low. On the other hand, it should be pointed out that the use of the occupational index is superior to that of the study of individual mobility in one respect. The index measures the mean occupational standing of *all* members of a group living in a city at a given time. Individual mobility studies record changes in occupational rank only for that minority that remain in a city for ten years or more. Thus while the index is limited in some ways, it is still a useful research tool, when supplemented by a detailed study of changes in specific occupations.

The procedure for calculating the occupational index is simple and straightforward. The first step is to compute the percentages of the total occupations of a given group that fall into the different occupational categories, ranked from 1 (professional workers) to 7 (domestic and personal servants). Next, multiply each percentage by the rank that it is categorized under, and add these products together. The index is then obtained by dividing this sum by the sum of the percentages of the seven categories and multiplying the entire result by 100. Or, to state this in mathematical terms:

The occupational index $= 100 \times \dfrac{1a + 2b + 3c + 4d + 5e + 6f + 7g}{a + b + c + d + e + f + g}$,

where $a =$ the percentage of the group in the professions,

$\qquad b =$ the percentage ranked as proprietors, managers, and officials,

$\qquad c =$ the percentage in clerical work, etc.

Theoretically, the occupational index used in this book can range from 100 (a hypothetical case in which all members of a group are professional workers) to 700 (a case where all workers are personal or domestic servants). In actuality, the occupational index almost always falls between 300 and 600.

Supplementary Tables

TABLE 21. *Area of birth of Ohio Negroes, 1900 and 1910*

Area of birth	1900		1910	
	Number	Percentage	Number	Percentage
Ohio	56,232	58.4	59,194	53.6
Middle West outside Ohio	2,218	2.3	2,714	2.8
Northeast	1,996	2.1	2,834	2.5
Upper South and Border	32,190	33.6	40,227	36.4
Lower South	3,026	3.1	4,565	4.1
West	50	0.1	114	0.1
Not specified or born abroad	764	0.8	1,149	1.0
Total	96,476	100.0	110,797	100.0

SOURCE: U.S. Bureau of the Census, *Negro Population in the United States, 1790–1915* (Washington, 1918), 75–79; U.S. *Twelfth Census, 1900* (Washington, 1902), I, pt. I, 702–5.

NOTE: *Middle West:* Michigan, Ohio, Indiana, Illinois, Iowa, Kansas, Wisconsin, Minnesota, Nebraska, North and South Dakota; *Northeast:* New England states, Pennsylvania, New York, New Jersey; *Upper South and Border:* Virginia, Kentucky, Tennessee, North Carolina, Maryland, West Virginia, District of Columbia, Missouri, Oklahoma, Delaware; *Lower South:* Georgia, South Carolina, Alabama, Mississippi, Louisiana, Texas, Florida, Arkansas; *West:* all other states.

TABLE 22. *Area of birth of Cleveland Negroes, 1910 and 1920*

Area of birth	1910		1920		Increase		
	Number	Percentage	Number	Percentage	Number	Percentage of Total	Percentage increase 1910–20
Born in Ohio	3,125	35.7	5,740	16.9	2,615	10.0	84.2
Born in other states	4,890	57.8	27,950	80.3	23,060	88.1	472.0
Foreign born	295	3.5	414	1.2	119	0.4	40.6
Others[a]	254	3.0	655	1.9	401	1.5	158.0
Total	8,564	100.0	34,759	100.0	26,195	100.0	307.0

SOURCE: U.S. Bureau of the Census, *Negro Population in the United States, 1790–1915* (Washington, 1918), 32.
[a] Includes those of undetermined nativity and those born in U.S. territories and possessions.

TABLE 23. *Increase in white and Negro populations in selected northern cities, 1910–20*

City	Negro population 1910	Negro population 1920	Negro increase, 1910–20 Number	Negro increase, 1910–20 Percentage	percentage increase in white population 1910–20
Detroit	5,741	40,838	35,097	611.3	107.0
CLEVELAND	8,448	34,451	26,003	307.8	38.1
Chicago	44,103	109,458	65,355	148.2	21.0
New York	91,709	152,467	60,758	66.3	16.9
Philadelphia	84,459	134,229	49,770	58.9	15.4
St. Louis	43,960	69,854	25,894	58.9	9.4
Cincinnati	19,639	30,079	10,440	53.2	7.9
Pittsburgh	25,623	37,725	12,102	47.2	8.3

SOURCE: U.S. Bureau of the Census, *Negroes in the United States, 1920–1932* (Washington, 1935), 55 (Table 10).

TABLE 24. *Area of birth of Ohio Negroes, 1910–20*

Area of birth	1920 Number	1920 Percentage	Increase, 1910–20 Number	Increase, 1910–20 Percentage of total
Ohio	66,836	36.3	7,642	10.6
Middle West outside Ohio	5,489	3.0	1,775	2.5
Northeast	4,843	2.7	2,009	2.8
Upper South and Border	62,674	34.0	22,447	31.2
Lower South	42,621	23.1	37,609	52.3
West	362	0.2	248	0.3
Not specified or born abroad	1,347	0.7	198	0.3
Total	184,172	100.0	71,928	100.0

SOURCE: U.S. *Fourteenth Census, 1920* (Washington, 1922), I, 637–41; U.S. Bureau of the Census, *Negro Population in the United States, 1790–1915*, 75–79.
NOTE: *Middle West:* Michigan, Ohio, Indiana, Illinois, Iowa, Kansas, Wisconsin, Minnesota, Nebraska, North and South Dakota; *Northeast:* New England states, Pennsylvania, New York, New Jersey; *Upper South and Border:* Virginia, Kentucky, Tennessee, North Carolina, Maryland, West Virginia, District of Columbia, Missouri, Oklahoma, Delaware; *Lower South:* Georgia, South Carolina, Alabama, Mississippi, Louisiana, Texas, Florida, Arkansas; *West:* all other states.

TABLE 25. *Census tracts with highest Negro percentages, Cleveland, 1910–30*

Census tract	Percentage Negro		
	1910	1920	1930
I-3	24.4	62.6	67.4
I-2	19.7	32.7	36.6
H-7	19.6	45.7	54.9
H-9	14.7	50.8	88.8
G-9	13.8a	18.5	17.4
G-1b	8.5	16.3	4.4
I-1b	8.4	5.4	0.7
J-1	6.2	25.4	63.3
I-6	5.9	42.0	53.0
L-6	5.6	6.8	8.9
G-7	5.1	3.8	0.7
I-5	3.1	26.0	25.5
H-8	3.1	28.5	52.4
J-2	2.8	32.5	48.7
M-6	2.8	20.8	81.1
M-2	2.8	2.3a	13.7
M-7	2.2	8.7	90.6
M-9	1.8	4.2	32.7
M-3	1.8	7.9	81.0
I-4	1.6	20.7	28.7
L-9	1.5	9.5	70.9
M-5	1.3	10.1	70.0
R-5	1.1a	5.0	4.0
M-4	0.9	6.4	76.1
I-8	0.8	20.9	75.7
M-8	0.4	7.1	78.3
I-7	0.4	38.5	75.5
J-3	0.4	11.7	49.1
N-7	0.4	3.3	30.6
N-1	0.4	3.5	25.4
G-4	0.3	6.4	16.4
S-2	—c	17.2	19.6
S-8	—d	12.4	13.8
U-1	—c	3.4	1.5

SOURCE: Howard W. Green, *Population Characteristics by Census Tracts* (Cleveland, 1931), 216–18, 231–32.

a Estimated; tract combined with one other tract for the year indicated.

b Denotes tract whose population declined drastically during the twenties due to industrialization.

c Accurate estimate impossible; tract combined with two or more other tracts for year indicated.

d The tract was not used by the Census Bureau for the year indicated.

TABLE 26. *Index of relative concentration of Negro males in selected occupations, Cleveland, 1870–1930*

Occupation	1870	1890	1910	1920	1930
Professionals					
Physicians and surgeons	0	82	50	56	53
Lawyers	0	33	74	19	38
Teachers	60	—	—	22	15
Clergymen	50	—	—	235	210
Musicians and music teachers	—	—	286	74	155
Proprietors, managers, and officials					
Building contractors	—	—	108	52	37
Manufacturers and officials	—	24	8	—	—
Retail dealers	19	9	18	20	29
Restaurant, lunchroom, and café keepers	—	32	—	95	81
Clerical workers					
Clerks in stores	—	—	20	49	28
Clerks (not in stores)	—	28	54	31	30
Salesmen	—	11	10	5	13
Insurance agents	0	—	6	15	52
Skilled workers					
Bakers	36	0	12	45	18
Blacksmiths	71	21	26	41	25
Brick and stone masons	78	153	133	84	58
Carpenters	81	48	45	42	41
Foremen and overseers	—	—	29	26	12
Compositors, linotypers, and typesetters	—	—	5	27	10
Machinists	—	19	18	23	15
Painters, glaziers, etc. (not in factory)	129[a]	45[a]	44	38	59
Plumbers	0	11	16	15	24
Shoemakers	74	9	16	18	55
Tailors	11	8	27	36	48
Pattern and mold makers	—	—	15	3	1
Barbers, hairdressers, and manicurists	1,620	1,010	463	180	139
Policemen	—	51	51	31	10
Semiskilled workers					
Semiskilled operatives in foundries and rolling mills	—	4[b]	33	105	65
Painters, glaziers, etc. (in factories)	—	—	7	43	46

Occupation	1870	1890	1910	1920	1930
Unskilled workers					
Longshoremen and stevedores	—	25	15	—	—
Porters in stores	—	514c	770d	480	392
Draymen, hackmen, and teamsters (all)	94	156	373	194	169
Domestic and personal service					
Chauffeurs	—	—	886	320	186e
Porters (except in stores)	—	—	2,900	1,380	1,000
Servants	260	2,120	1,320	432	317
Messenger, bundle, and office boys	—	—	120	79	93
Waiters	—	—	1,930	420	416

SOURCE: Thomas Goliber, "Cuyahoga Blacks: A Social and Demographic Study, 1850–1880" (M.A. thesis, Kent State University, 1972), 67–90 (data for black occupations in 1870); U.S. Census Bureau reports, 1870–1930.

NOTE: An index of 100 indicates that the proportion of blacks in an occupation was the same as the proportion of all males in the city in that occupation. Indexes below 100 indicate black underrepresentation in an occupation; indexes over 100 signify overrepresentation.

a Includes all painters and glaziers, whether in factories or not.
b Undifferentiated iron and steel workers.
c Messengers, packers, and porters.
d Laborers, porters, and helpers in stores.
e Includes truck and tractor drivers.

TABLE 27. *Index of relative concentration of Negro females in selected occupations, Cleveland, 1870–1930*

Occupation	1870	1890	1910	1920	1930
Professionals					
Teachers (all categories)	25	38	38	27	18
Nurses (trained)	—	—	23	14	8
Proprietors					
Boarding- and lodging-house keepers	244	305	152	173	129
Clerical workers					
Clerks in stores (including saleswomen)	—	13	9	20	11
Clerks (not in stores)	—	8	12	11	8
Stenographers and typists	—	0	3	2	5
Skilled workers					
Milliners	—	—	17	9	—
Semiskilled workers					
Housekeepers	—	85	112	105	132
Textile operatives (all)	—	0	—	31	13
Laundry operatives	—	0	13	510	416
Dressmakers and seamstresses (not in factory)	97	64	135	150	197
Unskilled workers					
All unskilled laborers	—	71	—	194	100
Domestic and personal service					
Charwomen	—	—	342	144	99
Laundresses (not in laundries)	781	605	503	643	514
Servants	65	141	300	432	421

SOURCE: Goliber, "Cuyahoga Blacks," 67–69; U.S. Census Bureau reports, 1870–1930.

TABLE 28. *Home ownership by racial and ethnic group, Cleveland, 1890*

	Total number of families	Percentage of families owning homes
Negroes (total)	690	14.8
Mulattoes only	329	17.9
Native whites (total)	17,938	30.3
English and Welsh immigrants	4,293	36.2
German immigrants	15,126	50.6
Irish immigrants	5,014	41.6
Italian immigrants	152	8.5
Norwegian, Swedish, and Danish immigrants	224	24.5
All Others	9,181	39.4
Total	52,947	39.1

SOURCE: U.S. Bureau of the Census, *Report on Farms and Homes: Proprietorship and Indebtedness* (Washington, 1896), 582, 598, 605.

NOTE: The category "Negroes (total)" includes mulattoes. The category "Native whites (total)" includes native whites of native parentage and native whites of foreign or mixed parentage.

Bibliographical Essay

Most of the chapters in this volume contain footnotes that are bibliographical in nature, and some of these footnotes include commentary on the references cited. It would be superfluous, then, to once again list every source in a formal bibliography. The sources which follow are those which bear directly upon the history of black Cleveland. For more complete citations and references to black communities in cities other than Cleveland, the reader should consult the extensive documentation in the text itself.

Unpublished-manuscript collections

Cleveland is virtually unique in having a large number of collections of manuscripts by blacks. Most of these are part of the black history collection at the Western Reserve Historical Society in Cleveland. Unpublished manuscripts used in this study include: the Walter L. Brown Papers, the Charles Waddell Chesnutt Papers, the Lethia C. Fleming Papers, the Charles Herbert Garvin Papers, the John Patterson Green Papers, the Phillis Wheatley Association Papers, the Cleveland Urban League Papers, the Walter B. Wright Scrapbooks, the Chester K. Gillespie Papers, and Thomas Fleming's 1932 autobiography, "My Rise and Persecution" (all at the Western Reserve Historical Society); the Charles Waddell Chesnutt Papers at Fisk University; the George A. Myers Papers at the Ohio Historical Society (Columbus, Ohio); and the Papers of the National Association for the Advancement of Colored People, Manuscript Division, Library of Congress. A small portion of "The Peoples of Cleveland," an unpublished Works Projects Administration study written in 1942 (copy in the Cleveland Public Library) also deals with black Cleveland.

Of these manuscript collections, the most valuable are the Green Papers, the Myers Papers, and the Papers of the National Association for the Advancement of Colored People. The Myers collection, in particular, is very large and contains correspondence not only with black leaders in Cleveland and other cities in Ohio but with influential Negroes in many other parts of the country as well. Most of the material in the NAACP Papers relating to Cleveland is in

the branch files (Containers G157 and G158), but there is some correspondence of value in Containers C65, C74, and C403. The Chesnutt Papers at
Fisk are also very useful, although many of the most important letters in this
collection are reprinted in Helen M. Chesnutt, *Charles Waddell Chesnutt:
Pioneer of the Color Line* (Chapel Hill, 1952). There is some interesting material relating to blacks in the medical profession in the Garvin Papers.

Cleveland before 1870

Sources on the early history of black Cleveland are not as plentiful as for
later periods. The *Annals of Cleveland* (Cleveland, 1937–38), a digest of the
city's early newspapers, contains occasional references to blacks and much
information on the slavery controversy. The Cleveland *Leader*, the city's
leading newspaper during the second half of the nineteenth century, is the
best general source of information on black activities and white racial attitudes. For a discussion of the Black Laws in Ohio, see Helen M. Thurston,
"The 1802 Constitutional Convention and [the] status of the Negro," *Ohio
History*, 81 (Winter–Spring 1972); Frank U. Quillin, *The Color Line in Ohio*
(Ann Arbor, 1913); and Charles T. Hickok, *The Negro in Ohio, 1802–1870*
(Cleveland, 1896). Franklin Johnson, *The Development of State Legislation
Concerning the Free Negro* (New York, 1918) contains a useful chronologi-
cal listing of legislation passed by Ohio and other states. The growth of aboli-
tionism and sympathy for the Negro in the Western Reserve is traced in A. G.
Riddle, "Rise of the Anti-Slavery Sentiment on the Western Reserve," *Maga-
zine of Western History*, 6 (1887); Karl Geiser, "The Western Reserve in the
Anti-Slavery Movement, 1840–1860," Mississippi Valley Historical Society
Proceedings, 5 (1911–12); and William C. Cochran, *The Western Reserve
and the Fugitive Slave Law* (Cleveland, 1920).

*North Into Freedom: The Autobiography of John Malvin, Free Negro,
1795–1880* (Cleveland, 1966), a reprint of the 1879 edition, edited by Allan
Peskin, is the only important first-person narrative written by a Cleveland
Negro in the nineteenth century. Though somewhat sketchy at points, it provides valuable information on the early years of the black community, and
Peskin's introduction and notes are useful in explicating the text and placing
Malvin's life in the proper context. There is additional information on
nineteenth-century black leaders in Harry E. Davis, "Early Colored Residents
of Cleveland," *Phylon*, 4 (July 1943), and in Russell H. Davis, *Memorable
Negroes in Cleveland's Past* (Cleveland, 1969), a volume of brief sketches of
prominent Cleveland Negroes. The early years of black politics in Cleveland
are discussed in Russell H. Davis, "The Negro in Cleveland Politics: Negro
Political Life Begins," Cleveland *Call and Post*, September 11, 1966. A valuable source on the residential patterns, occupations, and family structure of
Cleveland's early black community is Thomas J. Goliber's "'Cuyahoga Blacks:
A Social and Demographic Study, 1850–1880" (M.A. thesis, Kent State Uni-

versity, 1972), a study based chiefly on an analysis of manuscript census data. Unfortunately, there is no adequate general history of Cleveland that would help put black Cleveland in historical context. James H. Kennedy's *History of the City of Cleveland* (Cleveland, 1896) is a fair survey of the city's early years, but it contains only a few brief references to the Afro-American population. Slightly more useful, but still quite inadequate, is William Ganson Rose's *Cleveland: The Making of a City* (Cleveland, 1950), a volume that is more a collection of facts than a history.

The black community in transition, 1870–1915

In the late nineteenth and early twentieth centuries, Cleveland's white newspapers, the *Leader* and the *Plain Dealer*, began to take less interest in the city's black community and hence are of decreasing value as sources of information on blacks. Invaluable for an understanding of black Cleveland during these years are the city's black newspapers, the *Gazette*, the *Journal* (1903–12), and the *Advocate* (1914–22). The *Gazette*, which began publication in 1883 and did not cease until the death of its editor, Harry C. Smith, in 1941, is an excellent source, not only on black Cleveland but on the black communities of other Ohio cities as well. Because of Smith's militancy, the *Gazette* is usually the best source of information on civil rights activities and discrimination. The *Journal* and the *Advocate* were more more conservative in their approach to race problems and less prone to print news about black protest. All three newspapers contain a wealth of data on the social and cultural life of the city's Afro-American population.

Quillin, in *The Color Line in Ohio*, underestimated the degree of racial prejudice in Cleveland in 1913, although he was correct in stating that race relations were more harmonious in the Forest City than in most Ohio metropolises. An excellent corrective to Quillin is David Gerber's "Ohio and the Color Line: Racial Discrimination and Negro Responses in a Northern State, 1860–1915" (Ph.D. dissertation, Princeton University, 1971), which surveys discrimination, school segregation, racial violence, and several other variables of racial prejudice in a spectrum of Ohio cities.

There is probably more primary source material for the study of black leadership in Cleveland during the late nineteenth and early twentieth century than for any other city. The most valuable printed works include John P. Green, *Fact Stranger than Fiction: Seventy-Five Years of a Busy Life with Reminiscences of Many Great and Good Men* (Cleveland, 1920); Chesnutt, *Charles Waddell Chesnutt*; John Garraty, ed., *The Barber and the Historian: The Correspondence of George A. Myers and James Ford Rhodes, 1910–1923* (Columbus, 1956); and Jane Edna Hunter, *A Nickel and a Prayer* (Cleveland, 1940), which tells the story of the early years of the Phillis Wheatley Association from the point of view of the organization's founder. Useful on the relationship of George A. Myers with Mark Hanna is Henry E.

Siebert's "George A. Myers: Ohio Negro Leader and Political Ally of Marcus A. Hanna" (Senior Thesis, Princeton University, 1963). Cleveland's first black councilman, Thomas W. Fleming, tells the story of his political career in "My Rise and Persecution" (manuscript [1932], Western Reserve Historical Society). For brief sketches of lesser known black leaders, such publications as William J. Simmons, *Men of Mark* (Cleveland, 1887); Clement Richardson et al., eds., *The National Cyclopedia of the Colored Race* (Montgomery, Ala., 1919); and the various editions of *Who's Who in Colored America* (first published in 1927) proved useful, as did Davis's *Memorable Negroes in Cleveland's Past*. A scholarly article dealing with Cleveland's black leaders is Larry Cuban, "A Strategy for Racial Peace: Negro Leadership in Cleveland, 1900–1919," *Phylon*, 28 (Fall 1963). In overstressing the conservatism of Cleveland's black leaders during this period, Cuban carries a good point too far. Most of Cleveland's influential blacks were not militant, but they were not as uniformly accommodationist as Cuban implies.

The Great Migration and after, 1915–30

Cleveland's black weeklies, the *Gazette* and (prior to 1922) the *Advocate*, contain extensive information on all aspects of the black response to the Great Migration; and there are some clippings from the *Call*, the *Herald*, and the *Call and Post* in the Chester Gillespie Papers and the George Myers Papers. Langston Hughes's *The Big Sea* (New York, 1940) contains a discussion of increasing white hostility during World War I, and the Cleveland Chamber of Commerce's *Investigation of Housing Conditions of War Workers in Cleveland* (Cleveland, 1918) gives information on the housing and wages of black workers. John B. Abell, "The Negro in Industry," *Trade Winds*, March, 1924, surveys black workers in a dozen Cleveland firms.

For surveys of some of the more deleterious effects of the migration, see H. L. Rockwood, "Effect of Negro Migration on Community Health in Cleveland," National Council of Social Work, *Proceedings, 1926* (Boston, 1926), and two studies by Howard W. Green: *An Analysis of Girls Committed to the Girls' Industrial School by the Juvenile Court at Cleveland during a Six Year Period, 1920–25* Cleveland, 1929), and *An Analysis of Illegitimate Births in the City of Cleveland for 1926* (Cleveland, 1928). Also useful is Gordon Simpson, comp., *Economic Survey of Housing in Districts of the City of Cleveland Occupied Largely by Colored People* (Cleveland [1931]). Green, who served as director of the census in Cleveland for a number of years, also compiled several volumes of population data that are indispensable for the study of the growth and distribution of the black population of Cleveland during the 1910–30 period. They include *A Study of the Movement of the Negro Population of Cleveland* (Cleveland, 1924); *Natural Increase and Migration* (Cleveland, 1938); *Nine Years of Relief in Cleveland, 1928–1937* (Cleveland, 1937); *Population Characteristics by Census Tracts, Cleveland,*

Ohio, 1930 (Cleveland, 1931), which contains data from 1910 and 1920 as well; and *Population by Census Tracts, Cleveland and Vicinity, with Street Index* (Cleveland, 1931).

On the growth of the black church in Cleveland after 1915, data from the Cleveland *Gazette* should be supplemented by the scattered references in the Cleveland Foundation's *Cleveland Year Book, 1921* (Cleveland, 1921); George F. Bragg, *History of the Afro-American Group of the Episcopal Church* (Baltimore, 1922); John T. Gillard, *The Catholic Church and the American Negro* (Baltimore, 1929); and the *Antioch Missionary Baptist Church Golden Jubilee, 1893–1943* (n.p.[1943?]), which describes the growth of Cleveland's largest black congregation. A critical history of the development of Karamu House is badly needed. John Selby's *Beyond Civil Rights* (Cleveland, 1966) focuses too much on the lives of the founders of Karamu, Russell and Rowena Jelliffe, and not enough on the institution itself. There is some information on Karamu in Arna Bontemps and Jack Conroy, *Anyplace But Here* (New York, 1966). The histories of the Cleveland Urban League and the Phillis Wheatley Association are best approached through the unpublished minutes of the board of directors of those organizations, held at the Western Reserve Historical Society. There are ample materials on the early years of the Cleveland branch of the National Association for the Advancement of Colored People (including rare copies of the *Annual Reports* and the *Branch Bulletin*) in the NAACP Archives at the Library of Congress.

The best general sources on segregation and discrimination in Cleveland during the postwar period are the Cleveland *Gazette* and the branch files of the NAACP Papers. On hospital segregation and the attempt to build a separate black medical facility, see the Mercy Hospital Association of Cleveland pamphlet, *Does Cleveland Need a Negro-Manned Hospital?* (Cleveland [1927]), and Charles Garvin, "Pioneering in Cleveland," *The Woman's Voice*, 1 (September 1939). The successful conclusion of the drive to integrate City Hospital is discussed in Thomas F. Campbell, *Daniel E. Morgan, 1877–1949* (Cleveland, 1966). On the decline of equality in the Cleveland public schools, see Alonzo G. Grace, "The Effect of Negro Migration on the Cleveland Public School System" (Ph.D. dissertation, Western Reserve University, 1932), and Willard C. Richan, *Racial Isolation in the Cleveland Public Schools* (Cleveland, 1967). For an excellent, overall survey of racism in Cleveland on the eve of the Depression, see Charles W. Chesnutt, "The Negro in Cleveland," *The Clevelander*, 5 (November 1930).

William Giffin's valuable article, "Black Insurgency in the Republican Party of Ohio, 1920–1932," *Ohio History*, 82 (Winter–Spring, 1973) contains information on Cleveland as well as several other cities. While not dealing specifically with the period surveyed in this volume, Christopher G. Wye's "The New Deal and the Negro Community: Toward a Broader Conceptualization," *Journal of American History*, 59 (December 1972) and Wye's dissertation, "Midwest Ghetto: Patterns of Negro Life and Thought in Cleveland, Ohio, 1929–1945" (Kent State University, 1973), proved most useful in understanding the historical development of Cleveland's black community. A recent publication which deals extensively with the institutions and personalities, both prominent and obscure, of black Cleveland is Russell H. Davis, *Black Americans in Cleveland* (Washington, D.C., 1972). The first half of this volume contains much useful information on the period prior to 1930.

Index

Abolitionism: in Cleveland, 3–4, 5–7; in southern Ohio, 5; and egalitarianism, 7–9, 16; black, 25, 27, 28

Adams, Cyrus F., 119

Advocate (Cleveland): 100, 107, 176, 191; on black teachers, 62; on integrated colleges, 64; on Africa, 107–8; on streetcorner men, 111–12; on black migration, 159–60; on rent profiteering, 166; founded, 194; ideology of, 269–70

Africa: emigration to, 29; stereotypes of, 108n; interest in after 1915, 215, 216, 217–18, 228–32

African Methodist Episcopal churches, 94–95, 104

Afro-American League, 121, 132

Age distribution of ethnic and racial groups, 39

Ailer, Charles C., 208

Aliened American (Cleveland), 27, 29

Alpha Kappa Alpha sorority, 106

Amalgamated Association of Iron and Steel Workers, 197

American Federation of Labor, 69; and black workers, 67–68, 196–97

Anti-Mob Violence Act (Ohio), 132

Antioch Baptist Church: growth of, 94–95, 207; welfare work, 95–96, 253

Anti-Semitism, 170n

Attucks Republican Club, 145, 247

Bagnall, Robert W., 187, 243, 259, 260, 262, 268

Bailey, E. A., 168, 264

Bailey, Horace C., 95, 261

Baker, Newton D., 49, 123, 128, 135, 238, 246

Baker, Ray Stannard, 54, 114; as source on black communities, 55–56n

Baldwin Wallace College, 249

Baltimore, Md., blacks: occupations in 1870, 23

Baptist churches: growth of, 95, 207–8; welfare work of, 95–96, 253; and class structure, 96, 104

Barbering trade, blacks in: 18, 26; decline of, 75–76, 237; as elite occupation, 98, 123, 145, 147

Berthoff, Rowland, 96

Binga, Jesse, 84

Birmingham, Ala., 172

Birth of a Nation, The (film), 128, 176, 261

Black Laws: passed, 4–5; partially repealed, 7; opposed by Clevelanders, 7–8; blacks protest, 26, 28; last repealed, 121

Black Metropolis (Drake and Cayton), 91n, 146

Blossom, Dudley, 238

Blue, Welcome T., 83, 141, 192

Boston, Mass., blacks: family structure of, 11; occupations of, 23–24, 75n, 76, 77n; and race relations, 55; integration of, 62n, 93n; class structure of, 91, 105n; old elite of, 114, 136–37n; residential patterns of, 172; oppose use of "Negro," 241

Boyd, Albert D., 104; and alliance with

Introduction

I once spent an entire day looking for pomegranate concentrate. While this was somewhat enjoyable for one who loves food, grocery stores, and cooking, it was also frustrating. And eye opening. For part of what I discovered was that pomegranate concentrate can also be called dibs rumman, pomegranate molasses, and pomegranate paste.

My persistence rewarded me with a fabulous new ingredient and, even better, a whole new list of stores to shop.

In chef school I discovered some resources, too. I found out where to go to get knives sharpened; where to buy live fish; where to get oddball garnishing tools and heat-proof spatulas. Along the way I realized that most home cooks don't take advantage of Chicago's enormous choices. We are lucky enough to be a center for the food service industry and for ethnic cooking of all kinds.

If you had the stamina, you could make a cook's tour of Chicago that would take you from Korea to Poland to Japan to China to Southeast Asia to India in a weekend. While I wouldn't recommend that sort of whirlwind trip, I do recommend visiting one of our huge ethnic supermarkets. It is like visiting a foreign country for a day. You will see and smell and touch a whole different culture.

These days you can get many ingredients on the Internet, of course, but you can't sniff them, poke them, or ask the Asian lady next to you what to do with them. Sometimes shopping in a "foreign" country can be intimidating, so I've tried to give you advice on what to expect.

...where to go to get knives sharpened; where to buy live fish...

It has been an adventure. I've eaten stuff that was actually hair conditioner and sampled fruits that I found out later are poisonous unless cooked. I've also found flavors so wonderful, so different and delightful that I can no longer live without them. So whether you just need a source for risotto rice or ground sumac, or you want to go exploring, I hope this helps. May it also add some wonderful new flavors to your cooking and your life.

Naming Names

It is amazing how many different names exist for the same ingredient. One woman's jícama is another's yam bean is another's bengjuang. As a language freak, I find it fun to try and figure things out. I was thrilled when I learned that the squash called mirliton in Cajun cooking is the same one called chayote in Spanish and Buddha's hand in Chinese. I was amused to learn that pork floss is not part of a pig's dental hygiene, but rather a Chinese garnish of thin shreds of pork. And I love reading the hilarious English directions on a product from Japan or Korea.

...pork floss is not part of a pig's dental hygiene...

I realize not everyone enjoys this game, so I've listed alternate names when I'm aware of them. This becomes increasingly difficult with cultures that use a different alphabet. Transliterating names from Arabic or Chinese leaves room for interpretation. Muth dal is sometimes moth, or mot, or moath. Don't be put off by spelling differences. Try saying the word out loud, and if it sort of sounds like what you're looking for, it probably is.

Disclaimers

While every attempt was made to include a good cross-section of the largest sources, this book makes no claim at being definitive. Retail establishments close and change with great rapidity, so call before you go or you risk disappointment.

Small neighborhood sources were generally not included. This would have made the book hundreds of pages longer and immediately outdated. No stores were asked whether they wanted to be listed.

The recipes and tips were invented by the author unless it is otherwise indicated, and inspiration came from many cookbooks and friends who cook. The opinions expressed are mine, all mine. Most stores were visited only once or twice, so your experience may be very different.

Don't blame me if you eat something you shouldn't. I did, but it was never a problem because I tasted things in small quantities if I was unsure. Be aware that in many cultures, food is medicine. Some things, especially herbs, teas, and drinks can be potent (and taste bad).

How to Use This Book

When I started my research, I had visions of listing every store where each ingredient could be found. Hah! Too many variables. Things are in season or not. They are there one time and not the next, and besides, there are just too darn many. So ingredients are listed in chapters based on rather arbitrary categories. Some will be obvious. If you need truffle oil, look for a gourmet store; sushi rice will be found in a Japanese market; but there are a lot of delightful in-betweens. For instance, an Asian store is a great place to buy fresh fish and a farmers market may offer fresh Asian greens.

The index is designed to handle such multiple sources and also to be specific enough to help you find a particular ingredient or piece of equipment.

The "Top 10 Ingredients" listings for ethnic stores are there to give you ideas. They point out items that are unusually delicious, that often keep very well, and that fit into most cooking styles. They are the sort of products you should pick up when you visit that kind of store.

If you're looking for a particular ethnic ingredient, I suggest you browse the general category as well as checking the index. You may discover another name for what you want, a possible substitution, or a new ingredient to try.

What I hope you also discover is the joy of the chase. Finding exotic stuff like durian fruit and sea slugs and silk squash right here in the city is exhilarating. Visiting ethnic markets can quickly become habit forming. They're so much juicier than a regulation American supermarket with all its frozen dinners and shrink wrap. Sure ethnic markets smell a little peculiar sometimes, but so does food. Remember the first good whiff you got of garlic?

Another thing to remember is that ethnic cuisines have their own convenience products. Many of them are good. Try a jar of Thai curry paste or Mexican mole sauce. It's not the same as making it from scratch, but I assure you even some decent restaurants use these things, and it's an easy way to expand your weeknight repertoire.

Happy shopping.

> **Visiting ethnic markets can quickly become habit forming.**

GOURMET

(smoked salmon, cheese,
capers, and cornichons)

Gourmet

"Gourmet" has become an old-fashioned sounding word. These days the term is "foodie." The stores that specialize in gourmet products have changed a lot, too. Remember those tiny places with dusty jars of esoteric sauces you paid too much for and never used? Instead, we now enjoy bustling marketplaces that offer cheese, wine, bread, charcuterie, and plenty of service without the hoity-toity attitude.

Chicago is catching up with New York. We don't have a Dean & De Luca yet, though rumor has it one is on the way, but our gourmet stores carry all the high-end products along with midwestern specialties, like artisanal Wisconsin cheeses and local sausages. This is a list of some of what you'll find.

caper berries
capers
caviar
cheese, imported and arti-
    sanal
cornichons
crème fraîche
European (high-fat) butter
mustards: imported, and/or
    flavored with green
    peppercorns, other
    fruits and herbs

oils–
    grapeseed oils: plain
        and flavored
    olive oils: unfiltered,
        pressed with fruit
        (lemon, tangerine),
        flavored with herbs
    nut oils: hazelnut,
        pistachio, walnut
pâtés
proscuitto
smoked fish and seafood
tapenades: olive, arti-
    choke, red pepper, sun-
    dried tomato
terrines and mousses
truffle oil
truffle powder and paste
truffles
vinegars: aged balsamic,
    sherry, fruit and herb
    flavored, fancy wine
    vinegar (Cabernet,
    Merlot)

Gourmet Stores

Binny's Beverage Depot

213 W. Grand Ave.
312.332.0012

Binny's is a chain of wine and liquor stores, but this one also carries a variety of gourmet items and has an extensive selection of cheeses, too. (The other stores that I visited carried only a very limited selection of food items, but I didn't go to all of them.) The Grand Avenue store has the usual olive oils and jams, plus some harder-to-find things, including gourmet ice cream and the line of **Dahlia Exotic Flavoring Pastes**. You can buy little bottles of **truffle oil** for less than $10 (good if you're just trying it out) and also imported **truffles, truffle oil**, and **truffle cream**. Local producers are well-represented by **Frontera's line of salsas and Mexican foods**, as well as caviar from Chicago's **Carolyn Collins**. She distributes **American sturgeon caviar**, plus **flavored whitefish caviar** (pepper, citron), **salmon caviar**, and **tobikko** (Japanese flying fish roe). A deli features cured meats (**pancetta, soprasetta**) and almost a dozen **pâtés** and **terrines** sold by the pound.

Chalet Wine and Cheese

40 E. Delaware Pl.
312.787.8555

1531 E. 53rd St.
773.324.5000

Chalet has been around for decades. Most of the space is devoted to wine and some very interesting liquor, including 300-year-old cognacs and an extensive choice of good rum, tequila, and liqueurs. They also have an excellent assortment of cheese and knowledgeable sales folk to assist you. They stock **pâtés** and cute little **cornichons** to go with them. Oh, yeah, **caviar**, too, plus lots of sauces and condiments. There's **truffle oil, porcini paste, pinenut and pistachio oil**, and the newly-popular **olive oil pressed with citrus**. They carry both Italian and Californian versions. There are spices, **balsamic vinegars, sherry vinegars**, and **flavored vinegars** of all kinds. Lots of **pasta**, too, including **striped, sombrero-shaped**, and **squid ink**. I'd love to get a gift basket from here!

Foodstuffs

2106 Central St.
Evanston
847.328.7704

338 Park Ave.
Glencoe
847.835.5105

1456 Waukegan Rd.
Glenview
847.832.9999

255 Westminster Rd.
Lake Forest
847.234.6600

Foodstuffs offers an assortment of mouth-watering goodies. They do a brisk take-out business in sandwiches and salads. The Evanston store also has a wide variety of condiments, oils, vinegars, and other gourmet ingredients, both imported and domestic. You'll find products from many restaurant lines, including **Vong** and **Frontera**. There is a small assortment of **Asian and Middle Eastern specialties** like **Thai curry paste** and **tahini**, plus a dizzying array of **tapenades**, soup mixes, imported pasta, mustard, and more. You can purchase **Foodstuffs' frozen appetizers** (egg rolls, quiche, phyllo bites), prepared sushi, and

ready-to-cook seasoned and breaded fish and meat. Foodstuffs has a butcher shop and a selection of cheese as well.

Fox & Obel Food Market

401 E. Illinois St.
312.410.7301

Opened in 2001, this 22,000-square-foot premium food market offers much beyond the usual condiments, oils, and vinegars. There are **meats and fish smoked on premises**, a bakery, a **dry-aging room for beef**, and a produce department. A dairy case offers **European-style high-fat butter** and **crème fraîche**. There is a huge selection of **oils and ethnic specialties** from around the world. They take great pride in their **cheese department**, everything is fresh-cut, not shrink-wrapped. The butcher shop carries **foie gras**, **prime meat**, and specialty cuts, and the fish department displays **whole fish on ice** and then fillets to order. Fox & Obel is committed to a high level of service, so if you're looking for something special, ask if they'll stock it. They even promised me they'd try to get fresh wasabi. Fox & Obel has a café and prepared food, too.

Sam's Wines/Marcey St. Market

1720 N. Marcey St.
312.664.4394

If you've lived in the city any length of time you know Sam's. It was one of the first serious and seriously affordable wine places. The huge warehouse is loaded with wine and very hip clerks, and there's a gourmet section called the Marcey Street Market in the rear of the store. The cheese selection is huge and well-priced. In addition to the chefs' lines of sauces and condiments (**Vong**, **Bobby Flay**, **Rick Bayless**), there is an collection of vinegars, that includes aged **balsamic** and **sherry**. They also stock **gourmet salts**, including **Fleur de Sel** from France and **Malden** from England, **dried mushrooms**, canned **San Marzano tomatoes**, and an item I'd been looking for everywhere—**smoked paprika**.

Trader Joe's

17 W. Rand Rd.
Arlington Heights
847.506.0752

122 Ogden Ave.
Downers Grove
630.241.1662

680 Roosevelt Rd.
Glen Ellyn
630.858,5077

1407 Waukegan Rd.
Glenview
847.657.7821

735 Main St.
Lake Zurich
847.550.7827

577 Waukegan Rd.
Northbrook
847.498.9076

14924 S. La Grange Rd.
Orland Park
708.349.9021

This California-based chain is new to the area and expanding fast. In fact, Trader Joe's is going to be opening in the city fairly soon, reportedly in the Lakeview neighborhood.

Trader Joe's isn't like anyplace else. They are a full-service wine and grocery, but they have over 800 private label items. Trader

Joe's imports from all over the world and has products made to their specs. The quality is top-notch, and the prices are amazingly low. Selection is somewhat Californian with lots of salsa, low-fat things, organic produce, and a fair number of frozen prepared dishes. There's nothing tremendously esoteric, but you'll find good buys on sauces, vinegars, and the like.

To add to the California feel, the staff wears Hawaiian shirts and shorts and is very friendly.

Trotter's To Go
1337 W. Fullerton Ave.
773.868.6510

Charlie Trotter's latest endeavor offers carry-out foods prepared to the exquisite Trotter specifications. They also carry a high-end collection of gourmet condiments and ingredients. You'll find **artisanal cheeses**, grains, **forbidden rice**, **organic soba noodles**, soy sauces, and many different chefs' lines of products, alongside Charlie's. They have a small refrigerated case with the most gorgeous **white anchovies** I've ever seen. There are expensive aged vinegars, of course, and a small, but unique assortment of cooking equipment, including **wasabi graters** and beautiful, expensive **mandolines**. There is an open kitchen for watching the chefs at work and a variety of wines with suggestions on pairings.

And don't forget:

Treasure Island
Multiple locations

Yeah, it's a supermarket, but what a supermarket! They have fresh **chanterelles**, **Belgian chocolates**, and quite a decent selection of ethnic ingredients. The butcher shop is comprehensive. In stock last time I was there, were **Niman Ranch pork**, **foie gras**, and **smoked duck**, as well as **fresh duck breasts**.

Whole Foods
Multiple locations

Very similar to Treasure Island only with more emphasis on **organic and health food**. Whole Foods also runs a butcher shop and fish department dedicated to personal service. They will order what you want with advance notice and they **dry age meat on premises**. The produce department is well stocked with organic greens, and less common things like **blood oranges** and **fiddle-head ferns** in season.

Marshall Field's Marketplace
Multiple locations

Many Field's stores devote an entire floor to food and cooking equipment. They carry all the name brands like **Calphalon**, **Wusthof**, and **Kitchen Aid**. Also condiments, pasta, sauces, cook-books, and dishes, too. I tend to forget this wonderful resource for cooks even exists until I wander into Field's for something else. Even prices can be good on sale.

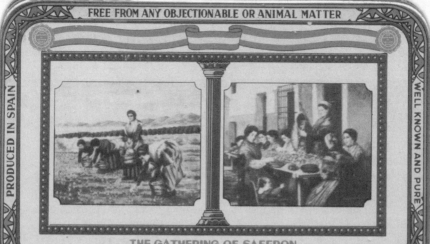

FREE FROM ANY OBJECTIONABLE OR ANIMAL MATTER

PRODUCED IN SPAIN

WELL KNOWN AND PURE

THE GATHERING OF SAFFRON
REGISTERED TRADE MARK

HeRBS
aND
SPiCeS

(saffron box, crystallized ginger,
sea salt, and salt cellars)

Herbs and Spices

Nothing improves your cooking quicker than using better, fresher (and more!) herbs and spices. Chicago is lucky enough to have quite a number of shops that specialize in just that.

Most dried herbs and spices retain their flavor for only about a year. Some have volatile oils that dissipate even faster. Go through your spice cupboard, open every jar and sniff. If it smells like nothing, it is. Toss it and buy new.

Many things (cayenne, chiles, poppy seed, sesame seed) keep their oomph longer if stored in the freezer. And the whole form of a spice lasts much longer, so grind whole peppercorns, allspice, cardamom, and nutmeg as needed.

Store herbs and spices in airtight jars or bags away from heat and light. (In other words, don't keep spices in a rack over the stove!)

All the stores listed will have the basics—dried oregano, basil, ginger, cinnamon, etc. So I'm only mentioning the less common ones. But if you've always bought your herbs and spices at the grocery store, try purchasing them at a specialty shop where things are fresher. The difference in flavor is substantial.

When looking for herbs for an ethnic recipe you're best off picking them up at the same store where you buy the rest of your ingredients.

ajowan (carom)
annatto seeds (achiote)
cardamom, whole green
    and/or decorticated
    (without the shell)
epazote
fenugreek
galangal
ginger, crystallized
grains of paradise
gumbo filé (sassafras)
juniper berries
kala jeera (black cumin)
kalonji (charnuska)
mace
mahlab, mahlebi (sour
    cherry pits)
saffron
star anise
sumac
turmeric
whole allspice
whole nutmeg
whole vanilla beans

Some Fresh-Ground Pepper??

green peppercorns
pink peppercorns
Sarawak peppercorns
Szechuan peppercorns (fagara)
Tellicherry peppercorns
white peppercorns

Remember the first time you had a waiter grind
fresh pepper on your salad with that huge pepper mill?
Or was it Julia Child who first convinced you fresh
ground was a whole lot better? Well, here's some
more info, so you can be an even bigger pepper snob.

Black peppercorns are not all the same. The ones
with the most developed flavor have been allowed to
ripen longer on the vine, so they tend to be bigger.
Tellicherry are considered the biggest and best Indian
peppercorns. BUT Sarawak peppercorns from Borneo
also have their fans (including me). They are dried a
different way and have a mellower, richer dimension.

Green peppercorns are the immature version of
the same plant and taste much milder. Whitepepper-
corns are the old folks of the family. They are left
to ripen the longest on the vine (so they're pricier).
Then their outer shell is removed. They're preferred
in most Asian cuisines and other recipes where specks
of black don't look appetizing. What about pink peppercorns and
Szechuan peppercorns you ask? They are not real peppercorns at
all since they come from totally different plants and only have
the name because they have the same shape.

Cracking Nutmeg

If you've only experienced dusty powdered nutmeg from a supermarket jar, freshly grated nutmeg will blow you away. No special equipment is required. Just rub a whole nutmeg against the small holes on your box grater. The aroma is fantastic—tropical, mysterious, sweet, and pungent. Try it in any cream sauce, with spinach, or on a baked sweet potato. Wow!

Herb and Spice Stores

Penzey's Spices

1138 W. Lake St.
Oak Park
708.848.7772

235 S. Washington St.
Naperville
630.355.7677
800.741.7787
www.penzeys.com

The premier mail order source for fresh, excellent spices now has retail stores in the Chicago area. If you've never received Penzey's catalog, call right now and get on their mailing list. Charlie Trotter even buys spices from Penzey's, so you know the quality is top-notch. Everything is FRESH. They offer just about every spice and dried herb, even some of the less common ones like **juniper berries** and **charnuska**. They also carry four kinds of ground **cinnamon** and seven different **peppercorns**. The differences can be a revelation. For instance, what we think of as cinnamon is actually **cassia**; real cinnamon is sweeter and milder tasting without that hot bite. The retail stores offer everything that's in the catalog. You can purchase jars or pre-weighed plastic bags. It is perfectly possible to spend 30 minutes just wandering around sniffing things.

It's All in the Family

Penzey's is owned and operated by Bill Penzey; The Spice House by his sister Patty Penzey-Erd and her husband. They compete with each other. Mom and Dad Penzey started things off with a retail business in Wisconsin years ago. Bill continued and built a mail-order business with a growing number of retail outlets. Patty built a retail business that sells some mail-order, too. Many of their products are identical. Must make for some spicy family gatherings.

The Spice House

1512 N. Wells St.
312.274.0378

1941 Central St.
Evanston
847.328.3711
www.thespicehouse.com

Flavored Coffee the Right Way

1. **Vanilla Coffee.** Cut a piece of fresh vanilla bean into a one-inch length and split it open. Toss it into the coffee filter with the ground coffee and brew as usual.

2. **Cardamom Coffee.** In parts of the Middle East they believe that coffee can sap your masculinity, unless cardamom is added. Don't know about that, but it tastes good. Crush two whole green cardamom pods and put into the ground beans and brew.

3. **Cinnamon Coffee.** Add a cinnamon stick to the brewing basket. You can retrieve and reuse the stick a few times before it loses flavor.

In Evanston for six years, the Spice House recently opened in Old Town as well. These charming old-fashioned stores sell dried herbs and spices in bulk. The good news is you can buy small quantities. The bad news is you have to decide how much you want by weight instead of just judging by the size of a jar. You have to get waited on, too, but that's usually a pleasure since the staff if friendly and knowledgeable. There are sample jars of everything for you to sniff, and lots of information is posted.

At this writing The Spice House carried a few items that Penzey's didn't, such as **fennel pollen**, **Tahitian vanilla beans**, **Aleppo pepper**, **Szechuan peppercorns**, **Fleur de Sel**, and **Hawaiian red sea salt**.

The Home Economist

419 N. La Grange Rd.
La Grange Park
708.352.1514

906 S. Northwest Hwy.
Barrington
847.382.4202

Church Point Plaza
9159 Gross Point Rd.
Skokie
847.674.7252

6382 Cass Ave.
Westmont
630.852.0214

Warehouse Store
J.B. San Filippo & Sons
2299 Busse Rd.
Elk Grove Village
847.593.2300

A chain of stores that carry mostly bulk bins of ingredients. It's a
bit of a hodgepodge: candies,
nuts, lentils, snack mixes, and
spices of all kinds, too (although
not as extensive a selection as
Penzey's or The Spice House).
Most things are sold by the
ounce.

You will find some otherwise
hard-to-locate items, especially in
the area of **baking supplies**. A
good place to go for **gum arabic**,
baker's ammonia, **citric acid**,
paste food colors, **extracts**
(way beyond vanilla–**kona
coffee**, **rum**), **TVP** (texturized
vegetable protein), **MSG**, **fructose**, **alum**, **sanding sugar**, and
other **decorating sprinkles and
sugars**.

Fresh Herbs

Most supermarkets sell fresh herbs in the produce section. They are a great convenience; however, they are pricey, not always fresh, and mostly hydroponically grown, which makes them rather bland tasting.

The best way to have fresh herbs available is to grow them yourself. Even without a backyard it's fairly easy to keep pots of rosemary, oregano, chives, and basil going. That way you don't have to buy an entire package of something just for a few sprigs. The other advantage to growing your own is that you can try some of the more exotic things, like **borage**, **lemon verbena**, **sorrel**, and **lavender** to name a few of my favorites.

See also the listings under **Southeast Asian** (p. 184) since those stores stock a selection of fresh herbs all year round. In fact the Argyle Street shops are the place to find **out-of-season basil** that is fresh and not too expensive.

Here are a few gardening stores that carry a selection of the more unusual culinary herbs. Check newspapers in May for yearly events like the Chicago Botanic Gardens herb sale and the Oak Park Conservatory herb sale.

Fertile Garden
1650 W. Diversey Ave.
773.929.9330

Gethsemane Garden Center
5739 N. Clark St.
773.878.5915

Pesche's
170 River Rd.
Des Plaines
847.299.1300

Platt Hill Nursery
222 W. Lake St.
Bloomingdale
630.529.9394

Ted's Greenhouse
16930 S. 84th Ave.
Tinley Park
708.532.3575

Saving Summer

I'll spare you another recipe for pesto, but did you know you can make pesto with many other leafy herbs besides basil? Parsley and cilantro work particularly well. Just chop them up in a food processor and add enough oil to hold them together. Freeze in an ice cube tray to make herb cubes.

Herb butter is easy, too. Chop by hand or machine almost any herb or combination of herbs (two or three tablespoons will do the trick) and add to a stick of softened butter. Mash it together in a bowl, use plastic wrap to shape it into a log, then wrap and freeze. You can serve your herb butter log on a special occasion, or just cut off a piece anytime to add great flavor to everything from muffins to steak.

You can even dry herbs in your microwave. Please proceed cautiously as I have started a few (minor) fires trying out this technique. Place herbs in a single layer between two paper towels. You can leave herbs on the stem, as they will crumble off more easily when dried. Nuke for no more than a minute to start. Peek and poke the herbs to see how they're doing. Then proceed in 20-second increments until the herbs are dry enough to crumble between your fingers. Store in a glass jar until you're ready to use.

Grilled Mustard-Herb Chicken
(Serves 6)

(This is a recipe everyone requests. It's an excellent way to take advantage of the fresh herbs in your garden or the market. Marinate the chicken the night or morning before for an easy weeknight dinner that's ready in minutes.)

1/2 to 3/4 C. chopped assorted fresh herbs
1/2 C. Dijon mustard
3/4 C. olive oil
1 tsp. salt
fresh ground pepper
6 boneless, skinless chicken breast halves (2-1/2 lbs.)

Chop the herbs roughly and use a mixture of basil, rosemary, tarragon, mint, and don't forget parsley. (It's cheap and flavorful, especially the flat-leaf kind.) Discard any really tough stems. Put the mustard in a bowl and whisk in the olive oil until the mixture is creamy. Then stir in the herbs, salt, and pepper.

Place the trimmed chicken breasts in a zip-top bag, add marinade, and squish around to coat completely. Cover and refrigerate for at least two hours or as long as overnight.

Remove from marinade and discard excess. Grill over medium fire until cooked through, about 10 minutes total. Don't over-cook! Cut and peek if you're not sure.

Serve sliced with mango salsa (p. 44).

Meat, Poultry, and Game

(veal and lamb chops)

Meat, Poultry, and Game

Your local butcher shop is to be cherished. These days even decent beef (choice grade) is hard to come by at the supermarket. It is beyond the scope of this book to seek out all the good local butchers. Part of what makes them good is the relationship you establish with the men or women who work there. Then not only will they order whatever you need, they'll make sure it's the best.

If you can't find a local source or don't have time to look, talk to the person behind the scenes at your big anonymous chain store. Ring that bell or buzzer and ask for what you want. There are sometimes real butchers in the back of the store who are quite delighted to give you personal service. Sometimes.

The stores included here are specialists and worth seeking out when you require an out-of-the-ordinary cut, quantity, or kind of meat or fish.

Ethnic stores are also good places to buy meat, so check the listings in the appropriate chapter, especially if you want variety meats (offal) or a cut that's frequently used in a particular cuisine.

For **fresh ham**, **pork belly**, **smoked butt**, **pig trotters**, or just about any other part of a pig, go to one of the Polish or Mexican markets.

Skirt steak and sometimes **hanger steak** are available in Latin American markets. You'll also find the more usual cuts of beef, and frequently they offer **choice grade**. Many of the bigger ones also sell **barbacoa** and **carnitas** on the weekends. These are meltingly tender pork cuts that are barbecued (for barbacoa) or just cooked slowly. Carnitas means "little meats" and is often used to fill tacos or enchiladas. Both are quite tasty and handy if you want to make a Mexican meal without spending a lot of time.

For **lamb**, try any of the Devon Avenue meat markets listed in the **Indian/ Pakistani** chapter (pp. 154–157). They offer good prices and will cut to order.

Veal shanks for **osso bucco** and other veal cuts, like breast and shoulder, are usually available at Italian markets.

Meat, Poultry, and Game Stores

Chicago Game and Gourmet

350 N. Ogden Ave.
312.455.1800
(wholesale)

These guys sell to high-end restaurants and do not have a retail store. They're listed here, however, because they are still a good resource. If you need **poussin, wild boar, foie gras, buffalo, ostrich**, or high-quality **venison**, call them. They may be able to sell to you directly if the quantity fits their wholesale specs. (For instance, some game birds are sold individually shrink-wrapped for the restaurant market, and you might be able to purchase them direct.) At the very least, they will be able to steer you to one of the retail establishments they deal with (**Whole Foods**, p. 12, is one) who can get you what you need.

Columbus Meat Market

906 W. Randolph St.
312.829.2480

One of the Randolph Street wholesalers also open to the public. They carry **prime** and **choice beef**, but for prime you need to order a **whole loin**, which they will then butcher into the cuts you want. What a smart way to stock your freezer! They can also order anything, and I do mean anything. I asked about **caul fat** (the fat netting they're always wrapping around things on "Iron Chef") and was told it would be no problem. "We even get bull penis for a restaurant that uses it in an authentic Jamaican soup."

Gepperth's Meat Market

1964 N. Halsted St.
773.549.3883

One of the oldest, most respected full-line butcher shops in the city. They will even **age beef** for you upon request. They carry **Hudson Vally foie gras**, but prefer a day's notice.

Nicholas Quality Meats

908 W. Randolph St.
312.563.0145

Though primarily wholesale, this market is open to the public and offers good prices on beef and pork. They also carry **rabbit**, **smoked meats**, and **shrimp**.

Olympic Meat Packers

810 W. Randolph St.
312.666.2222

This wholesale/retail operation specializes in package deals and posts different collections of meats on the walls. Prices start at about $50 and include some of everything—**beef** (short ribs, t-bones, ground beef), **pork** (ribs, pork chops), as well as **sausage** and even **tamales** and **pizza puffs**. You choose the assortment that suits your budget, tastes, and freezer capacity.

Paulina Market

3501 N. Lincoln Ave.
773.248.6272

Paulina Market began as an old time German neighborhood butcher shop and still carries many **homemade sausage** and **German specialties**, as well as **choice-grade meats**. They are service-oriented and will **age beef** if you ask. This is one of the butcher shops at which food stylists purchase their meat. (**Geppherth's**, p.27, is the other.)

Peoria Packing

1300 W. Lake St.
312.738.1800

A great place to buy **pork**, Peoria Packing is a wholesale business that has a store open to the public. You wear throw-away plastic gloves while checking out aisles of gorgeous cuts of meat on ice. They have every part of the pig, including whole, skin-on **fresh ham**, **ribs of every kind**, plus **trotters**, **chitterlings**, etc. Beef, including **liver**, **skirt steak**, and whole pieces of **round** are also stocked. A butcher is on premises to trim, or further break down your purchase into smaller cuts. They also have a good selection of **smoked meats**. Check their frequent ads in the *Chicago Sun-Times* food section for specials.

Live Poultry

Yes, you can find it in the city. My friend Mary Ann, in fact, ended up raising a chicken in her apartment. She took pity on the runt of the flock in the window of a Ukrainian Village store. "Cheep" as she was called, even provided Mary Ann with a eggs for a while.

I think it is respecful to remember that the meat we eat was once alive. It does not grow in plastic-wrapped styrofoam trays. Live poultry stores can be reminders of some of the unpleasant things that go with being a carnivore, however, so don't shop in one if you are squeamish.

On the other hand, the chickens in these stores are no worse off than those at factory farms. Certainly the meat is much fresher and the taste difference is noticeable.

These stores are also a good place to get **fresh quail**, **goose**, and **duck**, which you usually only find frozen, if at all, elsewhere.

Alliance Poultry Farms, Inc.

1636 W. Chicago Ave.
312.829.1458

Chicago Live Poultry

2611 S. Ridgeway Ave.
773.542.9451

6421 N. Western Ave.
773.381.1000

Chicken, **quail**, **turkey**, **ducks**, and **rabbits**, butchered to order. The South Side store is near the Mexican Little Village neighborhood; the North Side shop is just off Devon in the Indian/Pakistani area. The stores have the same name; I don't know whether they have the same owner.

John's Live Poultry and Egg Market

5955 W. Fullerton Ave.
773.622.2813

John's specializes in phone orders and has been providing freshly slaughtered Thanksgiving **turkeys** for decades. They also sell **chickens**, **geese**, **quail**, and their **eggs**. According to the clerk, most of the animals are raised on farms in Indiana.

FiSH aND SeaFOOD

(grouper from Isaacson L and Stein Fish Co)

Fish and Seafood

The fishmongers listed in this section are experts. Count on them to get you impeccably fresh, high-quality seafood and also to provide information. They can tell you where the fish came from, when it arrived, how to cook it, and sometimes even how it was caught and by whom. This is an important benefit when you're purchasing shellfish and you want to be confident that it came from unpolluted waters, or when you're planning to serve something out of the ordinary, like monkfish, for the first time and you need information on handling it. I'd probably buy **fresh oysters** and **softshell crabs** from one of these experts.

On the other hand, ethnic markets, particularly Asian ones, have a wide assortment and low prices, so check the listings under **Southeast Asian** (p.184), **China** (p.170) and **Japan** (p.204), especially:

Chicago Food Corporation (p. 206)

International Club (p.174)

Mitsuwa Marketplace (p. 204)

For **caviar** a gourmet shop is sometimes a good source. And **Petrossian caviar** is carried by Bloomingdale's as well as in Marshall Field's and Neiman Marcus specialty food departments. (Call ahead to the specific store to see what they stock.)

Smoked fish can be found in many of the **Eastern European** (p.103) and **Russian** (p.214) markets, especially:

Wally's International Market (p. 105)

Devon Fish Market/ Kashtan (p. 214)

Whole Foods (p. 12) and **Treasure Island** (p. 12) stores also carry an excellent selection of fresh seafood and will order things for you with advance notice.

Trout Meunière
(Serves 4)

Sounds fancy but you won't believe how simple this is. It works with whole trout or fillets of any delicate white fish. Sole Meunière is a French classic. I have seen it on chi-chi menus for big bucks and there's really nothing to it.

4 whole trout, or about 2 lbs. trout or sole fillets
or other mild white fish
about 1/2 C. flour, heavily seasoned with
salt, pepper, and a little thyme
2-4 T. unsalted butter, more if needed
2 lemons
fresh parsley, chopped

Spread out the flour on a platter and mix in the seasonings. Heat enough butter in a sauté pan (or pans) to thoroughly coat the bottom. Roll the fish in the seasoned flour, shake off excess, and fry until brown and crisp (about five minutes for skinny fillets, 5-7 minutes a side for whole trout).

Remove and keep warm. Pour off the burnt butter. Add another 2 T. to the pan; when it froths, squeeze in the lemon, swirl around, and pour over the fish. Sprinkle with parsley.

Serve with buttered noodles topped with poppyseeds.

Seafood Stores

Burhop's Seafood

609 W. North Ave.
312.642.8600

1515 Sheridan Rd.
Wilmette
847.256.6400

One of the first and best, Burhop's has been around for 75 years. They will order most anything for you. Cooking tips and recipes are happily provided and you can pick up **sauces**, **breading**, and accompaniments for your seafood dinner. Pre-prepared and ready to cook items are also available. There are free cooking classes on most Saturdays.

Captain Alex Seafood

8874 N. Milwaukee Ave.
Niles
847.803.8833

Friendly staff who know their stuff sell pretty much anything you could want at Captain Alex. There are boards posted with lists of fish, whether they're available

fresh or frozen, and the price. Some fresh fish is displayed on ice, but a lot is warehoused in the back since this is also a wholesale operation. A self-serve refrigerated case holds take-home items that are ready to cook, like **crab cakes** and **battered fish fillets**.

Di Cola's Seafood

10754 S. Western Ave.
773.238.7071

Southsiders have relied on Di Cola's since the 1930s. They carry prepared, to-go food in addition to a complete selection of **seafood that they will fillet**, or cut to your specifications.

Hagen's Fish Market

5635 W. Montrose Ave.
773.283.1944

A family business since 1946, Hagen's offers an array of fresh and frozen seafood, as well as prepared items, including **fried shrimp** and **calamari**. Their real specialty, though, is **seafood** they smoke themselves, such as smoked sable, salmon, chubs, whitefish, sturgeon, and shrimp. Theyll even smoke your own catch for you.

Isaacson L and Stein Fish Co.

800 W. Fulton Market
312.421.2444

In this place you feel like you're in a coastal town, buying off the dock. Isaacson's is a wholesaler, but they let retail customers walk around and look at, sniff, and touch (wearing gloves) displays of all kinds of fish on ice. They claim to carry 250 kinds. They almost always have **monkfish**, many kinds of **grouper**, **oysters**, **scallops**, and **skate**. While you get eye to eye with dinner, you can read signs that tell you where each fish came from. Choose the fish you want, bag it, and give it to one of the guys wearing a rubber apron and boots and have him clean it. They will also fillet, cut a big fish into steaks, whatever you like. On Saturdays they charge for some of these services and it is CROWDED. The staff is always friendly and patient with questions and seems to enjoy the stunned look on new customers' faces. Prices are excellent and there's even free parking in front or in a lot across the street.

Supreme Lobster and Seafood

220 E. North Ave.
Villa Park
630.834.FISH

A suburban wholesaler who also offers retail. A fine establishment if you live west, but the fish is behind glass and they don't have the huge variety of Isaacson's or even Captain Alex.

The Fish Guy Market

4423 N. Elston Ave.
773.283.7400

Bill Dugan, the proprietor, is charming, personable, and passionate about seafood. If he's there when you are, be sure to chat him up. He supplies some of the premier Chicago restaurants, like Trotters and the Ritz-Carlton. While the store is relatively small, he carries a wide variety and will get you pretty much anything you want. He will happily give you cooking advice as well. When I visited he had **monkfish**, **scallops in the shell**, **skate**, and **caviar**, among other things. Part of the place is a deli that offers prepared items, including some **very classy seafood salads**. A small selection of relevant equipment like **oyster knives** and **cedar planks** to cook on are also offered.

Good Morgan Kosher Fish Market

2948 W. Devon Ave.
773.764.8115

A kosher fishmarket at the western, Russian/Jewish end of the Devon shopping area. It's the place to go to get **ready-ground fish** for homemade gefilte fish.

Rubino's Seafood

735 W. Lake St.
312.258.0020 or 0021

A Fulton Market area wholesaler, specializing in **shellfish**, who will sell in quantity to retail customers. There is no sales area. You enter an office through hanging strips of plastic and order from a product and price list posted on the wall. Merchandise is warehoused in the back. It would be a good place to investigate if you were serving shrimp cocktail to a huge party. Call first to get minimums and place your order. They're not geared for walk-ins, but are perfectly friendly.

Roe, Roe, Roe Your Boat

Caviar, fish eggs, roe, whatever you call them, they are luxury ingredients, but there's more than one way to roe. To enjoy caviar, you needn't spend a bundle on the imported sturgeon kind.

Carolyn Collins Caviar: Chicago's caviar company (**www.collinscaviar.com**). Now run by daughter Rachel, Collins Caviar offers plain and flavored American caviar. Elegant choices include wasabi tobikko, caviar citron (with vodka), smoked golden caviar, and Hackelback sturgeon caviar. Mother-of-pearl caviar spoons are sold, too.

tobikko: I think of these as Japanese pop rocks. They are the (dyed) bright orange roe used in California rolls and other sushi. Not a lot of flavor, but plenty of texture and very affordable.

salmon roe: The big (1/4-inch diameter) red caviar that's served as sushi (ikura) is also tasty on its own or as a luxurious garnish for an omelet.

lumpfish caviar: These are the tiny black fish eggs you'll find in jarred caviar in the grocery store.

whitefish caviar (American golden): With slightly larger eggs than lumpfish, this can be very tasty. If you don't like the heavy deep-sea flavor of sturgeon caviar, you may actually prefer it.

PRODUCE

(bounty from the farmers market)

Farmers Markets

Chicago is finally catching up with New York in offering locally-grown produce to home cooks. Even with a short growing season, there are more wonderful vegetables and fruits than we dreamed of as city kids who thought peas came in cans. As more restaurants commit themselves to cooking with the seasons and using fresh local ingredients, we home cooks benefit from the availability of specialty greens, fresh herbs, heirloom tomatoes, exotic eggplant and squash varieties, and other perishable wonders that have to be enjoyed close to where they grow.

Every summer there are neighborhood markets as well as three or four downtown, sponsored by the city. To find them check the city's Web site: **www.ci.chi.il.us/consumer services**, or call the **Department of Consumer Affairs: 773.489.4180.**

Green City Market is a mostly organic market that is run as a private, not-for-profit organization. Supported by local chefs and committed to supporting sustainable agriculture, Green City Market sells meat, poultry, and cheese, in addition to fruits and veggies. They also sponsor cooking demonstrations and frequent fundraising events that feature celebrity chefs preparing the market's offerings.

In summer 2001, Green City Market was held Wednesdays in Lincoln Park along the path between Clark and Stockton streets. In winter the market moves indoors for a "Winter Pantry" held in 2001 at the **CHIC Cooking School** (p.73). Offerings include storage vegetables like beets and hard squash, greenhouse-grown salad fixings and herbs, as well as meats, cheeses, and breads. Check the newspaper for current schedules and locations.

Community-Supported Agriculture

Another way to enjoy our local bounty is to buy a share in an actual farm's harvest for the season. This is called subscription farming or CSA (community-supported agriculture). If you sign on, produce is delivered to a drop-off spot near your house, usually on a weekly basis for the season. There are various kinds of shares, so you can plan when and how much you receive (or find someone to share your share). You can even extend your subscription with some farms to receive deliveries of winter storage vegetables in November and December.

For information on farms that deliver in your area check these Web sites: **www.biodynamics.com/usda/** or **www.sare.org**.

Two local farms that participate are: **Angelic Organics, www.angelicorganics.com,** at **815.389.3106,** and **Prairie Crossing, www.prairiecrossing.com,** at **847.548.4030**

Pick-Your-Own Farms

A city person's excuse to get out in the country for a day. U-pick farms in the area have strawberries in the spring, pumpkins in the winter, and lots more in-between. Some of them also feature hayrides, tractor rides, and gift shops.

Check the University of Illinois Extension Web site: **www.urbanext.uiuc.edu/fresh** for listings of farms and what produce is available when.

Andrée's Swiss Chard & Pasta
(Serves 4-6)

8 strips of bacon (optional)
2 bunches Swiss chard, washed and chopped
3 cloves garlic, chopped
3 T. olive oil
I lb. fusilli (or other short pasta), cooked
1 T. Dijon mustard
2 T. white wine vinegar
1/4 C. grated Parmesan cheese
1/4 C. pine nuts, preferably toasted

Fry bacon until crisp. Drain and crumble, set aside. Sauté garlic and chard in olive oil until tender-crisp. In a large bowl, combine pasta with mustard and vinegar. Add cheese, chard, and bacon; toss well. Top with pine nuts.

Serve hot or at room temperature.

We Be Jammin'

If you're like me, you overbuy fruit. It's very seductive at the farmers market, so you bring home too much and it rots. Jam is the answer. The quickest way to make it is in the microwave. I'll spare you a lecture about low-pectin and high-pectin fruits. It doesn't matter much, as long as you don't mind runny preserves. If it's too gooey to spread on toast, you've made fruit sauce!

You need:

2 to 4 C. chopped fruit (strawberries, rhubarb, raspberries, plums, etc., or a mixture)

1 to 2 C. sugar (depending on the fruit and your taste)

1-2 tsp. lemon juice (optional)

A huge, humongous Pyrex measuring cup. 8 cups is perfect. If you don't have one, a microwave-safe casserole or soufflé dish will do. The container must be at least twice as big as the quantity of fruit since it will boil and bubble over.

Saran Wrap, a wooden spoon, and clean jars (right out of the dishwasher) to put the jam in.

Here's how:

1. Prepare the fruit. Wash and cut into bite-size pieces. If you are using stone fruit, like apricots or plums, leave the pits in the mix till after cooking. They add thickening and flavor.

2. Mix in the sugar. If the fruit is dry-ish, squash it some with a potato masher or other blunt instrument. You want a bit of juice to start things off.

3. Cover your container with Saran Wrap securely. No vents. No cheap plastic wrap. Nuke on high power for 4 to 8 minutes. Watch through the window. After about 4 minutes, the jam will bubble wildly, climb to the top, and start sneaking around the Wrap to drool on your microwave. How quickly this happens depends on all kinds of things: your microwave, the fruit, the phases of the moon. Don't be alarmed, just turn it off when it starts seriously leaking.

4. Then, stir. WATCH OUT!! IT'S HOTTER THAN HECK! Use oven mitts. CAREFULLY lift a corner of Saran Wrap that's away from you (THE STEAM IS HOTTER THAN HECK, TOO). Stir. The jam should boil for a total of 8 minutes, so put it back in the microwave and nuke in one or two minute spurts, stopping before it boils over too much. If you want to save the spilled jam, just scrape it up and return to the Pyrex (assuming your microwave was clean and not crusted with pizza sauce when you started).

5. Now uncover, stir, and nuke a couple of minutes at a time until you've cooked it about 5 minutes more. You are thickening the jam so it gels. Traditional jam-making does this by cooking for a very long time on the stove, or by using packaged pectin. There are times for tradition, but not if you have a quart of over-ripe berries and you have to go to work in the morning. As the jam thickens, your spoon will feel the weight more and start leaving a trail as you stir.

6. Add lemon juice to bring out the flavor and color, if you wish. Then pour into the clean jars. This is where a pour spout, like on the Pyrex, is useful.

That's it. You made jam. Try it tomorrow morning on toast. You will be very impressed with yourself. It will keep for at least a week in the fridge. Otherwise, put it in the freezer where it keeps for six months. You have not preserved these preserves, so they need to stay refrigerated or frozen.

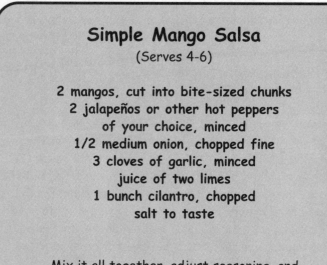

Simple Mango Salsa
(Serves 4-6)

2 mangos, cut into bite-sized chunks
2 jalapeños or other hot peppers
of your choice, minced
1/2 medium onion, chopped fine
3 cloves of garlic, minced
juice of two limes
1 bunch cilantro, chopped
salt to taste

Mix it all together, adjust seasoning, and
allow flavors to mingle for at least 30 minutes.

Taste and adjust seasoning again.

Serve with grilled or roasted meats. Also good as a dip.

Produce Stores

The stores listed specialize in produce and are also places to find good bargains on fruit and vegetables. For tropical things or ethnic specialties, see listings under **Southeast Asia** (p. 184), **Japan** (p. 204), **China** (p. 170), **Latin America** (p. 85), and **India/Pakistan** (p. 145).

Andy's Fruit Ranch

4725 N. Kedzie Ave.
773.583.2322

This one is worth making a detour for. Andy's seems to pride itself on offering the widest range of **fresh produce** anywhere in the city. You can purchase groceries and canned goods, including a good selection of condiments, dried legumes, and seasonings, but it's the produce that really shines. Here is a list of what was available the times I visited, but chances are if it is in season or in demand, Andy's will have it. The exceptions are specifically Asian items (no durian or lychees) and Indian items (no wing beans or tindora). At least not when I was there.

bitter melons
cactus fruit (tuna)
chayotes
cherimoya
daikon
green mangos
green papayas
guavas
Haitian mangos
horseradish
jícama
malanga (yautia, amarilla)
mamey
ñame (white yam)
Philippine mangos
plantains
pomelos
sour oranges
taro (dasheen, eddo)
tomatillos
young coconuts
yucca (cassava)

Berwyn Fruit Market

3811 S. Harlem Ave.
Berwyn
708.795.6670

A combination of Latin American, Eastern European, and Middle Eastern ingredients in one store. When I shop here, I come home with a world-tour of ingredients.

You can pick up **labna, ajvar, tomatillos**, Polish pickles, fresh **dill weed**, Produce is very cheap and the emphasis is on the Latin American. This is one of the few places that regularly has the spiny version of **Mexican chayote**. A full service butcher, too.

Carrot Top

**1430 Paddock Dr.
Northbrook
847.729.1450**
www.carrottopmarket.com

This produce market is hard to find, but worth seeking out if you live north. It's just off Willow Road south on Old Willow Road. You'll find exotic offerings— **chanterelle mushrooms, oyster mushrooms**, and **morels** in season, **passion fruit, lychees, baby artichokes**, and other **baby vegetables**. Carrot Top also carries fresh herbs, locally grown produce, and the usual lettuces, roots, and fruits. Another Carrot Top store next door carries meat, fish, and prepared food.

Northeastern Fruit

**6000 N. Lincoln Ave.
773.338.0610**

Tucked into a corner at the busy

Peterson/Lincoln intersection for generations, Northeastern Fruit has good prices on mainstream fruits and veggies, as well as a good selection of **Greek products**, including **trahina**, canned **grape leaves**, and jams.

Stanley's Fruits and Vegetables

**1558 N. Elston Ave.
773.276.8050**

Nothing too exotic, but good prices and an excellent assortment of in-season produce.

Ted's Fruit Market

**2840 W. Devon Ave.
773.743.6739**

Located where Devon Avenue transitions from "Golda Meir Blvd." to "Ghandi," this store's ethnic offerings are mixed— Middle Eastern, Greek, Balkan, with some Indian thrown in, too. In addition to a variety of produce, you'll find **ajvar**, Greek **jams**, including the hard to locate **bergamot, labna**, and **lentils**.

Overnight Pickled Green Beans
(4 appetizer servings)

1/2 lb. green beans (1-quart box from the farmers market)
1 C. white wine vinegar
1 C. water
1 T. salt (kosher preferred)
2 T. sugar
1 T. whole black peppercorns
1 T. whole coriander seed
2 tsp. whole brown or black mustard seed
1 hot green or red pepper, fresh or dried
1 bay leaf

Wash the beans and remove stem ends. Put the raw beans into a bowl or casserole large enough to hold the beans and the liquid. Tuck the hot pepper and bay leaf in with the beans.

Combine wine vinegar, water, sugar, salt, and whole spices. Bring to a simmer and simmer for five minutes. Pour hot liquid and spices over beans. The beans need to be submerged, so adjust the amount of liquid and the size of container accordingly.

Allow to cool to room temperature and then refrigerate.

The beans are ready to enjoy the next day. Letting them marinate for 48 hours is even better. Pack them as part of a picnic, serve as a munchy with drinks, or use in a salad. They even make a trendy martini garnish.

South Water Market

South 14th to 16th Streets
between Racine and Morgan

Not for the faint-of-heart or the late riser, South Water Market is Chicago's wholesale produce market. A long, low stretch of three buildings run east to west and parallel to each other. They were built in the 20s. Now they hover ghost-like and alone in the middle of emptiness waiting to go condo. Drive by in the afternoon and South Water feels abandoned. Come back at 3 a.m. and the joint's jumping.

photo by Eric Futran, ChefShots.com

The huge semis look anachronistic pulled up to the crumbling old facades that are more on the scale of horse and buggy. The stores are owned by families who've been in wholesale produce for generations. South Water is no longer an efficient site to do business, so the owners' association has plans to move soon. Chances are within a year or so the wrecker's ball will level the market, and an era and atmosphere will go with it.

If you go:

The market opens at midnight and runs till 10 or 11 a.m. "You gotta get there at 3 for the good stuff," I was told. I went at 6 a.m. Unless you're in the business or you're feeding an army, South Water is not a practical place to shop. They sell only by the case. I was also warned by many that it was not the kind of place for a "woman alone." (Made me really want to go!) So I took a friend. It didn't feel dangerous. Yes, people shout. There is very little room to maneuver, and fork-lift drivers cannot be expected to say excuse me when there is a gawking tourist blocking their path. You get out of their way. Quick.

The displays of chanterelles, melons, and peppers are beautiful, but it's the old photos on the wall, the ancient conveyer belts, the crumbling architecture, and, most of all, the people that are fascinating. Stay out of the way, watch your step, and if you are purchasing, negotiate price and quantity and *then* bring back your car to pick it up. And go before it's gone.

EQUIPMENT

(Benriner slicers)

Equipment

Next time you're tempted to give your credit card a workout at Williams-Sonoma, try a restaurant supply store instead. They're happy to sell to you, the home chef. They generally have a sales force that calls on restaurants, but their showrooms are usually retail stores that are open to the public and lots of fun. Many of them are only open Monday through Friday, 9 to 5. Call for hours.

For things like **sheet pans** (baking pans), **food storage containers**, and **gadgets** of all description, you can't beat 'em. You'll find some real bargains. They also carry things you'd have a hard time finding in a cookware store—from **ladles** in weird sizes (really tiny or huge), to enormous colanders, to **ramekins**, to catering-style **chafing dishes**, to heat-proof **spatulas** in any size and color. **Cutting boards** come in a rainbow of colors and are cheap enough to stock up on.

Paper goods are a deal. You can get a year's supply of straws for a buck. You can buy every kind of "to-go" container. None of these things would be worth the trip alone, but if you're picking up other items, why not stock up?

When it comes to **pots and pans**, you'll find good quality at reasonable prices. Especially if you're in need of large-capacity cookware. Be wary of the very reasonably-priced commercial aluminum pots and pans, however. They are perfectly okay 90 percent of the time, but they do react with some ingredients and turn cream sauces a very nasty gray color.

You'll find all sorts of delightful gadgets you never knew you needed. Better yet, simple tools like graters and melon ballers are often better made, sharper, and more efficient than the grocery-store versions. Proprietors are friendly and helpful (unless they're swamped with commercial clients), and you don't have to pretend you own a restaurant.

Small Equipment

butane torches
cutting boards, all sizes
    and colors
food storage containers,
    all sorts
garnishing tools
hand blenders
ladles
mandolines
melon ballers

nutmeg graters
oyster knives
parchment paper
pastry bags and tips
pastry brushes
pizza stones and peels
ramekins
rolling pins: French, marble
scales
sheet pans
silicon baking sheets (Sil-
pat)

skimmers
spatulas (heat-proof)
squirt bottles
steel gloves
stock pots
tamis
thermometers
tongs
V-slicers
whisks

Large Equipment

barstools
butcher block tables
carts
coffee brewers and urns
pot and pan racks
professional blenders,
toasters, processors,
slicers, mixers, etc.
shelving
stainless prep tables

How to Play on Your Mandoline (or V-Slicer).

Vegetable Chips

Try weird and wild veggies—taro, plantain, beets, turnips—any starchy tuber. The humble sweet potato also makes a great chip.

Peel and slice vegetables paper thin on your slicer. Dry thoroughly, heat 1-3 inches of oil to 350° in a deep pot. Fry chips in a single layer. (Always do beets last! They turn everything red.)

Remove with a skimmer when crisp and slightly colored. Salt immediately. Keep warm in a low oven.

You can also find the real restaurant professional items, like **deep fryers** and **Viking ranges**, in some of these stores, though most such equipment is not appropriate for home use. In fact, it's illegal to have a **professional range** in your home for fire safety reasons. Not only do they require a major, very expensive, make-a-hole in-your-wall vent, they are not insulated well enough to be safe. They're quite seductive, though, since at first blush the prices are reasonable. If you want a professional stove, you'll have to pay for a home version. (See the **Something's Cooking** store listing, p. 61.) Much of the other equipment is just too expensive for home use. There's usually no need to pay for heavy-duty versions of things like toasters and blenders.

One of my favorite finds at restaurant supply stores is the **prep tables**. These are tough stainless-steel tables used in restaurant kitchens and cooking schools. You can roll pastry right on them; they're pretty indestructible; and if you like the high tech look, they'll fit into your kitchen. Check them out if you're remodelling; they'd make a gorgeous island. They cost $150 and up, depending on size and accoutrements. (You can even find used ones on sale occasionally.) Customize with drawers, pot

racks, shelves, butcher block tops, and so forth.

Many of these stores also sell lovely, old-fashioned **John Boos** solid butcher block tables. You can also buy high-tech-looking wire shelving (Metro and other brands) that restaurants use in their store rooms.

For ethnic gadgets, like **sushi rollers** or **tortilla presses**, you're better off at a supermarket devoted to that cuisine. See the appropriate listing.

Equipment Stores

Alliance Paper and Food Service

913 W. Randolph St.
312.666.6424

A small place in the West Loop food-service neighborhood. They stock **restaurant-size containers** of **spices**, **salad dressings**, and canned goods, as well as paper products, including **parchment paper** sheets.

Chef's Catalog

3009 N. Clark St.
773.327.5210

151A Skokie Blvd.
Highland Park
847.831.1100

These retail outlets for a big catalog company carry a full selection of all the well-known brands of cookware and equipment, including **All-Clad**, **Calphalon**, **Cuisinart**, and **Kitchen-Aid**. It's a good place to buy **knives—Wusthof**, **Henckels**, and otherbrands— and all kinds of electronics, including **hand blenders**, **deep fryers**, and **food processors**. They have frequent sales with discounted prices.

Chefwear

3111 N. Knox Ave.
800.568.2433

Located over the factory in an industrial neighborhood, this outlet has good buys on **chef pants**, **coats**, **hats**, **shoes**, and **aprons**. Call first. Their hours are limited and it's hard to find. The chef's pants are comfortable, indestructible, and have lots of pockets.

Chiarugi Hardware

1449 W. Taylor St.
312.666.2235

This old-fashioned Italian hardware store is the place for **winemaking equipment**, like barrels, corks and chemicals. They sell huge **wine presses**, **citric acid**, **wine yeast**, **malt extract**, and **vinegar mothers** (to start your own batch of vinegar). They carry **Vittorio strainers**, **ravioli presses**, **cavatelli makers**, and of course, **pasta machines**.

Cost Plus World Market

1623 N. Sheffield Ave.
312.587.8037

2844 N. Broadway St.
773.477.9912

1725 Maple Ave.
Evantston
847.424.1022

145 Skokie Blvd.
Northbrook
847.509.1800

2155 W. 22nd St.
Oakbrook
630.573.9826

105 Orland Pl.
Orland Park
708.349.6111

3555 E. Main St.
St Charles
630.587.1011

1055 E. Golf Rd.
Schaumburg
847.413.0400

9454 Skokie Blvd.
Skokie
847.674.2241
www.costplusworldmarket.com

Cost Plus World Market is sort of like Pier One (imported products), only with a large selection of cooking equipment and supplies. They carry **canning jars**, baskets, **madeleine pans**, condiments, **spices** (Spice Hunter), **flavored vinegars**, oils, teas, **woks**, strainers, **gadgets**, **grill equipment**, **biscuit cutters**, and an eclectic bunch of serving ware and dishes. I've purchased cool square bamboo plates for noodles here as well as **cruets** for vinegar. Good prices.

Crate and Barrel

646 N. Michigan Ave.
312.787.5900

850 W. North Ave.
312.573.9800

Outlet store
800 W. North Ave.
312.787.4775

1240 Northbrook Court Mall
Northbrook
847.272.8920

40 Old Orchard Shopping Center
Skokie
847.674.6850

1515 Sheridan Rd.
Wilmette
847.256.2723

54 Oakbrook Center
Oak Brook
630.572.1300
www.crateandbarrel.com

Crate and Barrel was one of the first retailers to carry professional-quality cookware marketed to the home cook. The bright, uncluttered stores have all the name brands, including **Calphalon, Cuisinart**, and **Kitchen Aid**. You'll find an amazing assortment of kitchen **gadgets, cutlery, cookware, baking equipment**, and **electronics**.

Crate and Barrel is also justifiably famous for reasonably-priced, well-designed dishes, glasses, and other tabletop things.

A small but up-to-date collection of condiments and cookbooks rounds out the shopping experience.

Don Outlet Store
2525 N. Elston Ave.
773.489.7739

Edward Don is one of the biggest food service suppliers in the area and this is their retail outlet, so it's crowded with goodies. You'll find many geared toward the home cook, like **Emeril's line** of things and **Wilton cake decorating equipment**.

There's paperware, gadgets like **fish tweezers** (no, no, no, you use them to remove bones), **Microplane graters, pressure cookers**, and lots of pots.

GFS Marketplace
220 E. Roosevelt Rd.
Villa Park
630.832.3354

8146 S. Cicero Ave.
Burbank
708.424.4335

15606 S. Harlem Ave.
Orland Park
708.532.0794
www.gfsmarketplace.com
800.968.6525

A chain belonging to one of the big food service suppliers in Chicagoland. They have a small selection of equipment, but it's the place to go for **restaurant-size cans of tomato sauce** or **chocolate topping**. There are good buys on **paper and plastic goods**, and a frightening assortment of frozen prepared foods that restaurants use.

How to Paint a Plate

It looks like you went to chef school, but it's easy. In fact, I usually enlist the kids to paint the dessert plates at dinner parties.

1. Fill a plastic squirt bottle (available at any of these stores and also craft stores) with sauce, your own or store-bought, or some seedless jam thinned with liqueur.

2. Squiggle a design on the plate before you add the piece of pie or cake. Try circles, v's, whatever. If you want that spiderweb effect, do circles and then drag a knife through at right angles. This also works on top of things, like cheesecake.

3. For non-dessert items, use a squirt bottle of sauce to add spots or squiggles. Try colorful contrasts like dots of basil oil on top of a marinara sauce.

Gold Brothers

1132-50 W. Madison St.
312.666.1520

The downtown spot for chef
shopping. Parking is impossible,
and they are a bit less welcoming
than some places because
they're so busy with restaurant
customers. Still, they have—or
can get—anything. Don't miss
the interesting showroom of **used
restaurant equipment** and furniture, too.

Hi Mart of Chicago

5800 N. Pulaski Rd.
773.478.2550

This huge warehouse store was
quite a find. It's located in an
industrial park behind a fence
and gate, in back of a big, empty
lot. The sign says "Chicago Food
Corp.," which is the company that
owns and operates the huge
Korean market on Kimball with
the same name. You'd never
know Hi Mart was open to the
public, but it is. Just drive through
the gate and park near the sign
(in Korean) with the big "thumbs
up" design.

Inside you will find an impressive
array of restaurant equipment
and supplies. They have stock-

pots so big you could hide inside
them. There is an assortment
of **rice cookers** and **pressure
cookers.** You'll find most of the
usual pans and gadgets with the
emphasis on Asian things, such
as **sushi plates, china dipping
dishes, maki holders, tea sets,
bamboo steamers, bento
boxes,** and the best price I saw
anywhere for a **Benriner slicer.**
It's a wonderland. They even
sell those little **plastic grass
garnishes you get on sushi
plates!** Not to mention some
oddball items, too, including
car floor mats, slippers, and my
favorite brand of ginseng soap.
Don't miss it.

Krasny Supply

2829 N. Clybourn Ave.
773.477.5504

A well-established wholesaler
with a strong retail business as
well. Krasny carries **pots and
pans, glassware, gadgets,** and
some electrical equipment.

Marlinn Restaurant Supply

7250 S. Cicero Ave.
708.496.1700

A very pleasant store with lots of
things for the home cook, includ-

ing **Emeril's product line** and an excellent selection of **garnishing tools**, **V-slicers**, and **gadgets**. Expect good prices on professional aprons, dishes, and glasses. They carry bar supplies, **Wilton cake decorating equipment**, **stock pots**, **cutting boards**, and **heat-proof spatulas**, plus some exotica, like **escargot plates** and **teensy (1/4-inch diameter) cutters** in star and other shapes.

Olympic Store Fixtures

4758 S. Cicero Ave.
773.585.3755
773.585.3366

One of the first supply places I visited and quite a trip! A ton of **used equipment** culled from failed restaurants makes for one chaotic jumble of things all smooshed together in a small space. Used **deep fryers** and **popcorn machines** are displayed next to racks of **tongs** and **spatulas**, the usual selection of **commercial sauté pans** and **thermometers**. It's fun for types who enjoy digging through sale bins. The staff is very busy and will leave you alone to look, unless you ask for help (which you must do for a lot of small items behind the counter). Prices seem to be somewhat negotiable.

Pierce Chef Mart

9685 W. 55th St.
Countryside
708.354.1265

While Pierce carries a lot of **used restaurant equipment**, they also have a front room oriented toward the home cook. You'll find **baking supplies**, **pastry bags and tips**, **pepper mills**, and the like, as well as the usual **sheet pans**, **stock pots**, and **paper products**. The back room, however, is devoted to used equipment from out-of-business restaurants, meaning they sell everything from banged-up napkin holders and silverware to huge glass-door refrigerators like the kind in 7-11 stores. Most of this stuff (like **Hobart mixers** big enough to climb into) isn't appropriate for home chefs, but it's fun to look at.

Ramar Supply

8223 S. Harlem Ave.
Burbank
708.233.0808

Another worthy resource for all the usual stuff, but not as big an assortment as many places. There are some used things and lots of **plastic and paperware**.

Royal Industries

538 N. Milwaukee Ave.

312.733.4920

A manufacturer as well as a supplier, Royal is an excellent source for professional **pots and pans** as well as other restaurant-quality kitchen supplies.

Schweppe Foodservice Equipment

376 W. North Ave.

Lombard

630.627.3550

A very home-cook friendly place that even has "The Food Network" showing on television monitors. This is a big warehouse/showroom with just about everything you could imagine.

They carry all sizes of **ladles** and **tongs**, a huge selection of restaurant **dishes**, **ramekins**, **pizza peels**, **knives**, **colanders**, **mandolines**, **chafing dishes**, and, and... There are even **restaurant-size** packages of **condiments**, **soups**, and **spices**, as well as some some **chefs' clothes**. If you are in the western suburbs, don't miss it.

Something's Cooking

1131 W. Madison St.

312.455.8410

A showroom of professional appliances for home use, including **Viking**, **Garland**, **Gaggenau**, **Traulsen**, **Sub-Zero**, and more. Something's Cooking will give you the information you need about venting, safety, and such. The sad news is that professional equipment designed to be safe and legal for home use is quite expensive.

Superior Products Mfg. Company

1920 Beech St.

Broadview

708.344.6500

This is a "superstore" that is part of a huge national food service supplier based in Minnesota. It's located in an industrial neighborhood where they have a warehouse. Don't be intimidated, however; they are extremely nice and have a lovely showroom. And although it is not oriented towards home cooks, there is no minimum purchase required.

Superior stocks everything a restaurant needs and has a big catalog as well. You can purchase the usual **pots**, **pans**, **ladles**, and **strainers** off the rack in the showroom. Their assortment of **food storage containers** is particularly extensive. Choose clear, frosted, round, or square, in dozens of sizes.

This is also an excellent place to check out **prep tables**, since they have quite a few on display and will explain things to you, including how to order.

Sur La Table
54 E. Walton St.
312.337.0600
www.surlatable.com

This is the first Chicago retail outlet for a popular catalog company that offers an eclectic selection of equipment and serving ware. In addition to **All-Clad cookware** and **Henckels** knives, you'll find **Moroccan tangines** and **couscoussières**, as well as **Weck canning equipment**, **Kuhn Rikon pressure cookers**, and many items imported from France. They carry **Le Creuset** cast-iron cookware, **Provencal garlic pots**, **copper tarte tatin pans**, and much more. Call for a schedule of cooking classes.

Williams-Sonoma
700 N. Michigan Ave.
312.587.8080

900 N. Michigan Ave.
312.787.8991

Northbrook Court Mall
Northbrook
847.291.3626

Oak Brook Center
Oak Brook
630.571.2702

Renaissance Place
Highland Park
847.681.9615

Woodfield Mall
Schaumburg
847.619.0940

Old Orchard Mall
Skokie
847.933.9803

Market Square
Lake Forest
847.295.7045
www.williamssonoma.com

One of the oldest gourmet kitchen equipment stores and still one of the best. **Microplane graters, pasta machines, cappuccino machines, butane torches, mandolines, Kitchen-Aids Mixers**—they carry it all, including brand name cookware (**All-Clad, Calphalon**) and knives (**Wusthof, Henckels**).

There are also cookbooks, including a complete series of single-subject books published by Williams-Sonoma itself and a full line of gorgeous table linens, gourmet condiments, and ingredients to tempt you as well.

To top it off, Williams-Sonoma offers frequent cooking classes and has an extremely knowledgeable group of sales associates. You may be able to find some things cheaper elsewhere, but you won't find more inspiration anywhere.

Wilton Homewares

7511 S. Lemont Rd.
Darien
630.985.6000

All the Wilton cake and candy equipment is available in this outlet. For baking, you'll find **cake pans** in all sizes, **pastry bags and tips**, **paste food colors**, decorations, **equipment for** **wedding cakes**, plenty of gadgets, and the elusive **egg white powder**. For **candy making** they carry umpteen molds, flavorings, and decorating supplies, alongside all the essential ingredients.

Woks 'n' Things

2234 S. Wentworth Ave.
312.842.0701

An Asian cooking supply store in the heart of Chinatown. Here you'll find a huge selection of **woks, cleavers, steamers, strainers**, and **skimmers**, as well as tools for non-Asian cuisine. (You can't have too many strainers!) Check out the intricate **garnishing tools**, including the very elaborate (expensive) **vegetable cutters** that let you make carrots into butterflies or Chinese characters. They carry some books on garnishing, too.

The staff is quite knowledgeable and will help you choose a wok and explain how to cure it. Fellow shoppers are an interesting mix and often happy to chat about Asian cooking.

Knife Sharpening

Just do it. If you're still waiting for the cart with the bell to pull up in front of your house, give up. You need to take your knives to one of these establishments. It's easy, fast, and cheap. And with the possible exception of using good fresh spices, nothing will improve your cooking quicker. Dull knives are not only dangerous, they mash things up instead of slicing. You'll be amazed at how your knife skills improve when you're using a sharp one. (Don't try to sharpen those "Ginzus" though.)

Bagat Bros. Sharp Knife Service

7621 W. Roosevelt Rd.
Forest Park
708.366.2818

A tiny hole-in-the-wall just west of Harlem Ave. They sharpen knives for hundreds of restaurants, but are happy to oblige you, too, at very reasonable prices. Call first, but they usually open at 7 a.m. and close in the early afternoon. At this writing it cost a measly $1.50 to sharpen a 10-inch chef's knife.

Maestranzi Sharp Knife Service

4715 N. Ronald St.
Harwood Heights
708.867.7323

I didn't personally visit this place, but on the phone they gave me a cost of $2 to sharpen a 10-inch chef's knife. They will do it while you wait except at lunch time when the guys aren't there.

Northwestern Cutlery

810 W. Lake St.
312.421.3666
www.cutleryandmore.com

This place is a culinary institution located in the Fulton Market section of town, so while you're here, check out some of the other treasures nearby, like **Isaacson's** for fresh fish (p. 35).

In addition to sharpening knives, Northwestern sells them. There's a big display case of many brands, including **Henckels**, **Forschner**, and the ultra-cool **Japanese brands**.

They also carry tons of **gadgets** and quite a lot of **cookware**, so you can shop for equipment while you're getting sharpened.

The staff is friendly and fun,

albeit a bit macho. Ask one of the sales guys how sharp a knife is and he may just slice a hair on his arm in two to illustrate, while a co-worker looks on saying, "I hate when he does that."

(Japanese vegetable knife)

Top Ten Equipment Picks

1. V-slicers/mandolines* (p. 53)

2. instant-read thermometers

3. squirt bottles* (p. 58)

4. scales

5. tongs

6. chef's pants

7. heat-proof spatulas

8. handheld blenders

9. silicone sheets/parchment paper

10. restaurant sheet pans

Runners-up:

food storage containers
Microplane graters
butane torches
strainers in assorted sizes

*tip or recipe included

HEALTH FOOD

(rice cakes, sprouts,
and dried apples)

Health Food Ingredients and Stores

Although they are primarily vita-min stores, some of the bigger health food stores also stock hard-to-find food items. They make a good source for oddball grains, oils, vinegars, and any-thing to do with soy.

alfalfa seeds
amaranth
avocado oil
barley
blue cornmeal
carob chips
egg whites, powdered
flax seed
fructose
grits
groats
honey: unfiltered, tupelo,
    other varietals
kamut
kasha
lactose
millet
molasses: blackstrap
nut butters: macadamia,
    soy, almond, cashew
oat bran
quinoa
rice: wehani, japonica,
    brown basmati

rye
sea vegetables
soy cheeses
soy milk and powder
soy nuts
spelt
sprouting seeds and equip-
    ment
stevia
tahini
teff
tempeh, flavored
tofu, baked and flavored
vinegars: cider, brown
    rice, umeboshi
wheat germ
whole wheat

Fruitful Yield

7003 Cermak Rd.
Berwyn
708.788.9103

145 S. Bloomingdale Rd.
Bloomingdale
630.894.2553

229 W. Roosevelt Rd.
Lombard
630.629.9242

214 N. York Rd.
Elmhurst
630.530.1445

175 W. Golf Rd.
Schaumburg
847.882.2999

2129 W. 63rd St.
Downers Grove
630.969.7614

5005 Oakton St.
Skokie
847.679.8882

4334 E. Fox Valley Ctr. Dr.
Aurora
630.585.9200

Sherwyn's Health Food

645 W. Diversey Ave.
773.477.1934
www.sherwyns.com

A huge store with what is probably the city's widest selection of grains, nuts, fruits, soy products and frozen convenience health foods. They stock every kind of flour—**buckwheat**, **rye**, **oat**, **amaranth**, **chestnut**, and **tapioca**, and then some, as well as **whole wheat couscous**, many varieties of dried beans, and an assortment of **lentils** that includes **French, beluga, Spanish, green,** and **red**. The respectable Asian goods section contains **organic tamari** and **soy sauce**, plus **ume (red plum) vinegar** that is flavored with shiso and becoming a hot chef's ingredient. There's also a small selection of fresh produce and a good choice of equipment, including **dehydrators** and **juicers**.

Southtown Health Foods

2100 W. 95th St.
773.233.1856

A South Side institution that offers a small selection of **organic fruits and vegetables**, as well as grains, whole wheat flour, spices, and the requisite vitamins, minerals, and soy products.

Whole Foods
Multiple locations

In addition to an extensive array of **organic produce**, Whole Foods stocks **Asian specialties**, **whole grains in bulk**, and a full line of **soy products**.

COOKING SCHOOLS AND CLUBS

(chef's hat and pants)

Cooking Schools

Cooking classes can be recreational, professional, hands-on, or demonstration only. Many individuals/chefs teach an occasional class or series, and these offerings change constantly. The courses listed here are those with a regular location and a more-or-less year-round schedule. Be aware that most community colleges offer cooking classes, too, as do gourmet stores, wine shops, and supermarkets. The Chicago Botanic Gardens hosts a free summer Great Chef Series in their vegetable garden every weekend.

For a more comprehensive listing (over 100 last time) check the *Chicago Tribune* or *Chicago Sun-Times* in late August. They each publish an updated guide to cooking schools yearly.

Calphalon Culinary Center

1000 W. Washington St.
312.529.0100
www.calphalonculinarycenter. com

This brand-new 8,000-square-foot facility has three different teaching areas, including a hands-on classroom with cook-tops and video montiors for each student, as well as a library, wine cellar, and private dining room.

Chez Madelaine

425 Woodside Ave.
Hinsdale
630.655.0355
www.chezm.com

Classes on a variety of subjects, like healthy eating, French technique, and vegetarian cuisine.

Coachouse Gourmet

735 Glenview Rd.
Glenview
847.724.1521
www.coachousegourmet.com

Julie Kearney offers hands-on classes on such topics as hors d'oeuvres, entertaining, and quick gourmet meals.

The Chopping Block

1324 W. Webster Ave.
773.472.6700

www.thechoppingblock.net
The Chopping block holds lots of weekday, weekend, and evening classes to choose from, as well as private classes. You can take an individual class or a series. Ethnic cooking and menus for entertaining are offered. Equipment and ingredients are for sale at the school, too. There's **truffle oil**, **sherry vinegar**, **copper cookware**, **Microplane graters**, and gorgeous but pricey **Japanese knives**. They even have the very odd Asian "**Kewpie Mayo**." This product comes in a squeeze bottle and has a grotesquely cute kewpie on the front. It's used for sushi I'm told.

The Cooking and Hospitality Institute of Chicago (CHIC)

part of Le Cordon Bleu Culinary Program
361 W. Chestnut St.
312.944.2725
www.chicnet.org

Allow me a brief plug for my alma mater: It was taking CHIC's recreational classes that convinced me to pursue a professional diploma there. For the home cook, evening demos and hands-on classes are taught in the school's kitchens by chef-instructors with students helping out with the grunt work. You can also earn a degree or certificate in professional cooking or baking and you don't have to quit your day job. Classes are taught at all hours, including nights and weekends. The CHIC Café serves lunch daily, as well as weekend dinners and brunch. Students do the cooking as part of their study so prices are *very* reasonable and the food is mostly excellent.

Corner Cooks

507 Chestnut St.
Winnetka
847.441.0134
www.cornercooks.com

Proprietor Betsy Simson offers evening and weekend classes. You can also arrange to plan and cook (with professional help) a private dinner party in the charming dining room, something considered a good form of team-building for business people these days. On Friday nights the place turns into a restaurant with dinner served for one seating. Prepared foods made by Chef Larry Smith are available for take-out. In addition, they carry a small selection of **cookbooks** and condiments including **truffle oil** and **paste**.

Kendall College

2408 Orrington Ave.
Evanston
847.866.1300, x6360
www.kendall.edu

The other big private professional cooking school in Chicagoland (and arch-rival of CHIC) also offers programs for the non-professional. "Spice Up Your Life" classes run weeknights and Saturdays. Kendall has an open-to-the-public restaurant, too, for sampling students' work.

Oriental Market and Cooking School

2801 W. Howard St.
773.274.2826

Pansy and Chu-Yen Luke teach six-week courses on Chinese cooking, as well as single-session Saturday classes on Japanese, Vietnamese, Indonesian, and Thai food.

Wilton School of Cake Decorating and Confectionery Arts

2240 W. 75th St.
Woodridge
630.810.2211
www.wilton.com

Over 50 courses are offered at Wilton from cake decorating, fondant, pulled sugar confections, cake assembly, and Old World candy making, to starting a business. Individual classes or a course of instruction are available.

World Kitchen

66 E. Randolph St.
312.742.8497
www.worldkitchenchicago.org

These affordable classes are sponsored by the city. Some hands-on and some demo, these classes focus on ethnic cooking as well as basic skills and techniques. A summer-time roof garden provides a lovely setting for lessons in grilling.

Clubs and Organizations

American Institute of Wine and Food

312.440.9290

www.aiwfchicago.org

This national organization devoted to the exploration and celebration of food and wine was started decades ago by Julia Child and Robert Mondavi. The Chicago Chapter sponsors events, dinners, wine tastings, and excursions. There is a local newsletter for members.

ChicagoCooks.com

312.848.3644

www.chicagocooks.com

Proprietor Dana Benigno offers a Web-based resource for Chicago-area cooks. Membership gives you access to menus for entertaining, complete with prep lists, shopping lists, and suggestions for table decorations. The site also posts foodie events, news, farmers market locations, and other useful information for members and non-members alike.

Cooking with the Best Chefs

630.930.6001

www.bestchefs.com

A west suburban organization that sponsors cooking classes, restaurant tours, wine dinners, mushroom foraging, and cooking trips.

ChicaGourmets

Don Newcomb, president
708.383.7543

donaldnewcomb@home.com

A gourmet organization whose members plan events that let them experience new restaurants, cuisines, and the chefs who create them. Don Newcomb is well plugged into the Chicago culinary scene and has helped arrange many food-oriented lectures by visiting chefs and authors, so his is a good mailing list to be on.

The Culinary Historians of Chicago

info hotline:
773.955.5503
or contact:
Susan Ridgeway
815.439.3960
www.culinaryhistorians.org

Meetings are usually held monthly at the Chicago Historical Society; lectures and events relate to food history, ethnic cuisines, and the food business. Memberships and events are very reasonably priced.

Local Palate

3906 N. Broadway St.
773.472.8277

A free bi-monthly on all things related to food in the Midwest. You'll find it at bookstores, gourmet stores, Whole Foods, and the like. (Same places you pick up *The Reader*.) It covers artisanal products, restaurants, wine, food events, and more. If you need help finding it, or have an idea for a story, call my friend Christina Hansen, who is the publisher. And don't miss my columns on ingredients!

Slow Food

www.slowfood.com

An international organization begun in Italy devoted to promoting the sensual enjoyment of food and banishing the degrading effects of fast food. They sponsor local and national events on food education and tastings. For information on the Chicago chapter, e-mail: PortiaBL@yahoo.com

LATIN AMERICA

(guajes, tomatillos, peppers, and tortillas)

Latin American Ingredients

Chicago is a rich treasure trove of foods from Mexico, Central America, and South America. If you're used to the Mexican section at Jewel, a visit to a real Mexican (or other Latino) grocery may surprise you with its foreign feel and wealth of unidentifiable ingredients. It's a lot more fun, and you can expect better quality, selection, and prices than you get in a gringo store. So if you're looking for **fresh tortillas**, **dried chiles**, or just excellent quality herbs and meat, it's worth seeking out a nearby Latin American grocery, even if you never cook anything authentic at all.

shoulder as an example. I was understood completely. There's usually not a huge selection of seafood (at least compared to an Asian store), but you will almost always find raw, **head-on shrimp,** plus **sea bass**, **cod** or **snapper** and usually **mussels** or **clams**, too.

bacalao (dried cod)
beef tongue
carnitas, ready-made
chicharrónes (pork rinds)
chicken feet
chorizo sausage
cow feet
lamb hearts, liver

Meat/Fish

Meat is almost uniformly top quality in even small groceries. For one thing, they usually carry **"choice" grade**, which is a huge improvement over the "select" available in regular supermarkets. For another, there is a real live person standing behind the counter to assist you. Language can sometimes be a barrier, but there's always pointing and acting things out. I have found myself explaining the cut I wanted by using my own rump or

Carnitas and Barbacoa

Most stores with a full-service butcher shop prepare traditional meat dishes to take home from the deli. Carnitas is pork, slow-cooked until it's falling off the bone. Barbacoa is barbecue, but Mexican style. Each is utterly delicious and usually available only on weekends. They make great fillings for tamales or enchiladas, too.

pig, every part but the
oink: ears, heads,
tails, spine, trotters
shrimp, head-on
skirt steak
tripe

Produce

These shops are very good
places for veggies in general, as
well as specialty items. There is
an abundance of things you'd
expect like peppers and avoca-
dos, as well as excellent lettuces
and herbs. At any one time you
won't find all the items listed, only
those that are in season. (Fresh
chiles and herbs are included
here, dried ones in the spices
and seasonings list.)

boniato
calabaza
chamomile
chayote
cherimoya
chiles: Anaheim, arbol,
    habanero, jalapeño,
    perone, poblano,
    serrano
cilantro
epazote
garbanzos, fresh
green coconuts
guajes

guavas
huazontle
jamaica (hibiscus)
jícama
lita squash (a kind of zuc-
    chini)
malanga (yautia)
mangos
mint
ñame (white yam)
nopales (cactus paddles),
    whole, cleaned, and
    chopped
papayas
plantains
prickly pear fruit (tuna)
tamarillo
tamarind
tomatillos
verdolaga (purslane)
yucca (cassava)

Love That Lita

I'm not sure whether lita
squash (sometimes called cal-
abacita) is strictly a Mexican
import, but it's wonderful.
You'll find it in most Latino
groceries. It's shorter and
fatter than a zucchini with an
earthier, nuttier flavor and
less bitterness. The flesh is
crisp and dense and the seeds
unnoticeable. Use it wherever
you would regular zucchini.
It even tastes good raw.

Spices and Seasonings

achiote paste
achiote seeds
adobo seasoning
bouillon cubes: flavored
    with tomato, annatto,
    coriander
canela (Mexican cinnamon)
chamomile
chiles (dried): ancho, arbol,
    chipotle (red are mori-
    tas or colorados, brown
    are mecos), guajillo,
    pasilla
chipotles in adobo
hot sauces, all kinds
jamaica (hibiscus)
Mexican oregano
mole paste, vari-
    ous kinds
salsas, lots of
    unusual ones
tamarind paste

Julie's Ancho Pepper Dip

6 ancho chiles
1 T. minced garlic
2 T. chopped cilantro
1/2 C. sour cream
1 tsp. lime juice
salt and pepper

Reconstitute the anchos
by covering with boiling
water. Let stand at least 30
minutes. Drain. Clean peppers
by removing seeds and stems.
Puree in food processor with
garlic and cilantro. Combine
ancho puree, sour cream, and
lime juice. (Start with 2 tsp.
puree and add more for
deeper flavor.) Season. Serve
with crackers or veggies.

Chile Table of Correspondence

Dried	Fresh
ancho	poblano
chipotle (moritas, mecos)	jalapeño
pasilla	chilaca
guajillo	mirasol

In general, larger, rounder, thick-walled
chiles are milder than smaller, thin-walled
pointy ones. Individual variations exist:
some jalapeños are mild, others fairly hot.

Carbs

The land of corn. You will find many versions, from huge dried kernels often called "**mote**," to prepared **masa** to make your own tortillas and tamales. (Buy yourself a tortilla press. I was very humbled by trying to do it bare-handed. In fact, I am still humbled by trying to make them—even with a press.) Canned **hominy** is very versatile and can be used in soups, stews, and also tastes great sautéed with greens.

hominy, dried and
    canned
masa (prepared dough for
    tortillas or tamales)
masa harina (flour to make
    corn dough)
mote blanco (white dried
    field corn)
tortillas, all kinds

Rice and beans are also very important carbohydrate sources in these cuisines and most stores offer good prices on these staples. Since the turnover is huge, freshness is almost guaranteed. You'll discover many new kinds and colors of beans (including pink!), canned and dried.

beans: black, canary,
    coba, pink, pinto,
    white, kidney, dry or
    canned
habas (fava beans, broad
    beans)
pigeon peas (gandules) dry
    or canned
refried beans, canned
rice: medium grain, long
    grain, Valencia (pearl,
    short grain)

Groceries

chufa (tiger nut, earth
    chestnut)
corn husks
empanada wraps
guava paste/puree
huitlacoche (corn smut),
    canned
lard (usually the
    hydrogenated kind, talk
    to the butcher about
    buying the real thing)
mango paste/puree
panela (loaf-shaped brown
    sugar)
passion fruit paste/puree
pigeon peas
piloncillo (cone-shaped
    brown sugar)
plantain flour

Dairy

cajeta (caramel sauce made from goat's milk)
crema (Mexican sour cream)
dulce de leche (caramel sauce made from milk)

Mexican cheeses go by many different names and brands. The list here is far from definitive. In general "queso fresco" is mild, fresh, soft cheese; queso añejo is aged and harder. Queso fresco is good crumbled on top of things but won't melt. It's a nice addition to any kind of salad. Queso añejo is more like Parmesan and often grated onto things.

queso añejo (an aged version of queso fresco)
queso asadero (a melting cheese)
queso blanco (creamy white, cow's milk cheese)
queso Chihuahua
queso Cotija (hard, sharp, grating cheese)
queso criollo (yellow cheese similar to Muenster)
queso enchilado (queso añejo with a spicy red coating)

queso fresco (crumbly white mild cheese)
queso Oaxaca (a melting cheese, "Mexican mozzarella")
queso ranchero (same as queso fresco)

Miscellaneous

chicharrónes (pork rinds)
fava beans, spicy
Mexican chocolate (YUM!)
peanuts, spicy
pumpkin seeds and nuts, flavored with chiles, lime, etc.
tropical juices: guava, mango, etc.
tropical sodas: Jarritos and other brands

Equipment

lime squeezers
molcajetes (lava mortars)
molinillos (see photo)
comales (griddles)
tortilla presses

molinillo
(chocolate
frother)

Cheater's Tamales

Here's a sneaky modern way to enjoy tamales more often.
Also a great use for leftover roast chicken or pork.

**1 tub of La Guadalupana masa para tamales
dried corn husks, soaked in hot water
for at least an hour to soften
prepared salsa, homemade or store bought
fillings: cheese, corn, chicken, pork or beef,
in small chunks or shreds**

Set out all the ingredients and find a big
pot with a steamer insert (or one that will
hold a vegetable steamer) and that has a cover.

Lay a drained husk on a flat surface and spoon a heaping
tablespoon of the masa on it. Use your fingers to smear it
into a square layer in the middle of the husk leaving the
pointy ends naked. In the middle of the masa arrange a bit
of cheese and/or meat. Top with a spoon of salsa.

Wrap up the tamale by lifting the two long ends and folding
them over so the masa encloses the filling. Don't get too
concerned if a bit of filling leaks out or the job is not perfect.
Then fold over the pointy ends of the husk to make a package
and tie it shut with cotton twine or a strip of corn husk.
Set aside and go on the next one. You will get better at
adjusting the amount of filling and wrapping.

To cook, stand the tamales upright in the steamer. Touching
is OK, but they must be in a single layer. Put an inch or two
of water in the bottom and steam gently for an hour, adding
water to the pan if needed. Tamales are done when the
husk pulls away from the masa without sticking.

Tamales freeze well and reheat beautifully, so make lots!

Latin American Stores

Armitage Produce

3334 W. Armitage Ave.
773.486.8133

In the heart of Humboldt Park, this nice grocery caters to the needs of its Puerto Rican and Central American neighbors and has the biggest, best selection of **tropical tubers** I've seen— **malanga lila**, **malanga blanca**, **yucca**, and more. They're also worth the trip for the **breadfruit**, a good spice selection, the full-service butcher, and those big, flaky, crunchy, island-style crackers simply called **galletas**.

Cardenas

3922 N. Sheridan Rd.
773.525.5610

Around forever, this friendly, full-service Latin American grocery is not as big, slick, and new as some, but they'll probably have what you need. There's not a huge array of produce and herbs, but the mid-north location near the lake (with a parking lot!) makes Cardenas very convenient.

Carnicería Jimenez

3850 W. Fullerton Ave.
773.278.6769

4204 W. North Ave.
773.486.5805

2140 N. Western Ave.
773.235.0999

37 S. York Rd.
Bensenville
630.766.0353

A well-established chain of stores, mentioned in **Rick Bayless's** books (I've visited only the one on Fullerton),which is big, well-stocked, clean, and has a parking lot. You will find most anything you need, particularly good produce, lots of meat (all choice grade), a huge selection of seasonings and chile peppers (both fresh and dried), **frozen empanada dough**, **frozen tropical fruit pulps** (**mango**, **guava**, etc.), and some equipment. There is also a small restaurant attached.

Chicago Produce
3500 W. Lawrence Ave.
773.478.4325

Similar in size to Lindo Michoacán (p. 89) this store, as its name suggests, offers plentiful produce, including herbs, **tamarind, plantains, calabaza, jamaica,** and **yucca.** The butcher shop carries some unusual items, like **lamb hearts, pig tails, lamb liver,** and **lard.** To keep things interesting, there's even a small selection of Polish specialties.

Delray Farms
3239 W. Belmont Ave.
773.478.6958

5205 N. Broadway St.
773.334.2500

1701 W. Cermak Rd.
773.890.9200

6500 W. Fullerton Ave.
773.745.9600

2247 N. Milwaukee Ave.
773.772.0022

3311 W. 26th St.
773.762.2598

A chain of produce and grocery stores that are everywhere. I've listed only the city stores, but there are many more suburban ones. Not a bad place to start your shopping for Latin American ingredients as there is probably one near you. Delray carries **chiles, tomatillos, corn husks,** and all the other basics, and has a butcher shop. The prices are good, but the quality varies, so shop with care.

Dulcelandia
3300 W. 26th St.
773.522.3816

5117 S. Kedzie Ave.
773.737.6585

3855 W. Fullerton Ave.
773.235.7825

Okay, so this is not a grocery store, but it is loads of fun. It's a Mexican sweet shop with all sorts of goodies not available anywhere else. **Piñatas** hang from the ceiling and usually an employee walks around with free samples. You can buy **mango-flavored marshmallows, tamarind candy,** and all sorts of **by-the-pound sweets.** Try the "**Crunchitos,**" peanuts with a crunchy, spicy coating, a bit like beer nuts only LOTS tastier.

Fiesta Market

3925 W. Lawrence Ave.
773.478.2882

The very nice produce in this supermarket includes all the tubers (**boniato, yucca, yautia**), plus herbs like **epazote** and **huazontle**. They also carry **masa** from **La Guadalupana**, plus a full selection of the usual cheeses, canned goods, and meats.

Joe's Food and Liquor

3626 W. Lawrence Ave.
773.478.1078

A smallish grocery with a huge selection of **dried beans and corn**, a small selection of produce and meat, and many **Central American items**. They also prepare **roast pigs** for your fiesta!

La Casa Del Pueblo

1810 S. Blue Island Ave.
312.421.4640

A big, well-established market in the Pilsen neighborhood: clean, friendly, and with all the basics (though they didn't have pre-

pared masa when I visited). The store is now part of the Certi-Saver chain, which may be the reason it seems more American to me than the other Latino markets in Little Village or on the Northwest Side. That probably makes it a very good place to pick up your Cheerios and Tide at the same time as your epazote. They have a big deli, a good produce section (lots of **chiles**, fresh and dried), and a nice meat selection. Street parking, I suspect, may be a problem during busy times. La Casa operates a taqueria next door, and the famous Mexican bakery, **La Nopal**, is two doors down.

La Chiquita

3555 W. 26th St.
773.522.0950

2637 S. Pulaski Rd.
773.542.0950

9655 Franklin Ave.
Franklin Park
847.455.2724

A small chain with a selection and ambiance very similar to La Justicia (p. 88). You'll find fine produce (**guajes, fresh chiles, epazote**), a butcher shop, and all the standard **mole pastes**, salsas, cheeses, and beans.

La Guadalupana

"La Casa de la Masa"
3215 W. 26th St.
773.847.3191

4637 S. Archer Ave.
773.843.1722 or
dial 773-tamales

Tamale heaven. La Guadalupana is justifiably famous for prepared **tamales** and **masa** of all kinds. When you visit, proceed beyond the grocery section to the rear for masa and tamales. You can choose **masa for tortillas** or **masa for tamales** (either plain or sweet). Here you purchase masa by the pound, but La Guadalupana also distributes its products to most Mexican stores in the city. In fact, some have just appeared in my Oak Park Jewel! And don't leave without taking home some of their tamales. Fantastic. There are always four or five varieties and they are totally delicious.

La Justicia

3435 W. 26th St.
773.521.1593

3644 W. 26th St.
773.277.8120

Both these stores in the heart of the Mexican Little Village neighborhood have a restaurant attached. Both have a fairly complete choice of canned goods, cheese, produce, **chiles**, salsas, and so on, plus extensive butcher shops with every kind of **pork** product, **pig heads, cow feet.** Of course, huge slabs of **chicharrónes** (fried pork cracklings), are for sale on top of the meat counter, where blocks of **guava paste** are also displayed for some reason.

La Unica Foodmart

1515 W. Devon Ave.
773.274.7788

La Unica is unique. This fascinating store specializes in Central American and Cuban ingredients. When you first walk in you'll see **racks of chips**, not potato, but **plantain, taro,** and **yucca.** They have several varieties of **fruit paste**, like **guava** and **quince**, as well as syrups flavored with **passion fruit, tamarind, guava,** and more. One section is filled with dozens of different tins of fish: sardines, of course, in various sauces, but also **octopus, squid in its own ink, mussels, cockerel, scallops,** and more. The canned fruit is just as exotic. (Try canned **guava shells.**) There are flours and mixes to make breads and fritters, including **manioc flour, barley flour, bean flour,** and **pea flour**. Canned olives come stuffed with such things as tuna and hot peppers. **Yerba maté** (the South American drink) is here, as well as a big collection of medicinal teas and herbs.

There are many frozen prepared foods to choose from, too. The arepas (Columbian corn cakes) that I tried had an English muffin shape and a fresh corny flavor. Stocking **tamarillo, morro, guanabana,** and **mamey,** La Unica also has one of the widest varieties of frozen tropical fruit purees I've seen.

Finally, there's a small selection of equipment, plus a choice of beers and booze from Salvador, Peru, Honduras, and the Caribbean.

A restaurant is attached to the store and offers Cuban specialties at good prices, as well as tropical smoothies made from passion fruit, mango, and guava.

As you check out, check out the pomades, exotic soaps, and little tins of medicinal herbal salves across from the register.

Lindo Michoacán

3142 W. Lawrence Ave.
773.279.8834

Located in one of my favorite neighborhoods for food shopping—the area around Kedzie and Lawrence in Albany Park—this complete store has beautiful produce, including a big selection of Mexican items and herbs. Besides the usual **epazote,** you'll find (in season) **huazontle, guajes, pepicha,** and my favorite, **verdolaga (purslane)**. The complete meat department is next to a deli that offers **carnitas** and other specialties prepared on premises. Oh, yeah, there's a big parking lot, too.

Maxwell Street Market

1500 S. Canal St.
Sundays, year round
7 am to 3 pm (go early)

This is the new Maxwell Street open-air market, set up to replace the much-lamented old Maxwell Street. It's big, crowded (especially on nice days), and loaded with junk. As my mom used to say, if you like that sort of thing, it's just the sort of thing you'll like.

On my last visit, Maxwell Street

was somewhat short on produce and long on used tools and vacuum cleaners, but it is still great fun. You will find a good selection of dried and fresh **chiles** at a produce stand on the south end of the market, along with **jícama**, **tomatillos**, **guajes**, and **fresh garbanzos**.

The real reason to go, however, is the food stands. Don't miss the **papusas** at the north end of the market. These Salvadoran masa pancakes are filled with a choice of cheese, beans, chicharrónes, etc. Each one is hand-made and the woman who does it makes it look so easy! There are also several good places near the 14th Street entrance. You can see the food being prepared, so pick what looks good. A few stands have waitress service. It always looks like there's no room to sit, but there usually is. Tables are happily shared and if you show an interest, somebody will help you order or offer recommendations. Salsas and pickled vegetables are in big jars or pitchers on the table. Try something different. How wrong can you go when steak tacos cost a buck?

Pan American Foods

5617 N. Clark St.
773.275.7474

The "Foods" at this small grocery are **Central and South American specialties**. Of course, you can still get mainstream stuff, like beans, rice, and chiles, but in addition there's a large selection of **mote blanco**, dried corn for toasting, **plantain flour**, **horchata mixes**, and frozen **plantain leaves**. They carry some fresh produce and had **mamey** when I visited, but the wonderful and unusual choice of frozen tropical fruits— **guayaba** (**guava**), **mora** (Andean blackberry), **date palm**, **soursop**, **passion fruit**, and **mamey**—really shines. The staff is friendly, although not much English is spoken. There's a Salvadoran café attached.

Top Ten Latin American Ingredients

1. ancho, chipotle, and other dried peppers* (p. 80)

2. jalapeño, serrano, habanero, and other fresh peppers

3. lita squash* (p. 79)

4. masa* (p. 84)

5. Mexican chocolate

6. carnitas and barbacoa* (p. 78)

7. tropical fruit purees

8. mango* (p.44)

9. hominy

10. verdolaga (purslane)

*tip or recipe included

TIPS ON TROPICAL TUBERS

A visit to the produce department of any Latin American, Caribbean, African, or Asian store will present you with a number of lumpy, bumpy potato-like vegetables that may be new to you. Yucca, malanga, taro, and their tuberous relations are the ugly ducklings of the vegetable bin, but looks aren't everything.

These starchy, filling, pleasantly bland ingredients are the backbone of some African and Caribbean cuisines. Worldwide they are used more than the potato, and generally can be used in similar ways, so they are definitely worth getting to know, though that's not always easy.

Part of the problem is that each of them has many different names depending on the ethnicity of the person labeling them. To add to the confusion, they are often mislabeled or unlabeled, and most of them come in more than one variety.

Probably the most important shopping tip I can offer is this: Make sure that the tubers you take home are fresh. Purchase them in a market that has a lot of product displayed. Usually one or two samples will be cut open to reveal the interior and showcase its freshness. Please do squeeze—a fresh tuber is firm without soft spots.

These ingredients can be used many ways, so consult an ethnic cookbook or Web site for ideas. I can provide you with one foolproof recipe, however. They all make great deep-fried veggie chips! (See p. 53.)

YUCCA (also spelled yuca, often called cassava or manioc)

It can be boiled, baked, deep-fried, stewed, and used in dessert. Yucca is an important food every place it grows. Most Americans only know it in the form of tapioca. There are many kinds, and the bitter kind is poisonous if not cooked, so cook it! Yucca is a good side dish, simply boiled or steamed first, and then sautéed in olive oil with heaps of garlic.

MALANGA (also called yautia, cocoyam)

The many varieties are often labeled by the color inside (lila for lilac, blanca for white, etc). The outside is shaggy and ringed and looks a lot like taro with which it is often confused. Malanga makes tasty and pretty home-fried chips, especially the lilac version which has specks of color.

TARO (also called dasheen, eddo)

This tuber is also shaggy and ringed. The commonest kind here seems to be the small turnip-shaped taro. It is used to make Hawaiian poi among other things. The flavor is mild and nutty.

BONIATO (sometimes labeled batata or Cuban sweet potato)

A sweet potato, but with a texture that is fluffier and a flavor that is more like a baked potato than our sweet potato. The shape is bumpier and the skin is paler and patchier, but boniatos may be cooked in all the same ways as regular sweet potatoes and they're delicious.

For more information, consult *Uncommon Fruits and Vegetables*, by Elizabeth Schneider (see the bibliography, p. 228). She explains things clearly, offers recipes, and provides drawings.

All photos life-size.

taro, dasheen, eddo

malanga, yautia, cocoyam

boniato, batata,
Cuban sweet potato

malanga lila,
yautia

yucca, cassava,
manioc, tapioca

malanga blanca,
yautia

EASTERN EUROPE

(savoy cabbage)

Eastern European Ingredients

Chicago has a population of Poles second only to Warsaw. Not to mention a huge number of Lithuanians, Czechs, Estonians, and Russians. This provides a wonderful resource for cooks, even if they're not particularly interested in the cuisines of Eastern Europe. In a good Polish store, you'll find cuts of meat, mushrooms, honey, syrups, cheeses, grains, and spices you can't get elsewhere. And prices are generally quite low, too.

Meat and Fish

Their butcher shops are excellent and cheap. Even small stores have extensive delis with an assortment of very good bacon, lunch meats, and, of course, sausages galore.

calf liver
chicken gizzards
chicken, whole, smoked
deli meats, including
    headcheese and gypsy
    pork loin
fish, smoked: trout,
    salmon, whitefish
ham, fresh
herring, every kind
pork of any kind, includ-
    ing trotters and pork
    belly, smoked items
sausage, dozens of kinds
sweetbreads
tongue
tripe
veal bones for stock

The Best Scrambled Eggs in the World

fresh, organic eggs
fresh farmer's cheese (the kind in a tub)
salt, pepper, and chives
a few T. of cream or milk
butter for frying

Add 1 T. of cheese for every egg you're using. Whisk it into the eggs along with seasonings and cream or milk. Fry in butter. The cheese makes the eggs fluffy and delicious even if over-cooked.

Spices and Seasonings

Eastern European cuisine isn't known for its spices, but you will find an assortment of seasoning packets for making Polish-style fried chicken, **borscht**, etc., as well as a seasoning mix called **"Vegeta"** that is a popular blend of vegetables and MSG.

citric acid
dill, fresh
horseradish, fresh or jarred, with or without beets
sorrel, fresh
paprika, Hungarian
poppyseed
Vegeta

Carbs

Bakeries are usually quite good, especially for rye breads. Do try Lithuanian sourdough rye from the **Baltic Bakery**, a brand that's widely distributed.

barley, all kinds
buckwheat, toasted or not
kasha (buckwheat groats)
oats/oat bran
rye bread, pumpernickel
whole wheat, wheatberries

Groceries

The jams of Eastern Europe are delightful and come in exotic flavors like rose hip, aronia, and gooseberry. I used to think to get those you had to make them yourself. Honey is also taken seriously, as are pickles and pickled things.

exotic jams: aronia, gooseberry, rosehip

Lithuanian Potato Gratin
(Serves 6)

5 or 6 potatoes
1 jar (5 oz) horseradish
2 T. chopped fresh sage
salt and pepper
1 C. heavy cream
bread crumbs
1 T. cold butter in pieces

Preheat oven to 350°. Slice the potatoes paper thin. Put a layer in a shallow, buttered casserole. Smear with some horseradish and seasonings. Repeat until potatoes are used up. Pour on the cream, making holes with a knife so it penetrates all the layers. Top with crumbs, dot with butter, cover, and bake for about an hour. Uncover for last 15 min. to brown.

mushrooms, pickled
peppers, pickled
pierogis
sauerkraut

Dairy

Eastern European shops are the home of one of my favorite ingredients—fresh farmer's cheese. It is light, delicate, and fresh tasting. It comes in tubs like cottage cheese, but tastes more like ricotta. I add it to eggs, stuff it in crêpes and eat it straight.

farmer's cheese, soft or
    pressed
kefir
Polish cheeses
Scandinavian cheeses

Miscellaneous

I won't go into detail on the huge selection of **European candies and cookies** available, but these places have everything from my favorite chocolate-covered cherries in booze to awesome kolackys and dozens of kinds of hard candy with hilarious names ("lobster tails," "Eddy"). For the cook, there is an array of syrups—not the kind you put on pancakes, although you could—but fruit syrups that can be used for jazzing up seltzer water, making a meat glaze or sauce, or flavoring cheesecake.

European candies, cookies,
    and chocolate
fruit syrups: morello cher-
    ry, currant, rose hip,
    more
pierogis, frozen prepared

Drinks

These stores are great for juice drinks and teas, including medicinals. My daughter's Polish nanny used to give her **chamomile tea** as a baby to cure her colic. Sometimes it worked.

fruit and vegetable drinks,
    boxed: cherry, carrot,
    currant, etc.
kvas
teas: chamomile and more

Cham-Polski

A pretty drink and a nice change from ordinary white wine.

Pour a little fruit syrup (morello cherry or black currant are good) in a wine glass. Fill with champagne, white wine, or sparkling water.

Eastern European Stores

A-J Meats

3541 W. 99th St.
Evergreen Park
708.422.4130

This deli is tucked away on a side street on the South Side near St. Laurence H.S. The neighborhood is **Lithuanian** and so are the products. They carry the specialties that you'd get in any Polish store, plus some things that are uniquely Lithuanian.

Go for the ready-made **kugelis** and **bacon buns**, and at Christmas-time the dumplings used to make **shlisikai**, or poppyseed milk soup.

You'll also find **Polish and Lithuanian breads**, fried pastry, sausage of all descriptions, fresh sauerkraut, pickles, and the usual **farmer's cheese**. They carry baked goods from the **Baltic Bakery** and the **Racine Bakery**.

Andy's Deli

3055 N. Milwaukee Ave.
773.486.8160

A tiny store in Little Poland known mainly for meat and sausages (they have an excellent **house-smoked bacon**), though they do carry a few groceries.

Bobak's Sausage Company

5275 S. Archer Ave.
773.735.5334

A South Side favorite, Bobak's is a good-sized grocery with a restaurant attached. While the grocery selection is not quite as broad as it is at Wally's, you can find most of the same things, like lots of sausage, prepared foods, and an extensive meat section that carries **geese** and **ducks**.

Gene's Sausage Shop and Deli

5330 W. Belmont Ave.
773.777.6322

Though a little off the beaten (Polish) path, don't miss this large grocery, deli, and butcher. Customers line up at the counter for **pork belly**, **trotters**, and plenty of **house-prepared sausages**.

Gene's stocks an assortment of all kinds of sweets, grains, and seasonings (including **Vegeta**, of course), with notable selections of **European candies**, **fruit syrups**, **tort wafers**, and **jams** in flavors like **wild blackberry** and **aronia-apple**. The dairy case is small, but has the basics, including the usual brands of **farmer's cheese**. Almost an entire aisle is devoted to tinned fish: In addition to **sardines** in every imaginable oil and spice, they stock **sprats**, **herring**, and others.

Finally, they have a strong liquor and wine department, including unusual items like **chocolate vodka**, **peach liqueur** from France, and plenty of **Polish beer** and **vodka**.

Gilmart

5050 S. Archer Ave.
773.585.5514

Gilmart is east of Midway Airport, between Pulaski and Cicero. They are known for having great **Polish sausage**, but a complete deli/meat counter also offers **herring**, **house-cured bacon**, salads, and many cuts of pork. There is the expected variety of syrups, pickles, and jams in jars, as well as pickles (cucumber) and pickled fish in barrels. Prices are good and it is usually bustling. A small restuarant is tucked into a corner.

Halina's Polish Deli

6714-18 W. Belmont Ave.
773.685.8569

A small, but cute deli whose sign outside proclaims Halina's, "Winner of the Pierogi Fest, 1994." The frozen **pierogis** *are* excellent. They also have sausages, bacon, a small selection of jams, and grocery items.

Joe & Frank's Homemade Sausage

7147 W. Archer Ave.
773.586.0026

3334 N. Milwaukee Ave.
773.283.0310

8720 S. Ridgeland Ave.
Oak Lawn
708.599.3800

Though the biggest of these stores is the one on Archer, they all have excellent butcher shops, lots of **homemade sausages**, and the usual Polish specialties—**farmer's cheese**, syrups, pickles, etc. This is also where I found **mushroom powde**r, a tasty addition to homemade pasta among other things.

Kurowski Sausage Shop/Rich's Bakery

2976 N. Milwaukee Ave.
773.645.1692

Kurowski is a good-sized market with an especially comprehensive assortment of **sausages**, teas, and spices.

Teas include the Indian and Chinese varieties, as well as every sort of herbal, fruit tea and many unrecognizable combinations. They also have dieter's tea and other medicinal types.

Spice products include several variations on the all-purpose, ubiquitous **Vegeta**, which combines vegetable bits and MSG.

Mulica's Deli

3118 N. Milwaukee Ave.
773.777.7945

Beyond the usual spices and stuff, there is lots to drink at Mulica's. A large assortment of herbal teas is displayed, and **beer from Eastern Europe** is available by the single bottle, so this is a good place to try out some of the dozens of different brands.

Rich's Deli

857 N. Western Ave.
773.235.5263

Rich's is a neighborhood institution in the Ukrainian Village neighborhood. They have a meat counter, deli, and liquor. In grains, I found the usual **buckwheat**, as well as **spelt** and **barley**. They also carried **saltpeter**, **pork fat**, and lots of different breads.

Wally's International Market

6601 W. Irving Park Rd.
773.427.1616

3256 N. Milwaukee Ave.
773.736.1212

The original store on Milwaukee in Little Poland is a bit smaller and shabbier than the new improved Wally's on Irving Park, east of Oak Park Avenue.

This is a real supermarket. You will be overwhelmed and delighted with the assortment. The prices are very good, too.

Check out the **smoked fish**, the jars of **pickled things**, and the **jams**. The deli has more kinds of **sausages** than you knew existed, as well as a large assortment of **house-smoked meats**. They also prepare many of **their own cold cuts,** which are excellent and reasonably priced.

Wally's bakery is awesome. Try the **"Starapolski" bread**—a huge crusty loaf that smells wonderful and tastes even better.

Don't leave without some bread, jam, and **farmers' cheese** at least.

A minor warning: You need to put a quarter into a slot in order to get a shopping cart at the Irving Park Wally's.

You can also offer a shopper who's finished a quarter for her cart. You get the money back when you return the cart or "sell" it to someone else. (This can be confusing when you don't speak the language and folks start proferring quarters.)

Casmira's Pennycakes
(Makes about 12, 6-inch pennycakes. Can be doubled.)

My Lithuanian grandma called these thick crêpes pennycakes.

1 C. flour (preferably Wondra)
1 C. milk
3 eggs, preferably organic
pinch of freshly grated nutmeg (optional)
generous pinch of salt
4 T. melted butter, divided
farmer's cheese and smoked salmon for filling

Measure the flour into a bowl and add the milk gradually, whisking out as many lumps as you can. Minimizing lumps is the reason for Wondra Flour. (You'll find it in a tall canister in the flour section of most groceries.)

Whisk in the eggs one at a time, then stir in 2 T. of the melted butter, the salt, and nutmeg. You should have a pourable batter, thicker than heavy cream.

Heat a 5- or 6-inch non-stick frying pan over medium heat. Brush the surface with a little of the remaining butter. Pour a puddle of batter into the center of the pan. Tilt the pan to to spread the batter over the bottom. When the center begins to get dull (less than a minute), shake the pan to loosen the penny-cake. And this is the fun part, flip it! Yes, you can do it. Toss the pennycake by jerking the pan up and away and back towards you in one motion. Keep your eye on it so you can position the pan under it on the way down. You'll probably miss a few times, but have a utensil handy and unfold the messed up pennycake, or pick it off the ceiling, or let the dog have it. Let it cook for another 5 seconds and it's done. Cool on a rack. (Can be frozen.)

Put a small slice of smoked salmon and a tablespoon of fresh farmer's cheese in the middle of each pennycake, fold over the sides and roll into a package. Bake at 350° until cheese melts.

Stella's Stuffed Cabbage
(Serves 4)

1 head cabbage, washed, leaves separated
1 C. rice
2 eggs
1 onion chopped
1 T. butter or oil
1 lb. ground pork
1/2 lb. ground beef
1 carrot, shredded
1 tsp. Vegeta
salt and pepper to taste

prepared mushroom or tomato sauce

Pre-heat oven to 350°. Pull off cabbage leaves and cut out the hard center core section at the bottom of each one. Bring a big pot of water to boil. Meanwhile cook the rice in 2 C. of water until done. Put the cabbage leaves in the water and cook until wilted (5 minutes). Reserve the cooking water.

Heat the butter or oil in a sauté pan and cook the onion until limp, but not brown. Combine the meat, cooked rice, egg, carrot, and seasoning. Lay down each cabbage leaf and spoon on some filling. Fold over the sides and roll up into a package. Place in a baking dish seam-side down. When all the cabbage rolls are assembled, add 1-1/2 C. of the cabbage cooking water. Bake at 350° for about 45 minutes, or until the meat is cooked through.

Serve with mushroom and/or tomato sauce.

Helen Szajkovics's Famous Kolackys

Helen was from Bratislava, Czechoslovakia,
and her daughter, Pam, often treats lucky
friends to these rich, traditional cookies.

3 C. flour
3 egg yolks (separate and hold whites on side)
1/2 lb. butter
1/2 cake yeast or 1 packet of active dry yeast,
dissolved in 1/4 C. luke warm milk
1/4 pint sour cream
1 T. sugar

fruit filling:
purchase at any Polish store—your choice of
apricot, prune (povidla), raspberry, pineapple.

Preheat oven to 350°.

Mix all ingredients except fruit filling.

Let dough rest, covered with towel for an hour.

Roll out thin on floured board. Cut in squares,
fill with a small spoon of fruit filling. Cross
opposite corners; dab with water to hold together.

Place on cookie sheet. Brush with egg-white.
(Just whip with a fork, not a blender.)

Bake for 15-20 minutes or until golden brown.

Top Ten Eastern European Ingredients

1. farmer's cheese* (p. 100 & p. 107)

2. fruit syrups* (p. 102)

3. house-cured bacon and sausage

4. jams and fruit fillings* (p. 109)

5. pork, especially fresh ham, butt

6. smoked fish* (p. 107)

7. horseradish* (p. 101)

8. honey

9. pierogi (they're not an ingredient, but...)

10. whole wheat (wheatberries)

*tip or recipe included

ITALY

(radicchio and pizzelle)

Italian Ingredients

Italian is usually the first cuisine we think of as Mediterranean. Certainly Italian cooking has been mainstream for a long time, especially here in Chicago, land of pizza and Italian beef. Many ingredients like **fresh basil**, instant **polenta**, **pine nuts**, and **risotto rice** are available at almost every grocery store. Therefore, the markets included have something special to offer—either more exotic ingredients or a better selection or both. I'm aware that there are dozens of local Italian delis that escaped my notice and/or selection criteria, so apologies if your favorite was left out.

Meat and Fish

Usually a big Italian market will carry a slightly skewed choice—the steak and chicken you'd find in a regular market, but also more **deli meats**, **veal**, and **lamb**. Same with seafood, though these stores are generally great places for **sardines** and **squid**.

Fish and Seafood:
anchovies, in salt, in tins, or by the pound
baccalà (salt cod)
clams
mussels
octopus
sardines, fresh
squid

Meat:
rabbit, often frozen
veal breasts
veal cutlets
veal shanks (osso bucco)

Cured Meat:
bresaola (cured raw beef)
pancetta: regular (round) or smoked (strips)
prosciutto: crudo and prosciutto di Parma (cured, but uncooked)
prosciutto cotto (cooked)
sausages, homemade: all kinds depending on the region of the maker

Produce

We'll skip the obvious eggplants and peppers, but know that all these relatively ordinary items are cheap and good.

artichokes, baby
arugula

broccoli raab (rapini)
cardoons (cardi)
chicory
dandelion
escarole
fava beans
fennel (finocchio)
figs, fresh
olives, uncured
radicchio

Spices and Seasonings

balsamic vinegars: red,
    white, aged
basil, fresh
caper berries
capers, in brine or salt-
    packed
Italian parsley, fresh
oregano, fresh
rosemary, fresh
sage, fresh
syrups: Torani and other
    brands; almond,
    hazelnut, and other
    flavors
wine vinegars

You Don't Have to Baby Baby Artichokes

If you love the flavor of artichoke but hate the time-intensive task of trimming and de-choking, try the baby version available in the spring. No bigger than a real baby's fist (but a lot pointier), they're very easy to handle because they haven't yet developed a fuzzy choke or all those tough outer leaves. Just whack off the top and stem and cut them in half or quarters and they're good to go. They are an excellent addition to pasta with pesto.

Genna's Spinach Risotto

5 C. chicken broth (low sodium preferred)
2 T. olive oil
1 medium onion, chopped small
2 tsp. minced garlic
1 C. raw Arborio rice
1 tsp. dried basil
1 bunch fresh spinach, washed and chopped (one box frozen)
salt and pepper to taste
1/2 C. fresh grated Reggiano Parmesan
1/8 tsp. fresh ground nutmeg

Heat all the broth and keep it just below a simmer for the duration. Heat the oil in another wider pan. Add the onion and cook until softened, then add the garlic. In 30 seconds, put in the raw rice and stir it around for a minute.

Now comes the fun part. Put a ladle full of hot broth into the rice and stir. When the rice absorbs it, add more. The rice mixture should stay at a low simmer. Don't worry. This is really hard to screw up as long as you don't let the rice dry out and burn. Add the basil when you feel like it. (You can use fresh basil, but don't add that till the end of the cooking.)

Taste and season after 15 minutes. When the rice is soft on the outside but still hard in the middle, stir in the spinach.

Keep adding broth and checking the doneness of the rice. It's difficult to be precise about amounts and timing since it depends on the rice, the size of the pan, and the vibes of the person stirring. The whole process takes between 20 and 40 minutes. You may not use all the broth or you may run out. If so, use water or white wine.

The risotto is done when just cooked through. Turn off the heat, add the Parmesan and nutmeg, and adjust the seasoning.

Carbs

farro (spelt)
flours: 00 (hard flour,
    like semolina), chest-
    nut, chickpea (ceci),
    semolina (pasta flour)
pasta: squid ink, orchietti,
    many wild shapes and
    imported brands
pizza crusts, ready to top
pizza dough, for pizza,
    focaccia, or calzones
polenta, instant or regular
rice: Arborio, Carnaroli,
    Vialone Nano (all for
    risotto)

Groceries

artichoke paste
beans: borlotti, cannellini,
    lupini
cannoli shells
chestnuts
olive paste, green and
    black
pesto, green or red
porcini mushrooms, dried
roasted peppers
tomatoes, San Marzano
    canned
tomatoes, sun-dried

Dairy

Cheeses:
Asiago
Bel Paese
Fontina
Gorgonzola
Grana Padano
mascarpone
mozzarella: fresh cow's
    milk, buffalo milk
    (mozzarella di bufala),
    smoked
pecorino Romano
Reggiano Parmesan
ricotta
ricotta salata
Stracchino
Taleggio

Is Real Reggiano Worth It?

Yes. You can be sure you're
buying the real thing by
checking the rind to see the
word "Reggiano" stamped
there in pinpricks. Enjoy this
luscious treat on its own,
paired with fruit and wine, as
well as grating it over your
pasta. Grana Padano is similar,
cheaper, and fine for most
cooking, but not as tasty.

Caprese Salad

This classic combination of fresh mozzarella, tomato, and basil is so perfect it doesn't really need a recipe. In tomato season, I can (and have) eaten Caprese for breakfast, lunch, and dinner. I consider myself an expert. Here's what I've learned:

1. The quality of mozzarella varies wildly. The best is usually made where it's sold. It should be soft, not mushy, and should exude cream when you cut into it. **Caputo Cheese Market** (p. 118) makes a good one.

2. Fresh mozzarella is sold covered by a water/whey liquid. When you store mozzarella in your refrigerator at home, you should keep it in a container filled with water. Change the water daily if you don't eat it all up immediately.

3. Don't even bother making Caprese unless you have really fresh flavorful tomatoes. Ditto basil.

4. The very best dressing is simply salt, pepper, and a drizzle of aged balsamic vinegar (the pricey kind). Balsamic vinaigrette is also good and has the advantage of letting you pass the dressing at the table so everyone can use what they want. Leftovers keep better undressed.

5. Making your own mozzarella is sort of fun, but it takes a gallon of milk to make a lousy 3/4 of a pound! One experiment convinced me that store-bought is not only better, it's worth every penny.

6. You can create a stunning salad with combinations of different color tomatoes interspersed with different kinds of basil. Or try cherry tomatoes, whole basil leaves, and bocconcini (little balls), skewered shish kebab style for a stylish hand-held salad.

Broccoli Raab and Polenta
(Serves 4)

Quick cooking polenta (enough for four or more)
1/2 C. grated Parmesan or Asiago cheese
2 T. butter
salt and pepper to taste

1 large bunch of broccoli raab
(or substitute chard, spinach, or mustard greens)
3 cloves garlic, minced
3 T. olive oil
2 tsp. of balsamic vinegar
2 tsp. of soy sauce
1/4 C. pine nuts, preferably toasted
salt and pepper to taste

I am somewhat embarrassed to admit to using instant polenta, but for a weeknight supper it's a lifesaver. If you have the time, do it the long way.

Wash the broccoli raab and chop it into bite-size pieces. Heat a big sauté pan, add the oil, then the garlic. After 30 seconds put in the thicker stem sections of broccoli raab (or other greens), stir to coat with oil and garlic, then cover for 5 minutes to help the greens cook. Uncover and add the leafy parts. Stir again and cook until the desired degree of tenderness is reached. Season with balsamic vinegar, soy sauce, salt, and pepper.

Meanwhile make the polenta. Bring the salted water to a boil and add the polenta in a steady stream while stirring. When the polenta is thick enough, turn off the heat, add the butter and grated cheese, season, and cover to keep warm.

Top a big scoop of polenta with the broccoli raab and sprinkle pine nuts on top. Easy and delicious.

Italian Stores

Bari Foods

1120 W. Grand Ave.
312.666.0730

Bari has been around forever and with good reason. It's a small store, but jam-packed with imported Italian goods. They make their own sauces and deli items, and they are excellent. Stop by **D'Amato's Bakery** next door (1124 W. Grand) for some real old-fashioned Italian bread while you're at it.

Caputo Cheese Market

1931 N. 15th Ave.
Melrose Park
708.450.0074

Although it's down an industrial side street off North Avenue and just west of First Avenue, Caputo's is worth seeking out for good prices on all kinds of cheeses from **Manchego** and cheddar to a huge choice of Italian ones. They make their own fresh **mozzarella** and **ricotta**. It is also an Italian grocery with **prosciutto**, deli meats, prepared food, spices, and the usual canned and dried Italian items. (No relation to the other Caputo's.)

Caputo's

2560 N. Harlem Ave.
Elmwood Park
708.453.0155

1250 Lake St.
Hanover Park
630.372.2800

240 W. Lake St
Addison
630.543.0151

Caputo's is an institution—a must for anyone who cooks. They have a huge and well-priced selection of produce, an awesome Italian deli, plus fish and meat. The sign outside used to proclaim, "If we don't have it you don't need it."

Produce is their forte and you'll find not only hard to locate Italian items like baby artichokes and escarole, but also **Latin American** and **Asian produce**, like **persimmons** and **malanga**. You can buy by the case, too—strawberries, figs, uncured olives—whatever's in season.

Caputo's grocery aisles offer a lot of **Polish items** (farmer's cheese!) and a fair selection of **Middle Eastern** and **Latin**

American foods. The Bella Romana brand is Caputo's own, and provides real bargains on canned Italian goods and pasta.

The deli (be sure to take a number) displays wonderful homemade sausages, imported **prosciutto**, all kinds of olives and prepared salads, as well as the classics. The bakery shelves hold just about every local brand of Italian bread, so it's a good place to try the different kinds.

The place is always a zoo. The main store on Harlem recently remodeled to double its size and it's just as jammed as ever. Negotiating a shopping cart is a trick and finding parking in the lot can be a challenge. It's fun if you're in the mood, since the clientele is a diverse mix, but if you can help it, don't go on Saturday or Sunday afternoon.

Conte di Savoia
1438 W. Taylor St.
312.666.3471

A lovely store in the old Italian Taylor Street neighborhood. Not huge, but nice. They have an upscale deli with a good selection of **cheese**. You'll also find **truffle oil**, **aged balsamic vinegar**, **canned chestnuts**, and exotic pastas like **salmon tagliatelle**. The liquor section has

Italian specialties like **Limoncello** and **Cynar**.

Convito Italiano
1515 Sheridan Rd.
Wilmette
847.251.3654
www.convitoitaliano.com

Convito is a restaurant, deli, and Italian gourmet shop. For starters, there's a wide selection of oils and vinegars—**aged balsamics, olive oils pressed with lemon and other citrus fruits, truffle oils**, and **nut and grapeseed oils**. They also stock three kinds of **risotto rice**—**Arborio**, **Carnaroli**, and **Vialone Nano**, in addition to high-end pastas, canned **San Marzano tomatoes**, and gourmet sauces and condiments of all kinds. The deli displays a small selection of mainly Italian cheese, sausage, and a large choice of prepared foods.

D'Andrea Italian Market
7055 W. Cermak Rd.
Berwyn
708.484.8121

Tucked away at the eastern end of a mall (the one with the

sculpture that consists of cars on a huge skewer), D'Andrea has been around serving the near western suburbs for decades. The narrow aisles are packed with pastas, **risotto rices** (**Arborio** and **Carnaroli**), and other canned imported Italian goods. **Fresh mozzarella, ricotta, Reggiano Parmesan, prosciutto, homemade sausages**, and antipasti are highlights of the big, full-service deli. Prepared sauces, frozen ravioli, pizzas, and **pizza dough** are also on hand.

Gino's Italian Imports

3420-22 N. Harlem Ave.
773.745.8310

In the "Piazza Italia" on Harlem, this small Italian grocery and deli also carries some equipment. When I visited they had imported pasta serving dishes, as well as huge $300 grinders. (I'm not sure for what.) There were a couple of odd choices on the shelves, like **maté**, the South American tea-like drink. Next door is a fresh pasta shop, where you can purchase homemade **pumpkin ravioli, rottoli**, and more.

Isola Imports

1321 W. Grand Ave.
312.421.9490

A high-end deli devoted to the Italian gourmet. You'll find a wide range of **balsamic vinegars**, including one aged for 100 years. They carry **fresh truffles** and **mozzarella di bufala** as well as more mundane pastas, sauces, and olive oils. An entire display rack is devoted to **truffle paste, truffle oil, truffle vinegar**, and the like.

Joseph's Food Market

8235 W. Irving Park Rd.
773.625.0118

A large deli and grocery at the far western end of Irving Park Road. All the staples are here (**anchovies, porcini, balsamic, semolina**, etc.), and while the meat/fish department is small, it carries **rabbit** and **octopus**. The produce section is modest, but they have **fig trees** and **basil plants** for sale in the summer. The variety of equipment, however, goes way beyond the usual. You'll find **pasta machines**, of course, but also **cavatelli makers, espresso machines, Vittorio strainers**, huge expensive **wine presses**, and a "**torchietto spremi**," which is, according to the directions posted, "a food squeezer to flatten for preservation or extract oil and liquids."

L'Appetito
875 N. Michigan Ave.
312.337.0691

30 E. Huron St.
312.787.9881

A small deli/grocery downtown. They do a booming business in sandwiches at lunchtime, but also carry a modest assortment of Italian necessities like **Arborio rice**, **Reggiano**, etc.

The Pasta Shoppe, Inc.
3755-59 N. Harlem Ave.
Elmwood Park
773.736.7477

This is a tiny store that specializes in homemade fresh and dried pasta. They also carry some Italian cheese. It's included because it's on Harlem in Italian Elmwood Park, near Caputo's and the other stores, and if you're in the neighborhood...

Top Ten Italian Ingredients

1. Arborio rice* (p. 114)

2. Reggiano Parmesan* (p. 115)

3. basil* (p. 116)

4. fresh mozzarella* (p. 116)

5. baby artichokes* (p. 113)

6. proscuitto de Parma

7. balsamic vinegar* (p. 116 & p. 117)

8. broccoli raab (rapini)* (p. 117)

9. ready-to-use pizza dough

10. polenta* (p. 117)

*tip or recipe included

GReeCe aNd THe Middle eAST

(fresh fava beans)

Greek and Middle Eastern Ingredients

Whether the store is owned by an Assyrian, Jordanian, Lebanese, or Greek, a Middle Eastern grocery is a wonderful place for the home cook. The **pita bread** and **feta** alone are worth the trip. Nuts, dried fruits, and olives are fresh and cheap. There are wonderful spice blends, **rose water**, **phyllo sheets**, and plenty more.

Meat and Fish

Usually these stores are relatively small and at best carry deli items and prepared sausages—**soujouk** and **basturma** (dried beef). Go to one of the halal butcher shops on Devon (p.154) for **lamb** or **goat**.

cod roe, smoked taramasalata

Produce

Middle Eastern groceries don't offer much in this category either. I think most places just don't have the turnover or the space to handle perishables in quantity. They do have a few unusual things in season, however, often stocked at the front of the store.

currants (real ones, the California ones are actually small raisins)
dates, many kinds
figs
nuts: pine nuts, walnuts, almonds (fresh), hazelnuts, pistachios, more
olives, all kinds

Spices and Seasonings

Here's where these shops become a gold mine for cooks, as they have many things you just don't find other places. Sometimes items are not marked in English. Then there are the spice blends spelled many mysterious ways, often with unidentifiable ingredients, and "house" blends which can vary greatly from place to place. The famous **ras el hanout** includes at least 20 spices and means "head of the shop" because each version was put together according to the owner's unique recipe. There

Pomegranate Chicken

(Serves 4)

2 whole, boneless skinless chicken breasts
1-1/2 C. walnuts
1/4 C. flour
2 eggs, beaten lightly
2-4 T. olive oil
1/4 C. pomegranate concentrate
1-1/2 C. chicken stock
salt and pepper

Rinse and separate the chicken into four pieces. Flatten by removing the tenderloin (that little skinny part underneath) and then covering with plastic wrap and pounding until thickness is fairly even, about 1/2-inch. Chop the walnuts coarsely with the flour in a food processor. Put the egg and the walnut mix into separate shallow dishes. Salt and pepper each chicken piece, then dip into beaten egg, followed by the walnut coating. Press the coating onto both sides so it sticks.

Heat the oil in a sauté pan. Add the chicken and brown both sides. Cook through, about 10 to 15 minutes total. Don't crowd the pan and don't worry about some walnut mixture falling off (it thickens the sauce). Remove the chicken and keep warm.

Add the chicken stock and pomegranate concentrate to the pan. Cook, scraping up the brown bits, for about 5 minutes until the sauce thickens slightly. Taste and adjust seasoning. Pour over the chicken and serve.

are many herbs that are sold for medicinal purposes rather than for cooking, so if you don't recognize something, but want to try it, ask. (Herbs can be strong medicine.)

Fortunately, at least in my experience, the proprietors of many shops speak English and are happy to answer questions, give you recipes and opinions, and generally talk your ear off!

angelica
baharat (blend of nutmeg,
    peppercorns, coriander,
    cumin, clove, paprika)
cardamom
citric acid
fenugreek
harissa (Tunisian chile
    sauce with red chiles,
    cumin, coriander, mint,
    caraway, and more)
hibiscus
lemons, dried
limes, dried
mango powder (amchoor)
mastic
molukhia (Jew's mallow)
orange blossom water
pomegranate concentrate
    (pomegranate molasses)
rose water
sesame
sumac
syrups: almond, tamarind,
    mulberry
tabil (blend of coriander,
    caraway, garlic, and
    chile)
tahini (sesame paste)
tamarind paste
verjus (sour grape juice or
    grape vinegar)
zaatar (blend of sumac,
    thyme, and sesame)

Carbs

basmati rice
bulghur wheat: coarse,
    medium, fine
chickpea flour
couscous
freekah (green cracked
    wheat)
Israeli couscous (the big
    kind)
lentils: brown, red, yellow
rishta (pasta)

Groceries

almonds, raw
amardine (dried apricot
    in sheets)
beans: brown, fava
carob molasses
cashews, raw
grape leaves
halvah
honeys: date, sage, more
kishke
melon seeds, many kinds
phyllo, in sheets and in
    shreds
pistachios, raw or roasted
preserves: rose, pistachio
    bitter orange, fig

Spinach/Cheese Phyllo Triangles
(Makes 6-10 appetizer servings)

1 box frozen chopped spinach,
thawed and squeezed dry
1 T. olive oil
1/2 onion chopped
1 egg
1/2 C. crumbled feta
1/2 C. farmer's cheese or ricotta
salt and pepper to taste
2 tsp. dill weed
1/2 box of phyllo sheets
1/2 stick butter, melted

Make the filling first. Sauté the onion in oil for a few minutes. Add the squeezed spinach and cook another minute or two. In a bowl mix the cheeses with the seasoning and egg, then add the cooled spinach mixture. Mixture can be refrigerated for a few days in a covered container.

Preheat oven to 350°. Clear a large work surface, place the melted butter in a dish with a pastry brush, get the baking sheet out, and dampen a clean dishtowel to cover the phyllo. Unroll the dough and cut it the long way into strips about 3 inches wide (a pizza cutter works well). Remove one single strip from the stack. Immediately cover the rest. Brush gently with the butter. Place a teaspoon of filling near one short end about an inch from the edge. Fold the corner over to cover the filling and make a triangle. Keep folding and making triangles, like folding a flag, until you've used up the strip. Trim off any extra and place on baking sheet with the loose end down. Continue until you fill the baking sheet and use up the filling and phyllo. Bake for 15 to 20 minutes until puffed and golden.

"Phun" with Phyllo

Phyllo (or filo) is paper-thin pastry. You buy sheets of it rolled up in a box from the refrigerated or freezer section of any Middle Eastern or Greek store. There are two tricks to working with Phyllo:

1. It dries out in a heart beat, so keep it covered with a damp cloth as you work.

2. Don't get upset when it rips; just cover up with another sheet.

Phyllo is versatile. Roll a buttered layer around apples and sugar for strudel. Cut into circles or squares and stuff into muffin tins, one buttered layer at a time to make puff pastry cups that can be filled with almost anything sweet or savory. One traditional recipe is on the previous page.

Dairy

cheese: feta (many kinds), kasseri, touloum
kefir
labna (yogurt cream cheese)
yogurt

Bagels and Labna

In the refrigerated dairy case, you'll find cartons of labna, the cream cheese of the Middle East. It tastes like cream cheese with an attitude (a sour attitude). Try it anywhere you would normally use cream cheese. Or smear some on toasted bread, crackers, or pita; drizzle on olive oil; and top with coarse salt and fresh cracked pepper for a delicious new take on cheese and crackers.

Miscellaneous

baklava
Jordan (candy-coated)
    almonds
lavosh
pita bread, white or
    wheat, many sizes
Turkish delight (rahat
    loukoum)

Rahat Loukoum

Turkish delight as it is called in English is a
legendary sweet that everyone should try at least
once. Kind of a clear, gummy candy coated in sugar,
it comes in wonderful flavors like rose, pistachio,
and mastic. There is an entire song about it in
"Kismet" where it features in a seduction. It is
also a magical, addictive candy offered to children
by the bad witch in C.S. Lewis's Narnia series.
Nothing can live up to all this, of course, but it
is tasty. Sort of a cross between gummy bears
and Jello. And it's extremely pretty.

Tomato-Red Lentil Soup
(Serves 4-6)

This recipe is my attempt to create a soup similar to one served at Reza's restaurant. The secret ingredient is sumac. Sumac is a sour spice used almost like salt in some parts of the Middle East. It's also an ingredient of zaatar, a table seasoning frequently sprinkled on flat breads.

2 T. olive or vegetable oil
1 medium onion, chopped
1 large stalk celery, chopped
1 medium carrot chopped
2 cloves garlic, minced
1 large can (28 oz.) chopped tomatoes
4 C. chicken stock or broth
1/2 C. red lentils
2 T. dried parsley (or one bunch fresh, chopped)
salt and pepper to taste
1-2 tsp. sumac (to taste)
juice of 1 small lemon (optional)

Heat the oil in a soup pot over medium heat. Add the onion, celery, and carrot, and cook until softened (a few minutes). Add the garlic, then in a minute add the tomatoes and chicken stock.

Simmer for about 20 minutes, season, and let cool. Puree the soup, then strain it back into the pot. This removes tomato skins and most seeds. Add the lentils and return to a low simmer.

Taste a lentil in about 15 minutes to see if it's tender. If not, continue cooking, but don't let them get mushy. Add the sumac and parsley. Taste for seasoning and add lemon juice if you like.

Serve with a dollop of yogurt on top.

Greek and Middle Eastern Stores

Al-Khyam Bakery and Grocery
4738 N. Kedzie Ave.
773.583.3077

Al-Khyam makes the best **pita** bread. In fact, it's carried in many other stores, but as long as you're here, buy it at the source. This cram-packed grocery has all the Middle Eastern basics—**pomegranate concentrate**, **soujouk sausage**, **labna**, plus lots of canned goods, including the largest selection of **canned favas** in the world. There's even a small meat counter.

Arax Foods
9017 N. Milwaukee Ave. Niles
847.966.1808

A clean, brightly lit store that prides itself on stocking ingredients for all the Mideastern cuisines—**Persian, Jordanian, Armenian, Egyptian, Turkish, Palestinian**. You will find the best selection of **spice mixes** here alongside single-note herbs and spices of all kinds. There

are bins of snacks and nuts, a well-stocked freezer case, **jams**, a deli for **cheese**, and a good selection of bakery goods, as well as the usual items.

Athens Grocery
324 S. Halsted St.
312.332.6737

A Greektown landmark since the 60s. After lunch or dinner on Halsted, stop here to pick up **feta**, **Greek oregano**, olive oil, canned goods, and groceries.

Best Turkish Foods
2816 W. Devon Ave.
773.764.5093
www.bestturkishfood.com

A pretty little shop tucked into the Indian/Pakistani majority on Devon Avenue. A small deli features Turkish cheeses (like **kasseri**) and meat specialties (**soujouk**, **basturma**). The jam-packed shelves hold Turkish coffees, teas, interesting jams and preserves, and packaged mixes for **bulghur pilaf** and such.

This is the best place to buy your **Turkish delight** as they stock several kinds. Ask one of the friendly clerks for a recommendation or go for the expensive one.

Brillakis
9061 N. Courtland Ave.
Niles
847.966.1250

The emphasis here is on **Greek** specialties, including **liquors** and **liqueurs** (a great selection of **ouzo**). They also carry many brands of **phyllo**, **giant limas**, and **cracked wheat**.

Devon Food Market
2958 W. Devon Ave.
773.381.0021

This small grocery located at the western end of Devon (where the Russian stores are) is an ethnic hybrid, but carries mostly Middle Eastern specialties, including sheets of dried apricot (**amardine**), **tahini**, and such.

Holy Land Bakery and Grocery
4806 N. Kedzie Ave.
773.588.3306

This delightful store has been around for years and it's easy to see why. It's well-stocked and the staff is helpful. Ask for Jarad, who will answer questions, talk politics, and even provide recipes. They carry a good range of **grains**, **nuts**, **jams**, and **sweets**, including the usual bins of **bulghur**. There's an excellent deli loaded with **olives** and **cheeses**, and a good choice of **yogurt**, **labna**, spices and condiments, including the all important **pomegranate concentrate**. They also stock a mysterious-looking, cone-shaped ingredient called **lektc**. It's made of yogurt and goats milk and is grated and used in stews, according to Jarad.

One of the best parts is you can stop at Holy Land and then visit **Clark Market** across the street for Korean food (p. 207) and the big Latin American market, **Lindo Michoacán** on Lawrence (p. 89). All without moving your car! (See **Delicious Day Trips** chapter, pp. 218-219.)

International Food and Meat Market

8747 S. Ridgeland Ave.
Oak Lawn
708.233.9999

Located in a South Side strip mall and hard to spot, this is small store that doesn't have a lot of "tourists" and seems to cater to ethnic customers who are (I'm guessing) Palestinians. They have all the basics—spices, grains, **tahini, labna**. If you live southwest, it's a real find.

Middle East Bakery and Grocery

1512 W. Foster Ave.
773.561.2224

In addition to fresh pita and a selection of pastry, this store offers all the staples. You'll find **couscous, lentils, dried fruits and nuts, bulghur, labna,** and a large assortment of **spices** packaged in-house, including **sumac** and **zaatar**. The Andersonville location makes for good shopping and eating nearby, but lousy parking.

Pars Persian Store

5260 N. Clark St.
773.769.6635

This store has been smack dab in the middle of Scandinavian Andersonville for a long time and is a good place to stop off before or after dining at Reza's (Persian) or Ann Sathers (Swedish).

The Pars inventory includes many herbs and spices, **couscous, tamarind, pomegranate concentrate**, and other staples. They also have jarred **harissa** and a wider-than-average collection of flavoring "waters." Besides the traditional **rose** and **orange blossom waters**, Pars offers **cumin, sweetbrier**, and **peppermint waters**.

There are fresh barrels of nuts and seeds up front. At the time of my visit they had a fruit called **seyjid** which looked like a pale date, was said to be good for cleansing the digestive tract, and is a traditional food for Persian New Year's feasts.

In addition to food, they stock books, dishes, medicinal herbs, and even **hookahs**!

Ted's Fruit Market

2840 W. Devon Ave.
773.743.6739

A large store on multi-cultural Devon that sells a good selection of produce and a huge assortment of breads, including **Ukranian ryes**, as well as many **Middle Eastern flat breads** and **pitas**. Greek specialties are well represented in the grocery section. There are pastas, including **trahina**, **Greek jams**, **honeys** of all kinds, and much more. You'll also find a selection of Middle Eastern **yogurt**, **labna**, and **kefir**.

Top Ten Greek/Middle Eastern Ingredients

1. couscous

2. phyllo dough* (p. 127 & p. 128)

3. pomegranate concentrate (pomegranate molasses)* (p. 125)

4. labna* (p. 128)

5. sumac* (p. 130)

6. pita bread

7. feta cheese* (p. 127)

8. bulghur wheat

9. olives

10. dates

*tip or recipe included

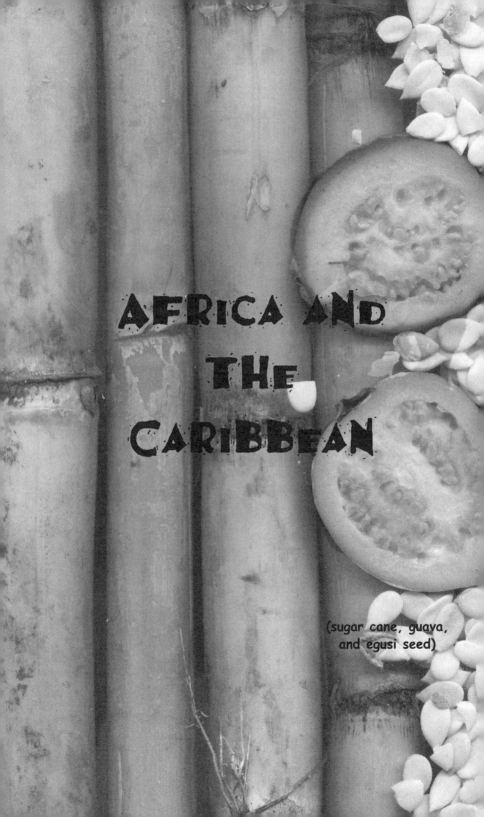

AFRICA AND THE CARIBBEAN

(sugar cane, guava, and egusi seed)

African and Caribbean Ingredients

This is a big category and a slippery one. It comprises everything from Jamaican jerk to Haitian curry and Nigerian egusi soup. Many ingredients overlap with those listed under Latin America because many items (**yucca** and **guava**, for instance) are used by several cultures. You will find stores listed under **Latin America** that specialize in Cuban (**La Unica**, p. 88) and Puerto Rican (**Armitage Produce**, p. 85), although you'll also find many of those ingredients here.

Meat and Fish

Go to African and Caribbean shops for **offal**, **cow feet**, **goat feet**, **pig tails**, and many smoked versions of these things. Although fresh seafood is part of these cuisines, the choices are limited compared with Asian stores. There is, however, a large variety of **smoked and dried fish**.

chicharrónes (pork rinds)
conch, frozen
cow feet
fish, smoked
goat, fresh or smoked
pig tails and snouts
salt fish, dried
salt pork
shrimp, dried

Produce

Tropical fruits and vegetables abound, and there is almost always a good selection of greens, peppers, and tropical tubers. (See **Tips on Tropical Tubers**, p. 93.) Yams in various sizes and colors are a primary carbohydrate source in most of these cuisines. (The various flours made from them are listed under carbs.)

boniato (batata, Cuban
    sweet potato)
breadfruit
chayote (christophene,
    mirliton)
chiles: habanero, Scotch
    bonnet
dasheen (taro)
guava
June plum (Jamaica plum)
mamey
okra
peanuts, green
plantains: green, black

quenepa (Spanish lime,
    mamoncillo, mamones)
sour orange
sugar cane
tomatillos

yams: white, yellow, Ghana
yautia (malanga, cocoyam)
yucca (cassava)

Guava Guidelines

Guava is my favorite fruit flavor, tropical and mysterious, without that over-ripe, decadent taste you sometimes get in mangos or papayas. The flavor and scent are tangy sweet with flowery overtones.

Fresh guava is often available here. While there are many varieties and the flesh can vary in color from almost white to hot pink, the kind usually sold in Chicago is small (2- to 3-inch diameter) and green on the outside with a lovely pink inside. You can recognize it by sniffing. I've always been disappointed with the taste of the fresh fruit (they tend to be VERY seedy and rather bland), but they sure make the kitchen smell good.

Guava puree is in the freezer case in Caribbean or Latin American stores. It makes an excellent smoothie or sauce.

Guava jam is also a good glaze or ice cream topping.

Guava juice is available most everywhere. It's delicious, but a beige color instead of the gaudy pink of the fruit.

Guava paste comes in a brick shape and tastes wonderful paired with cheddar cheese (sounds strange, but it's a perfect match).

140

Spices and Seasonings

achiote
allspice (called pimento or
    Jamaican pepper)
annatto
canela (soft-stick cinna-
    mon)
cassareep (flavored, con-
    centrated cassava juice)
curry powder, West
    Indian
criolla seasoning
egusi seed (squash seed)
filé (sassafras powder)
hot sauces, dozens of dif-
    ferent kinds
jerk seasonings and pastes
kichela (green mango chut-
    ney)
piloncillo (brown sugar
    cones)
sofrito (a tomato-based
    seasoning sauce)
solomon gundy (herring
    paste)
tamarind
turbinado sugar

Carbs

Gari is cassava (yucca) flour and comes in sour or sweet versions. It is the basis for Jamaican **bama** bread and for **egba**, a classic Nigerian starch dish. You will also see something labeled "**farinha**," It's not Cream of Wheat, but another term for the same dried cassava flour. Toasted and flavored with palm oil, it is called "**farofa**," a crunchy sprinkle used on top of many Brazilian dishes.

cane syrup/juice
cassava meal
corn flour
cornmeal: white, yellow,
    coarse, fine, hominy
    grits
couscous de manioc
    (attieké, cassava cous-
    cous)
fu fu (foo foo) flour (dried
    pounded flour from
    yams, plantains, corn,
    or rice)
gari, sour or sweet
kenkey (fermented corn
    meal cakes, found in
    the freezer)
millet

Groceries

ackee, canned (a creamy
    white tropical fruit
    used in Jamaican
    Salt Fish and Ackee)
banana leaves, frozen

callalloo (soup made from taro greens)
cassava leaves, frozen
dende (palm oil)
gandules (pigeon peas, gun-goo peas)
jute leaves, frozen
pickled hot peppers
rice flour

semolina
tropical fruit purees: mango, passionfruit, guava
tropical jams: guava, coconut, passion fruit
zomi (spiced palm oil)

In Praise of Plantains

Sometimes called the cooking banana or plátano, this relative of the regular sweet banana is versatile and delicious. Usually available in various stages of ripeness, plantains are cooked in stews or boiled like potatoes when green. When ripe the skin turns black, but the fruit inside retains a firm texture. The flavor is somewhere between banana, squash, and potato. Green ones will ripen gradually so you can enjoy them at many stages. What an obliging fruit!

Breakfast Plantains

Peel a black-ripe plantain, cut into 3-inch lengths, and then slice vertically. Sauté in a non-stick pan with a melted butter until both sides are browned. Season with salt, pepper, lime juice, and some cayenne, if you're feeling frisky.

Dessert Plantains

Cut a black-ripe plantain (unpeeled) in half vertically. Spread a little butter on both sides. Dot with brown sugar, and cinnamon or nutmeg. Cover with plastic wrap and microwave on full power for 2-3 minutes until butter melts and sugar caramelizes. Serve with ice cream and/or rum sauce.

African and Caribbean Stores

La Fruitería

**8909 S. Commercial Ave.
773.768.4969**

A well-stocked grocery with a friendly, helpful staff, specializing in African and Caribbean ingredients (particularly Jamaican and Haitian). Produce is fresh and plentiful and includes all the tropical tubers (**yucca, yautia,** and **yellow, white,** and **Ghana yams**). They carry **fresh guava, breadfruit, sour orange, mamey, "June plum,"** and **quenepas** (also called mamones) in season.

Spices are available in amazing variety, from some I didn't recognize (**ukazi, obgono, suya pepper, pitter**) to dozens of mixed spices for **jerk, Haitian curry,** and the complete line of **Walker's Woods-brand Jamaican pastes and spices,** as well as the **Ocho Rios-brand** from Miami. There is a small frozen section with tropical fruit pulps and a butcher shop that offers **cow feet, smoked goat feet,** and **pig tails** alongside more pedestrian items. They sell smoked fish ("boney fish"), dried fish, and shrimp, but they direct customers to a shop across the street for fresh fish.

Old World Market

**5129 N. Broadway St.
773.777.7945**

This is a Caribbean/African market in yet another strip mall, only a few steps away from the Southeast Asian Broadway-Argyle corridor. They carry African, Jamaican, and Caribbean foods, spices, and condiments. It's not a huge store, but it is packed with exotic stuff and lots of fun.

The odor of dried fish hits you when you walk in, so take a minute to get over it. Then go slowly down the aisles and check out **dende (palm oil), zomi (spiced palm oil), oil beans, tiger nuts, gari (cassava flour),** many kinds of **fu fu flour,** frozen **palm hearts** and **jute leaves,** and teensy **pickled peppers** that would look great in a martini.

Pick up **cassareep** (concentrated cassava juice used in stews), dried **bitterleaf** (used in stews and African palaver sauce), **Jamaican jerk spices**, and the whole, very good line of **Walker's Wood Jamaican products**, too.

If you are interested in African or Caribbean cooking in the slightest, don't miss this place.

Rogers Park Fruit Market

**7401 N. Clark St.
773.262.3663**

It was a tough call as to whether this multi-ethnic place should be listed here or in the produce section. It's a microcosm of the melting-pot-nature of Rogers Park. There is a huge selection of fruits and vegetables, including the exotic, like **mamey** and **bitter orange**. There are **green coconuts**, **yautia**, **yucca**, plus four different kinds of **yams**. **Plantains** are available at every stage of ripeness and there is a good choice of Latin American vegetables, including **purslane**, **tomatillos**, **epazote**, and **nopales**.

A complete butcher shop offers **pig tails** and **snouts** in addition to the usual cuts of beef. There is a small selection of fish, too.

Last but not least, one of the best assortments of **Jamaican ingre-** dients is here: all the **jerk sauces** and **criolla sauces**, as well as jarred **escabèche sauce** and an array of **hot sauces**, including some I didn't see elsewhere, like **papaya-habanero**.

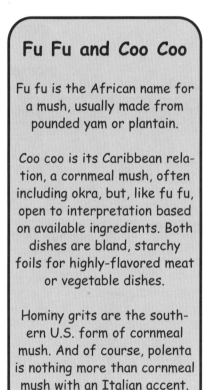

Fu Fu and Coo Coo

Fu fu is the African name for a mush, usually made from pounded yam or plantain.

Coo coo is its Caribbean relation, a cornmeal mush, often including okra, but, like fu fu, open to interpretation based on available ingredients. Both dishes are bland, starchy foils for highly-flavored meat or vegetable dishes.

Hominy grits are the southern U.S. form of cornmeal mush. And of course, polenta is nothing more than cornmeal mush with an Italian accent.

Top Ten
African/Caribbean
Ingredients

1. guava* (p. 139)

2. plantain* (p. 143)

3. jerk seasoning

4. boniato

5. sour orange

6. papaya-habanero hot sauce

7. yucca (cassava)

8. coconut

9. cornmeal or grits* (p. 143)

10. dende (palm oil)

*tip or recipe included

Indian and Pakistani Ingredients

My first experience of Indian cuisine left me enraptured. These were tastes and also fragrances I'd never experienced before. It seemed to me I was eating perfume. No one handles spices with more subtlety and panache than an Indian or Pakistani cook. And there's no place better to buy your **saffron, cardamom**, or **cinnamon** than in what some Chicagoans call Little India—Devon Avenue. Devon has been designated "Ghandi Marg" for this stretch from about 2200 West to 2600 West.

Wandering east and west of Western Avenue on Devon and stopping at the dozens of groceries and produce markets, you'll find that these cuisines believe in spices, fresh produce, more kinds of grains and flours than you dreamed of, and impeccably fresh meat.

Don't forget to stop for lunch while you're at it. Many new sweet shops have sprung up, and they offer lots of snack/sandwich-type fare in addition to exotic desserts.

Devon is a good place to stock up on **cashews, peanuts**, and the like, as well as **spices** and **lentils**. The street is also lined with electronics shops that carry

rice cookers and **pressure cookers** of all kinds and sizes Many seem to be named "Ghandi Electronics." They come and go with some rapidity so I haven't provided listings for them.

This is definitely a destination for cooks, even if they never cook Indian. Allow enough time to explore. People are generally friendly and will answer questions if they speak enough English. Many shops are closed on Tuesdays.

Meat and Fish

There are dozens of butcher shops along Devon and most advertise themselves as "**halal/zabiha**." This is the Muslim version of kosher meat. The halal part of the equation means it is a type of meat allowed (i.e., not pork). The zabiha designates the way it is slaughtered to meet Muslim requirements. It's interesting that they are extremely close to kosher regulations. In fact, I've been told that a kosher kitchen would accept zabiha meat if kosher were unavailable, rather than use the ordinary supermarket kind. The quality is usually very good, especially the lamb. They will butcher to order.

INDIA AND PAKISTAN

(pappadams, mace, cardamom, and cinnamon)

fish: pomfret, shrimp, prawns, hilsa, ruhu, surmai, more, all frozen.
goat and kid
lamb, all kinds and cuts

Produce

Millions of Indians are vegetarians, so the produce at their groceries is varied and good. While there is some overlap with Asian cuisines, there are also unique vegetables and herbs.

amaranth
banana blossoms
bottle gourds
chickpeas, fresh
curry leaves
karela (bitter melon)
lemongrass
long beans (yard long beans, snake beans)
lotus root
mangos, green mangos
methi (fenugreek leaves)
mooli (daikon)
paan leaves (betel leaf)
parval (a gourd)
plantains
pomegranates
quinces
sinqua (luffa, silk squash)
star fruit (carambola)

tamarillo
taro
tindora (like a cucumber/ zucchini)
turmeric, fresh white (zedoary)
turmeric, fresh yellow
tuvar beans (Indian green beans)
valor beans
young coconuts (white, with conical tops)
winter melons

5 Things to Do with Cilantro or Mint Chutney

1. Use it as a sandwich spread. (Mint chutney on leftover Thanksgiving turkey is divine.)

2. Serve as a dip (as is, or mixed with sour cream or yogurt) for pita, pappadam, or vegetables.

3. Mix with mayo and use in tuna, chicken, potato, or egg salad.

4. Add it to salad dressings.

5. Heat and use as a sauce for fish or chicken.

Spices and Seasonings

These are the best reason to visit Devon Avenue. The stores' selections are vast, their turnover is fast so things are fresh, and the prices are hard to beat.

Whole Spices:
allspice
anise seed (saunf)
caraway
cardamom: green, black
celery seed
chiles
cinnamon
cloves
coriander
cumin
dill seed
fennel seed
mace
mustard seed
nutmeg
peppercorns
poppy seed, white
saffron
sesame seed
star anise

Indian Spices:
ajowan
amchoor (mango powder)
anardana (pomegranate seed)
asafoetida, powdered (hing)
black salt
cassia leaf
fenugreek
haldi (turmeric)
kala jeera (black cumin, royal cumin)
kokum
nigella (kalonji, black onion seed, charnuska)
salam leaf (Indonesian bay leaf)
tamarind, paste or block

The idea of **"curry"** is British, not Indian. The root word means a sauce to serve with rice. There are hundreds of kinds of spice mixtures in Indian/Pakistani cuisines, from the incendiary to the delicate. All-purpose **curry powder** is a fine English invention made to bring Indian flavors to non-Indian cooks. It is not truly representative of Indian food.

On store shelves you'll find many pre-mixed spices, as well as ready-made sauces.

One of my favorite convenience products is **garlic-ginger paste**. A jar in the fridge is incredibly handy. After all, who always has fresh garlic and ginger on hand, and also has enough time to chop or grate it?

In general the word "**masala**" indicates a mix of spices.

chaat masala (salty, spicy, sour. The name means "finger-licking.")
garam masala (slightly sweet with coriander, cinnamon, cumin, and cardamom)
panch phoron (a Bengali five-spice blend)

tandoori masala (hot and sour with cumin and coriander)
tikka masala, vindaloo masala, and many, many more

There are also cooking pastes and sauces for everything from **balti** to **vindaloo**. Mostly good. Directions in English are usually included.

Finger Lickin' Potatoes

1-1/2 lbs. red potatoes, boiled until tender, then peeled and cut into chunks
2 T. oil
2 T. butter
2 tsp. garlic-ginger paste (or use fresh)
2-4 tsp. chaat masala (to taste)
salt and pepper (to taste)
lemon wedges for serving

This riff on Indian street food is addictive. Make sure you have good quality, fresh chaat masala with dried mango listed as one of the main ingredients. Alternately you can use amchoor powder, which is dried mango, and add other spices of your choosing. Think of these as slightly exotic hash browns, and feel free to improvise, adding tomato, onion, whatever.

Heat vegetable oil and butter in a sauté pan. Add the ginger/garlic and stir. In 30 seconds, add the chunks of potatoes and masala. Stir to combine, then leave to brown for 5-10 minutes. Turn with a spatula, scraping up the flavorful crust and brown the other side. Adjust seasoning. (You may not need salt and pepper.) Serve with wedges of lemon.

Carbs

It's easy to be overwhelmed by the selection of **lentils**, **flours**, **rice**, and **bread**, happily overwhelmed. Legumes are king here and you'll find beautiful, cheap **lentils** in every color and configuration.

"Dal" is the word used to describe all dried peas, beans, and pulses. Things are complicated by the different names, not to mention spellings. Sometimes toor dal is toover dal or achar, for instance. Many can be bought either whole or split, skinned or not. Some dals are called "gram" to make it even weirder. The good news is, other than having different cooking times, they are more or less interchangeable. Herewith, a superficial lesson:

channa dal (made from chickpeas)
masoor dal (red lentils)
moong dal (mung beans, sold split or whole)
toor dal (yellow lentils, also called pigeon peas)
urad dal (black lentils)

Bread is often sold frozen as well as fresh, and it's the next best thing to making your own. Many kinds also come in more than one variety or with different flavorings (cumin, saffron, etc), but these are four of the basics:

chapati
naan
pappadam
paratha

The Pleasures of Pappadam

Pappadam is a round, cracker-thin Indian bread made of lentil flour. It comes in packages of 10 or more, either plain or flavored with garlic, pepper, or my favorite, ajowan. Most every store carries at least one brand.

Before serving pappadam, they need to be cooked to puff and crisp. The simplest way to do this is in the microwave.

Nuke at full power in a single layer for 15 to 30 seconds. When they curl a bit and color a little, they're ready.

Serve them with chutney as a cocktail snack, or try them as a base for a salad.

I won't pretend to understand all the flours of the region. Suffice it to say that Indians make flour out of just about everything, including wheat. Here are some of those you'll find.

atta flour (basic wheat)
besan flour (gram flour, made from a kind of chickpea)
corn flour
dokra flour (a mix of besan and rice flour)
raggi and bajri flours– (made from millet)
rice flour
semolina (hard wheat)

Indian **basmati rice** is world-famous and you'll find a zillion brands in any of the listed stores. The two main types are **"Patna"** and **"Dehraduni,"** the latter being the more expensive and higher quality. They are named after the region where they're grown.

All rice is a good buy; the only catch is you usually have to purchase a sack of at least 10 pounds. Go with a friend and share. You can find **brown basmati** as well, in smaller quantities than the white. It's delicious but takes longer to cook. You'll also find puffed rice for snacking and flattened rice, called **poha**, to deep fry or use in desserts.

Perfumed Basmati

2 C. basmati rice
2-1/2 C. water
pinch of salt
2 green cardamom pods
2-inch cinnamon stick

Rinse the rice in several changes of water, then soak in cold water for 30 minutes. Put drained rice and other ingredients in a saucepan and bring to a boil. Then turn heat very low, cover, and cook for 15 minutes. Turn off the heat and let it sit another 10 minutes. No peeking. Remove the spices, fluff with a fork, and serve.

If you are cooking more or less rice, you will have to adjust the amount of water, but it is NOT proportional. Try this trick: With the rice in a pan, add enough water to come up to the first knuckle on your index finger when you place your finger on top of the rice. I don't know why, but it works.

Groceries

Indian and Pakistani shops stock a delicious collection of chutneys, pickles, and more. If you like hot, you're really in luck. The Indian version of "pickle" is usually made from a citrus fruit and the hot versions are blazing. The cooking sauces are generally pretty good and save a huge amount of time. Canned and/or frozen versions of Indian desserts and vegetables are also available.

chutneys: mango, cilantro, mint, eggplant, combos
cooking sauces: tandoori, rogan josh, korma, and more
ghee (Indian version of clarified butter. "Usli ghee" is real butter. There are also vegetable oil imitations.)
jaggery (a kind of sugar)
mustard oil (It will say, "for external use only." This is because the FDA has decreed it may be a health risk.)
orange blossom water
pickles: lime, lemon, mango, tamarind, combos, everything but kosher dill!
rose water
varak (edible gold or silver in thin sheets. Ask at the check-out. It's expensive).

Miscellaneous

Look to Indian and Pakistani shops when you want a new and different cocktail nibble. I've listed only a few of the many crunchy, salty, spicy snacks you'll find.

channa (spiced roasted chickpeas)
chivda (puffed rice)
sev (chickpea-noodle bits)

Indian ice cream called **kulfi** comes in exotic flavors like saffron and rose. It also comes in individual-size containers. Just unmold on a dessert plate for a classy, but instant dessert.

Stop by a sweet shop and pick up some **barfi**, the unfortunate name for Indian fudge. It comes in many flavors like ginger and cashew. You'll also find **ladoos**, big, sugary balls kind of like donuts, and cheese-sweets like **rosogollas**.

Julie's Super Twangy Tamarind Pie
"Looks real ugly, tastes real pretty"

9-inch pie shell (store bought is fine)
1-1/2 C. sugar
1/3 C. cornstarch
1-1/2 C. water
3 egg yolks, slightly beaten
2 tsp. lime peel (or more)
1/2 C. lime juice (or more)
2-3 T. tamarind concentrate
(or more, depending on your twang tolerance)
3 egg whites
1/4 tsp. cream of tartar
6 T. sugar
1/2 tsp. vanilla

Bake pie shell and keep oven at 400°.

Filling:
Mix sugar and cornstarch in saucepan. Gradually stir in
water. Cook over medium heat, stirring constantly until
mixture thickens and boils. Boil and stir one minute. Stir 1/3
to 1/2 of hot mixture slowly into egg yolks. Blend tempered
egg yolk mixture back into saucepan. Boil and stir one more
minute until thick and creamy. Remove from heat, add lime juice,
lime peel, and tamarind (to taste, but it should be pretty sour
as meringue will sweeten it up). Pour into cooked shell.

Meringue:
Beat egg white and cream of tartar until foamy. Beat in
sugar, 1 T. at a time. Continue beating until stiff. Beat in
vanilla. Spoon meringue over pie filling while still hot, spread
to edges of crust, filling cracks. Lightly touch and lift
meringue with ladle/spoon to create cool shapes/bumps.

Bake 10 minutes or until raised part of meringue
starts to brown. Cool thoroughly and serve.

Indian and Pakistani Stores

Awami Bazaar and Zabiha Meat

2350 W. Devon Ave.
773.274.9600

Primarily a butcher shop (and a nice big one, too), but they do carry some groceries and spices.

Bismillah Meat and Grocery

2742 W. Devon Ave.
773.761.1700

A grocery with a butcher shop and the standard selection of seasonings.

Chicago Halal Meat

2243 W. Devon Ave.
773.743.6934

Another butcher shop for zabiha/halal lamb, etc.

Fish Corner

6408 N. Campbell Ave.
773.262.7173

The charming proprietor, Mr. Ahmed, will be happy to talk to you about the collection of mostly frozen fish he carries. It is imported from Bangladesh, India, Thailand, and Pakistan, among other places. He has reasonably-priced **tiger shrimp** from Thailand, plus frozen **ruhu**, **pomfret**, **hilsa**, **poa**, and **surmai** **(kingfish)**, to name a few.

Fresh Farms

2626 W. Devon Ave.
773.764.3557

This grocery probably has the biggest produce selection in the area. It's the place for **methi leaves** and **fresh turmeric**, as well as every kind of green and fruit. You'll find **green mangos**, **young coconuts**, **fresh young ginger**, and much more depending on the season. Many products, like mangos, can be bought by the case.

They also carry cheeses (many kinds of **feta**), the usual **pickles**, **chutneys**, and **spices**, and many different kinds of flatbread, including **pita, naan,** and **chapati** from a variety of bakeries.

Farm City Meat and Farm Supermarket
2255-57 W. Devon Ave.
773.274.2255 (meat)
773.274.6355 (market)

Two adjacent stores that are connected. One is a very, very busy butcher shop. They carry beef as well as lamb, chicken, etc. The grocery next door stocks Middle Eastern specialties and Indian/ Pakistani foods. You'll find **pomegranate concentrate, giant limas, rose petal spread, grape leaves, cracked wheat, whole wheat,** and **bulghur.** They even have some Mexican products. Very ecumenical.

House of Laziza
2537 W. Devon Ave.
773.262.6566

A small Pakistani grocery that is primarily a butcher shop.

Jai Hind Plaza
2658 W. Devon Ave.
773.973.3400

The small selection of grocery items in this store is overshadowed by the wide array of equipment. There are long wooden tongs, cutting boards with feet, Indian rolling pins, **idli** steamers, flat **"tava"** steel skillets, stainless pots in many sizes, serving dishes, and other interesting gadgets.

J.K. Grocers
2552 W. Devon Ave.
773.262.7600

Another grocer who carries the expected array of **dals, spices,** and **chutneys.** Many stores have the same products, and one reason is that their customers spend a lot of time comparison-price shopping. If you're purchasing in quantity check sale prices. They vary from store to store on many of the most popular items.

Kamdar Plaza
2646 W. Devon Ave.
773.338.8100

This place offers a sweet counter in addition to shelves of **spices, dals,** and **chutneys.**

Lawando's Grocery and Meat

2244 W. Devon Ave.
312.262.1222

It looks like an everyday supermarket, but Lowando's stocks Indian specialties as well as a good selection of Middle Eastern stuff, like **sumac** and **grape leaves**.

Madni Mart

2440 W. Devon Ave.
773.761.4626

Madni is located at the eastern end of Devon, and like its many neighbors competes for the Indian/Pakistani grocery business with good prices on the usual **spices**, **dals**, and **chutneys**.

Mehrab Meat & Grocery

2445 W. Devon Ave.
773.764.3737

As with many stores along Devon this place is a butcher shop in back with a grocery in front. And like the rest, it offers a decent selection of the usual grocery items.

Mubarak Grocers and Meat

2522 W. Devon Ave.
773.743.3889

Mubarak is nothing out of the ordinary, but offers most of the basic groceries for Indian/Pakistani cooking and a halal/zabiha butcher shop.

Noor Meat Market

2505 W. Devon Ave.
773.274.6667
773.973.7860

Noor is primarily a butcher shop, and I've purchased excellent lamb here. They also make their own Indian-style pickles and stock some equipment as well—**tava skillets**, pots and pans, and gadgets.

Patel Brothers

2610 W. Devon Ave.
773.262.7777

2554 W. Devon Ave.
773.764.1857

This is the definitive Indian grocery store. The Patels were

Devon Avenue pioneers and actually own a lot of Devon Avenue I'm told. They also have outposts in many other cities. The stores are clean, well laid out, and have everything in the way of **spices**, **flours**, **dals**, **chutneys**, **pappadams**, other breads, and canned goods.

All the flours like **atta**, **besan**, and **dokra** are here, plus a modest assortment of cooking gear.

The bigger store at 2610 also carries a good selection of Indian specialty produce, like **tuvar** and **valor beans**, **fresh methi**, and **tindora**. Best of all, it has a center aisle filled with bins of bulk Indian snack items—over 80 varieties—like **sev**, **channa**, and **boondi** to name a few. You can mix and match as you like. Fun!

The staff in both stores will try to answer questions or offer help if you look lost. Note that these stores are totally jammed on the weekend.

Par Birdie Foods (Khan Brothers)
2234 W. Devon Ave.
773.274.1750

This grocery has a golfer on the sign leftover from who knows when, hence the name "Par Birdie." It is now an all-purpose grocery store with the emphasis on **Indian/Pakistani** and **Middle Eastern** ingredients. You'll find **dals**, **atta flour**, **basmati**, as well as **sumac**, **rose water**, and such. They do have **spices** and **chutneys**, but not as good a selection as at Patel Brothers and some others. You can pick up staples like baby food and detergents, however.

Super Fruit Market
2405 W. Devon Ave.
773.338.7120

The emphasis here is on produce, from Indian specialties, like **silk squash** and **opo**, to ordinary items like oranges and peppers. There is also a butcher shop and a representative selection of Indo-Pak seasonings, spices, and canned goods.

World Fruit Market
2434 W. Devon Ave.
773.508.0700

A produce store with some interesting sidelines, World Fruit carries African **fu fu flour** and some **Latin American goods** in addition to Indian/Pakistani groceries. Their big deli is a mixed bag. It even offers salami.

Cheater's Tandoori Chicken

A great weeknight grilling dish if you can
remember to put together the marinade
in the morning or the night before.

3-4 T. prepared Indian tandoori paste from a jar

1 C. plain yogurt (preferably whole milk)

**2 whole boneless, skinless chicken breasts,
divided into 4 half-breast pieces**

Rinse off and clean the chicken and cut 2 or 3
shallow slits in each piece. For the marinade, mix
together the yogurt and 3-4 T. tandoori paste (check
the directions on the bottle). Slather it over the
chicken, rubbing it into the slits. Refrigerate at
least 3 hours. Then remove from marinade and grill
about five minutes a side. Serve with wedges of lemon,
basmati rice, pappadam, chutney, and a green veggie
for a fast, yummy, but inauthentic Indian dinner.

Top Ten Indian/Pakistani Ingredients

1. red lentils* (p. 130)

2. basmati rice* (p. 151)

3. whole cardamom* (p. 151)

4. chaat masala* (p. 149)

5. saffron

6. tamarind concentrate* (p. 153)

7. tandoori paste* (p. 158)

8. pappadam* (p. 150)

9. mint and cilantro chutneys* (p.147 & p. 150)

10. lemon pickle

*tip or recipe included

CHINA

(tofu and dried mushrooms)

Chinese Ingredients

For many of us, Chinese was the first "foreign" meal we experienced. It was Chinese cooking America-style, of course, and in most restaurants, it still is. We are more sophisticated now and understand there's a difference between Szechuan and Cantonese. But reading a really good authentic cookbook, like *The Chinese Kitchen*, by Eileen Yin-Fei Lo, makes you realize how little you know. Her recipes for what we consider Chinese classics (but have only tasted in hybrid form), like "moo-goo-gai pan," are a revelation. I highly recommend it.

Chinese grocery stores seem both more foreign and more assimilated than other Asian stores. Many of the ingredients are familiar. They've been with us since Chung King first canned chop suey. On the other hand, nobody does the exotic better than the Chinese. You can pick up **shark fin**, **bird's nest**, **fish lips**, and **thousand-year-old eggs** on your shopping trip. Better yet you can get higher quality staples like **oyster sauce** (the brand *does* make a difference), as well as more sophisticated forms of old standbys. **Mushroom soy sauce**, for instance, is a wonderful addition to any cook's pantry.

If you've only visited the old Chinatown on the South Side, do try one of the bigger, newer markets elsewhere in the city. They don't have the atmosphere, but they do have the goods.

Fish and Seafood

Really fresh fish is alive. We all know this, but the Chinese markets act on it. Even some of the smaller ones will have tanks of swimming fish and you can usually find **live crabs**, too. Shrimp, while not alive, are cheap and good, and best of all, easy to find uncooked and often with their heads on, which gives better flavor to sauces and soups.

Fresh Fish and Seafood:
clams
crabs, live: blue,
    Dungeness, others
eels
flounder
lobster
mackerel
octopus
oysters
shrimp, head-on
snails

squid
tilapia

Frozen Seafood:
crab legs
crab meat
jellyfish
oyster meat
prawns
...plus frozen versions of
    most fresh items

Dried Seafood:
abalone
anchovies
fish lips
fish maw (air bladder)
jellyfish
octopus
scallops (conpoy)
sea cucumber
shark fin
squid

Basic Asian Marinade

1/4 C. soy sauce
(mushroom is good)
3 cloves garlic, minced
1-inch piece of ginger,
    minced
2 T. oyster sauce
2 tsp. sesame oil
2 T. peanut or olive oil
3 T. red wine vinegar
freshly ground pepper

Mix everything together and
use to marinate steak, pork,
or chicken. Particularly good
on flank steak for the grill
and pork tenderloin roast.

Meat

In the Chinese kitchen meat
most often means pork. Poultry
is important and you'll find good
whole chickens as well as the
harder to find **quail**, **squabs**,
geese, and **ducks** (frozen).

chicken: including
    feet, gizzards

pork: including snouts,
    tails, backbones
quail eggs

Many groceries display prepared
meats—barbecued chicken,
duck, ribs, and pieces of pork
near their fresh meat. This is
a great way to experience
Peking duck or **soy sauce
chicken** without going to the
trouble of making it. You'll also
find flattened duck, called **dried
duck,** in the refrigerated case
or hanging with his friends.

Produce

You will always find plenty of greens and many members of the broccoli/cabbage family in Chinese stores. Don't be put off by odd names or seeing flowers on the greens. They are mostly interchangeable with the more familiar spinach, kale, and regular broccoli. The standards for judging them are the same, too. Look for a bright color, no wilting, and a perky leaf.

amaranth
baby bok choy
bitter melons
bok choy
bottle gourds
chives: yellow, flowering
choy sum (flowering cabbage)
daikon
durian
gai choy (mustard cabbage)
gai lan (chinese broccoli)
ginger, young ginger
horned water chestnut (water caltrop)
jícama
kabocha squash
kohlrabi
kumquats
kun choy (chinese celery)
litchis

long beans
lotus root
luffa (silk squash)
mushrooms: enoki, oyster, shiitake
napa cabbage (Chinese cabbage)
pea shoots
rambutans
sprouts
tai goo choy (flat cabbage, tatsoi)
taro
tsu goo (Chinese arrowhead)
Vietnamese spinach (slippery vegetable)
water chestnuts
winter melons

You will often find Southeast Asian ingredients like **lemongrass** and **green papaya** as well, especially in bigger stores.

Spices and Seasonings

bean sauce
black vinegar (Chinkiang)
char siu sauce (barbecue paste)
Chinese five-spice powder

fish sauce (most places)
hoisin sauce
lemon sauce
oyster sauce
pickled mudfish
plum sauce
rice vinegar
rock sugar
salted (preserved) black
    beans
sesame paste
sesame seeds
shrimp paste
soy sauce: dark, light,
    mushroom
Sriracha (it's everywhere)
star anise
Szechuan peppercorns
XO sauce

Magic Beans

Salted black beans, also
called fermented or pre-
served black beans, are the
original form of soy flavoring.
You'll find them packed in
plastic bags or jars. Once you
take a whiff of their winey,
magical aroma, you'll want to
use them everywhere. They
are delicious added to all
kinds of stir fries and work
particularly well with vegetables. Just crush with some
garlic and ginger and cook.

zizyphus (jujube, Chinese
    red dates)

Carbs

Visit Chinese stores to stock
up on all sorts of rice (usually
in 10 lb. or larger sacks), every
kind of noodle, and lots of "Cup
O' Noodle"-type products, too.
Look in the refrigerated or
frozen section for the fresh
(not dried) noodles. They are
a treat and also quicker than
dried. Especially try the kind
called **fresh rice noodles**
(sometimes they are made with
rice, sometimes wheat.) They
come in folded sheets, plastic
wrapped. You then cut the
sheets into noodles of whatever
width you want.

bean thread noodles
    (cellophane noodles)
glutinous (sticky) rice
glutinous rice flour
jasmine rice
mein (wheat flour noo-
    dles), fresh or dried
potato starch (flour)
ramen
red rice
rice flour
rice noodles: fresh (chow
    fun), dried rice
    sticks, or vermicelli

soba (buckwheat noodles)
somen (wheat noodles)
tapioca pearls
tapioca starch (flour)
udon noodles
water chestnut flour
wheat starch (non-
   glutinous flour)

Groceries

adzuki (red beans)
anchovies and other
   fish, dried
agar-agar
bird's nest (for soup)
black sesame seeds
chestnuts, dried
cloud ear fungus (black
   fungus, tree fungus)
ginger, crystallized
ginkgo nuts
hair vegetable (black
   moss)
jackfruit
jellyfish, dried
lily buds
longan
lotus root
lotus seeds
lychees
mock duck (wheat gluten)
mung beans
mushrooms, dried: black,

shiitake, wood ear
persimmons, dried
pork floss (pork fu)
preserved plums
preserved vegetables
   (radishes, kohlrabi)
rice papers
rice vinegar
sesame paste
shark fin
spring roll wrappers
water chestnuts
watermelon seeds
white fungus (silver fun-
   gus)
wonton wrappers

Four Non-Asian Ways to Use Asian Wraps

1. Use round wonton skins to make ravioli.

2. Stuff wonton skins into greased mini muffin tins and bake, then fill for hors d'oeuvres.

3. Cut into strips and deep fry for garnishing soup or salad

4. Wrap a fish fillet in rice paper and bake until crisp.

Soy Products

bean curd sheets
dried soybeans
fermented (preserved)
    bean curd
pressed bean curd
tofu, all forms, including
    fried and tofu pockets

Miscellaneous

exotic drinks: grass jelly,
    bird's nest, etc.
jellies: litchi, durian, etc.
ginger candies
rice candies (edible wrap-
    pers)
shrimp chips (crackers)
teas, medicinal and other-
    wise
tea drinks, canned

Noodle Nests

Fried in hot oil, bean thread (cellophane) noodles puff up
to a crunchy, tangled nest perfect for serving things.

1. Pull apart noodles and flatten into a disk shape.
You may have to wet them with hot water to do this,
but make sure they are *completely* dry before frying
or you risk a splattering, fiery, dangerous mess.

2. Heat 2 inches of vegetable oil in a deep
wok or other heavy pan until it shimmers.

3. Carefully place the noodle nests into the oil. In a
matter of seconds they will magically puff up and crisp.

4. Drain on paper towels and keep warm. Top with
stir-fried vegetables, or, my favorite, crab and spinach
cooked briefly with garlic, ginger, and some soy sauce.
Save stray noodle bits to sprinkle on top for garnish.

Quick, Easy Five-Spice Squash Rings
(Serves 4)

2 delicata (sweet potato) squash
1-2 T. olive oil
1-2 tsp. Chinese five-spice powder
salt and freshly ground pepper to taste

Pre-heat oven to 350°. Line a baking sheet with foil.
Slice the squash into 1/2-inch thick rounds. Remove the
pith and seeds. (Using a serrated grapefruit spoon makes this
easy.) Lay rings on the foil and brush with oil. Sprinkle with the
five-spice powder, salt, and pepper. Bake for 20-30 minutes.

Fresh Rice Noodles
(Serves 6)

1 package fresh rice noodles
3 T. peanut oil
1 T. each minced garlic and ginger
1 bunch green onions, chopped, including green parts
2 C. quick cooking vegetables
(Asian greens, thin asparagus, small
pieces of broccoli, or a combination)
meat (chicken, pork, or beef),
in small pieces (optional)
1/4 C. soy (mushroom is nice)
2 T. oyster sauce or hot bean paste
1 tsp. sesame oil
1/2 C. bean sprouts

Cut the noodles into strips, without unfolding.
Make the strips as narrow or wide as you like.
Half an inch works well. Place in a colander and pour
boiling water over to loosen them. (Skip this step if
they are very fresh and have not been refrigerated.)

Stir fry garlic and ginger in 1 T. oil. Add meat and
cook until almost done. Remove and reserve meat,
then add 2 T. oil and veggies (slowest cooking first)
and stir-fry until crisp tender. Add noodles and soy
sauce, oyster sauce, and sesame oil. Stir fry, separating
noodles. Add bean sprouts. Adjust seasoning (adding hot
sauce, more soy sauce, or a squeeze of lemon) and serve.

Chinese Stores

Chinatown

The original old Chinatown at Cermak and Wentworth is a great place to visit, especially with out-of-towners or kids in tow. If you've been spoiled by big Asian markets, though, the grocery stores at first seem a bit disappointing. They're small and usually crowded. But they also seem more authentic and you can pick up most anything you'd need in one place or another. You'll find plenty of bakeries, herbal stores, and places to buy fancy chopsticks or porcelain rice bowls, not to mention great places to eat!

The names of some of the stores change rapidly, so don't get hung up on finding the exact name listed. The nice thing about Chinatown is that it's a community, so even if one store closes, there's another to pick up the slack. Just wander up and down Wentworth and you'll find everything you want.

I usually park on Wentworth, south of the Dragon Gate and east of the new (comparatively) Chinatown Square Mall. It's free street parking. There is also a pay parking lot a bit closer to Cermak on Wentworth.

A & J Housewares
2125-A S. China Pl.
312.567.9908

This may belong under equipment, but it's not worth the trip unless you're in the area anyway. It's in the mall, across from **Mayflower Food** (p. 172). Among the usual souvenirs, you'll find sauce dishes, **rice cookers**, tea pots, **Benriner slicers**, strainers, peelers, and gadgets of all kinds.

Aji Ichiban
2117-A S. China Pl.
312.328.9998

An Asian candy store that's a real treat. Most things are sold by the pound and there are plenty of free samples. The choices are exotic—dozens of kinds of **preserved plums**, including one called "preserved thinking milk plum." Nobody could explain the name, but it tasted good. You can also try **dried kumquats**, **star fruit**, and **guava**; **fish and shrimp candies**; and many **exotic flavors of marshmallows**.

Chicago Food Market

2245 S. Wentworth Ave.
312.842.4361.

Emphasis here is on fresh (live) fish. They also carry some meat and a modest selection of groceries.

Dong Kee Company

2252 S. Wentworth Ave.
773.225.6340

A grocery and gift shop with canned and dry goods; a decent assortment of dried noodles; soy sauce, **oyster sauce**, and other condiments; plus **fortune and almond cookies**. Two whole rooms are devoted to dishes, **woks**, cooking utensils, and souvenirs, including the biggest, most **hideously wonderful piggy banks** you've ever seen.

Wing Cheong Trading

2317 S. Wentworth Ave.
312.808.1199

Another small store that's packed with a bit of everything, including fresh (live) fish, some meat, and a butcher to cut it for you. Last time I visited they had **live crabs**, **snails**, and **turtles**—fairly large ones. You'll find some produce and the obligatory assortment of dried noodles and canned goods.

Hong Kong Noodle Company

2350 S. Wentworth Ave.
312.842.0480

This is a real noodle factory that has been a Chinatown fixture as long as I can remember. Luckily they sell retail, too. You can buy three sizes of **dried wheat noodles**, **fresh noodles** (only early in the day), and **fried "chow mein" noodles** like you get in the can only lots fresher and better. These are so good that my daughter and I scarfed up a half pound right out of the bag before we got home. They'd probably be good sprinkled on things, too, if you don't eat them all first. This is a factory, not a store, so don't think you're in the wrong place when you walk in. You order by the pound at the service desk and the clerks are friendly and accomodating. **Egg roll and wonton wrappers** are also available and everything is an amazing bargain.

Kwok Chiu Market

211 W. 23rd St.
(closed Wednesday)

A very clean, small meat market, just off Wentworth dealing in every kind of **pork**, including **pork intestine** and **pork blood**, plus **Smithfield hams**, **ducks** and **geese** with head and feet attached, some fresh and frozen fish, chicken, **tripe**, and even some very fresh-looking vegetables. Not a tourist stop.

Mayflower Food Company

2104 S. Archer Ave.
312.326.7440
312.326.7450

An always-packed store with narrow aisles at the east end of Chinatown Square Mall. Mayflower recently expanded and added a large aisle of frozen items (**dumplings**, **fish balls**, **frozen shrimp**, and fish), as well as more packaged goods.

It smells a little funky when you first enter because there are bins of **dried shrimp and fish** right inside the door, as well as a mysterious collection of glass jars filled with **dried medicinal herbs**, like **angelica root**, **radix** and "semen euryales," whatever that is. Don't be deterred. This is a fun place, off the beaten tourist path.

There is meat, produce, including fresh **lotus root**, and **long beans**, **fresh rice noodles**, a wide variety of frozen items, plus the usual groceries. Things seem to have high turnover here.

Check out **Yin Wall City** next door, too. It is a **medicinal-herbal store** and fascinating. They offer every kind of **dried scallop** and **abalone** (some cost $600/lb.!), as well as **dried seahorse** and **deer antlers**.

Tai Wah Grocery

2226 S. Wentworth Ave.
773.326.4120

Barbecued ducks and pork hang in the window of this crowded, tiny store that has almost everything. There's fresh meat and live fish (a modest selection), **live crabs**, all sorts of **dried fish** and **squid**, plus the usual canned goods and sauces and even some produce.

Wing Lee Co.
Corner of Wentworth Ave. and Alexander St.

I think of this as the no-name produce shop. The sign saying Wing Lee was gone on my last visit, but the store was still busy ringing up sales of groceries and all kinds of produce to Chinese shoppers. They had **fresh water chestnuts**, a large selection of greens, and even **durian** last time I was there.

Elsewhere (not Chinatown)

Diho Market
665 Pasquinelli Dr.
Westmont
630.323.1668

6120 W. Dempster St.
Morton Grove
847.965.8688

A real find and kind of hard to find, Diho is in a mall, tucked behind another mall near the Ogden exit off Route 83. It is a full service Chinese/Asian grocery with plenty of everything

Chinese and some Japanese and Southeast Asian items, too.

Diho has one of the best arrays of **Chinese liquors** and **liqueurs**, many of which are used in cooking. There are several varieties of **Shaoxing wine** in cute ceramic bottles, plus **sakes**, and some interesting alcoholic potions like **ginseng au cognac**. Hmmm.

You'll discover an awesome selection of frozen foods—lots of "balls" of all kinds: rice balls, pork balls, sesame balls. There are frozen fish, meats, and even frozen boned **duck feet** in addition to a big selection of fresh meat and fish. Unusual cuts like **chicken feet**, **pig ears**, two kinds of **tripe**, and **turkey gizzards** are available, as well as live **tilapia**, **blue crab**, **sushi fish**, and lots more. They even have pre-packaged combinations for **fire pot cooking**.

The extensive tea assortment is heavy on medicinals, with tea for everything from diabetes to allergies.

The produce department is on the small side, but has the usual **Asian greens** and vegetables. They also sell seeds to grow your own in the spring.

International Club

4000 W. 40th St.
773.927.0100

Oh my! This is an amazing place—sort of like Sam's Club, only for Asian food. It is located in the midst of an industrial corridor just south of I-55 on Pulaski Road (which is 4000 west). You'll see a huge sign on your right as you travel southbound over the hill by the Com Ed plant on Pulaski. It says "Five Continents International Club." Turn at the Burger King. There is a small parking lot in front that is often crowded with trucks. You are required to be a member ($18 per year at this writing), but if you ask at the desk they will give you a trial pass and you can shop. (You just pay 5 percent more.)

This enormous warehouse store sells cartons of noodles and drinks, institutional-size tins of oil, huge sacks of **dried mushrooms**, and the like to the restaurants around town. There are smaller sizes of everything, too, so don't freak when you first enter. I can happily wander the aisles for hours and always find something new. They carry dozens of brands of **soy sauce** and **fish sauce** and canned **water chestnuts** and **bamboo**

shoots that are superior to the poor dusty things you find in the supermarket. The prices are very good, even on small quantities. They have sections devoted to **Latin American, Japanese, Thai, African**, and even **Jamaican cooking**, though selections are limited.

The drink variety alone is good for 30 minutes of browsing. There are **bird's nest drinks**, every kind of tea in a can, little paper juice boxes in exotic flavors like **tamarind** and **litchi**. They also have **Jarritos drinks** from Mexico, **Coco Rico** coconut soda (my fave), and **Ting**, a Jamaican grapefruit soda that is a cult favorite.

After you've wandered the grocery aisles and loaded your cart, you come to the fresh produce. Pick up **bok choy**, **yu choy**, or **fresh water chestnuts**. There are also big self-serve bins of **sprouts** and **bamboo shoots** (both **summer** and **winter** kind). At first I thought these were fresh shoots. They're not. They're just sold by the pound instead of in a can. **Fresh bamboo shoots** are sometimes available and look like, no surprise, fat green pointed shoots, but they have to be peeled and boiled for quite a while to eliminate prussic acid.

On the other side of one of those "doors" made of strips of hanging plastic, you'll find more produce, as well as a full-service **butcher shop** and **fish market**. It's a large bright room filled with dozens of aquariums that are home to many kinds of live **seafood**. There is always **tilapia**, **crab**, **lobster**, **catfish**, and whatever else is seasonal.

I guess because this is a discount warehouse, you have to bag your own groceries, so don't be shocked when they hand you a bunch of plastic bags and send you on your way. I am always amazed at how much stuff I bought for how little money, so I don't mind doing a little work.

Richwell Market
1835 S. Canal St.
312.492.7030

A brand-new, full-service market about a mile from Chinatown, near Lawrence Fisheries (with a parking lot!). Grab a mango smoothie from the attached juice bar while you shop.

You'll find a serve-yourself candy selection in bins (fun for the kids). There are prepared foods, mainly **barbecued pork**, **barbecued duck**, and **pressed duck**. A butcher shop offers every part of the pig, whole chicken, and **chicken feet**, and the seafood department consists of four well-stocked fish tanks, plus **live snails**, **crabs**, and **clams**.

Ginseng and dried **abalone** are stocked in the (expensive) medicinal section up front. In the small, but complete produce department you'll find **durian**, **litchi**, and **silk squash**. The grocery assortment includes Vietnamese items and some Filipino products, too, like **coco vinegar** and **palm vinegar**.

Oriental Food Market and Cooking School
2801 W. Howard St.
773.274.2826

This well-respected cooking school (p. 74) has been on Howard Street for years teaching courses in Chinese, Thai, and other Asian cuisines. Their small, but well-stocked store carries many of the grocery basics (**Szechuan peppercorns**, **mushroom soy sauce**), as well as some things in frozen form (**rice noodles**, **wonton wrappers**). The proprietor is a cooking expert and is happy to answer questions. You can even buy a **used rickshaw** for $1,200!

Woks 'n' Things
2234 S. Wentworth Ave.
773.842.0701
See listing in **Equipment** (p. 63).

Top Ten Chinese Ingredients

1. salted (fermented) black beans* (p. 165)

2. oyster sauce* (p. 163 & p. 169)

3. mushroom soy sauce* (p. 163 & p. 169)

4. Shaoxing wine

5. chili paste with garlic

6. greens, especially gai lan (Chinese broccoli) and others in the broccoli/cabbage family

7. five-spice powder* (p. 168)

8. fresh noodles, especially rice noodles* (p. 169)

9. wonton wrappers* (p. 166)

10. bean thread (cellophane) noodles* (p. 168)

*tip or recipe included

SOUTHEAST ASIA

(spring roll wrappers and
kaffir lime leaves)

Southeast Asian Ingredients

We are very lucky to have such a wealth of Vietnamese and Thai markets in Chicagoland. Not only do these folks love food, they love freshness. You'll find great produce, fish, and meat in markets in which the ambiance runs the gamut from somewhat seedy to very posh.

Fish and Seafood

Vietnamese and Thai markets are great places to go for fish in all forms. From a simple fillet of sole to **live crabs** to **frozen sea squirt**, if it swims, floats, or crawls on the bottom, chances are they have it. This is handy when you're looking for a good price on something mainstream like **crab legs**, or when you need exotica, like **sea urchin roe**.

There's often a bewildering array of fresh fish on ice, right out in the open so you can pick your own. You are also expected to choose your own crabs or shellfish. (Do like the natives and grab the ones that are the liveliest.) This is sometimes a bit daunting if the names of the fish are not in English. Be forewarned that fish is not cleaned the way we're used to, either. After all, the head and the liver are delicacies in these cultures. Many kinds of

dried fish and a huge selection of canned items that include all sorts of **smoked and seasoned sardines, mackerel**, and **shellfish** are also on hand.

Fresh Fish and Seafood:
butterfish
clams, live
crab legs
crab meat
crabs, live
eel
mackerel
mussels, live
oysters, live
pomfret
sea bass
skate
snails
sole
squid
tilefish
...and many more

Frozen Seafood:
cuttlefish
jellyfish
kingfish
octopus
oysters
periwinkles
prawns, head-on

sea cucumber
sea urchin
shrimp, head-on
squid

Dried Seafood:
anchovies
eel
mackerel
shrimp

Meat

At South East Asian stores the meat is a trifle mysterious. **Organ meats** from organs you never thought about before are displayed next to normal cuts. Good buys are available especially on pork items, like tenderloin, whole pork shoulder with the skin on, fresh hams, and hocks. Many places obviously butcher their meat on the premises.

chicken: feet, gizzards,
    other parts
beef: blood—often frozen—
    sometimes in chunks
    (don't ask), tendon,
    liver, tripe
pork: tongue, kidney,
    heart, uterus, spleen,
    trotters
quail eggs

Chef Tim's Vietnamese-Style Pork Tenderloin
(Serves 6)

3 lbs. pork tenderloin

Marinade:
1 C. sugar
1/4 C. water
additional 1/4 C. water
4 tsp. soy sauce
4 tsp. fish sauce
1/4 C. veg. oil
Make caramel with the sugar and water by heating in a heavy pan without stirring. Let cool slightly and stir in other ingredients. (The use of caramel with meat is traditional and scrumptious.) Marinate meat for several hours or overnight. Grill.

Dipping Sauce:
1 1/2 T. chili-garlic sauce
1 tsp. minced garlic
1/4 C. rice vinegar
1/3 C. sugar
1/2 tsp. salt
1 T. cornstarch dissolved in
1/3 C. water
2 T. chopped cilantro
Mix together everything but the cilantro. Heat until thickened, then add cilantro.

Serve at room temperature. Drizzle some dipping sauce over meat and greens. Serve extra on the side.

Green Papaya Salad
(Serves 4-6)

1 medium green papaya
1/4 C. frozen French-cut green beans, thawed
2 hot peppers, in tiny slivers
3 cloves garlic, minced
3 T. fish sauce
3 T. sugar
juice of 2 limes
1/4 C. roasted peanuts

I adore this stuff. It is hot and sweet and crunchy and sour and chewy and refreshing. So I whittled the recipe down to an easy version that is halfway between Thai and Vietnamese. If you are really lazy, buy pre-cut papaya, which saves even more time.

Cut the papaya in half vertically, scrape out the seeds, and peel. Shred in a food processor. Combine with green beans and peppers. Whisk together everything else, except peanuts, and mix in. Serve topped with peanuts.

Produce

Shop these markets for **Asian greens** in abundance and many **fresh herbs**. Vietnamese meals feature a "table salad" that is mostly fresh herbs. Identifying things is not always easy, especially since the names are different depending on language, dialect, and, if you're lucky enough to find something in English, the whim of a translator. Availability depends on the season, too. I've had good luck asking other shoppers. Even if they don't speak much English they'll point to what they think is tasty and try to communicate with you. It's actually hard to go wrong. Sniffing tells you a lot. Don't wait till you have a Southeast Asian menu in mind either; most greens can be used in any stir fry or side dish. When in doubt, sauté in oil with garlic.

amaranth
banana flowers
bitter melons
bok choy
chive flowers
daikon
durian
fuzzy melons

gai choy (mustard greens)
gai lan (Chinese broccoli)
galangal
gau ma (Vietnamese spinach)
ginger: regular, young, or
    stem ginger
green papaya
herbs, fresh: Vietnamese
    cilantro, holy basil, Thai
    (anise) basil, mint
kaffir lime leaves
lemongrass
long beans
longan
lotus root
luffa
opo squash
pandan leaves
water chestnuts
water spinach (ong choy,
    kangkong)
wing beans
young coconuts
yu choy (flowering cabbage)

Spices and Seasonings

Fish sauce rules. There are many brands and styles. Southeast Asian cooks also use a fabulous chile sauce called **Sriracha** that has a rooster on the label. It is hot and sweet and works with anything from stir fries to roasted veggies. Still it is only one of a dizzying array of chile sauces and pastes available. Ditto soy sauces and vinegars.

chili-garlic sauce: Sriracha
    and others

Storage Tip

Lemongrass and kaffir lime leaves freeze well. (There is a change in texture, but not in flavor.) So don't hesitate to buy more than you need immediately. It is also easy to root lemongrass. Just put fresh stems in water. Plant in a pot once roots appear. Keep in a warm place.

Julie's Roasted Veggies with Sriracha

Peeled (or not), 1-inch chunks of sweet potato and carrot
1 part Sriracha
2 parts olive oil

Mix together Sriracha and oil. Add veggies and toss to coat. Bake at 400° until done (about 30-40 minutes). Hot, sweet, spicy, yummy!

crab paste
fish paste
fish sauce
soy sauce: dark, light,
    citrus
tamarind concentrate
vinegars: coconut, lemon,
    Chinkiang

Carbs

Noodles and wraps are ubiquitous, and most stores carry not
only the Southeast Asian things
like rice paper, but also Pan-
Asian items like **soba** and
gyoza skins.

You'll find flour of all kinds and a
collection of **ready-to-use
mixes for crêpes, dumplings,**
and other fare.

panko (bread crumbs)
rice: glutinous (sweet),
    jasmine, sweet brown
rice flour: regular,
    glutinous (sweet)
rice noodles: fresh (gway
    tiaow in Thai), rice
    stick, rice vermicelli,
    jantaboon noodles (wide
    rice stick)
rice papers
roasted rice powder
tapioca pearls

tapioca starch
tapioca starch noodles
wheat noodles: soba (buck-
    wheat), somen, udon
yam (sweet potato) noodles

Groceries

All sorts of **tropical fruits** are
readily found in cans at these
groceries. Many you've never
heard of before, like **palm fruit.**
Personally I think they mostly
taste sickeningly sweet, but they
sure can turn a fruit salad into a
conversation piece. **Pickled
items** present an array of martini
garnishes you won't find elsewhere. There are aisles devoted
to **seaweed** and **dried vegetables.**

banana buds, pickled or
    plain
daikon, pickled
flavorings: pandanus (bai
    toey), rose water
fried shallots, onions
halo halo (Filipino fruit
    salad)
jackfruit
litchi
longan
loquat
MSG
palm fruit

peppers, pickled
preserved (1,000-year-
old) eggs
rock sugar
seaweed: wakame, nori
wheat gluten

Soy/Dairy

edamame (soy beans),
fresh or frozen
fermented bean curd
soy milk
tofu, every kind

Miscellaneous

coffee drinks, all kinds
ginger, crystallized
jellies: litchi and others
Poky cookies (YUM!)
teas, medicinal and others

Equipment

bamboo steamers
clay pots
cleavers
stone mortars, large
sushi rolling mats
wok

Chicken Bites That Bite Back
(Serves 4-6)

2 whole boneless, skinless
chicken breasts
1 C. plain yogurt
(not non-fat)
1/4 C. Sriracha
flour/cornmeal
salt and pepper

Cut the chicken into nugget size pieces. Mix yogurt and Sriracha. Pour over chicken, coating thoroughly. Marinate, refrigerated, for at least an hour and up to 10.

Prepare a plate with flour or a cornmeal flour mix for dusting. Season it generously with salt and pepper. Add a bit of chile powder if you want extra spicy.

Heat a wide skillet. Add olive oil to a depth of 1/8 inch. (If you prefer, these can also be deep fried.)

Remove chicken pieces from marinade; shake off excess. Roll in flour to coat lightly. Fry until golden and cooked through. Keep warm in a low oven until ready to serve.

Southeast Asian Stores

The area around Argyle and Broadway is sometimes called the new Chinatown. It isn't Chinese at all, of course, but Southeast Asian. This is a wonderful place to come to eat and shop. You'll find everything you've been dreaming of in terms of Thai and Vietnamese ingredients and many things you'd never dream up.

Plan on spending time exploring. While the area around the L-stop on Argyle is on the seedy side, the stores are delightful. You can get a delicious (and cheap) bowl of noodles at dozens of places. Check out the great Thai food and gorgeous pastries at **Thai Pastry** (4925 N. Broadway, 773.784.5399). And stop at one of the many butcher shop/delis to pick up a soy-cooked chicken or roasted duck to go so you don't have to cook when you get home exhausted after your adventure. **Vinh Phat BBQ** (4940 N. Sheridan, 773.878.8688) is legendary (and closed Thursday).

Hoa Nam Grocery

1101-3 W. Argyle St.
773.275.9157

This is the smaller of the two groceries on Argyle. They proffer all things Vietnamese, plus lots of Thai ingredients (**green papaya**), fresh Asian greens, and a smattering of Chinese, Filipino, and Japanese products.

Tai Nam Market

4925 N. Broadway St.
(in the Thai Mall)
773.275.5666

A very clean, big supermarket with excellent produce and greens, although most are plastic-wrapped and hard to sniff. Choose from a large assortment of fresh Vietnamese herbs and vegetables, including **rau ma** (**pennywort**) and **ong choy** (**water spinach**), a narrow-leafed green with crunchy stems that a fellow shopper turned me on to. Quite tasty. Some vegetables are even labeled in English.

The fresh fish selection is extensive and easy to examine as it's all laid out on ice. Some prepared food is also available, especially bakery goods which come in gorgeous, garish colors. Look for a decent selection of equipment, including **rice cookers**, **V-slicers**, etc., and crossover Chinese, Filipino, and Japanese products, too.

Thai Grocery

5014 N. Broadway St.
773.769.0800
773.561.5345

One of the original Thai stores in the neighborhood and the model for the truly wonderful book, *The Asian Grocery Store Demystified*, by Linda Bladholm. Thai Grocery is smaller than most, but packed with groceries, produce, fresh fish, and meat. The nicest **green papaya** you'll find is here, and there's a deli section in back with prepared Thai foods. The staff is extremely helpful and even introduced me to an imported gadget that's designed to shred green papaya.

Thaong Xa My A (Broadway Supermarket)

4879 N. Broadway St.
773.334.3838

A nice big market in a mall with parking (provided the lot's not full), Broadway Supermarket has a varied assortment of foodstuffs and is a fun place to browse. Cases full of unusual frozen food (including **dragon fruit**) share the aisles with a wide-ranging choice of produce. They carry many exotic fruits, even **durian**, as well as greens and herbs, plus a good selection of fish—**live tilapia**, **clams**, **oysters**, and much more, including a fairly large offering of Japanese products (**panko**, **wasabi**), as well as some Chinese and Filipino ones.

This must be the place where a lot of restaurants shop as they have a huge variety of equipment, serving dishes, and institutional sizes of products. **Woks**, **bamboo steamers**, **rice cookers**, **clay pots**, **fish scalers**, and **stone mortars** are among the delights for sale.

Trung Viet Supermarket

4936-42 N. Sheridan Rd.
773.561.0042
773.561.0131

On Sheridan Road, just south of Argyle, this store is easy to miss. It has a parking lot directly in front. (Don't get too excited; the parking lot is small and usually filled.) While the junk-filled windows make it look most unpromising from outside, inside the store is fairly clean and rather large. It offers very good prices on the usual items and has a wide selection of sauces, **rice papers**, and frozen foods. Lots of frozen fish are available along with a good selection of fresh, including **crabs** and **flounder**. The butcher shop even carried **skin-on pork shoulder**, which is hard to find.

Trung Viet has **green papaya already shredded** in a self-serve barrel to purchase by the pound, as well as whole papayas. Many herbs, like **saw-leaf herb** and **basil**, are well-priced even in January. Another great find here was **fresh garlic**, the kind you get in spring at the farmers market with the greens still attached (and a lot of the dirt, too). It looks like an overgrown green onion, but one smell and you'll recognize it. Delicious.

Viet Hoa Plaza

1051 W. Argyle St.
(no phone listed)

Very similar to **Hoa Nam** (p. 184), which is just to the west on Argyle, but bigger and with a more supermarket-y feel. While perusing their good selection of greens, groceries, noodles, and fish, I actually came upon fresh **sea cucumber** here (quite startling!), as well as **live snails** and **clams**. They have a large offering of Filipino ingredients (**banana sauce** and **halo halo**) and some equipment, too— **clay pots**, **V-slicers**, and the ubiquitous (in Asian stores at least) **ice-shavers**.

Viet Hoa is conveniently located very close to the Argyle L-stop on the red line.

Top Ten Southeast Asian Ingredients

1. Sriracha sauce* (p. 181 & p. 183)

2. lemongrass* (p. 181)

3. fresh greens and herbs* (p. 179)

4. fish sauce* (p. 179 & p. 180)

5. rice papers

6. frozen shredded coconut

7. fresh fish

8. green papaya* (p. 180)

9. prepared curry paste

10. canned coconut milk

*tip or recipe included

KNOWING YOUR NOODLES

The choice of noodles in an Asian store is overwhelming. While I've never met a noodle I didn't like, it helps to have an idea of the commonest types on your shopping trips. English spelling is idiosyncratic at best. Noodle names are made even more arcane by virtue of different languages (and different dialects!) that may each have more than one word to describe the same basic noodle.

Sometimes noodles are even labeled "alimentary paste." This really threw me the first time I saw it. Then I read that it is a holdover from an old U.S law forbidding any product without egg to be called a noodle. Go figure.

The following list is far from definitive. It's a starting place to help you begin to untangle the many strands of noodle cookery. In addition to the wheat and rice noodles mentioned here, there are also noodles made from mung beans, cornstarch, tofu, yams, and potatoes among other edibles.

The photos that follow are all life-size to give you an idea of the look of different kinds of noodles. Don't take them too literally though, since the hundreds of real world noodles don't always conform to these nice, neat categories.

For further explanation and helpful drawings, consult *The Asian Grocery Store Demystified,* by Linda Bladholm. (See the bibiliography, p. 228)

NOODLES MADE FROM WHEAT:

Chinese mein (also spelled mian):
Made with or without egg, flat or round, fresh or dried. Sold in bundles or arranged in nests.

Japanese somen:
Made from wheat flour and oil, these thin, dried noodles are usually sold tied in neat-looking bundles with ribbon or paper tape.

Japanese udon:
Round or flat noodles of various widths made of wheat flour and water. They are sold dry or fresh, often with a packet of seasoning mix to make soup.

Japanese soba, Korean buckwheat (naengmyon):
Made from buckwheat and some regular wheat flour. The unique, nutty flavor works well in cold dishes. The Korean version is chewier. (See recipe on p. 203.)

Ramen or **chuka soba**:
Curly nests of instant noodles familiar to all from "Cup O' Noodles." Usually sold in single-serving sizes with seasoning packets in a multitude of flavors.

NOODLES MADE FROM RICE:

Rice sticks:
Flat or round, fat or skinny, fresh or dried. These pale, almost see-through noodles are particularly popular in Southeast Asian cuisines. Used in pad Thai and Vietnamese pho.

Fresh Rice Noodles:
Also called chow fun (Chinese), gway tiaow (Thai), or river rice noodles, these very perishable noodles come folded up in uncut sheets. You'll find them in bakeries or with the baked goods. (See recipe on p. 169.)

Fresh Noodles

Cantonese egg noodles (mein)

fresh rice noodles

Wheat Noodles

yacamein

soba

somen

wheat vermice

Rice Noodles

thin rice sticks

flat medium rice sticks

rice vermicelli

JAPAN, KOREA, AND THE PHILIPPINES

(octopus and lotus root)

Japanese, Korean, and Filipino Ingredients

Lumping these three cuisines together is convenient and arbitrary. They are together because many ingredients are common to all three and also because they tend to carry at least some of each other's specialties (less true of Filipino stores).

The Korean shopping scene in Chicago was a revelation to me who knew next to nothing about the culture or the food. You'll find huge supermarkets to get lost in. Some have **"salad bars"** of ingredients that are sold by the pound and are totally unrecognizable. There are often sacks of **red pepper** so huge it would take two big guys to carry them. The fish is impeccably fresh, the produce is gorgeous and varied. Sure, they have **kimchee** (dozens of kinds), but there is so much more! And perhaps because it is a highly-developed cuisine that we are less familiar with, a trip to a Korean market feels like a foreign vacation that you don't have to leave the city to experience.

As for Japanese groceries, some can be found at health food stores or gourmet markets (**seaweeds**, **nori**, **wasabi**, and other mainstream items). To find a real Japanese supermarket, you have to go to Arlington Heights (at least to the best of my knowledge).

There is a fairly large Filipino population in Chicago, though, much of it is assimilated, so there aren't as many strictly Filipino groceries as there are Korean. Filipino food is fascinating and worth seeking out because it is a blend of so many influences, from Spanish (with a little Mexican thrown in) to Southeast Asian, with side trips through China and India.

Fish and Seafood

All three types of stores have an excellent selection of seafood. Japanese product is the most cleaned and prepped (and the most expensive).

Fresh Fish and Seafood:
clams
crabs, live
flounder
mackerel
octopus
oysters

pomfret
shrimp
squid
tilapia, live

Japanese Specialties:
baby octopus
eels
pollack roe
salmon roe
scallops in the shell
sushi fish: including uni,
    eel, clams, octopus
tobikko (flying fish roe)
tuna
uni (sea urchin roe)

Frozen Seafood:
beltfish
clam meat
crab meat
croaker
milkfish
octopus
oyster meat
pollack
rex sole
sand dab
sea cucumber
sea snails
sea squirt
skate

Dried Seafood:
anchovies

cuttlefish
jellyfish
sardines
squid
tilefish

Meat

Small but interesting selections
of meat can be found in all of
these stores. The Japanese
cuts are exquisite, beautifully
and symetrically arranged.
Koreans have very good beef,
because they use it for tableside
barbecue among other things.
This list doesn't include the stuff
you can get anywhere, like
chicken, which is also available.

beef feet
beef tendons (shins)
flank steak
longaniza (Filipino sausage)
oxtail
pampana (Filipino sausage)
sukiyaki beef and pork
    (Japanese)
tripe
various bones and offal

Korean Specialties:
beef bulgogi meat (usually
    sirloin)
beef ribs (kalbi)
sliced pork belly

Produce

All these stores carry a good selection of fresh produce. The Japanese is the most beautiful and most expensive. There are greens of all kinds, of course, and exotic fruits in season. If you want to be sure to get a particular ingredient for an ethnic dish, it's better to go to the appropriate store, but there are certain things they all carry, like Asian eggplants, daikon, and assorted mushrooms

banana flowers
bitter melons
daikon
edamame (soy beans)
ginkgo nuts
gobo (burdock)
jute leaves
kabocha (pumpkin-like
    squash)
Korean melons (delicious)
long beans
lotus root
luffa (silk squash)
mitsuba (trefoil)
mushrooms: enoki, oyster,
    nametake, shiitake
myoga (ginger buds)
naga-imo (mountain yam)
pea shoots
perilla leaves
persimmons

sata-imo (taro)
shungiko (chrysanthemum
    leaves)
sprouts
ume (green plums, pickled
    to make umeboshi)

Wasabi Mayo

1 T. wasabi
1/4 C. mayo
(Adjust amounts to taste.)

Wasabi mayo can be used anywhere you'd use regular mayo. It really perks up a tuna salad and is also a great dip for crudités. Try it as a coating for fish: sprinkle with bread crumbs and bake or broil.

Spices and Seasonings

rice vinegar
sea salt
soy sauce: light, dark,
    mushroom
soybean paste
Sriracha sauce

Japanese Specialties:
furikake (seasoning blends)
ichimi togarashi (dried
    ground red chiles)
memmi (noodle-dipping
    sauce)
mirin
ponzu (citrus soy dipping
    sauce)
sansho (Japanese pepper)
shabu shabu sauce
shichimi (7-spice season-
    ing, shichimi togarashi)
tamari
tonkatsu sauce
wasabi

Korean Specialties:
brown rice vinegar
bulgogi sauce
denjang (soybean paste)
fish sauce
gochujang (hot pepper
    paste)
grape vinegar
perilla oil
persimmon vinegar
red pepper powder

Filipino Specialties:
banana sauce
cane vinegar
kecap manis
nipa sap (coconut palm
    vinegar)
toyomansi (soy sauce)

The Wonders of Banana Sauce

It's bright red and has the consistency of ketchup. It even tastes like ketchup without the vinegar, but it's made from bananas!

Carbs

bean thread noodles
harusume sai fun noodles
    (potato starch noodles)
pancit noodles (Filipino
    noodles)
rice (all kinds)
rice flour
rice flour, glutinous

A Rice Primer

short grain rice: Japanese and Korean,"sushi rice," sticks together, but is *not* the same as sticky (sweet) rice.

medium grain rice: all purpose (Calrose, Nishiki).

long grain rice: Chinese and Thai, fluffy, separate grains, jasmine or regular American.

sweet rice: sticky or gluti-nous rice, short grain, used in sweets and as table rice in northern Thailand.

rice noodles: fresh, rice stick, vermicelli
shirataki noodles (gelatin noodles for in sukiyaki)
wheat noodles: chukasoba (ramen), soba (buckwheat), somen
yam noodles (Korean)

Groceries

Most Japanese items are carried by Korean stores (and vice versa, but less so). Filipino stores are probably closer to Southeast Asian in this category.

adzuki (red beans)
barley, pressed
bean cakes
daikon, pickled
dashi (soup) mix
fish cakes
fish, pickled
ginger, pickled
garlic, pickled
katsuobushi (bonito flakes)
kimchee
konyaku (yam cakes)
mugwort flour
mushrooms, dried
panko (bread crumbs)
red bean paste
seaweed: nori, wakame, hijiki, kombu

tapioca pearls
tempura mix
umeboshi (pickled plum)
veggies, pickled, all kinds

Filipino Specialties:
acorn starch
annatto
baitop shell, canned
coconut, frozen shredded
coconut milk, canned
cod intestines
ginseng
green bean starch sheets
halo halo (fruit dessert)
jackfruit
lumpia, frozen
lumpia wrappers
palm fruit, canned
purple yam jam
purple yam powder
red eggs, preserved
taro stems, dried
tuna, canned with red pepper

Soy Products

atsuage (fried tofu)
miso:
    akamiso (brown),
    mamemiso (soybean)
    shiromiso (white),
natto (fermented beans)

nigari (the coagulant used
   to make tofu)
soybean powder, fermented
soybean powder, roasted
soy milk
tofu, all kinds
tofu "pockets"
yuba (beancurd skin)

Miso Misconceptions

1. It's not just soybeans.
In fact only mamemiso is
all soybeans. The others
are primarily rice-based.

2. What is called "white"
miso is really yellow.

3. It's not just for soup.
Add miso to marinades,
salad dressings, sauces, and
stir fries for a deep, rich
flavor (and good nutrition).

Equipment

The bigger stores have a pretty
good assortment of cooking
tools. Japanese shops tend to
be more expensive (and perhaps offer higher quality), and
you can also pick up amusing
children's dishes decorated with
characters from Japanese ani-
mated TV series there.

bamboo strainers and
   steamers
chopsticks
clay pots
crocks (for pickling, etc.)
rectangular skillets
   (Japanese omelet pans)
rice cookers
suribachi and surikogi
   (Japanese mortar and
   pestle)
sushi mats

Miscellaneous

The snacks and sweets available in these markets are fascinating, usually more interesting looking than good tasting, although I'm seriously considering trying to get a mainstream U.S. distributorship for **Poky cookies**. These luscious little sticks coated with chocolate or chocolate and nuts are eaten up instantly at our house. I suspect they would look good doing duty as fancy garnishes for desserts, too, but we keep eating them before I can try it.

The larger Korean stores stock drinks of all kinds. (And we think the idea of putting herbs and protein in a can of soda is new!) There are medicinals that promise energy, weight loss, and even **"sexy" drinks**. But the Japanese "Pocari Sweat" wins the prize for unappetizing name. It's a Gatorade-type drink.

cinnamon punch
citron tea
ginkgo nut tea
honey tea
Korean drinks: crushed
    pear drink, mulberry
    drink, pine bud drink,
    pumpkin gruel, "sexy"
    drinks
Morning Rice drink

Poky cookies
rice cracker snack mixes
shrimp crackers
wasabi peas

Cold and Spicy Soba Noodles
(Serves 6)

Soba noodles are the brown buckwheat kind that in Japan are often served on a slatted bamboo dish with a dipping sauce on the side. They have a nice nutty flavor on their own, but are great paired with hot chile paste and lots of garlic. For this recipe I took the liberty of combining the noodles with a sauce instead of serving it separately. It's no longer very Japanese I suppose, but it's very tasty (And you don't have to wash as many dishes.)

1 lb. dried soba (buckwheat noodles)
2 shallots sliced (or one bunch green onions, sliced with most of the green part)
1/4 C. soy sauce
1/4 C. rice vinegar
1-1/2 T. (about 8 cloves) minced garlic
1 T. minced fresh ginger
3 tsp. sesame oil
3 tsp. chili-garlic paste
1 T. sake (optional)

Cook the noodles in lots of rapidly boiling water until done but not mushy, about 4 minutes. Consult package directions if in English, but don't trust them as they often give too long a time. Drain and rinse in cool water.

Combine the rest of the ingredients and mix with the cooled noodles. Refrigerate at least several hours, or even overnight. These go great with grilled meats of all kinds and they're not bad for breakfast either.

Japanese Stores

Mitsuwa Marketplace

100 E. Algonquin Rd.
Arlington Heights
847.956.6699

You'll see the Asian-style roof peeking out from behind the parking lot at the corner of Algonquin and Arlington Heights Roads. Mitsuwa used to be called Yaohan. It is an all-under-one-roof Japanese shopping center and not to be missed. Plan on spending the entire morning or afternoon.

As you enter, there is a shop with Japanese serving ware on your left. A liquor store next to it offers a wide selection of **sake**, **plum wine**, and other goodies.

On your right you enter the supermarket through an amazing produce section, featuring everything Japanese, including the more esoteric, like fresh **ume**. (The kind pickled to make umeboshi. Don't try to eat them raw, like I did. They're supposedly poisonous, although fortunately they are also inedible!)

This is the place to get fresh **mushrooms**, **shungiku** (**chrysanthemum leaves**), and **gobo** (**burdock**). **Miso** and **tofu** come in more brands and varieties than you'll see anywhere else. If you like **pickled things**, you've come to the right place. A special deli case displays a jewel-like array of **pickled eggplant**, **carrot**, **burdock**, and dozens of flavors of **pickled daikon**. If it's a weekend, you may even be treated to samples.

The back of the store is lined with refrigerator and freezer cases loaded with impeccable fish and meat. All the ingredients for **sushi** are here, including **octopus**, **surf clams**, **tobikko** (the bright orange **flying fish roe** used in California rolls), **unagi** (**grilled eel**), and more.

The cooking equipment includes some items that made me smile. Pick up a **Hello Kitty waffle iron** or **toaster**, or a special attachment to add a bidet function to your toilet. There are also more practical things, like **sushi mats** and pots and pans.

When you're through shopping, and please allow plenty of time to peruse the many aisles of noodles, rice, seaweed, and sauces, visit the food court for lunch. Go for sushi or a bowl of udon. There's even a "Hippo" bakery that sells Japanese croissants.

True World Market

3 S. Arlington Hts. Rd.
(at Higgins)
Elk Grove Village
847.806.1200

Also a fish market (Sea World) and grocery at:
3217-3223 Lake Ave.
Glenview
847.256.4404
847.256.7010

Somewhat smaller than Mitsuwa, True World is still a full-service Japanese supermarket. They also do a booming carry-out business in **sushi** and **sashimi**.

You'll find pretty much the same stuff as at Mitsuwa in terms of produce, groceries, and meat. There's just a little less of it, which can be a good thing if you're short of time.

They carry equipment, too, including a lot of **Japanese kidstuff**, like Sailor Moon chopsticks. I picked up cute porcelain soup spoons decorated with Japanese writing and cartoon vegetables.

Sushi Mats Aren't Just for Sushi.

A sushi mat makes a great device for rolling up all kinds of things, such as spinach.

Blanch and season spinach, squeeze out most of the water, and then roll it into a cylinder in a mat lined with plastic wrap. You'll get a neat, dense spinach roll you can slice into pretty serving-size pieces. You can even roll it around a filling of chopped, sautéed mushrooms.

Korean Stores

Arirang Supermarket

4017 W. Lawrence Ave.
773.777.2400

I almost drove away from this place thinking it was closed down, since the burglar gates were up over the windows. Glad I didn't. Inside it's big and clean.

Arirang offers a comprehensive selection of all things Korean, even **liquor** and medicinals. There is a **"salad bar"** (with lots of kinds of **kimchee** and many unrecognizable things), and a deli with prepared items, but there's no place to eat.

Chicago Food Corporation

3333 N. Kimball Ave.
773.478.5566

This definitive Korean supermarket is being discovered by non-Koreans, especially on weekends. They come for the good prices as much as the authentic food, I suspect. It's located almost on the Kimball off-ramp of the Kennedy. You'll see the big sign in Korean and English. The small parking lot is in front and usually jammed, but they often have attendants to direct traffic.

Everything Korean is here, and most things Japanese. The outside walk is jammed with huge bags of rice and cartons of fruit. A selection of sweets, including the yummy **maltose/sesame candy**, greets you on entering.

The produce department offers good buys on garlic, shallots, herbs, and **Asian greens**. Be sure to try **Korean melons** in season and the very crunchy, wet white pears when they're around.

An awesome selection of fresh and frozen seafood tempts with good prices on ordinary things and a world of exotic offerings. There is an entire aisle of different **seaweeds**, another with sauces and condiments, and much more.

You'll find two refrigerators full of various kinds of **kimchee**, and a "salad bar" that allows you to take small portions of strange-looking prepared dishes. An adjoining room is filled with dishes, cookware, and gadgets. You'll find **Benriner slicers**, big ceramic **crocks** to make kimchee (or whatever you want), dishes, **mortars and pestles**, **sushi** rolling mats, and cute little plastic Japanese-style lunch boxes with badly translated English on them.

Towards the rear is a small eating area with an open kitchen and a picture menu on the wall. Try pibimpap, a rice and vegetable dish with an egg on top.

Kimchee, 160 Different Ways

As I stood paralyzed with indecision in front of a refrigerator full of jars of different kinds of kimchee, a kind fellow shopper pointed me to basic cabbage kimchee and warned me that the green onion kind is the hottest. Although there are labels, names are spelled many ways. Just look at the ingredients and take your chances.

Here are a few of the over 160 kinds, from a book by the Korean tourist organization:

T'ongbaecch'u kimchee
whole cabbage
Oisobaegi kimchee
stuffed cucumber
Kkaktugi kimchee
diced radish (daikon)
Nabak kimchee
radish and cabbage

The spelling varies wildly, I just call it bim-bam-bop and they seem to understand.

Clark Market
Albany Park Mall
4853-55 N. Kedzie Ave.
(no phone listed)

Clark Market is large, but not as huge as Chicago Food Corp. All the Korean necessities are here: **hot bean paste**, **pickled garlic**, and **kimchee**, as well as a good assortment of Japanese ingredients. This is where I found an amazing convenience product—cooked rice in aseptic (non-refrigerated) packs. It was not bad and sure beat Minute Rice in terms of flavor (easier, too).

Hyundai Supermarket
2837 Pfingston Rd.
Glenview
847.559.1618

In a mall at the corner of Willow and Pfingston Roads. This good-sized market carries produce, meat, fish, and has a large deli offering prepared foods.

Kimball Food

3445 N. Kimball Ave.
773.539.5553

Hidden away on an industrial side street this market is quite near to Chicago Food Corp. Kimball Foods isn't as big, but it has a very nice butcher shop/ fish market, as well as decent produce and good prices. It also has the best selection of bizarre drinks. Pick up a six pack of **"sexy drink"** for a bachelor(ette) party.

Lawrence Fruit Market

3318 W. Bryn Mawr Ave.
773.279.8020

A small, older place in the heart of the Korean neighborhood that offers a representative selection of Korean foods.

Song Do Market

282 E. Golf Rd.
Arlington Heights
847.718.1010
847.718.1919

A smallish Korean grocery near the big Japanese stores in Arlington Heights. Expect to find the usual **sweet potato noodles** and **kimchee**. There is a fairly extensive deli featuring Korean pancakes, vegetable dishes, and other specialties to take out. They also had barrels of sea weed-like stuff displayed in the back, which I didn't recognize.

Filipino Stores

Philippine Market

5750 N. California Ave.
(no phone listed)

In a mostly residential area, this small strip-mall store is a bit seedy but stocks most of the basics, like **pancit**, **red eggs**, and the beloved **banana sauce**.

Uni-Mart (Philippine Plaza)

5845 N. Clark St.
773.561.8667

7315 W. Dempster Ave.
Niles
847.663.8388

1038 W. Golf Rd.
Hoffman Estates
874.755.1082

Located in a strip mall on busy Clark Street, the Chicago store is not huge, but it is packed with merchandise. The grocery on Dempster is larger but very similar in terms of merchandise.

Bakery goods abound and tempt the shopper with unusual looking cakes, cookies, and breads. The small, exotic produce department at the Clark St. store carried (when I was there) fresh **jute leaves**, **taro leaves**, and **banana flowers** as well as the usual **taro**, **bitter melon**, and **long beans**.

There is some fresh fish on ice—**silverfish** (these look like noodles with eyes), **squid, butterfish**, and others, as well as a small meat department. Aisles are filled with Filipino noodles (**pancit**), sauces (**toyomansi**), and canned tropical fruit treats, including **halo halo** and the gorgeous **purple yam jam** that unfortunately doesn't really taste like much.

Both the Clark and Dempster stores carry an array of prepared foods and will fry fish for you to order for take outs. (I didn't visit Hoffman Estates.)

Top Ten Japanese, Korean, and Filipino Ingredients

1. wasabi* (p. 198)

2. panko bread crumbs

3. short-grain Japanese rice* (p. 199)

4. miso* (p. 201)

5. soba noodles* (p. 203)

6. citrus (yuzu) soy

7. furikake seasoning blends

8. Korean melon

9. kimchee* (p. 207)

10. banana sauce* (p. 199)

*tip or recipe included

A MIXED BAG

BAG

OTHER ETHNIC STORES, NUTS, AND COOKBOOKS

(almonds, hazelnuts, pecans, and walnuts)

Miscellaneous Ethnic Stores

German:

Meyer's Delicatessen

4750 N. Lincoln Ave.
773.561.3377
www.delicatessenmeyer.com
This is a real (wonderful) throw-back to a time when sausage was made at the butcher shop and Lincoln Square was a heavily German neighborhood. The brats and wurst you find here are not anything like the grocery store version. They're plump and still attached to each other. There's **knackwurst**, **veal** and **Sheboygan-style brats**, **blood sausage**, and **wieners** (Meyer's, not Oscar Meyer's). The sales-girls speak German and wear little white lacy caps. The patrons frequently speak German, too. The deli is gorgeous and holds **herring**, **cheeses**, and some prepared foods. There is a good selection of **German and Alsatian wine**, imported beer, and liquor. Don't miss all the chocolate, European candies, and imported jams, either.

Scandinavian:

Andersonville, the traditional Scandinavian neighborhood around Clark and Foster, is the place to go for **lingonberries** and **lutefisk**. (A newer, Middle Eastern presence has brought diversity with stores like **Pars Persian Store**, p. 133.) While you're in the area, stop by **Ann Sather's** restaurant (Swedish, 5207 N. Clark), especially for breakfast, or **Reza's** (Persian, 5255 N. Clark) restaurant for lunch or dinner. And don't forget dessert at **The Swedish Bakery** (5348 N. Clark).

Erickson's Delicatessen

5250 N. Clark St.
773.561.5634

This is the smaller of the two Scandinavian delis in Andersonville. They carry an excellent assortment of cheeses (**gouda**, **havarti**), **flatbreads**, **lingonberries**, **cod and herring paste**, **lefse**, and **lutefisk**.

Wikstrom's Gourmet Food

5247 N. Clark St.
773.275.6100
www.wikstromsgourmet.com

This deli's small café draws a huge lunch business with its excellent sandwiches. Wikstrom's Scandinavian specialities include **lutefisk, lefse, Swedish brown beans, lingonberries** (jarred or frozen), **herring paste, cod paste**, and imported **flatbreads**.

Irish:

Winston's Market

4701 W. 63rd St.
773.767.4353

7961 W. 159th St.
Tinley Park
630.663.7500

Winston's is a South Side favorite famous for **corned beef** and **Irish soda bread**. Actually all their meat is quite popular. They make **"bangers"** (Irish/English sausages), **black and white "puddings"** (breakfast sausages), **pickled pork**, and **smoked pork butt**. All these items are seasoned but uncooked. There is also an assortment of imported goods including **marmite, HP Sauce, YR Sauce, Irish oats, canned marrofat peas, salad cream**, candies, and jams. The Chicago store is tiny and the prep kitchen is in the back. The Tinley Park market is much larger and has a restaurant as well as **Irish dishware** and even jewelry for sale.

Russian:

A & T International

2858 W. Devon Ave.
773.973.2642

This little shop is primarily a Ukrainian bakery. Once the wonderful odors hit you, I defy you to leave without a loaf of bread. In addition to an **assortment of authentic rye, sourdough**, and other breads and pastries, they carry deli meats, **honey of all sorts, jams**, and other grocery imports.

Devon Fish Market/Kashtan

2740 W. Devon Ave.
773.338.9080

This is a Russian store specializing in **smoked fish**, with an enormous selection that included kinds I've never seen elsewhere. There's **smoked cod, salmon,** and **trout**, of course, but also **smoked flounder, pike, carp, turbot, sturgeon,** and more that I couldn't identify. Grocery shelves hold **Russian bread,** condiments, **canned fish,** and **dried smelt.**

Globus International Deli

2909 W. Devon Ave.
773.973.7970

This small deli at the Russian end of Devon offers a selection of meats and **smoked fish, kefir,** and also some packaged goods, including the usual honey, jam, and tea.

Three Sisters Delicatessen

2854 W. Devon Ave.
773.465.6695

A busy, crowded establishment where you'll hear mainly Russian spoken. Of course, **smoked fish** of all sorts, is a big seller, sold whole or by the pound, but Three Sisters is a complete deli and also stocks many kinds of **sausages**, pickles, breads from various bakeries that specialize in Eastern European styles, and a good assortment of **jarred fish, mushrooms, relishes,** and **jams**.

Balkan:

Devon Market
1440 W. Devon Ave.
773.338.2572

This place looks like a perfectly ordinary supermarket outside, but inside it's a bustling combination Balkan (Bulgarian, Serbian, Hungarian) and Latin American grocery. Expect to find several kinds of **ajvar**, a red-pepper-based vegetable spread, plus peppers stuffed with cabbage, **smoked beef, Hungarian pickles**, and an assortment of **syrups** and **fruit and vegetable drinks in boxes**, including some not seen elsewhere, such as blueberry. Grains like **buckwheat, millet,** and **barley** are fresh, as is the produce with the requisite peppers, tubers, and fruits. The fairly big butcher shop makes **their own sausage** and **smoked salmon**, and the seafood selection includes **head-on shrimp** and a tank of **live tilapia.**

Nuts:

Ricci & Company
162-164 W. Superior St.
312.787.7660

A wholesale nut merchant that is open to the public, Ricci carries just about **any nut you could want**, any way you could want it. Almonds come blanched or not, sliced, slivered or whole, for instance. Prices are good and quality is top-notch. Ricci also has dried fruit, candy, soy nuts, and chocolate covered coffee beans. Limited weekday hours, call first.

Nuts on Clark
3830 N. Clark St.
773.549.6622

Purveyors of **bulk nuts and candies of all kinds**, as well as the **caramel corn** for which they are famous.

Cookbooks:

Certainly buying recent cookbooks at any bookstore is easy enough. (The on-line discount source **www.ecookbooks.com** has some bargains.) There is a growing interest in old cookbooks that have been out-of-print for years. They have become collectibles and are often found in antique stores.

After-Words Bookstore

23 E. Illinois St.
312.464.6641

Head downstairs to the used book department for an eclectic assortment of old, but not antique cookbooks. They may not be collectibles yet, but the prices are good.

The Frugal Muse

7511 Lemont Rd.
Chestnut Court
Shopping Center
Darien
630.427.1140

This bookstore is pretty far out in the burbs, but offers one of the best selections of used cookbooks I've seen anywhere. The prices are incredibly low. They also discount new books, music, and videos. **Wilton Homewares** (p. 63) is in the same mall.

Kay's Treasured Books

847.256.4459
kaysbooks@aol.com

Not a retail store but a knowledgeable local source that has more than 3,000 out-of-print cookbooks in stock. If you're looking for a particular volume, give Kay Sullivan a call. She says she has a 95 percent success rate with searches.

Little Treasures

7446 W. Madison St.
Forest Park
708.366.0098

A large collection of old cookbooks (amidst the antique jewelry and bric-a-brac) makes this an enjoyable destination for cookbook lovers. You'll find classic sets like *The Foods of the World* Time-Life Series and early editions of Julia Child and *The Joy of Cooking*, as well as lots of interesting but unknown volumes. The staff will help you find something specific or just let you browse. Remember to bring your checkbook or cash as they do not accept credit cards.

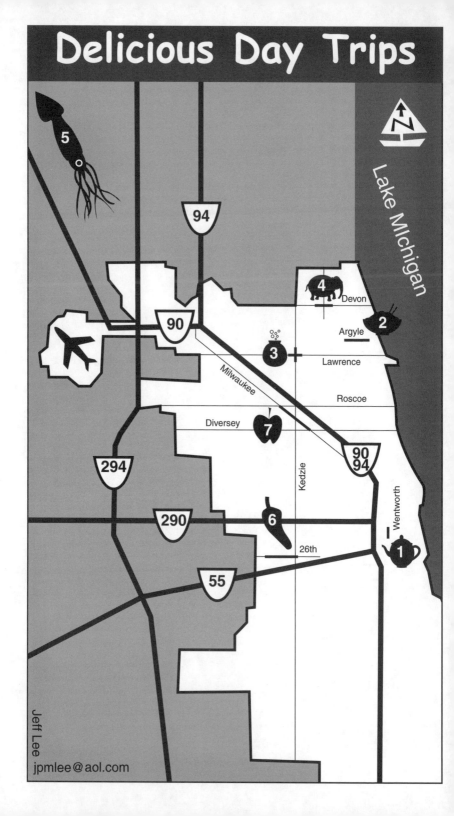

Spend the day in a foreign country without leaving town. Shop, gawk, eat, and learn a little of the language without spending much money.

Chinatown. Make sure to visit **Ten Ren Tea** shop and the **Hong Kong Noodle Company** on Wentworth Avenue. Don't miss the "modern" mall at the north end. It has good, less touristy stores. (pp. 170–173)

Southeast Asia. Wander Argyle Street from Broadway east to Sheridan Road Stop for a bowl of noodles. Then head south on Broadway to visit one of the big supermarkets— **Tai Nam** or **Thaong Xa My A**. (pp. 184–186)

The Kedzie/Lawrence melting pot. For exotic produce don't miss **Andy's Fruit Ranch** (p. 45). On the east side of Kedzie you'll find Middle Eastern shops and restaurants. **Clark Market** is Korean (p. 207) and **Lindo Michoacán** can supply Latin American ingredients (p. 89).

Little India. Devon Avenue from 2200 to 2600 west is packed with Indian/Pakistani grocers, spice shops, sari stores, halal butchers, and restaurants (pp. 154–157); and Jewish, Russian, Middle Eastern, and Balkan spots, too.

Mitsuwa Marketplace. Arlington Heights. It's only one store, but it's a Japanese shopping center. Groceries, fish, booze, and equipment. Best of all there's a food court that features sushi, noodles and a Japanese bakery. (p. 204)

Little Village. This Mexican neighborhood that runs from 3200 to 3500 west on 26th Street is centered around a pink welcome arch at 26th and Albany Avenue. You'll find supermarkets, restaurants, nightclubs, and on summer weekends a fiesta mood. (pp. 86–88)

Milwaukee Avenue. Blending old and new establishments, this Polish shopping neighborhood stretches from Diversey to Roscoe. Discover great sausage, bacon, and beer. When hunger hits, head to the famous **Czerwone Jabluszko**, "**Red Apple**," (3123 N. Milwaukee) for an overflowing buffet of Polish specialties. (pp. 103–106)

A DRINK WITH THAT?

(filters, corks, and corkscrew)

Coffee and Tea

Coffee is easy to find these days. The few shops listed here are the real local specialists. Don't forget the ethnic stores for coffee and tea, either. Polish and Asian markets are great resources for herbal and medicinal teas. Latino stores carry espresso and South American coffees. Vietnamese stores have French Market style coffee with chicory (the French influence I guess). Canned coffee and tea drinks are also available in most Asian stores and a nice change from Arizona Iced Tea.

Intelligentsia

3123 N. Broadway St.
773.348.8058
www.intelligentsiacoffee.com

Intelligentsia **roasts its own coffee** and does its own **tea blending**, and will even roast to order. It's where many local restaurants and gourmet stores acquire their house blends.

Coffee and Tea Exchange

3311 N. Broadway St.
773.528.2241
www.coffeeandtea.com

Around since 1978, long before the coffee boom, these guys have been **roasting and selling dozens of blends of coffee and tea** to Chicagoans.

Ten Ren Tea

2247 S. Wentworth Ave.
312.842.1171

This Chinatown store devoted to imported teas has a small tea room for tasting, lots of packaged teas, and **hundreds of varieties by the pound**. Try the "bubble teas," flavored tea drinks with tapioca pearls added for texture that you drink through a staw. (A very hot trend in L.A., I've read.)

Todd & Holland Tea Merchants

7577 Lake St.
River Forest
708.488.1136
www.todd-holland.com

Tea is the story at Todd & Holland. They are knowledgeable, friendly, and have an enormous selection of **whole leaf tea**, plus pots, cozies, and other tea-related ware.

Brewing and Winemaking Supplies

These retailers carry all the chemicals and hardware for making wine or home-brewing. You'll also find the "mother" you need to start your own batch of vinegar fermenting.

See also the listing for **Chiarugi Hardware** in the **Equipment** chapter (p. 55).

Bev Art Brewer and Winemaker Supply

10035 S. Western Ave.
773.233.7579
www.bev-art.com

This supply company is a pet shop, too, so don't think you've got the wrong address. Just pop inside and go through to the adjoining store. They sell a full panoply of equipment and ingredients and also teach classes and sponsor events related to brewing and wine making. In fact, Bev Art traditionally brews up a special beer every year for folks to sample during the South Side St. Patrick's Day Parade.

Chicagoland Winemakers

689 W. North Ave.
Elmhurst
800.226.2739
www.cwinemaker.com

A mail order source as well as a retail store, Chicagoland Winemakers offers special package deals for beginners who wish to try their hand at making wine or beer. In addition you can order anything you need in terms of equipment or ingredients. They also carry **cordial extracts** and **soft drink flavors**.

Wine Stores

A far from definitive listing of some of Chicago's wine shops. These establishments offer everyday wines, plus access to more interesting bottles. And whether big (**Sam's** at 33,000 square feet) or small (**Howard's Wine Cellar**), they all offer tastings, information and a knowledgeable staff to assist you.

Binny's Beverage Depot

213 W. Grand Ave
312.332.0012

3000 N. Clark St.
773.935.9400
www.binnys.com

See the listing under **Gourmet** (p. 9) for more information. Also in Niles, Skokie, Schaumburg, Highland Park, Elmwood Park, and Buffalo Grove.

BIN 36

339 N. Dearborn St. (Marina City)
312.755.9463
www.bin36.com

A restaurant/wine bar that is also a retail store.

Chalet Wine and Cheese

40 E. Delaware Pl.
312.787.8555

See the listing under **Gourmet** (p. 9) for more information.

Chicago Wine School

2001 S. Halsted St.
312.266.9463
www.wineschool.com

Not a store, but a school that features everything from one-night seminars to comprehensive five-week courses.

Fine Wine Brokers
4621 N. Lincoln Ave.
773.989.8166

House of Glunz
1206 N. Wells St.
312.642.3000
www.houseofglunz.com

Howard's Wine Cellar
1244 W. Belmont Ave.
773.248.3766

Randolph Wine Cellars
1415 W. Randolph St.
312.942.1212

An adjoining wine bar lets you try before you buy and offers food, including **cheese flights**.

Sam's Wine and Spirits
1720 N. Marcey St.
312.664.4394
www.samswine.com

Sam's was one of the first warehouse-style wine stores. It also houses a gourmet store, the **Marcey Street Market** (p. 11).

Schaefer's Wines, Foods and Spirits
9965 Gross Point Rd.
Skokie
847.673.5711
www.schaefers.com

Schaefer's has a well-attended **tasting of wine and food** every Saturday.

The Wine Crier
2070 N Clybourn
773.404.8684
www.thewinecrier.com

Wine Discount Center
1826-1/2 N. Elston Ave.
773.489.3454
www.winediscountcenter.com

LEFTOVERS

Bibliography
and Indexes

Bibliography

REFERENCES:

Bladholm, Linda. *The Asian Grocery Store Demystified*. Los Angeles: Renaissance Books, 2000.

_____. *Latin & Caribbean Grocery Stores Demystified*. Los Angeles: Renaissance Books, 2001.

_____. *The Indian Grocery Store Demystified*. Los Angeles: Renaissance Books, 2000.

Cost, Bruce. *Asian Ingredients*. New York: Harper Collins Publishers, Quill, 2000.

Davidson, Alan. *The Oxford Companion to Food*. Oxford, England: Oxford University Press, 1999.

Grigson, Sophie. *Gourmet Ingredients*. New York: Van Nostrand Reinhold, 1991.

Haddix, Carol Mighton and Sherman Kaplan. *Cook's Marketplace Chicago*. San Francisco: 101 Productions, 1996.

_____, editor. *Ethnic Chicago Cookbook*. Lincolnwood: NTC/ Contemporary Publishing Group, Contemporary Books, 1999.

Herbst, Sharon Tyler. *Food Lover's Companion*. New York: Barron's Educational Series, 1995.

Lindberg, Richard. *Ethnic Chicago: A Complete Guide to the Many Faces and Cultures of Chicago*. Lincolnwood: NTC/Contemporary Publishing Company, Passport Books, 1997.

Morgan, Lane. *The Ethnic Market Food Guide*. New York: Penguin Putnam, Berkley Publishing Company, 1977.

Norman, Jill. *The Complete Book of Spices*. London: Viking Studio Books, 1990.

Ross, Rosa Lo San. *Beyond Bok Choy*. New York: Workman Publishing Company, Inc., Artisan, 1996.

Schneider, Elizabeth. *Uncommon Fruits and Vegetables: A Commonsense Guide*. New York: William Morrow and Co., 1986.

Werle, Loukie and Jill Cox. *Ingredients*. Cologne, Germany: Konemann Berlagsgesellschaft, 2000.

Whiteman, Kate. *A Cook's Guide to Italian Ingredients*. New York: Annex Publishing, Lorenz Books, 2000.

Wood, Rebecca. *The New Whole Foods Encyclopedia*. New York: Penguin Putnam,1999.

ETHNIC COOKBOOKS:

Asian—

Brennan, Jennifer. *The Original Thai Cookbook*. New York: Berkley Publishing, 1981.

Coultrip-Davis, Deborah and Young Sook Ramsay. *Flavors of Korea, Delicious Vegetarian Cuisine*. Summertown, TN: Book Publishing Co., 1998.

Lo, Eileen Yin-Fei. *The Chinese Kitchen*. New York: William Morrow, 1999.

Loha-Unchit, Kasma. *It Rains Fishes: Legends, Traditions and the Joys of Thai Cooking*. Rohnert Park, CA: Pomegranate Artbooks, 1994.

Shimbo, Hiroko.*The Japanese Kitchen*. Boston: The Harvard Common Press, 2000.

Trang, Corinne. *Authentic Vietnamese Cooking*. New York: Simon & Schuster, 1999.

Caribbean/African—

Harris, Jessica B. *Iron Pots & Wooden Spoons*. New York: A Fireside Book, Simon and Schuster, 1989.

Ortiz, Elizabeth Lambert. *The Complete Book of Caribbean Cooking*. New York: M. Evans & Co., 1973.

Indian—

Jaffrey, Madhur. *Flavors of India*. Seattle: West 175 Publishing, 1995.

_____. *Indian Cooking*. New York: Barron's Educational Series, 1982.

_____. *Spice Kitchen*. New York: Carol Southern Books, 1993.

Latin American—

Bayless, Rick. *The Mexican Kitchen*. New York: Scribner, 1996.

Ortiz, Elisabeth Lambert. *The Complete Book of Mexican Cooking*. New York: M. Evans & Co., 1967.

Zaslavsky, Nancy. *A Cook's Tour of Mexico*. New York: St. Martin's Press, 1995.

Mediterranean/Middle Eastern—

Hazan, Marcella. *The Classic Italian Cookbook*. New York: Ballantine Books, 1973.

LaPlace, Viana and Evan Kleiman. *Cucina Rustica*. New York: William Morrow and Co., 1990.

Roden, Claudia. *A Book of Middle Eastern Food*. New York: Vintage Books, A Division of Random House,1968.

Jaffrey, Madhur. *World of the East Vegetarian Cooking*. New York: Alfred A. Knopf, 1981.

Recipe Index

Stores, Clubs, and Organizations Index

Equipment Index

Ingredients Index

About the Author

photo by
Tamara Bell

Marilyn Pocius has been writing, cooking, and eating weird things all her life.

Growing up on the Southwest Side, Pocius learned that Chicago is a collection of ethnic neighborhoods (hers was Lithuanian). Her earliest culinary memories are Lithuanian black bread, which she still loves, and pickled herring, which she still hates.

At the University of Wisconsin she studied French, Chinese, and Russian, and graduated with a B.A. in Linguistics. Her career as an advertising agency creative director gave her an opportunity to write television commercials for national accounts like Kraft, Kellogg's, and M & M Mars.

She has done food writing for the *Chicago Tribune*, EthnicGrocer.com, the National Restaurant Association Educational Foundation, and *Local Palate*, among others. Since 2001 she has authored the food column "In Season" and has been a regular contributor to 48 *Pioneer Press* papers.

Pocius recently sharpened her skills and her knives at The Cooking and Hospitality Institute of Chicago (CHIC) where she earned the right to be called "chef." She currently lives with her daughter, Genevieve, her calico cat, Sophie, and her mutt, Purdie. She is an amateur herbalist and organic gardener and likes to grow unusual vegetables and exotic herbs. She is also active in the local food scene and a member of AIWF and Culinary Historians of Chicago.

Lake Claremont Press

Celebrating what's distinctive about Chicago's history, culture, geography, spirit, and lore. Join us in preserving the past, exploring the present, and ensuring a future sense of place for our corner of the globe.

Regional History

NEW!
Near West Side Stories:
Struggles for Community in Chicago's
Maxwell Street Neighborhood
Carolyn Eastwood
1-893121-09-7, Spring 2002, softcover,
360 pages, 113 historic and contemporary
photos, $17.95.
Recommended by *Chicago* magazine.

NEW!
Chicago's Midway Airport:
The First Seventy-Five Years
Christopher Lynch
1-893121-18-6, Spring 2002, softcover,
10" x 8", 200 pages, 140 historic photos,
$19.95.
Look for the audiobook in late 2002.

Great Chicago Fires:
Historic Blazes That Shaped a City
David Cowan
1-893121-07-0, August 2001, softcover,
10" x 8", 167 pages, 86 historic and
contemporary photos, $19.95.
By the author of *To Sleep with the
Angels*.

The Chicago River:
A Natural and Unnatural History
Libby Hill
1-893121-02-X, August 2000, softcover,
302 pages, 78 historic and contemporary
maps and photos, $16.95.
Winner of the 2001 American Regional
History Publishing Award (1st Place—
Midwest). Winner of the 2000 Midwest
Publishers Association Award (2nd
Place—History).

Hollywood on Lake Michigan: 100
Years of Chicago and the Movies
Arnie Bernstein
foreword by George Tillman, Jr.
0-9642426-2-1, December 1998,
softcover, 364 pages, 80 historic and
contemporary photos, $15
Winner of the 2000 American Regional
History Publishing Award (1st Place—
Midwest).

"The Movies Are": Carl Sandburg's
Film Reviews and Essays, 1920-1928
edited by Arnie Bernstein
introduction by Roger Ebert
1-893121-05-4, October 2000, softcover,
397 pages, 72 historic photos and
artifacts, $17.95.

Literary Chicago: A Book
Lover's Tour of the Windy City
Greg Holden
1-893121-01-1, March 2001, softcover,
332 pages, 83 photos, 11 maps and
walking tours, $15.95.
As seen in the *Chicago Tribune* and
the *Chicago Sun-Times*.

Ghosts and Graveyards

Chicago Haunts
Ursula Bielski
0-9642426-7-2, October 1998, softcover,
277 pages, 29 photos, $15.
Our best-seller—an all-round favorite!

More Chicago Haunts:
Scenes from Myth and Memory
Ursula Bielski
1-893121-04-6, October 2000, softcover,
312 pages, 50 photos, $15.
50 all new stories.

Graveyards of Chicago:
The People, History, Art, and
Lore of Cook County Cemeteries
Matt Hucke and Ursula Bielski
0-9642426-4-8, November 1999,
softcover, 228 pages, 168 photos, $15.
By the creator of the award-winning
www.graveyards.com.

Haunted Michigan:
Recent Encounters with Active Spirits
Rev. Gerald S. Hunter
1-893121-10-0, October 2000, softcover,
207 pages, 20 photos, $12.95.

More Haunted Michigan
Rev. Gerald S. Hunter
1-893121-29-1, October 2002, softcover,
$15.

Guidebooks by Locals

Ticket to Everywhere: The Best of *Detours* Travel Column
Dave Hoekstra
1-893121-11-9, November 2000, softcover, 227 pages, 70 photos, 9 maps, $15.95.
Explore offbeat and overlooked Americana with Hoekstra's 66 road trips through the Midwest and along Route 66.

NEW EDITION!
A Native's Guide to Chicago, 4th Edition
Lake Claremont Press
edited by Sharon Woodhouse
1-893121-23-2, Summer 2002, softcover, 400 pages, photos, maps, $15.
Named "Best Guidebook for Locals"!

A Native's Guide to Northwest Indiana
Mark Skertic
1-893121-08-9, Summer 2002, softcover, photos, maps, $15.

Let our "Native's Guide" series be your personal tour guide to the best our suburbs have to offer.

A Native's Guide to Chicago's Northern Suburbs
Jason Fargo
0-9642426-8-0, June 1999, softcover, 207 pages, photos, maps, $12.95.

A Native's Guide to Chicago's Northwest Suburbs
Martin A. Bartels
1-893121-00-3, August 1999, softcover, 315 pages, photos, maps, $12.95.

A Native's Guide to Chicago's Western Suburbs
Laura Mazzuca Toops and John W. Toops, Jr.
0-9642426-6-4, August 1999, softcover, 210 pages, photos, maps, $12.95.

A Native's Guide to Chicago's South Suburbs
Christina Bultinck and Christy Johnston
0-9642426-1-3, June 1999, softcover, 242 pages, photos, maps, $12.95.

How to Order Our Books

Lake Claremont Press books can be found at Chicagoland bookstores and online at Amazon.com, bn.com, and others.

Order directly from us by mail, phone, fax, or e-mail.
All of our books have a no-hassle, 100% money-back guarantee.

Enjoy these discounts when you order several titles:
2 books—10% off total, 3–4 books—20% off, 5–9 books—25% off, 10+ books—40% off. Please inquire about case discounts.

Illinois residents, add 8.75% sales tax.

Shipping is $2.50 for the first book and $.50 for each additional book, with a maximum charge of $8.

Lake Claremont Press
4650 N. Rockwell St.
Chicago, IL 60625
773-583-7800 (phone)
773-583-7877 (fax)
www.lakeclaremont.com
lcp@lakeclaremont.com

Also from Lake Claremont Press

Near West Side Stories: Struggles for Community in Chicago's Maxwell Street Neighborhood
Carolyn Eastwood

Chicago's Midway Airport: The First Seventy-Five Years
Christopher Lynch

Great Chicago Fires: Historic Blazes That Shaped a City
David Cowan

The Chicago River: A Natural and Unnatural History
Libby Hill

Literary Chicago: A Book Lover's Tour of the Windy City
Greg Holden

Chicago Haunts and More Chicago Haunts: Scenes from Myth and Memory
Ursula Bielski

Haunted Michigan: Recent Encounters with Active Spirits and More Haunted Michigan
Rev. Gerald S. Hunter

Graveyards of Chicago: The People, History, Art, and Lore of Cook County Cemeteries
Matt Hucke and Ursula Bielski

Hollywood on Lake Michigan: 100 Years of Chicago and the Movies
Arnie Bernstein

"The Movies Are": Carl Sandburg's Film Reviews and Essays, 1920-1928
edited by Arnie Bernstein

Ticket to Everywhere: The Best of *Detours* Travel Column
Dave Hoekstra

Coming Soon

A Native's Guide to Northwest Indiana
Mark Skertic

A Native's Guide to Chicago, 4th Edition
Lake Claremont Press

The Hoofs and Guns of the Storm: Chicago's Civil War Connections
Arnie Bernstein

Traces of Checagou: Mammoths, Mounds, Forts, and the Fur Trade in Northern Illinois
Christina and Nicole Bultinck

Muldoon: A True Chicago Ghost Story
Rocco A. Facchini

Creepy Chicago
(*Chicago Haunts* for kids)
Ursula Bielski

Finding Your Chicago Ancestors
Grace DuMelle

The Politics of Recreation
Charles Shaw